Social Justice in the Stories of Jesus

Social Justice in the Stories of Jesus

The Ethical Challenge of the Parables

Matthew E. Gordley

Pittsburgh, PA
United States

WILEY Blackwell

This edition first published 2024
© 2024 John Wiley & Sons Ltd

All rights reserved. No part of this publication may be reproduced, stored in a retrieval system, or transmitted, in any form or by any means, electronic, mechanical, photocopying, recording or otherwise, except as permitted by law. Advice on how to obtain permission to reuse material from this title is available at http://www.wiley.com/go/permissions.

The right of Matthew E. Gordley to be identified as the author of this work has been asserted in accordance with law.

Registered Offices
John Wiley & Sons, Inc., 111 River Street, Hoboken, NJ 07030, USA
John Wiley & Sons Ltd, The Atrium, Southern Gate, Chichester, West Sussex, PO19 8SQ, UK

For details of our global editorial offices, customer services, and more information about Wiley products visit us at www.wiley.com.

Wiley also publishes its books in a variety of electronic formats and by print-on-demand. Some content that appears in standard print versions of this book may not be available in other formats.

Trademarks: Wiley and the Wiley logo are trademarks or registered trademarks of John Wiley & Sons, Inc. and/or its affiliates in the United States and other countries and may not be used without written permission. All other trademarks are the property of their respective owners. John Wiley & Sons, Inc. is not associated with any product or vendor mentioned in this book.

Limit of Liability/Disclaimer of Warranty
While the publisher and authors have used their best efforts in preparing this work, they make no representations or warranties with respect to the accuracy or completeness of the contents of this work and specifically disclaim all warranties, including without limitation any implied warranties of merchantability or fitness for a particular purpose. No warranty may be created or extended by sales representatives, written sales materials or promotional statements for this work. This work is sold with the understanding that the publisher is not engaged in rendering professional services. The advice and strategies contained herein may not be suitable for your situation. You should consult with a specialist where appropriate. The fact that an organization, website, or product is referred to in this work as a citation and/or potential source of further information does not mean that the publisher and authors endorse the information or services the organization, website, or product may provide or recommendations it may make. Further, readers should be aware that websites listed in this work may have changed or disappeared between when this work was written and when it is read. Neither the publisher nor authors shall be liable for any loss of profit or any other commercial damages, including but not limited to special, incidental, consequential, or other damages.

Library of Congress Cataloging-in-Publication Data
Names: Gordley, Matthew E., 1972- author.
Title: Social justice in the stories of Jesus : the ethical challenge of the parables / Matthew E. Gordley.
Description: Hoboken, NJ : John Wiley & Sons Ltd., 2024. | Includes bibliographical references.
Identifiers: LCCN 2023026391 (print) | LCCN 2023026392 (ebook) |
    ISBN 9781119884026 (paperback) | ISBN 9781119884033 (pdf) | ISBN 9781119884040 (epub)
Subjects: LCSH: Jesus Christ--Parables. | Bible--Parables. | Social justice--Religious aspects--
    Christianity. | Christian sociology.
Classification: LCC BT375.3 .G67 2024 (print) | LCC BT375.3 (ebook) | DDC 226.8/06--dc23/
    eng/20230817
LC record available at https://lccn.loc.gov/2023026391
LC ebook record available at https://lccn.loc.gov/2023026392

Cover Image: © juanljones/Getty Images
Cover Design: Wiley

Set in 10/13pt PalatinoLTStd by Integra Software Services Pvt. Ltd, Pondicherry, India

SKY10068720_030524

In memory of
Jack Conroy
Michael Palmer
Rae Ann Hirsh

Contents

Preface	xi
Acknowledgment	xiii
1 Reading the Parables through the Lens of Social Justice	1
1. Introduction	1
2. What Are Parables?	8
3. Why Parables?	13
4. The Parables as They Were Originally Heard	17
5. Parables and Mercy: An Entry Point into Social Justice	20
6. Exploring the Ethical Implications of the Parables through a Social Justice Lens	24
7. Reading the Parables through the Lens of Social Justice: A Proposal	32
2 Encountering the World and Words of Jesus	39
1. Introduction	39
2. Exploring Other Worlds: Some Key Concepts	41
3. The World of Jesus	42
Religious Context: Early Judaism	42
Sociopolitical Context: An Advanced Agrarian Society within the Roman Empire	54

Contents

4.	The Words of Jesus	60
5.	Words about Jesus	73
	The Actions and Example of Jesus	74
	Death and Resurrection	75
6.	Postscript: Jesus and Crucified Peoples Today	78

3 The Parable of the Good Samaritan (Luke 10:25–37)   83

1.	Introduction	83
2.	The Text: Parable of the Good Samaritan (Luke 10:25–37)	85
3.	Our First Step: Grasp the Story	85
4.	Our Second Step: Going Deeper through Asking Questions	87
	What Can We Know about the Characters?	87
	Good Samaritan … and Bad Jews?	90
5.	Our Third Step: Spot the Twist	92
6.	Our Fourth Step: Consider the Metaphor	94
7.	Our Fifth Step: Articulate the Challenge	98
8.	Our Final Step: Consider Implications	102
	Physical Care for Those in Need: The Corporal Works of Mercy	103
	The Natural World	105
	The Humanity of Our Enemies	106

4 Lost Sheep, Lost Coin (Luke 15:4–10)   109

1.	Introduction	109
2.	The Text: Lost Sheep, Lost Coin (Luke 15:4–10)	110
3.	Our First Step: Grasp the Stories	110
4.	Our Second Step: Ask Questions to Gain Understanding	112
	What Glimpse Does Each Parable Give Us into Economic Realities in the First Century?	113
5.	Our Third Step: Spot the Twist	115
6.	Our Fourth Step: Consider the Metaphor	118
	Lost and Found	123
	Communal Rejoicing	124
7.	Our Fifth Step: Articulate the Challenge	126
8.	Our Sixth Step: Consider Implications	129

Contents

5 The Lost Sons (Luke 15:11–32) — 136

1. Introduction — 136
2. The Text: The Lost Sons (Luke 15:11–32) — 136
3. Our First Step: Grasp the Story — 137
4. Our Second Step: Ask Questions to Gain Understanding — 142
5. Our Third Step: Spot the Twist — 151
6. Our Fourth Step: Consider the Metaphor — 153
7. Our Fifth Step: Articulate the Challenge — 157
8. Our Sixth Step: Consider implications — 163

6 The Parable of the Mustard Seed (Mark 4:30–32) — 174

1. Introduction — 174
2. The Text: The Parable of the Mustard Seed (Mark 4:30–32) — 176
3. Our First Step: Grasp the Story — 176
4. Our Second Step: Ask Good Questions — 178
5. Our Third Step: Spot the Twist — 183
6. Our Fourth Step: Consider the Metaphor — 184
7. Our Fifth Step: Articulate the Challenge — 187
8. Our Sixth Step: Consider Implications — 192

7 The Pharisee and the Tax Collector (Luke 18:9–14) — 202

1. Introduction — 202
2. The Text: The Pharisee and the Tax Collector (Luke 18:9–14) — 203
3. Our First Step: Grasp the Story — 203
4. Our Second Step: Ask Questions to Gain Understanding — 207
5. Our Third Step: Spot the Twist — 214
6. Our Fourth Step: Consider the Metaphor — 215
7. Our Fifth Step: Articulate the Challenge — 219
8. Our Sixth Step: Consider Implications — 221

8 The Laborers in the Vineyard (Matthew 20:1–16) — 232

1. Introduction — 232
2. The Text: The Laborers in the Vineyard (Matthew 20:1–16) — 233
3. Our First Step: Grasp the Story — 233
4. Our Second Step: Ask Questions to Gain Understanding — 235

Contents

5.	Our Third Step: Spot the Twist	238
6.	Our Fourth Step: Consider the Metaphor	240
7.	Our Fifth Step: Articulate the Challenge	245
	Jon Sobrino and Ignacio Ellacuría	246
8.	Our Sixth Step: Consider Implications	248

9 The Rich Man and Lazarus (Luke 16:19–31)   257

1.	Introduction	257
2.	The Text: The Rich Man and Lazarus (Luke 16:19–31)	258
3.	Our First Step: Grasp the Story	259
4.	Our Second Step: Going Deeper through Asking Questions	261
5.	Our Third Step: Spot the Twist	266
6.	Our Fourth Step: Consider the Metaphor	268
7.	Our Fifth Step: Articulate the Challenge	274
8.	Our Final Step: Consider Implications	277

Conclusion: Living into Our Humanity and Cultivating an Ethic of Love, Mercy, and Justice   282

1.	Introduction	282
2.	Summary of the Parables	285
3.	Shared Themes throughout the Parables of Jesus	288
4.	Conversation Partners	294
5.	An Ethic of Love, Mercy, and Justice	302

Appendix 1: Sisters of Mercy Reflections on the Parables   309

Appendix 2: Questions for Individual Study and Group Discussion   326

Bibliography   333

Index   341

Preface

This is a very different book for me. Although like my previous books this is a work of academic scholarship, in this volume I engage not only the words of the New Testament but also the world we all share today. In seeking to make explicit connections between the teaching of Jesus and our current context, I have had to move significantly out of my scholarly comfort zone. But this is a book I had to write. First, for the obvious reason that I believe that the teaching of Jesus in the parables has something to say to us today with regard to matters of social justice. Second, because I am increasingly convinced that many of the people claiming to be followers of Jesus today have, perhaps unknowingly, embraced some very bad ways of reading and understanding the Bible. These bad ways of interpreting the Bible have been used to lend support to ways of living out their "Christian" faith and ways of being in the world that appear to me to be very much at odds with the kinds of compassionate, merciful, and loving ways that Jesus promoted. In my experience, it has often been Christians seeking to live "according to the Bible" who have inflicted serious harm on others whether through explicit messages of exclusion and hatred, implicit messages devaluing the humanity of others who do not measure up to certain standards, or complicity with oppressive systems of exploitation and abuse. In my experience growing up as a Christian, I have witnessed firsthand the

Preface

ways in which "biblical" messages and institutions inflict a uniquely painful kind of damage on individuals, pushing them off a path of authentic spiritual growth and well-being, and severely limiting their ability to thrive or live into their full humanity. The purpose of this book is to share an informed, contextual way of reading the parables that I hope can serve as a corrective to some common mis-readings of the Bible and their corresponding mis-applications in real life. My experiences in Christian churches and Christian academic institutions from a variety of traditions, as well as my training and research as a scholar of Christianity and Judaism in antiquity, have given me a perspective that I think can be helpful in our current times.

Acknowledgments

I have many people to thank who contributed to this book. First, I extend my heartfelt gratitude to the Sisters of Mercy whose collective efforts of embodying the mercy of Jesus in this world have resulted in hospitals, schools, colleges, universities, and other service organizations that today serve hundreds of thousands of people and represent millions of lives impacted for good. I am particularly grateful to the eight Sisters who contributed parable reflections that are now included in this volume: Mary-Paula Cancienne, Anne Curtis, Mary Kay Dobrovolny, Diane Guerin, Marilyn Lacey, Cynthia Serjak, Judy Schubert, and Sheila Carney. I felt it was critical for individuals who live out this teaching on a daily basis to be able to give voice to the spirit that animates their work. To Sister Sheila Carney, I owe an exceptional debt of gratitude not only for recruiting the other Sisters in support of this volume but also for her incredible work at Carlow University of welcoming newcomers like me into the wider community of mercy higher education. I am comforted to know that wherever I may go in life, I will now always be part of the "Circle of Mercy." In this regard, I also acknowledge Maureen Crossen and Jack Alverson who generously shared with me their understanding of teaching theology in the spirit of mercy, and who helped me consider the parables as an important instructional tool in the teaching of Jesus about mercy.

Thank you also to the Carlow University MFA in Creative Writing community for ongoing inspiration and support of me as a fellow

Acknowledgments

writer in spirit—and for inviting me to share my writing. Along those lines, I also want to express my gratitude to so many of my colleagues at Carlow, and especially within the College of Arts and Sciences, who integrate their scholarly expertise with a genuine commitment to social justice and a deep love for students—and who, by their example and willingness to engage across disciplinary boundaries, have challenged me to view my own scholarship and academic work in exciting new ways. For candid conversations both challenging my views and expanding my perspective, I am so grateful. I must also thank my executive assistant, Ada Lovo-Martinez, whose exceptional attention to the details of our work and to matters of academic administration are matched only by her kindness and embodiment of Carlow's spirit of mercy. Without the support of all of the above, this book could never have been written.

Thanks are due also to the editorial and production teams at Wiley Blackwell and to the anonymous reviewers who provided such essential feedback and recommendations on earlier versions. I am deeply grateful for all of their support and wisdom. Special thanks to David Aune who provided invaluable feedback in early stages that helped shape this project in a fruitful direction and who has been a mentor, teacher, and friend since the beginning of my scholarly career. Many thanks to Néstor Medina and his colleagues at Emmanuel College of the University of Victoria for arranging time for me to work on the final stages of this project in their beautiful and welcoming setting within the University of Toronto.

I want to express my most profound and highest thanks to my family, Janine, Jack, Aidan, and Noah, as the people in this world closest to my heart. Thank you for your support and encouragement throughout the many years of working on this project, and for the many lively discussions around social justice, faith, religion, and life that have helped reshape the way I think about all of these issues. You all continue to be my inspiration in so many ways. And to Janine: thank you especially for your unfailing support of this book during very challenging years of your own. There is still no one else I would have rather gone off the deep end with.

Acknowledgments

This book is dedicated to the memory of three remarkable individuals, each of whom influenced my life in significant ways as colleagues, collaborators, mentors, and friends:

- Jack Conroy who I remember for his laughter, intellect, love for learning, generosity of spirit, and unfailing belief in me.
- Michael Palmer who I remember for his wisdom, wit, calming leadership in times of crisis, and mentoring role in my life.
- Rae Ann Hirsh who I remember for her unquenchable positive spirit, ability to make those around her feel uniquely treasured, and (case in point!) naming a butterfly after me.

With their passing in 2022, I continue to reflect on the extent to which each of these individuals improved countless lives through their quiet and intentional work of teaching, scholarship, and service, and, even more importantly, their friendship and love. I aspire in my daily life and work to carry forward so much of what they each shared with me. My hope is that through this book you will encounter a little bit of their spirit even as I now carry them in my heart.

Matthew E. Gordley
Ascension Day, 2023
Pittsburgh

1

Reading the Parables through the Lens of Social Justice

"He sighed and whistled, bending his old head. He said, 'You can't conceive, my child, nor can I or anyone the ... appalling ... strangeness of the mercy of God.'"[1]

1. Introduction

The longer I study and teach about the parables, the more uneasy I become. Scared may even be a better word for it, if I am being honest. I know this may seem an odd way to begin but bear with me. Two things unsettle me.

First, recognizing that parables are notoriously difficult to interpret and that they are "stories with intent" as one writer calls them, I am afraid that I may be missing the point. As a person of faith who has spent many years studying the Bible, teaching it as a professor, and working at an educational institution with deep roots in the Christian tradition, it is troubling to think that I might actually miss the point of the parables. Looking at their complex history of interpretation it is clear that others have done so. And it is a real possibility that I might too.

---

[1] Graham Greene, *Brighton Rock* (Penguin Classics; New York: Penguin Books, 2004), 268.

Social Justice in the Stories of Jesus: The Ethical Challenge of the Parables, First Edition.
Matthew E. Gordley.
© 2024 John Wiley & Sons Ltd. Published 2024 by John Wiley & Sons Ltd.

Chapter 1

Second, and still more unsettling, recognizing that in the parables Jesus calls his listeners to live a radical new kind of life marked by mercy, justice, valuing of community, and forgiveness (the values associated with what Jesus called the "kingdom of God"), I am afraid that I may *not* be missing the point. The kind of human existence to which Jesus calls his followers is one that sounds appealing—who wouldn't want to be on the receiving end of divine mercy?—but also carries with it significant obligations to others. If we take seriously the message of Jesus in the parables, then we are called to recognize that there are harmful prejudices within us that need to be challenged and there are demanding, new actions that we need to take. These attitudes and actions relate not only to ourselves but to the world around us. Moving toward a life marked by mercy, justice, community, and forgiveness means embracing a commitment to the flourishing of all people. And in a world where only some are flourishing and many are suffering, and where complex societal forces dehumanize and degrade, and where ideologies and beliefs divide, the parables challenge us to think differently and live differently. Mercy, justice, community, and forgiveness—the themes of many of the parables—call us to care for our neighbors, whoever they may be. Their call is a call to restoring those who are broken and making whole those whose dignity has been lost. If I am not missing the point, then the call of Jesus in the parables is an appeal to recognize that it is only in living a life of concern for others' wellbeing that one is able to live fully into one's own humanity, and thus live in the way of "the kingdom." Scary.

Of course, not everyone who reads the parables takes away such a message of other-concern and solidarity with our fellow humans in the here and now. As metaphorical stories there is an almost limitless plurality of interpretations that are possible for the parables and what they convey about the kingdom of God. But the "religious" element of the parables (I mean, they are found in the Bible and on the lips of Jesus who is a religious teacher, right?) has led many readers to find in them a spiritual message rather than an ethical one. In this line of thinking the parables teach primarily about spiritual realities like salvation, getting into heaven, and gaining eternal life. One quick example is the parable of the laborers in the vineyard who receive their

Reading the Parables through the Lens of Social Justice

wages at the end of the day in Matthew 20:1–16.[2] A common "spiritual" interpretation understands this parable as really being a message about salvation, becoming a Christian, and receiving eternal life. Overlooked entirely are the this-worldly dynamics of the complex relationship of the landowner, the laborers, and the societal obligations the characters had toward one another within the harsh realities of the agrarian economy of Jesus's day. By ignoring the concrete details of the parable and spiritualizing the message, many interpreters throughout history have unintentionally "domesticated" the parables—ignoring their ethical implications and making them easier to live with.[3] Yet if one takes seriously the explicit teachings of Jesus about social concerns together with his actions on behalf of the poor, the oppressed, and the marginalized, one can see that the parables themselves also deal with these same concerns about the human experience in this world. As Michael Cook explains, "Parables … raise in an acute and striking way the question of how concrete and specific was Jesus' own concern for justice."[4] In this way, and importantly for anyone who wishes to understand the historical Jesus and his concerns in their context, "Parables bring us to the very heart of Jesus' ministry."[5]

While spiritual interpretations of the parables abound, throughout history there have also been those who have taken seriously the ethical challenge of the parables and come to this point of recognition of their social implications. Whether theologians, philosophers, writers, ministers, or activists, they have read the parables, heard the call to live fully into their own humanity, and were moved to devote their energies and activities for others. At my university—a school founded by the Sisters of Mercy and that continues to be animated by their spirit—I have encountered some of these heroic people, some in person, and some through their legacies of writing and action. Teaching the parables in such a context I have made an important discovery: it is not just whether

---

[2] See the discussion of this parable in Chapter 8.

[3] Amy-Jill Levine, *Short Stories by Jesus: The Enigmatic Parables of a Controversial Rabbi* (New York: HarperOne, 2014), 3–4.

[4] Michael L. Cook, "Jesus' Parables and the Faith that Does Justice," *Studies in the Spirituality of Jesuits* 24, no. 5 (1992): 4.

[5] Cook, "Jesus' Parables," 3.

Chapter 1

we read the parables or even how we read the parables that impact our understanding of their message. It is also *who we read them with* that matters. And reading the parables with the reflective and action-oriented Sisters of Mercy led me to some startling moments of fresh insight about the mercy of God as both a spiritual reality and a practical one.

Engaging with the parables in my current setting also challenged me to wrestle with the kind of mercy that the parables invite us to show to ourselves and to others. In this way I have come to see that the message of the parables is both personal and communal, with implications for my own personal faith but also for matters of societal importance and social justice. So this book has grown out of my own context and experiences. I have written it as an invitation to you not only to read the parables, but to read the parables in conversation with some of these individuals who have grappled with the message of Jesus and brought it to life in their generation in their own way. By doing so we will consider together the claims of mercy on us and on our world; claims that seem more urgent with each day that passes.

The context in which this book is being written in the United States in the 2020s calls attention to ways that mercy is needed more now than ever. An important aspect of mercy, as we will see, involves the simple act of seeing the need of human beings around us. In a global pandemic and its aftermath, inequities in our society have been brought into sharp focus. Before vaccines were available all of us could see human dignity being compromised in essential workers, often people of color, who contracted the coronavirus and died from it at rates disproportional to the rest of society. Police brutality, use of excessive force, and killing of black people are continuing to occur at alarming rates. The murder of George Floyd by a white police officer in 2020 seems to have been a tipping point for many white Americans who were forced to come to grips with the reality that racism impacts the lives of black and brown Americans on a daily basis throughout their lives. Americans of all backgrounds have had no choice but to see these realities. Yet each person's response, and our collective response, are still being enacted and written.

Beyond what is happening in the United States, the world itself is facing unprecedented challenges which call for responses of mercy. The growing gap between the poor and the wealthy, the disproportional impact of climate change on the poorest, violence against women and

4

Reading the Parables through the Lens of Social Justice

children, and ongoing military conflicts are impacting literally billions of our fellow humans. These global crises call for our attention and call for us to respond. Can we respond with mercy? How? And what would it look like if mercy were animating our responses to what we see around us and experience ourselves? With these questions we can see that we are facing not only religious questions, but ethical ones. What is the right thing to do in our time?

Author and activist Jim Wallis refers to the present moment in US history with its multiple crises of racism, gun violence, white nationalism, intolerance, and political and social discord as a "Bonhoeffer moment"—referring to the German theologian and pastor who served, preached, and wrote during the rise of Hitler in Nazi Germany.[6] Dietrich Bonhoeffer explored what faith in Jesus meant in response to the rising authoritarianism and evils perpetrated by the Nazis. In an era in which large sectors of Christian churches failed to offer any meaningful critique or resistance to the Nazi agenda, Bonhoeffer was ultimately imprisoned for his resistance efforts and killed in a German prison just weeks before the end of World War II. Wallis suggests that individuals who consider themselves followers of Jesus should ask Bonhoeffer's question, "Who is Jesus Christ for us today?" This question requires those who identify as Christian to ask what the teaching and message of Jesus means in the current context and current historical situation. In particular it invites consideration of whether following God may require Christians to resist in some way the direction our society is moving or even to actively disobey unjust laws. Wallis writes, "We need to understand Jesus and his teachings to shape how we respond to this historical and moral crisis if those of us who call ourselves 'followers of Jesus' want to keep calling ourselves that with any credibility."[7]

In the parables we come face to face with the central message of Jesus. Through them we will see that Jesus invites his followers to act in ways that promote the dignity of every human. The short stories of Jesus invite all readers to see the needs around us, and to respond with compassion. They invite us to question our assumptions and our sense of

---

[6] Jim Wallis, *Christ in Crisis? Why We Need to Reclaim Jesus* (San Francisco: HarperOne, 2019), 184–186.

[7] Wallis, *Christ in Crisis*, 186.

Chapter 1

who is deserving of God's favor and who is undeserving, who is right and who is wrong, and see the world and its people in new ways. The parables challenge readers to see and feel the suffering of others, and to act to alleviate it. They invite us to envision a world in which people act in ways that promote human connection and foster communities where everyone thrives.

In short, the parables invite us to live in mercy—to live with compassion and love in light of the reality of what Jesus called the "kingdom of God." The parables remind us that in every moment of life we either need to show mercy to others or we need mercy shown to us. Oftentimes both. And at different times one more than the other. And it is through living out mercy and living in mercy that we can live into our full humanity. If we close ourselves off from this kind of genuine concern—whether showing it or receiving it—we close ourselves off to a part of what it means to be human. So in a very real way, the parables of Jesus offer a challenging invitation to embrace our full humanity. And in so doing, to change the world for the better through what might be called an ethic of love.

So this book is an invitation and you are the one who is invited. You are invited to enter into a conversation—one that literally goes back two thousand years. This conversation is a two-way dialogue between Jesus and his listeners. Jesus taught in parables and through them offered the world a challenging message about what it means to be human—human in the fullest sense of the word. For Jesus, this was a message about a radical kind of life: a life marked by mercy as a defining characteristic. His listeners responded in different ways, of course. Some dismissed his teaching, missing the point or being unwilling to struggle with its meaning. Some sought to understand his teaching and to wrestle with its implications for their lives. They asked questions and engaged in dialogue and discussion about what it all meant. That dialogue has continued through the centuries as readers in each generation have encountered the parables in new contexts and in new circumstances. You are now part of this ongoing dialogue. Each chapter of this book is an invitation to explore a parable and consider its significance at the time of its original telling and also its significance today in our time. Through engaging with these stories we all are invited to consider how mercy might be a part of our world, our communities, our relationships, and our individual lives today. We all are invited to consider what it means to be more humane and more fully human.

Reading the Parables through the Lens of Social Justice

In this introductory chapter we will lay a foundation for entering into the conversation. First, we will need to understand a little bit about what parables are and why Jesus used them as a primary vehicle for his message. Second, we will need to consider why it is important to think about the original meaning of the parables as they were understood by the first-century listeners. We will see that if we want to understand what they may mean for us in the "here and now," it will be helpful first to grapple with what they meant "then and there." Third, we will introduce a major theme that runs through the parables—mercy—and meet Jon Sobrino, a figure who has understood this message in a striking way as a matter of life and death. His insight into the social implications of the teaching of Jesus in the parables will prepare us for our fourth task: exploring the idea of reading the parables through the lens of social justice. With all of the above perspectives in mind, we will wrap up this introduction by outlining a process of reading the parables that will enable us to appreciate the original message of the parables and to consider their ethical implications for our contemporary contexts. We will use this process in the remainder of the book to look together at eight parables of Jesus in conversation with influential thinkers in social justice.

When it comes to interpreting the parables, author Barbara Green uses two images of a butterfly that I find very apt as we begin this study.[8] The first image is that of a butterfly preserved in a display case complete with arrows and pins pointing to various aspects of the butterfly's physical characteristics. Quite analytical. The second is an image of a live butterfly gracefully fluttering through the air: awe inspiring and uplifting to behold. Both types of beholding a butterfly have their place, though we probably have our preference for one or the other. For the truly curious, the analytical view can enhance our appreciation of the butterfly in motion, and vice versa. In the same way, we can look at parables in two very different ways. In this book, my goal is for us to be able to look at them in both ways in order to gain the benefit that each way of perceiving offers. In each chapter I will provide some analytical pointers to the features of each parable that we will examine: the parable in a display case. But each chapter will also engage with key thinkers, writers, and

---

[8] Barbara Green, *Like a Tree Planted: An Exploration of Psalms and Parables through Metaphor* (Collegeville, MN: Liturgical Press, 1997), 10.

Chapter 1

activists who have sought to put the message of the parables into action in their own way. Whether in their writings or in their communities, these are individuals who draw our attention to issues of social justice and the ethical implications inherent in the parables. As we engage the parables and these individuals, we will be challenged ourselves to consider enacting the kind of mercy the parables call us to. Through this process in each chapter I hope that we will not only understand the parables better, but capture a glimpse of the beauty of each parable in flight.

2.   What Are Parables?

According to the Gospels—the books of the New Testament that tell us about the life, ministry, death, and resurrection of Jesus—parables are a type of teaching method that Jesus used extensively. Here we will take a look at what a parable is and how parables convey their teaching in some very unique ways.

As a starting point we can begin with New Testament scholar Amy Jill Levine's clever reference to the parables as "short stories by Jesus."[9] This is a fitting description in many ways. Most of the parables are given in story form. They have memorable characters (a good Samaritan, a prodigal son, a farmer sowing seed, a king hosting a wedding banquet). They have plots that develop, some in quite dramatic ways. And like good stories, they are interesting to listen to. However, if we approach the parables expecting to encounter a short story such as we might read today, we will be surprised by a couple of things. First, some of these "short stories" are very, *very* short—as short as one or two sentences. Second, though these "short stories" have memorable characters, in all but one parable the characters are not named. This creates an interesting dynamic as well, reading about anonymous characters who are often more like general types rather than specific individuals. On these bases alone, our concept of "story" does not quite capture what we are reading when we read a parable. Further complicating matters, some of the teachings that are called parables by the gospel writers are not stories at all but really just clever comparisons.

---

[9]   Levine, *Short Stories*.

Reading the Parables through the Lens of Social Justice

The original Greek term from which we get the English word parable carries with it the connotation of a comparison: putting two different things alongside of each other. This is useful to know as we read the parables. They are not simply stories with a point. Instead, they are comparisons of two unlike things to bring out some truth about one or the other. Understanding what that truth is is the hard part. Mary Ann Getty-Sullivan puts it this way: "The parables describe what is unknown in terms of what is known. Parables use the language of analogy and comparison."[10] Through a simple story about what is known and familiar, the point of parables is to tell us about something external to the story; something that is unknown, perhaps unfamiliar, but is the important point of the parable—more important than the story itself. As literature professor Leland Ryken writes, "The parable is a story that means what it says and something besides."[11]

When Jesus introduces his teaching with a phrase like "Listen to another parable…" (Matthew 21:33) he is, in effect, saying, "Listen to this comparison, and see what you make of it." In another place, Jesus starts out even more explicitly about the comparative nature of what he is saying: "The kingdom of God may be compared to…" (Matt. 22:2). What follows next is a parable. And just as parables invite the reader to do the work of comparison in different ways, so too do they end in a range of ways. Sometimes parables end with a question. At other times they end abruptly, inviting the listener to imagine where the story goes from there (e.g., Matt. 21:40).

In this vein we can see that for a formal definition of parables, Arland Hultgren's is a good one: "A parable is a figure of speech in which a comparison is made between God's kingdom, actions, or expectations and something in this world, real or imagined."[12] In this book we will focus mostly on parables that are of the narrative or story type. Another type of parable is called a similitude, in which a simple comparison is made without all the features of narrative. Using this definition of parable there are about thirty-eight parables of Jesus recorded in the New Testament.

[10] Mary Ann Getty-Sullivan, *Parables of the Kingdom: Jesus and the Use of Parables in the Synoptic Tradition* (Collegeville, MN: Liturgical Press, 2007), 3.
[11] Leland Ryken, *How to Read the Bible as Literature* (Grand Rapids: Zondervan, 1984), 145.
[12] Arland J. Hultgren, *The Parables of Jesus: A Commentary* (The Bible in its World; Grand Rapids: Eerdmans, 2000), 3.

Chapter 1

As a kind of folk discourse common in the ancient world, parables are a creative medium that is uniquely suited to convey a provocative message in a simple and even disarming way. One intriguing point about parables is that they require the reader or hearer to really think about what might appear at first glance to be a relatively simple interaction. Of course, if the reader or hearer is not interested in really understanding, he or she can leave it at face value. But the point of a parable is to use a comparison to help the listener gain some insight, and then to do the hard work of considering how that insight may be true in the listener's own life. Through this act of comparison parables "metaphorically redescribe our world" and invite us to a fresh awareness of how things are or how they might be.[13] And then, in view of that insight, the listener is invited to consider what action, attitude, or thought might need to change in order to live in line with the mercy of God and the reality of God's love for all of humanity.

In these acts of narrative comparison it is important to recognize that there is a range of ways in which the comparison works. Some parables can be understood as allegories where each element of the story has a specific corresponding meaning in another sphere. The parable of the sower is most often understood in this way since an allegorical interpretation is provided by Jesus himself in Matthew's Gospel (see Matt. 13:1–9 and 18–23). Most parables, however, are not allegories (though as we will see many have been interpreted that way throughout history). Rather, parables are more often metaphorical in the sense that it is the story as a whole that conveys the meaning, not the individual parts. Many of the overarching images Jesus uses did have familiar allegorical meanings that would have been readily understood by his audiences. These just would not be the kind of complex and detailed allegories sometimes seen in the interpretation of the parables by early theologians in the Patristic period. New Testament scholar Raymond Brown explains, "Simple allegory and metaphor, and allegories already familiar to his hearer from the Old Testament—these lay within his [Jesus's] illustrative range."[14] For example, for listeners familiar with the Jewish Scriptures where writers compare the people of Israel to a vineyard (see, for example, Ps 80:8–10 or Isaiah 5:1–7), a story about a landowner and his vineyard would carry obvious connotations as

---

[13] Green, *Like a Tree Planted*, 10.

[14] Raymond E. Brown, *New Testament Essays* (Garden City, NY: Image Books, 1968), 323.

10

Reading the Parables through the Lens of Social Justice

being potentially a story about God and God's people. Similarly, with the biblical emphasis on God as king or God as a father, one might expect a parable about a king or a father to represent God. Those images sometimes *do* and sometimes *do not* seem to carry those meanings in the parables of Jesus. Often the parables challenge readers' presuppositions about those generic characters, inviting readers to wrestle with the differences. Thus, instead of asking whether a parable is an allegory or not, it will be more beneficial to note the range of degrees to which the narrative details may be understood to be allegorical, and to recognize the ways this varies from one parable to another.[15]

In this process of comparison, it is important to note also that parables show both what God is like and unlike. The comparisons can work two ways. And readers must be careful not to identify every act or deed or word of characters in a parable as expressing what God is like. The point may be that God is like one particular aspect of the story, but not others. Understanding this subtle dynamic is important, and it is where the process of interpretation, and interpretation in conversation with others, comes into play.

To take one quick example, in the parable of the great banquet in Luke 14:15–24, Jesus tells a parable about the kingdom of God, after someone dining with him proclaims, "Blessed is anyone who will eat bread in the kingdom of God!" The parable concerns a master who gives a great banquet and invites many people. We might expect that the banquet represents the kingdom of God and that the master represents God. Thus, we may expect to learn something about God from the actions of the master. However, the parable goes on to show the master getting increasingly angry as individuals make excuses to avoid the banquet and do not willingly come to it. Finally, the master tells his servant to force people to come to the banquet, and also that those who would not accept the invitation will never dine with him again. These descriptions of anger, forcing people against their will, and holding a grudge clearly do not align with the explicit teaching about God from the rest of Scripture as a compassionate parent, or even from other

---

[15] Carey explains this noting that, "Every parable has elements that map onto realities beyond the world of the parable, but not every parable is an allegory. We discover that not all parables are alike." See Greg Carey, *Stories Jesus Told: How to Read a Parable* (Nashville: Abingdon, 2019), 102.

Chapter 1

parables comparing God to someone who goes out himself and actively seeks what has been lost. This jarring parable should cause us to remember that parables both reveal what God is like and unlike. In this case, the parable gives us pause, and we can be grateful that God is not like that angry and spiteful dinner host. At the same time, what does this reveal about the kingdom of God? It may indeed be like a banquet which people choose not to attend, even though there is plenty of room and everyone, from the least to the greatest, is welcome. As a listener to such a parable I might then ask where I see myself in the parable: have I accepted the invitation, or am I like those who make excuses and prioritize other things over the kingdom? Or in a different vein, is there some area of life in which I myself am an angry, spiteful host toward people around me? The challenge of the parable is often found in our response, not in linking every character in the story to what God is like.

As an aside here, we might also ask why the master had such a difficult time getting people to come to his banquet. As listeners to this intriguing story we can only imagine. Maybe he was a terrible host. Maybe he was a tyrant. Maybe his (very obvious) anger issues were well known. Matthew's Gospel includes an even more extreme retelling of this parable with the host as a murderous king who sends troops to destroy those who would not attend and who had previously murdered his messengers (Matthew 22:1–14). Since the servants ultimately brought in whoever they could find off the streets, one man ended up there without a wedding robe. When the man cannot explain why he is not properly dressed the vengeful host gets even *more* unhinged (if that were possible!) and says to the servants: "Bind him hand and foot, and throw him into the outer darkness, where there will be weeping and gnashing of teeth" (v. 13). Wait, what?! Again we are confronted with a gripping story that does not go as we expect it will. The challenge is to wrestle with what the parable says to us while recognizing that every detail is not a word picture of what God is like. The comparison of the parable invites us to consider critically what is being brought into focus.

So we see that a parable is a comparison, and often a narrative one, which draws the listener in with an interesting scenario built around experiences familiar to the audience. While the story may be interesting in and of itself, it is the comparison to another reality which is where the challenge for listeners lies. In this sense we can talk about the internal coherence of the story itself which is referred to by parables scholar Dan

Reading the Parables through the Lens of Social Justice

Otto Via as the "in meaning." At the same time, we can consider the realities in the reader's world to which the story is pointing as capturing the "through meaning."[16] It is this challenge to the listener's values, this "more besides," that is of ultimate importance. But as we will see, unless we understand the realities of the actual story itself as much as possible—the in meaning—, we will be at a loss in considering the full range of challenge that a parable may offer to us today—the through meaning.

3. Why Parables?

As we start out on this exploration of the parables we should pause for a moment to consider why it was that Jesus taught in parables. From our modern vantage point we can see a number of reasons why this method of teaching was particularly effective. First, parables are entertaining—everyone loves listening to a good story. In this way parables are an effective way of capturing peoples' interest. Second, parables are memorable. Unlike a sermon or classroom lecture it is much easier to remember a story. One can recall a story and reflect on it. One can also retell it. And that is exactly what has happened with the parables: they have now been told and retold for centuries.

Beyond just being entertaining and memorable, a third reason for Jesus's teaching in parables is that parables have the power to engage the mind on a deep level. On the level of the story being told, they involve the imagination of the listener in picturing the scene that is unfolding. And because they move in the realm of comparison rather than straightforward assertion, they also require the listener to think and actively question what is going on in the story and why. And here is the brilliant effect of a parable which is captured well by C. H. Dodd:

> At its simplest, the parable is a metaphor or simile drawn from nature or common life, arresting the hearer by its vividness or strangeness, and leaving the mind in sufficient doubt to its precise application to tease the mind into active thought.[17]

---

[16] Dan Otto Via, *The Parables: Their Literary and Existential Dimension* (Philadelphia: Fortress, 1967), 83–84.

[17] C. H. Dodd, *The Parables of the Kingdom* (Glasgow: Fount Paperbacks, 1961), 16.

Chapter 1

This "leaving the mind in sufficient doubt" is a key aspect of what parables do in such a unique way. Because of this puzzling dimension of parables, Howard Thurman half-jokingly referred to parables as "can openers for the mind."[18] They get the listener thinking about how such an interesting concrete, this-worldly occurrence can reflect a spiritual meaning. Whether one wants to or not, when listening to parables one almost automatically begins to ask questions such as: What is the comparison that Jesus is making here? What does this story have to do with understanding God, other people, or myself in relation to them? Where do I see myself in the parable? Metaphor has the capability to engage the mind in deeper and more powerful ways than other more direct forms of communication.

Fourth, parables have the power to engage the heart. Though they feature common occurrences and scenes, they often contain a twist that brings an element of surprise and which may cause an emotional response in the reader. The twist is often what makes the parable interesting or even disturbing. In addition to engaging the imagination of the listener, this element of a parable is one that holds the potential to engage the emotions. Greg Carey refers to this feature as a "hook" and what he describes as "a point at which the story jumps off the rails of normalcy."[19] The banquet parables noted above are great examples of parables where a fairly standard scene becomes anything but. And such a departure from audience expectations invites further consideration of both the story itself and one's own emotional response to it. It is also commonly in that twist or surprise element that the significance of the parable is to be found. Carey puts it this way: "A parable's hook challenges us to open our imaginations to the possibility that the things of God are not as we'd expect. Parables with hooks refuse to wrap spiritual lessons in fancy paper and tie them up with a pretty bow."[20]

Fifth, because of the above dynamics, the parables are a disarming way to raise difficult issues. They cause the listener to let her guard down as she thinks about the features of the story. And suddenly, when she realizes the significance of the parable, she is faced with a challenge of accepting it or not. Green notes how parables "sidle up" to us

[18] Howard Thurman, *Sermons on the Parables* (Maryknoll, NY: Orbis Books, 2018), 8.
[19] Carey, *Stories Jesus Told*, xi.
[20] Carey, *Stories Jesus Told*, 105.

Reading the Parables through the Lens of Social Justice

innocently and then "blindside us, suddenly disclosing to us something we might have screened out had we seen it coming."[21] This is much different than starting with a difficult truth and trying to explain it directly. In this way, parables are an indirect and less threatening way of inviting listeners to consider challenging realities. Crossan cleverly notes: "Parables are traps for thought and lures for participation."[22] He uses the phrase "participatory pedagogy" to describe the ways parables invite the listener to engage with their significance. Megan McKenna suggests that parables are the "arrows of God" that have the capacity to pierce the hearts of listeners.[23] What each of these writers is getting at is the unique way in which parables draw readers into a consideration of their own values, often without their realizing it until it is too late.

The features above combine together to suggest the power of parables to engage a listener at multiple levels of their consciousness, including the mind, the heart, and the imagination. For teaching religious ethical concepts that his listeners would not only remember but enact, Jesus chose a very powerful instructional tool. Ethicist and theologian Lisa Sowle-Cahill explains, "To be practically effective, theological and ethical ideals must grip people and communities at more than an intellectual or theoretical level. They must have an imaginative and affective appeal."[24] The power of parables is found in that they possess this very quality.

The gospel writers tell us that Jesus had other reasons for speaking in parables. Matthew, Mark, and Luke each recount that Jesus explained his use of parables to the disciples (see Mark 4:10–12; Luke 8:9–10; Matt. 13:10–17, 34–35). Notably, Matthew, Mark, and Luke's explanations

---

[21] Green, *Like a Tree Planted*, 20.

[22] John Dominic Crossan, *The Power of Parable: How Fiction by Jesus Became Fiction about Jesus* (New York: HarperOne, 2012), 244.

[23] Megan McKenna, *Parables: The Arrows of God* (Maryknoll, NY: Orbis Books, 1994).

[24] Lisa Sowle Cahill, *Global Justice, Christology and Christian Ethics* (New Studies in Christian Ethics; New York: Cambridge University 2013), 6. Along these lines Cahill also notes theologian Jon Sobrino's linking of orthodoxy (right thinking) and orthopraxis (right acting) with what he calls *orthopathy* (right feeling): "To do what is right requires an attraction to the good, commitment to its reality, and the imagination to see possibilities of goodness that stretch beyond present conditions" (7). Thus the importance of symbol, story, art, music, and ritual in promoting ethical values.

Chapter 1

each connect the use of parables with fulfillment of prophetic expectations as Jesus quotes from Isa 6:9–10 and Ps 78:2. The passage in Isaiah speaks of listeners whose hearts are hard and who refuse to hear the message of healing and forgiveness—a passage that was likely very important to the gospel writers themselves as they wrestled with issues in their own day of who would or would not accept the message about Jesus. The verse from Ps 78 suggests that Jesus's use of parables was a fulfillment of prophecy:

> Jesus told the crowds all these things in parables; without a parable he told them nothing. This was to fulfill what had been spoken through the prophet: "I will open my mouth to speak in parables; I will proclaim what has been hidden from the foundation of the world."
>
> (Matt. 13:34–35 citing Ps 78:2)

Matthew clearly understood that Jesus's choice to use parables was a visible demonstration of the arrival of the new age, the kingdom of heaven, and that it was what the prophets had foretold. Seen in these ways, teaching in parables takes on some added depth of significance. We will consider this dimension of the significance of parables more fully in the next chapter.

Finally, we can add one additional reason for parables. Concepts like the "kingdom of God" and the "kingdom of heaven" are ultimately divine mysteries that exceed human understanding. "God" is ultimately beyond human understanding in any direct sense. The divine exceeds the capacity of human language, so analogy and comparison are needed. These are spiritual realities that cannot be seen and observed around us with just our five senses. They are mysteries that cannot be directly described. As Carey puts it: "The parables call us to look through them to other realities."[25] Parables, through the language of comparison, give insight into unknown things by comparison with things that are known. Hultgren explains, "The verbal images and the behavior of the metaphorical figures described are more powerful than propositional language about God could convey."[26] Norman Perrin puts it even more directly: "The parables of Jesus mediated to the hearer

[25] Carey, *Stories Jesus Told*, 106.
[26] Hultgren, *Parables of Jesus*, 10.

16

Reading the Parables through the Lens of Social Justice

an experience of the Kingdom of God."[27] Through parables readers come into contact with deep truths in ways that are less amenable to direct assertion, but nonetheless very real.

4. The Parables as They Were Originally Heard

Reading the parables of Jesus in the twenty-first century requires us to be aware of several things that we may not immediately recognize. First, it is important to keep in mind that the daily life experiences and worldview assumptions of Jesus's first-century Jewish audience were very likely quite different from the daily experiences and worldview assumptions of any of us reading the parables today. That means that if we are to try to understand what Jesus intended his first audiences to "get" out of his parables, what the challenge was that he intended to convey, we will need to make a concerted effort to understand the perspectives and experiences of first-century people. Since the parables involve stories which include things like farms, vineyards, slaves, kings, and sheep, those of us with no day-to-day experience of these things need to do a little bit of work to understand them and their significance to first-century life. That is not easy, but it is possible thanks to the research of historians, archaeologists, anthropologists, and others who have studied life in the ancient world. We will get to some of those details of ancient life later, but for now it is important simply to recognize that "our" world and "our" assumptions about life may be quite different from those of Jesus's listeners. At the very least, we should not assume that our own views or experiences are normative. If we can recognize that and keep it in mind, we can avoid the trap of assuming we know the meaning of a parable just by taking it at face value.

Second, if it is hard to get back into a first-century mindset, there is another complication. When we read the parables in the Gospels, we are not hearing the stories directly from the lips of Jesus. Instead, we are reading the parables given to us in ways based on the purposes and understanding of each gospel writer whether Matthew, Mark, or Luke.

---

[27] Norman Perrin, *Jesus and the Language of the Kingdom: Symbol and Metaphor in New Testament Interpretation* (Philadelphia: Fortress, 1976), 56.

Chapter 1

The Gospels were written in the generations after Jesus, only after the disciples had been telling and retelling the parables for many years. Since parables are open to a variety of interpretations (that is part of the challenge of parables—they get us to think and consider how the parable applies to us), we need to keep in mind that the particular interpretation that one of the gospel writers gives to the parable may not be the only possible one. When Jesus originally spoke the parable, what did he mean? What range of possibilities did he have in mind for his listeners?

In some instances the gospel writers will give us the interpretation of a parable. We may have cause to wonder, though, whether that interpretation was Jesus's intention or was an explanatory comment by the gospel writer. The gospel writers were communicating about Jesus with a message that was suited for their day, decades after Jesus first taught the crowds in parables. By this time communities of Jesus-followers had been formed and new sets of issues had arisen within these communities. The gospel writers conveyed their understanding about the reality of Jesus and his teaching, but certainly did so in ways that were designed to speak to the needs of their audiences. We might keep this in mind as we consider the significance of any particular parable: it may have had different significance at different points in its being told and retold.

There is a third challenge to reading the parables as they were originally heard. We may have some unrecognized biases and assumptions about these parables which unconsciously shape how we interpret them. This is particularly true with regard to how some parables have been interpreted, in some cases for centuries, in ways which present a false picture of first-century Judaism. "Anti-Judaism" is a word that describes approaches to reading the New Testament that denigrate and devalue Jewish belief and practice.[28] This is seen most readily in assumptions that Judaism was legalistic, hard-hearted, unmerciful, and hypocritical (often represented by Pharisees in the parables), while Jesus and Christians, by sharp contrast, brought a message of love, mercy, and grace. When the good character in a parable is understood to represent Christians, and the bad character is understood to represent Jews, then it is easy to fall into the trap of adopting an anti-Jewish interpretation.

---

[28] For readers for whom this is a new concept, "anti-Judaism" as understood here with regard to Jewish religion is distinct from "anti-Semitism," which is a racist ideology. But the two are obviously closely related as one often justifies the other.

18

Reading the Parables through the Lens of Social Justice

But there are serious problems with that approach. The first problem is that Jesus was Jewish and not a Christian. Christianity did not exist when Jesus was speaking to his audiences and sharing the parables. "Christianity" as a religion only developed as followers of Jesus formed communities of faith in Jesus after his death and resurrection. Even then, the first followers of Jesus were Jews. So when Jesus spoke to the crowds, he was a Jewish teacher speaking to Jewish listeners. Rather than trying to contrast "bad" Judaism with "good" Christianity, Jesus was challenging Jewish listeners to put into practice the kinds of teachings that were already part of Judaism. And that is the second problem with anti-Judaism: the teachings of Jesus were not in contrast to Jewish teaching but are drawn directly out of Jewish teaching. Love, grace, compassion, forgiveness, and mercy are all part of the rich tapestry of Jewish teaching found in the Jewish Scriptures, which Christians came to refer to as the Old Testament.

With this in mind, we will need to be cautious about using the parables to bolster one group's legitimacy at the expense of another group. One writer who has done a good job of helping contemporary readers understand and resist anti-Judaism is Amy-Jill Levine. In several of the parables we study, we will turn to her insights about the deeply Jewish nature of the parables to help us ensure that we are hearing the parables as they were originally heard. And it is important to recognize that this is not just a matter of getting interpretation "right." There are significant ethical and practical implications to reading parables well. Dominic Crossan observes, "The trajectory of human violence escalates almost inevitably from the ideological through the rhetorical to the physical."[29] Interpreting the parables in anti-Jewish or other ways that dehumanize, whether intentionally or unintentionally, is a first step on this trajectory of human violence. Sadly, one can see this trajectory illustrated in the shooter at the Tree of Life Synagogue in Pittsburgh. In his online rantings against Jews, New Testament scripture was directly quoted as justifying his beliefs and actions. It is thus incumbent on anyone who wishes to interpret the parables of Jesus to be mindful of this reality and to ensure that the good news about Jesus is not distorted by being read through a lens of hate that is completely out of line with what Jesus was about.

[29] Crossan, *Power of Parable*, 247.

Chapter 1

With the above considerations in mind about cultural distance and cultural assumptions, it is clear that interpreting parables is a challenging task that happens on several levels. In considering the meaning of parables, Hultgren identifies two types of translation that must occur. By "translation" he is not speaking simply about moving from the language of the Gospels (Greek) to our language. Instead he is speaking about conveying the message of the parables across the divide of two millennia. The first type of translation, cultural translation, is the work of moving from the worldview of the ancient listeners to a contemporary worldview. The second type of translation is translation from one mode of discourse to another—in this case from parable speech to declarative speech. As Hultgren puts it, this is a move "from one mode of expression (parable) to another (descriptive discourse)."[30] He suggests that in both processes there will naturally be some loss from the original impact—and we need to keep this in mind for each parable we explore. Given the power and imagery of the parables, and the changing nature of culture, the parables present an opportunity for fresh interpretation in every generation and culture. In fact, they require it. What might have been "lost in translation" in an earlier generation may be able to be recovered anew through the act of reading together in our present moment with all that it entails.

5. Parables and Mercy: An Entry Point into Social Justice

As we will see, through the parables Jesus touches on many different aspects of what it means to be fully human and to live according to the values of the kingdom of God. Topics include fundamental things like forgiveness, humility, generosity, compassion and priorities. One theme that is prominent in the parables is the notion of mercy. Mercy is brought into view sometimes explicitly (i.e. the word "mercy" is used in many parables) and sometimes implicitly in the parables. While there are many parables which speak to mercy—both the mercy of God and the imperative for us to be merciful to one another—one parable stands out

---

[30] Hultgren, *Parables of Jesus*, 17.

Reading the Parables through the Lens of Social Justice

from the rest in this area, and that is the parable of the Good Samaritan. This parable, found in Luke 10:25–37, is among the most well-known of Jesus's parables, with a character whose description has become synonymous in Western culture with one who helps others in times of need. We will examine this parable in detail in Chapter 3. For now, we will note the centrality of mercy in this parable. The whole point of this parable revolves around the recognition that the one who is the true neighbor to the injured man is "the one who had *mercy* on him" (Lk 10:37). As we will see, the twist in this parable is not as often recognized, however: the one who was merciful was the one Jesus's original listeners would least expect to show it. And so Jesus complicates things and provides a more challenging picture of mercy than simply the notion of helping someone in need.

Mercy is certainly well-known as a dimension of Christian faith. It is also common, to some degree, in contemporary culture. Catholics may be familiar with what are called the corporal works of mercy and the spiritual works of mercy.[31] The importance of mercy today can be seen by the books and titles that have come out in recent years. From Bryan Stevenson's *Just Mercy*, a powerful book and movie, to Pope Francis's first book as pope, *The Name of God Is Mercy*, it is clear that mercy themes resonate with our world today. Even John Grisham's latest thriller bears the title, *A Time for Mercy*. Surprisingly though, as recently as 2014 Cardinal Walter Kaspar could claim that mercy as a theological concept had been "criminally neglected" and that the results were "catastrophic." He wrote, "What is now required is to think through anew the entire teaching about God's attributes and, in the process, to allow mercy to assume its proper place."[32] Engaging the parables with an eye toward understanding mercy themes is an important aspect of allowing mercy to assume its proper place. Indeed, Jesus famously taught that "blessed are the merciful." What does it mean to live a life of mercy in our current climate? And what is mercy really? Is it an attitude? Is it an action? Is it a feeling we have toward others? These are some of the questions that the parables will help us to answer. Of course, they do

---

[31] See James F. Keenan, *The Works of Mercy: The Heart of Catholicism* (Lanham: Rowman & Littlefield, 2017).

[32] Walter Kasper and William Madges, *Mercy: The Essence of the Gospel and the Key to Christian Life* (New York: Paulist Press, 2014).

Chapter 1

not define mercy for us; as parables they offer us metaphors in motion that invite us to think more deeply about what mercy really is.

Theologian Jon Sobrino has written some of the most insightful works on the concept of mercy, and his insights will help us as we wrestle with the concept of mercy throughout this book. Sobrino is a Jesuit theologian from El Salvador whose writings focus on bringing into reality the promises of the kingdom of God, particularly for those in the world who are poor, oppressed, and suffering. He is associated with what has been called "liberation theology," an understanding of the good news of Jesus that seeks not only to promote the embrace of biblical values and teachings at a personal level but also to promote political structures and systems that can make those promises a reality for the poor. The practical, political dimensions of liberation theology have sometimes brought this form of teaching into conflict with expressions of theology which are less threatening to the status quo. The emphasis on fostering systemic change as a practical implication of the message of Jesus has also brought liberation theology into conflict with corrupt and oppressive governments, particularly in Latin America. So much so that Sobrino's work has become a matter of life and death. Such risks are common in countries with authoritarian regimes where those who speak out are imprisoned, killed, or simply disappear. As one instance of this harsh reality, six colleagues at Sobrino's university in El Salvador, including a bishop, were murdered by government sponsored killers in 1989. Sobrino was away at the time, and so his life was spared. But this horrific crime impacted him greatly, and much of his work has been dedicated to promoting the positive vision of social change for which his colleagues died. The reality of the struggle in his country to bring about systemic change, and the threat that Christian theology potentially poses to those in power, are both very real and ongoing. Living out God's mercy in such an environment is difficult for many reasons.

Given this challenging context, Sobrino has written a lot on issues relating to the poor and the wealthy, the oppressed and the oppressor, the victim and the victimizer. He draws on deep theological resources to understand the complex interrelationship between individual sin, collective sin (the sin of a community or society in fostering inhumane conditions for others), and the dehumanizing values that often prevail in our world. He also attends to the possibilities for forgiveness of those agents of great evil who themselves are dehumanized by those forces.

Reading the Parables through the Lens of Social Justice

Sobrino ultimately promotes a vision of reality in which the values of equality, solidarity and the brotherhood and sisterhood of all peoples are guiding principles. For purposes of our study of the parables, it is important to note the very strong connections between Sobrino's teaching and the teaching of Jesus through the parables.

Sobrino draws deeply from the parable of the Good Samaritan (Luke 10:25–37) as an illustration and explanation of what mercy is all about.[33] In short, he views mercy as the natural human response to the suffering of another person. One who shows mercy is one who is living into their full humanity. The Samaritan in the parable cares for the injured person not out of duty to obey a command but out of compassion. He allowed himself to be moved because he saw, really saw, the suffering of his fellow human. On the flip side, one who does not show mercy and is not moved to feel deeply and take action to help another in need may be closing off an important dimension of what it means to be fully human. Even worse, based on his context of facing evil head-on in Latin America, Sobrino talks about not only those who overlook mercy but also those who actively work against mercy, "who are governed by the principle of active anti-mercy."[34] In the parable of the Good Samaritan, that negative principle might be seen to be embodied in the robbers and thieves who cause the suffering of the traveler. In light of that reality, Sobrino suggests that those who would live out the principle of mercy in their lives today must not only show mercy but must also work against anti-mercy in order for mercy to become the "enduring mercy" which leads to love. For Sobrino, confronting anti-mercy "means necessarily stepping into society's conflicts, running personal and institutional risks."[35] To be merciful in this sense is a challenging call to see where human dignity is being compromised in the world around us, to identify with those in need, and to work alongside them to restore their dignity as fellow human beings.

We have engaged here briefly with Sobrino's insights as one example of considering what it can look like to read the parables through a lens of social justice. We can now turn toward a broader overview of how it is that we can consider the ethical implications of the parables today.

---

[33] For the full analysis of this parable, see Chapter 3.

[34] Jon Sobrino, *The Principle of Mercy: Taking the Crucified People from the Cross* (Maryknoll, NY: Orbis Books, 1994), 179.

[35] Sobrino, *Principle of Mercy*, 179.

Chapter 1

6. Exploring the Ethical Implications of the Parables through a Social Justice Lens

As we have begun to recognize, through metaphor, imagery, and story, the parables prompt listeners to consider questions of mercy, justice, community, and forgiveness as they invite them to consider a way of being that recognizes the dignity of every person and what it means to live into being fully human. The nature of parables with their surprising twists and their surplus of meaning ensures that listeners in every time and place can reflect on what the message of a given parable might suggest in their own lives and their own circumstances. You may not have thought of it this way, but the process of moving from the "then and there" of the original story Jesus told to the "here and now" implications for today is a process of ethical reasoning. If readers do take the teaching of Jesus seriously as carrying some weight today (whether as committed followers of Jesus or as those who simply recognize the potential for some contemporary relevance in his message) an implicit question they are asked to consider is, "What is the right thing to do in light of this parable?" This book is a conversation partner that invites readers to work through the process of ethical reasoning together, showing some ways this has been done effectively and offering some tools for doing the work afresh.

The process of ethical reflection on the parables begins with "biblical interpretation"—an entire field in its own right. In the pages ahead we will be concerned with a process of interpretation that, while not a recipe for success, is a guide for the journey. Interpreting any ancient text is a challenge, but especially one that is as revered and sacred to Christians as "the Bible." When it comes to interpreting the parables, we will see that the process is even more challenging since, as we have already seen, we are dealing with metaphors and trying to translate cultural meanings across two millennia of historical and cultural change.

While the process begins with biblical interpretation it does not stop there. It continues on to include investigation of one's own social location and situation, in light of the teaching of a given parable. This is where we make the move to ethical implications and wrestling with what a particular parables means for us in the "here and now." We might say that with this step we move from interrogating the parable to allowing the parable to interrogate us. As we will see, throughout

24

Reading the Parables through the Lens of Social Justice

history there have been many Christians who have seen in the teachings of Jesus a call to bring about change not only in their individual lives but in their society. Like Jon Sobrino, there have been many who have been passionate about identifying places where human dignity has been compromised and finding ways to restore it. Reading the parables with these thinkers, we will consider the ethical implications along with them and see what we can learn both from the parables themselves and from our fellow interpreters.

Richard B. Hays is a New Testament scholar who has been influential in shaping New Testament ethics as a theological discipline. He advocates thinking through the interpretive and ethical reasoning processes outlined above as four tasks of New Testament ethics.[36] The first two tasks address the "then and there" while the second two speak to the "here and now." These tasks are: (1) the descriptive task: reading a passage carefully and understanding what it actually says; (2) the synthetic task: placing the particular text in conversation with the rest of the Bible in light of the guiding focal images of the New Testament;[37] (3) the hermeneutical task: relating the text to our current situation through an integrative act of the imagination; and (4) the pragmatic task: actually living out the text. For Hays, "The value of our exegesis and hermeneutics will be tested by their capacity to produce persons and communities whose character is commensurate with Jesus Christ and thereby pleasing to God."[38] While Hays's is obviously a Christian approach to this process, the method is not an exclusionary one. With an emphasis on interpreting texts in context and within community, interested readers from any faith tradition can engage this process to consider how the ethical teachings of Jesus may offer rich material for reflection on issues of character formation and community today.

It is safe to say that with regard to the biblical message and its ethical implications each generation has had to wrestle with the interpretive

---

[36] Richard B. Hays, *The Moral Vision of the New Testament: Community, Cross, New Creation: A Contemporary Introduction to New Testament Ethics* (San Francisco: HarperSanFrancisco, 1996).

[37] For Hays these guiding images of the New Testament are the focal images of community, cross, and new creation. Given our narrower focus on the parables of Jesus, we will see that a different set of themes emerge within this smaller set of texts, but with multiple connection points to the larger themes of the New Testament.

[38] Hays, *Moral Vision*, 7.

Chapter 1

and ethical reasoning process themselves, making sense of the message of Jesus in their own day. It is also safe to say that it is not always done as consciously, as neatly, or with as explicit attention to a process such as Hays outlines. Nevertheless, for two thousand years people have been working through a very similar practice in interpreting not only the parables of Jesus, but the entire message of Jesus and the message *about* Jesus contained within the New Testament and within the teaching and tradition of the Christian church.

Though it goes far beyond the scope of this book to consider the differing ways that ethical interpretation of the message of Jesus has been approached through history, one can readily observe the kinds of shifts that occur from one era to another as culture, education, geographical location, and social and political realities change the context in which the Bible is read. As an example, we do not need to look any farther than Jesus and the first and second generation of his followers. The ethical teaching of Jesus in his own time was geared to the concerns of Jews in a particular time and place who were reckoning with the reality of the Roman occupation of Palestine in light of their understanding of the covenant promises, the Jewish scriptures, and the importance of the worship of God centered in the Temple. Yet the not-so-much-later teachings of Paul about Jesus, while drawing on that framework, were geared to a much wider set of concerns related to Jews of the diaspora (i.e. outside of the boundaries of the land of Israel) and non-Jews who were embracing the message about Jesus and gathering in communities together throughout the Roman Empire. Within another century, the dominant discourse of early Christian writers which had already moved from an initially Jewish framework to a Hellenistic-Jewish one, would engage a new context in which Christian thinkers like Clement of Alexandria and Origen were explaining Christian teaching in light of the Greek classical tradition. In each new generation these ongoing and expanding engagements with historical, cultural, and political realities have required and invited new understandings of the message of Jesus—new enactments of Hays's hermeneutic and pragmatic tasks.[39]

---

[39] The story of the development of Christian ethics over the centuries is a fascinating one. For an overview of the interrelationship between church history, ethics, and Christian ethics, see Samuel Wells, et al., *Introducing Christian Ethics* (Hoboken, NJ: Wiley Blackwell, 2017), esp chs 2–4.

Reading the Parables through the Lens of Social Justice

As readers today approach interpreting the parables for our own current contexts in the turbulent 2020s and beyond, we can work through a process of interpretation that includes the four tasks that Hays outlined. What is exciting at this point in history is the opportunity to consider the tools and perspectives that have become available to us through the work of individuals who have brought new approaches to the study of the Bible and to the study of our own times. Alongside centuries of tradition, more recent critical explorations of social realities and societal forces that have shaped our modern world have given rise to some new lenses through which to see the message of Jesus and see our own lives. These include but are not limited to:

- Theologies of liberation, drawn from the experiences of people like Sobrino, which seek to take seriously the societal implications of the good news about Jesus for the poor, marginalized, and oppressed, originally focusing on South America but now looking at global realities;
- Black theology which looks at the message of Jesus and its complex interrelationship with slavery and racism particularly within Black and Brown communities in North America;
- Feminist and womanist theologies which take a similar approach recognizing the patriarchal structures which guide Western society and serve to continue a legacy of silencing or diminishing the voices of women, particularly women of color;
- Post-colonial approaches which examine the legacies of colonization and the ongoing dynamics of the colonizer and the colonized; and
- De-colonial and de-colonizing approaches which actively seek to give voice and place to cultures and traditions which colonial mindsets have devalued and pushed to the margins.

We will have the opportunity to engage in more detail with insights from many of these approaches, and individuals who have developed and applied them, in the chapters that follow.

For now it is important to note that what each of these approaches has in common is careful attention to matters of social justice. Ethical concepts related to social justice include looking at individuals and communities, understanding one's social location, and exploring power

Chapter 1

dynamics, oppression, and the societal forces that contribute to human suffering or promote human flourishing. While dominant discourses give attention to those with privilege and power, these various approaches seek to understand the position of those without privilege and without power. Scholars use different terminology to express these social dynamics whether referring to the marginalized, the oppressed, the disinherited, the colonized, the under-privileged, or the victimized. Further, these approaches recognize that for one to be oppressed, there must be an oppressor; for one to be colonized there must be a colonizer; and so on. As we will see, the ethical implications of these approaches engage the realities and dynamics of both groups, and also recognize the complexity of individual and communal dynamics. One can be both oppressor and oppressed. One can be both victim and victimizer. The concept of intersectionality—an analytical tool that "investigates how intersecting power relations influence social relations across diverse societies"—brings to light the ways in which identity is complex and how various aspects of one's identity can impact how one experiences the world.[40]

As just one example of how these more recent approaches invite ethical exploration of our current realities, womanist ethicist and theologian Emilie Townes expresses this well. The following short paragraph introduces some important concepts around the need to recognize one's own social location and inevitable biases, noting that all discourse comes from a particular place with particular perspectives:

> A womanist perspective argues that because all discourse is rooted in the social location of those who speak (or are silent or silenced), such discourse is particular and ultimately biased. The task of womanist ethics is to recognize the biases within particularity and work with them to explore the rootedness of social location and the demands for faithful reflection and witness in light of the gospel demands for justice and wholeness.[41]

[40] Patricia Hill Collins and Sirma Bilge, *Intersectionality* (Key Concepts; Cambridge, UK; Medford, MA: Polity Press, 2020), 4.

[41] Emilie M. Townes, "Ethics as an Art of Doing the Work Our Souls Must Have," in *Womanist Theological Ethics: A Reader* (eds. Cannon, et al.; *Library of Theological Ethics*; Louisville, KY: Westminster John Knox Press, 2011), 35–50, here 37.

Reading the Parables through the Lens of Social Justice

As Townes suggests, the goal of examining social location, bias, and related aspects of human experience in this way is to move toward "faithful reflection and witness." Understanding the particularity of our own experiences, and making room for the very different experiences of others, creates a space where faithful reflection on the parables of Jesus can occur with an openness to learn from one another.

Writing a generation prior to Townes, Howard Thurman—teacher, author, mystic, and mentor to the leaders of the Civil Rights movement—connected such concerns back to the person of Jesus. Thurman points out what modern Christians sometimes overlook: that Jesus himself was among the marginalized. Further, though it has not always been heard this way, the message of Jesus was one from the marginalized to the marginalized. Thurman explains,

> It seems clear that Jesus understood the anatomy of the relationship between his people and the Romans, and he interpreted that relationship against the background of the profoundest ethical insight of his own religious faith as he has found it in the heart of the prophets of Israel. The solution which Jesus found for himself and for Israel, as they faced the hostility of the Greco-Roman world, becomes the word and work of redemption *for all the cast-down people in every generation and in every age ...* Wherever his spirit appears, the oppressed gather fresh courage; for he announced the good news that fear, hypocrisy, and hatred, the three hounds of hell that track the trail of the disinherited, need have no dominion over them.[42]

Rather than responding to social situations of marginalization with fear, deception, and hatred, Thurman shows how Jesus challenged his followers to embody a "love-ethic" which was countercultural and ultimately cost him his life. Such an ethic of love required as a starting point a "common sharing of a sense of mutual worth and value" grounded in authentic human to human exchange; it includes a deep and difficult recognition of the humanity of both the oppressed and the oppressor.[43] With these insights, Thurman is able to connect the

---

[42]   Howard Thurman, *Jesus and the Disinherited* (Boston, MA: Beacon Press, 1996), 18–19 (italics added for emphasis).

[43]   Thurman, *Jesus and the Disinherited*, 79, 90.

Chapter 1

experience and message of Jesus in his context with the experience and needs of the disinherited in contemporary times.

Each of these recent approaches has brought important new questions and considerations to bear on thinking about contemporary ethical issues. Focusing as they do on social dynamics and the implications of Christian beliefs related to human dignity, mercy, and justice, it is clear that these writers offer perspectives that will help us with the "here and now" considerations of the implications of Jesus's parables for today (what Hays referred to above as the hermeneutic task). However, it is important to notice that these social justice perspectives will also help with the "then and there" analysis, the first parts of our interpretive process which seek to understand the parables' meanings in the first century. This is possible because the dynamics of social power and oppression were very much a reality in the first century. As Townes observed above, "All discourse is rooted in the social location of those who speak."[44] When we attend to questions about those social relationships in the time of Jesus, we can gain new insight into the parables.

Of course, the specific social and historical dynamics in our days which have given rise to liberation theologies, feminist theologies, and post-colonial and de-colonial approaches are far removed from the social and historical dynamics of Jesus's day. So it needs to be clear that we cannot simply import ethical imperatives or critical concerns of these approaches back into the teaching of Jesus. In doing so we would risk doing violence to the teaching of Jesus in the name of justice.[45] However, what is possible and of immense value is to engage the questions and perspectives that these approaches provide to give us new insight into the particular social dynamics that were at play in the time of Jesus—a time of empire, patriarchy, and economic upheaval. As we

---

[44] Townes, "Ethics as an Art," 37.

[45] Such a concern about anachronistically reading our own perspectives into the message of Jesus is significant. We should note, however, that using the dominant discourses of Western theological approaches from the Enlightenment already runs that risk of importing the values and ideals of far-removed times and places into the teaching of Jesus. The anti-Judaism that we mentioned above is just one example. See NT Wright's observation about ethics in Paul as another: N. T. Wright, *Paul and the Faithfulness of God* (Minneapolis: Fortress, 2013), 24.

30

Reading the Parables through the Lens of Social Justice

will see, rather than just bringing an otherworldly spiritual message, the teaching of Jesus was deeply connected to concrete social realities where injustice needed to be challenged. As William Herzog explains, "Jesus' ministry was concerned with political and economic issues. Matters of justice were not peripheral to a spiritual gospel but were at the heart of his proclamation and practice."[46] This observation yields the conclusion that "justice was at the center of Jesus' spirituality" and that "Jesus' proclamation of the reign of God, including its attendant theology and ethics, grew out of his social analysis."[47] Contemporary tools of social analysis can give us a hand in understanding the message of Jesus in its time as a message that was both spiritual in nature (intended to lift the human spirit) and grounded in the needs he observed around him (intended to bring about real change in the present).

In the chapters ahead, with each parable we explore we will work through a process of interpretation that engages the parable in its first-century context. We will also bring to bear the thoughts of individuals who can help us engage an aspect of that parable in our contemporary context. In this way, we will model an approach that allows the parable to speak for itself in its context, and an approach which uses critical lenses to look at what the teaching of the parable might mean for us today. This will enact a process of ethical reasoning in conversation with some very influential Christian thinkers, writers, and activists.

The apostle Paul, our earliest interpreter of the Jesus tradition, had a great deal to say about ethics, character, and virtue. He famously summed things up this way: "And now these three remain: faith, hope and love. And the greatest of these is love" (1 Cor 13:13). We will see that these themes are woven together within the parables. While "love" may seem to be a rather squishy concept to our modern ears, we will see that the love referred to in the New Testament (from the Greek *agape*) is a specific kind of love. It is a love that is geared toward seeking the good of others and is closely connected to the mercy themes we noted above.

---

[46] William R. Herzog, *Parables as Subversive Speech: Jesus as Pedagogue of the Oppressed* (Louisville, KY: Westminster/John Knox, 1994), 264.

[47] Herzog, *Parables as Subversive Speech*, 264.

Chapter 1

Bishop Michael Curry, Presiding Bishop of the Episcopal Church and one of our conversation partners in this book, puts it this way: "Love is a firm commitment to act for the well-being of someone other than yourself" and "a commitment to seek the good and to work for the good and welfare of others."[48] Seeking the good and working for the good of others brings us directly into the realm of ethics as we consider what is "the good" in any given situation. Curry goes on to explain the expanding circles of obligation that such a love places on those who accept it:

> It doesn't stop at our front door or our neighborhood, our religion or race, or our state's or your country's border. This is one great fellowship of love throughout the whole wide earth, as the hymn goes. It often calls us to step outside of what we thought our boundaries were, or what others expect of us. It calls for us to sacrifice, not because doing so feels good, but because it's the right thing to do.[49]

With these lines, Curry explicitly connects the biblical message of love with ethics: "the right thing to do." In the pages that follow, we will seek to connect informed study of the parables of Jesus with engaged reflection on the significance of those parables for our actions in the world today. In the final section of this chapter, we conclude with a short outline of a framework for how we can profitably read the parables today through the lens of social justice.

7. Reading the Parables through the Lens of Social Justice: A Proposal

Over the centuries many, many volumes have been written about the parables and how to interpret them. The recommendations here are not a "new and improved" way to read the parables but rather an attempt to highlight some of the key components of careful reading that can lead

[48] Michael B. Curry and Sara Grace, *Love is the Way: Holding onto Hope in Troubling Times* (New York: Avery, 2020), 14, 23.
[49] Curry and Grace, *Love is the Way*, 23.

Reading the Parables through the Lens of Social Justice

to the startling and fresh insights to which the parables invite us. This process can also be seen to follow the basic impulse of Hays's four interpretive tasks for New Testament ethics although focusing here mostly on his "descriptive task" (understanding the text) and his "hermeneutic task" (imagining its implications for our time and place). While these are enumerated as steps in order, many of these interpretive activities will be happening simultaneously as we read and re-read the parables to understand them. Even so, each step deserves its own attention in the process, recognizing that it is interconnected with the others.

1) Grasp the story
As with reading of any biblical text, before trying to interpret it is important initially simply to try to understand what is happening in the text. In the case of parables, it is important first to try to grasp the basics of each individual story. Who are the main characters? What actions do they undertake? What is the conflict or turning point? What is the outcome? Why do they act the way they do in the story? It can also be important to understand the circumstances in which Jesus is telling this parable. Understanding the literary context can help shed light on how the gospel writer wanted the reader to understand the parable.

2) Ask questions to gain understanding
Since the parables are set in an ancient, agrarian culture that is vastly different than ours, we must identify those aspects of the parable that are not immediately understandable to us and ask good questions so that we can make sure we are not overlooking an important dimension or misunderstanding something important. In addition, questions about the social dynamics at play within the parables are particularly important. While being careful not to force our contemporary concerns into the text, modern theologies of liberation and other post-modern approaches can help us ask questions about dynamics of power, status, privilege, and economic realities in the world of the text that the predominantly euro-centric, Western tradition of biblical interpretation has not normally prioritized. Asking good questions about what the parable conveyed in its original social, cultural, and economic setting can help open up new ways of understanding the parable in our own time.

Chapter 1

3) Spot the twist
As we have noted, parables often have a twist—something that catches the reader off guard or signals that the parable is not just an entertaining story. Identifying that moment or aspect of the parable that introduces a new twist can help us hone in on where in the parable we might identify the challenge of this parable.

4) Consider the metaphor
Once we understand the basics of the story (step one), have some initial questions about the parable (step two), and have a sense of where the parable offers a twist on conventional thought (step three), we can then turn to thinking about what the comparative aspect of the parable entails. Careful consideration of what two things are being set alongside each other for comparison can help get us to the challenge aspect of the parable, the "something besides." Returning to the image of parables as a butterfly in motion that captures our attention, Barbara Green writes, "A parable is a narrative metaphor—a metaphor in motion—that by the peculiar working of its juxtaposed elements startles the mind into fresh awareness."[50] To understand the "peculiar working" of a parable we need to consider carefully what elements are juxtaposed and how they work together to create meaning. This is where both the imagination and the emotions connect with the story and begin to connect the story to the real word of the listener. The metaphor is the place where Jesus chose to actively enter the world of the listener to enable the listener to be able to engage with his vision of faith and community.[51]

5) Articulate the challenge
Once we grasp the story, the context, and the comparison we might then try to put into words what the parable is challenging readers to do, think, or feel differently. This is that second type of translation where the significance is translated from story speech to declarative speech. How does the vision of the world that the parable shows us challenge our own assumptions about the way things are or the way things ought

[50] Green, *Like a Tree Planted*, 10.
[51] On the power of imagery in the teaching of Jesus, see Chapter 6, "Pictures and images in the teaching of Jesus," pp. 85–104 in Anthony C. Thiselton, *The Power of Pictures in Christian Thought: The Use and Abuse of Images in the Bible and Theology* (London: SPCK Publishing, 2018).

34

Reading the Parables through the Lens of Social Justice

to be? In light of the purposes of this volume, we will be looking here especially to articulate the challenge in terms of where mercy, justice, and values relating to human dignity, human flourishing, and well-being may be at play. With this parable how did Jesus seek to transform his listeners' view of the world and invite them to imagine the world in a new way? Because of the nature of metaphor the challenge often takes the form of several related threads that are interrelated and can be interwoven as we consider the point of a parable.

6) Consider implications

Once we have understood the basic elements of the parable and have made an effort to articulate its challenge, we can then allow ourselves and our world to be interrogated by the parable. Is there a value or human principle in the parable that we are being called to return to? What does this mean for me? What does this mean for my community? What does it mean for the world around me? It is here where the insights of theologians, ethicists, activists, social critics, and socially engaged scholars can help us look at the world around us with attention to power dynamics, systems of oppression, and other subtle factors that may be less visible to some of us depending on our position and privilege. It is with these insights that we can hope to see the butterfly in flight as Jesus's ethic of love, mercy, and justice finds its way into practice in our lives and out communities.

As we move toward considering implications in contemporary social issues, it will become clear that we will move beyond what the parables explicitly teach. Moving away from the biblical text in this way may be of concern to some readers, particularly those who might see this as using the biblical text as a "springboard" to jump into whatever issue comes to mind. However, such a move is necessary if we are to have any chance of bringing the ethical insights of Jesus to bear on concrete issues of our time—issues that were not even contemplated in the first century. As we explore issues like racism, economic injustice, human rights, and environmental justice we will see that, although the specific nature of these issues today is not addressed in the parables, the underlying themes of human dignity, love, justice, and mercy have enduring relevance. We thus will use an "integrative act of the imagination" to give attention to how the message of Jesus in the parables can invite us to engage the world around us in new ways.

Chapter 1

It is a process like this that lies behind each of the chapters ahead of us. I hope you will accept this invitation to engage with the parables, to encounter the teaching of Jesus, and to dialogue with others about what God's mercy means for all of us in our present day.

One final caveat. In exploring the eight parables under discussion here, it will become evident that this is a selective analysis. One reason for choosing these eight parables is that I have been inspired by the work of Amy-Jill Levine in her *Short Stories by Jesus* which I regularly use as a textbook in my own course on the parables. As noted already her treatment of many of these same parables provides a rich context for understanding the anti-Jewish bent of much of the history of interpretation; for appreciating the parables in their context; and for considering contemporary implications. Though my conclusions do not always align with hers, readers can find across her volume and mine a commitment to these same intentional approaches. In particular, by referring to her work on anti-Judaism in these parables I have been able to build on that position and take additional steps in outlining the contemporary implications in relation to other conversation partners Levine does not engage. Our different volumes on the same parables thus show the plurality of meaning that can be found in the parables. These same approaches have great potential to be brought to bear on the remainder of the parables and it will be exciting to see how other readers, writers, and activists take us further down the road in engaging social justice in the stories of Jesus for future generations.

Works Cited in Chapter 1

Brown, Raymond E. *New Testament Essays*. Garden City, NY: Image Books, 1968.
Cahill, Lisa Sowle. *Global Justice, Christology and Christian Ethics*. New Studies in Christian Ethics. New York: Cambridge University, 2013.
Carey, Greg. *Stories Jesus Told: How to Read a Parable*. First ed. Nashville: Abingdon, 2019.
Cook, Michael L. "Jesus' Parables and the Faith that Does Justice." *Studies in the Spirituality of Jesuits* 24, no. 5 (1992): 1–35.
Crossan, John Dominic. *The Power of Parable: How Fiction by Jesus Became Fiction about Jesus*. New York: HarperOne, 2012.
Curry, Michael B. and Sara Grace. *Love is the Way: Holding onto Hope in Troubling Times*. New York: Avery, 2020.

36

Reading the Parables through the Lens of Social Justice

Dodd, C. H. *The Parables of the Kingdom*. Revised ed. Glasgow: Fount Paperbacks, 1961.

Getty-Sullivan, Mary Ann. *Parables of the Kingdom: Jesus and the Use of Parables in the Synoptic Tradition*. Collegeville, MN: Liturgical Press, 2007.

Green, Barbara. *Like a Tree Planted: An Exploration of Psalms and Parables through Metaphor*. Collegeville, MN: Liturgical Press, 1997.

Greene, Graham. *Brighton Rock*. Deluxe ed., Penguin Classics. New York: Penguin Books, 2004.

Hays, Richard B. *The Moral Vision of the New Testament: Community, Cross, New Creation: A Contemporary Introduction to New Testament Ethics*. First ed. San Francisco: HarperSanFrancisco, 1996.

Herzog, William R. *Parables as Subversive Speech: Jesus as Pedagogue of the Oppressed*. Louisville, KY: Westminster/John Knox, 1994.

Hill Collins, Patricia and Sirma Bilge. *Intersectionality*. Second ed. Key Concepts. Cambridge, UK; Medford, MA: Polity Press, 2020.

Hultgren, Arland J. *The Parables of Jesus: A Commentary. The Bible in Its World*. Grand Rapids: Eerdmans, 2000.

Kasper, Walter and William Madges. *Mercy: The Essence of the Gospel and the Key to Christian Life*. New York: Paulist Press, 2014.

Keenan, James F. *The Works of Mercy: The Heart of Catholicism*. Third ed. Lanham: Rowman & Littlefield, 2017.

Levine, Amy-Jill. *Short Stories by Jesus: The Enigmatic Parables of a Controversial Rabbi*. New York: HarperOne, 2014.

McKenna, Megan. *Parables: The Arrows of God*. Maryknoll, NY: Orbis Books, 1994.

Perrin, Norman. *Jesus and the Language of the Kingdom: Symbol and Metaphor in New Testament Interpretation*. Philadelphia: Fortress, 1976.

Ryken, Leland. *How to Read the Bible as Literature*. Grand Rapids: Zondervan, 1984.

Sobrino, Jon. *The Principle of Mercy: Taking the Crucified People from the Cross*. Maryknoll, NY: Orbis Books, 1994.

Thiselton, Anthony C. *The Power of Pictures in Christian Thought: The Use and Abuse of Images in the Bible and Theology*. London: SPCK Publishing, 2018.

Thurman, Howard. *Jesus and the Disinherited*. Boston, MA: Beacon Press, 1996.

Thurman, Howard. *Sermons on the Parables*. Maryknoll, NY: Orbis Books, 2018.

Townes, Emilie M. "Ethics as an Art of Doing the Work Our Souls Must Have," Pages 35–50 in *Womanist Theological Ethics: A Reader*. Edited by Katie G. Cannon, Emilie Maureen Townes, and Angela D. Sims. of *Library of Theological Ethics*. Louisville, KY: Westminster John Knox Press, 2011.

Via, Dan Otto. *The Parables: Their Literary and Existential Dimension*. Philadelphia: Fortress, 1967.

Chapter 1

Wallis, Jim. *Christ in Crisis? Why We Need to Reclaim Jesus*. First ed. San Francisco: HarperOne, 2019.

Wells, Samuel, Ben Quash, and Rebekah Ann Eklund. *Introducing Christian Ethics*. Second ed. Hoboken, NJ: Wiley Blackwell, 2017.

Wright, N. T. *Paul and the Faithfulness of God*. Minneapolis: Fortress, 2013.

2

Encountering the World and Words of Jesus

1. Introduction

Jesus lived and taught in a fascinating period of human history—the first century CE in the era of the Roman Empire—and his parables reflect the richness and complexity of that age. Dedicated in the Jerusalem temple and raised in a Jewish household with stories and traditions of figures such as Abraham, Moses, King David, and King Solomon, Jesus's life and message find their most meaningful context within the world of first-century Judaism. The Judaism of this period, however, was shaped not only by its own history and heritage but by another ever-present reality: the Roman Empire. In the first century the land of Israel was under the rule of Rome such that Jesus's entire life was lived in lands under the control of the Roman emperor. Since the emperor claimed a religious status approaching that of a deity this reality had significant religious implications. It also raised many questions about the covenant promises of God to the people of Israel and when and how they would be fulfilled. In addition, the reality of Roman rule had very practical day-to-day implications as the heavy taxation system impacted the economic and social worlds of people under its rule particularly in urban centers (like Jerusalem) but also in rural and

---

Social Justice in the Stories of Jesus: The Ethical Challenge of the Parables, First Edition.
Matthew E. Gordley.
© 2024 John Wiley & Sons Ltd. Published 2024 by John Wiley & Sons Ltd.

Chapter 2

agrarian lands like Galilee. Undergirding all of this was the now centuries-long spread of Greek culture throughout the Mediterranean which had begun with Alexander the Great and continued unabated with Romans, Jews, and (later) Christians adopting many aspects of Hellenism, resisting others, but ultimately being shaped by it in lasting ways. Though the parables of Jesus have outlasted the world in which Jesus composed them, these short, compelling stories have their origin and find their place in that complex and multi-faceted cultural world. To understand them better, it will help greatly to understand the world from which they come.

Since we cannot do justice here to the complexity of first-century Roman Palestine, this chapter has the more modest goal of sketching out some of the important historical, cultural, and religious features associated with the time and place in which Jesus lived. The present chapter will also draw attention to the topics that were essential elements of the teaching of Jesus according to the Gospels. Our ultimate aim is to be able to understand the message of the parables within these larger contexts: both the historical and cultural context in which Jesus taught, but also the context of his overall message of which the parables are just one part. While the parables were a key part of his teaching, we will see that Jesus conveyed his message of good news through many other means, including dialogue, questions and answers, sermons, and maxims, as well as through specific actions such as healing, performing miracles, and casting out demons. Just as importantly, Jesus conveyed central elements of his message through simple daily actions—actions as basic as eating and drinking. If we can come to understand a little about the overall message of Jesus, we will be in a much better position to understand the teaching of the parables.

Prior to laying out aspects of Jesus's message, we will spend some pages setting the context in which he lived and taught. As we have already noted in Chapter 1, consideration of the historical and cultural context of the parables is crucial for getting a grasp of the message of any given parable. The message of Jesus, while understood by Christians to be a timeless message for all peoples everywhere, was delivered in a very particular context to a very particular group of people facing a very particular set of challenges. To help us draw potential "universal" concepts and ethical implications from his message, it will be important to ensure that we take sufficient account of the real people

Encountering the World and Words of Jesus

and "particular" challenges that Jesus addressed. Further, for readers who approach the parables without necessarily embracing them as part of their own religious tradition but who read them with an eye toward understanding their message and the ways in which they have captured the imaginations of readers for two-thousand years, this step of grounding the parables in their original social and cultural context is vital.

After exploring the world of Jesus and the words of Jesus, we will then look briefly at words "about" Jesus, considering briefly how the earliest Christians spoke about Jesus, his message, and his work. This will lead us to engage with some contemporary writers who have connected the message of Jesus to the needs of the world today. Some of these will be individuals we will reconnect with in the chapters that follow, so this will give a preview and some context for including them as dialogue partners later on.

2. Exploring Other Worlds: Some Key Concepts

From our own individual experiences of growing up and living in a particular time in history and place in the world, we know that the time and place in which a person lives has a major impact on their life. The events of our lives and our interpretation of and responses to those events are deeply shaped by the culture in which we live. As anthropology and the social sciences have shown us, our culture largely shapes us without our even knowing it, so that certain things we accept as foundational or values we hold seem "natural" while other assumptions, beliefs, or values can seem odd and even foolish. Interacting with someone from another culture can bring up feelings of anxiety, confusion, and opportunities for misunderstanding based on cultural expectations. Even worse, if left unexamined we can go through life with the feeling that our own culture and way of seeing the world is somehow better than others, or even the best: a notion referred to as ethnocentrism. Pride in one's own culture is common to people across many cultures, but when an unconscious belief of the supremacy of one culture is joined with some form of power within a particular cultural group, there is a real risk of a cultural hegemony expressed in the starkest example through historical practices of colonization and

Chapter 2

colonialism. By contrast, cultural humility is a stance of openness to others which recognizes that, while I may not fully understand another person's culture, I can recognize that it is as important to them as mine is to me. Further, I can recognize that I can learn from other cultures and that my experience of the world can be enriched by the manifold expressions of creativity that can only be experienced through cultures other than my own.[1]

If we extend an understanding about ourselves in our own cultures to individuals in other cultures, we then recognize that a deep appreciation of the significance of any person's life requires an ability to understand that person's accomplishments within their time and place, and within their particular culture. And this is certainly true with as well-known a figure as Jesus. To understand his life and his message, it is imperative to have some basic knowledge of his time and place so we can understand how his life and message made sense in that world. Thus, before turning to the words of Jesus, we turn first to the world of Jesus.

3.   The World of Jesus

Religious Context: Early Judaism

Since Jesus is the central figure of the Christian religion, it is likely that readers unfamiliar with the contours of the world of Jesus would expect that the religious upbringing of Jesus is an important aspect of understanding his role in what would become the Christian faith. And they would be correct! What they may not immediately expect, however, is that the Judaism of Jesus's day was complex and multi-faceted. United by ancient traditions, a body of sacred writings, and a shared history, by the first century CE there was a considerable amount of diversity as to what it meant to be a Jew and to practice one's faith in reliance on the God of Israel. The writings of ancient historians, as well as writings

---

[1]   For a helpful approach to these concepts around engagement with people of other cultures, see Edward J. Brantmeier and Noorie K. Brantmeier, *Culturally Competent Engagement: A Mindful Approach* (Charlotte, NC: IAP, Information Age Publishing, Inc., 2020).

Encountering the World and Words of Jesus

produced by various sects within Judaism of this period, allow us to understand that within the frame of "Judaism" could be found a wide range of views, beliefs, and practices. Rather than outline all the groups, we will here take a look at some of the key themes around which Jewish thought cohered.[2] Some of these also are the areas around which a diversity of views developed, and many of these come into view in the parables.

As we engage with trying to provide a broad-brush overview of early Judaism, it is important to note what we said above about engaging other cultures on their own terms. The need for a stance of openness and humility applies not only to interactions with people with differing lived experiences from ours in our own time and place, but also in our efforts to understand people and cultures of other eras. We introduced the issue of anti-Judaism in the introduction, and it is an issue that has unfortunately been present in biblical scholarship and historical research into ancient Judaism, particularly in early-twentieth-century German scholarship. Anti-Judaism is essentially a negative mindset toward the Jewish faith, often expressed through caricature, misrepresentation, and attribution of negative characteristics. It is different from anti-Semitism which is a racist ideology, but the two are inter-related.

The subtleties of anti-Judaism in historical study of the New Testament exceed what can be discussed here. However, we can note the importance of two things. First, it is critical to make every effort to understand first-century Judaism on its own terms before evaluating it on other terms. This entails bringing an open mind to what the sources tell us about Jewish faith in the time of Jesus, and an awareness of stereotypes we may bring with us to the analytical task. Second, we should beware of imposing external frameworks that limit the potential for a text to "speak for itself," which is to be interpreted on its own terms and within its own frame of reference. A powerful example of this is found in certain types of biblical studies which seek to get behind the text as it has been passed on to us to uncover a supposed original and authentic early form.

---

[2] For an excellent overview of Judaism in the ancient world, see James C. VanderKam, *An Introduction to Early Judaism* (Grand Rapids: Eerdmans, 2003). See also James C. VanderKam, "Judaism in the Land of Israel," in *The Eerdmans Dictionary of Early Judaism* (eds. Collins and Harlow; Grand Rapids: Eerdmans, 2010), 57–76. See also the essays and entries in the same volume.

Chapter 2

This process of analyzing a text to understand its history of development, changes over time, and editorial reshaping of tradition is a valid angle of inquiry. However, working off the assumption that there is an original, authentic (=good) expression of ideas which later had become corrupted (=bad) and through which we must seek to find the original, is emphatically not taking the text as we have it on its own terms.[3] While not readily apparent on the surface, such an approach can be shown to derive from racialized ways of viewing the world. In particular, it is explicitly linked to early-twentieth-century German views of purity, authenticity, and concerns about mixed races and racial purity. In contemporary scholarship this dynamic can also be seen in approaches that elevate Greek philosophy and the Western tradition and approaches as an ideal, with other ways of knowing (whether Eastern, African, or Semitic) as somehow inferior to the ideal type. While such ways of assessing ancient texts can be subtle and unintentional, we here simply draw awareness to the reality that this dynamic exists, even among those who seek to read ancient texts in as favorable a way as possible, with a commitment to human dignity and equity. At the very least we can be attentive to when we feel an impulse to put down a particular idea or expression, and ask ourselves to consider the cause and potential impact.

One God

Central to the Judaism of Jesus's day was the belief that the God of Israel was the one true God. One of the major claims of the Jewish faith is expressed in what is called the *shema* (Hebrew for "hear," the first word of the following verse): "Hear, O Israel, the Lord our God, the Lord is one" (Deut. 6:4). This one God is the creator of all things and the ruler of all. Of critical importance to Judaism is that this is not just some deity out there in the universe, but a deity who cares deeply about this

---

[3] Shawn Kelley, *Racializing Jesus: Race, Ideology, and the Formation of Modern Biblical Scholarship* (Biblical Limits; New York: Routledge, 2002). As Kelley shows, Heideggerian categories of authenticity and corruption "reflect the racial anxieties of the Weimar Republic and that they implicitly yet forcefully endorse the racialized politics of post-First World War German fascism. They are, in short, anachronistic, structurally racialized, and quietly antiSemitic. They necessarily pull the discourse of biblical scholarship in an ignoble direction, and they do so despite the genuinely benign intentions of current scholarship" (213).

44

Encountering the World and Words of Jesus

world. And the idea that the Lord is "our God" alludes to the special covenantal relationship that God established with Abraham and his descendants. The covenant is thus a critical element of understanding early Jewish views of the divine-human relationship.

When Jesus refers to God in his teaching, as a Jewish teacher speaking to a Jewish audience, it is with this shared understanding of God as the "one true God" which is in view even if not always explicitly stated. In response to a question about the greatest commandment Jesus cites the entire *shema* in Mark 12:29–30, demonstrating not only his familiarity with it, but its centrality in his own teaching. Jesus answers that the greatest command is to "love the Lord your God with all your heart, and with all your soul, and with all your mind, and with all your strength." Interestingly, though we believe many of the parables to be about the divine-human relationship, the parables rarely mention God directly. However, like the Jewish scriptures and early Jewish writings which use many different terms and images to describe God, the parables seem to do the same. Common Jewish images of God include references to God as a king, master, shepherd, father, and owner of a vineyard. Each of these images just mentioned finds a place in the parables, inviting us to wonder whether, for example, a king in a particular parable is intended to make us think of God by comparison, or just to think of human kings and what they are like. And even though God is rarely mentioned explicitly in the parables the concept of the "kingdom of God" is a frequent topic of the parables and of Jesus's teaching in general. This is an important phrase that we will return to below.

The Covenant

The concept of the covenant refers to the belief that the creator God had specifically chosen the people of Israel—the descendants of Abraham— for a special purpose, namely, to bless them and to bless the world through them (Gen. 12:1–3). The covenant is outlined in the Hebrew Bible and, like ancient treaties between two parties, outlines the responsibilities of each party, the benefits of keeping the commitments, and the negative results of failing to honor those commitments. Although there are several places within the Jewish scriptures where God reaches a solemn agreement with a particular person or group of people, it is the covenant with Abraham that characterizes his descendants as

Chapter 2

having a special relationship with God: a relationship with obligations on both parties, and consequences for failing to meet the obligations (see Gen. 17:1–14). The covenant is renewed in the time of Moses and includes the giving of the Torah, the Law (Ex 34:27–32). In addition to the Abrahamic covenant and its renewal with Moses, a covenant with David establishes that David's son, Solomon, will build the temple and that David's line will continue to rule "forever."[4] In addition, with the writings of the prophets during periods when the rulers of Israel were not living up to the covenant obligations, we see reference to a new covenant which God will make (Jer 31:31).

With these various expressions of the covenant, we can see the importance of the concepts of the people of Israel, their obligations to God as outlined in the Law of Moses, the establishment of the Davidic line of rulers, and the expectation of a new covenant to come. Demonstrating the importance of the covenant for the gospel writers, the Gospel of Luke is framed with references to the covenant (Luke 1:72) and the new covenant initiated by Jesus (Luke 22:20). Thus, even when the covenant tradition is not explicitly called out within the text, the covenant is assumed to be in effect. Further, each of these important elements of the covenant tradition finds a place within the teaching of Jesus and they collectively provide an essential context for the parables.

The Law of Moses and the Jewish Scriptures

As mentioned above a key part of the covenant was the special provision of God's instruction to God's people through Moses. In addition to the famous "ten commandments" the Jewish scriptures delineate the first five books of the Bible as the Books of Moses, which can also be referred to as the Torah, the Pentateuch, or simply, the law. As a critical element of the covenant and being considered part of the sacred writings, the interpretation and application of the law became a crucial matter for Jewish life and practice for each succeeding generation. Children were taught the Torah from an early age, and the Jewish educational system centered around the importance of the law. In addition to the

---

[4] In 2 Sam 7:13 the Lord tells David about Solomon: "He shall build a house for my name, and I will establish the throne of his kingdom forever," and in v. 16, "Your house and your kingdom shall be made sure forever before me; your throne shall be established forever."

Encountering the World and Words of Jesus

written law an important tradition developed referred to as the "oral Torah"—a way of understanding and interpreting the written Torah in line with its intent that was later claimed to have been passed down from Moses alongside the written Torah. In first-century Judaism, both the written Torah and oral traditions of interpretation were circulating. Some of these traditions are preserved for us as they were written down and witnessed to in other Jewish writings; others are only hinted at in our sources. By the first century the Jewish scriptures, sometimes referred to today as the Hebrew Bible or the Old Testament (a Christian term), included not only the Torah but also the writings and the prophets. Called the *TaNaKh* in Judaism, sometimes the entire collection of Jewish sacred writings can simply be referred to as the Torah.

Jesus demonstrated familiarity with each of these aspects of scripture, and studies of the teachings of Jesus often address the connections between the Jewish scriptures and what came to be recorded in the Christian Gospels included in the New Testament. Jesus refers to "the law," "the law of Moses," "Moses," or "the prophets" numerous times in his teaching and discussions, often in matters of controversy. One of Jesus's most well-known expressions involves his one sentence summary of the Torah: "In everything do to others as you would have them do to you; for this is the law and the prophets." (Matt. 7:12). Jesus also explicitly defined his own mission in reference to the law: "Do not think that I have come to abolish the law or the prophets; I have come not to abolish but to fulfill" (Matt. 5:17). This claim is noteworthy in light of explicit ways that Jesus spoke and acted against some of the contemporary interpretations of the law. Notably for our purposes, the parable of the Good Samaritan (Luke 10:25–37) is told in response to a question about the meaning of one of the two greatest commands of the law: to "love thy neighbor as thyself" (found in Lev. 19:18). In addition, the parable of the Rich Man and Lazarus (Luke 16:19–31) explicitly references the critical importance of "Moses and the prophets" twice, demonstrating the high status of the Jewish scriptures even within the fictional scenes described in the imaginal world of the parables.

Worship of God: Tabernacle, Temple, and Synagogue

The Jewish scriptures make it clear that the one creator God is to be the sole recipient of human worship. In the biblical context worship of God

Chapter 2

includes such activities as prayer, praise, songs, psalms, offerings, service, and sacrifice. Worship of God through sacrifice in the Jewish tradition originally occurred at the tabernacle in the wilderness in the era of Moses. Tabernacle worship continued in various iterations through the time of David. With the building of the temple in Jerusalem by Solomon, David's son, sacrifice occurred at the temple. Within the twelve tribes of Israel, the Levites were given the role of serving in the tabernacle and then the temple. By the time of Jesus, the temple that stood in Jerusalem was the "second temple" as the temple built by Solomon had been destroyed by the Babylonians centuries earlier. This second temple was constructed by Jews who returned from exile at the end of the sixth century BCE and was later renovated extensively in a massive construction project under King Herod in the first century BCE. Temple sacrifices continued through and after the time of Jesus and ultimately ceased with the destruction of the second temple by the Romans in 70 CE.[5]

In addition to the temple in Jerusalem, Jewish devotion and communal worship found expression in synagogues located in many cities both in the land of Judaea and throughout the diaspora. While there was not a fixed kind of worship that occurred within the synagogues in the first century CE, the extant literary, inscriptional, and archaeological evidence indicates that synagogue services generally included Torah reading, reading of the prophets, instruction in matters of Jewish faith and tradition, and sermons. Synagogues also likely included times of communal prayer, although the hard evidence for such a practice is surprisingly lacking until later periods.[6]

Not surprisingly, the temple and synagogues both played an important role in both the life and teaching of Jesus. In the Gospel of Luke, for example, the birth of Jesus and the childhood narratives are framed with references to events occurring in the temple (see Luke 2:22–38 and 2:41–50). Later, it is Jesus's prophetic action of driving out the money changers at the temple that ultimately leads to his crucifixion. Jesus also uses a play on words recorded in several of the Gospels to create

---

[5] Lee I. Levine, "Temple, Jerusalem," in *The Eerdmans Dictionary of Early Judaism* (eds. Collins and Harlow; Grand Rapids: Eerdmans, 2010), 1281–1291.

[6] Lee I. Levine, *The Ancient Synagogue: The First Thousand Years* (New Haven: Yale University Press, 2005). See especially chapter five, "The Second Temple Synagogue—Its Roles and Functions," pp. 124–159.

Encountering the World and Words of Jesus

ambiguity about whether he was referring to the Jerusalem temple, or the temple of his own body (John 2:19; cf. Mk 14;58). As for the synagogue, Jesus first announces his ministry with a reading from Isaiah which takes place in a synagogue (Luke 4:16–21). Turning to the parables, the temple is explicitly referenced as the setting of the parable of the Pharisee and the tax collector (Luke 18:9–14). But it is not only the physical spaces that are represented but also the personnel associated with these institutions. Notably, a priest and a Levite, both of whom are temple personnel, are two important characters in the parable of the Good Samaritan.

Jerusalem and the Land of Israel

An important aspect of the covenant involved the land which God gifted to Abraham and his descendants. Within this covenant understanding and since the land was part of the covenant, one of the possible eventualities from Israel's failure to remain faithful to the covenant was exile from the land. And indeed, exile was an experience of the Israelites recorded in the Hebrew Bible as they are invaded by foreign powers, resulting in the destruction of Solomon's temple. While Jewish history also includes a return from exile and a rebuilding of the temple, the theme of exile remained a central one. Even in the time of Jesus, covenant blessings and curses due to disobedience were cited as the reasons behind the invasion of the Romans (see *Pss Sol* 2, for example).

By the first century CE, Jewish communities could be found throughout the Greek and Roman world with important centers of Jewish learning in Alexandria and other places. These diaspora communities outside of the land of Israel preserved their Jewish heritage while also adapting in a variety of ways to the cultures and places in which they found themselves. Readers familiar with the New Testament and the missionary journeys of the Apostle Paul recognize that the early work of establishing communities of followers of Jesus was interconnected with already established Jewish faith communities and synagogues in a variety of Greek and Roman cities throughout the Mediterranean world. At the same time, because of the importance of the temple, Jewish worship of God was conceptually centered in the major urban center of Jerusalem where the temple was located. Scholars thus distinguish between what

49

Chapter 2

is sometimes called Hellenistic Judaism (Judaism as it was practiced throughout the Greco-Roman world outside of the land of Israel) and Palestinian Judaism (Judaism as practiced in the land of Israel). A variety of religious festivals, prescribed in the Torah, brought thousands of visitors to Jerusalem throughout the year. According to the Gospels Jesus and his disciples visited Jerusalem during the festivals. Though many Jews in the diaspora would never visit Jerusalem, it nevertheless held an important conceptual place within Judaism.

As we read in the Gospels about Jesus and his engagement with contested issues within Jewish belief and practice, it is important to note that the Gospels themselves were composed in the diaspora context. Thus, even though intended in some cases for Jewish-Christian audiences, they did not assume readers' familiarity with everything that occurred in Jerusalem relative to Jewish faith and practice. In addition, though recounting traditions passed on from the lifetime of Jesus, they reached their final form only decades later, when Christian communities of faith were already established. Thus, their frame of reference at times reflects concerns of their later generation rather than the generation of Jesus. Their frame of reference also reflects issues of the diaspora, at times, more so than the issues current in Jerusalem at the time of Jesus.[7]

The Prophetic Tradition

Within the Jewish scriptures are found a collection of books called "the prophets." These are writings named according to the prophet they are associated with such as Isaiah, Jeremiah, Hosea, and Amos. These were individuals who at various times in Israel's history called Israel and its rulers to live up to the obligations of the covenant. These obligations included both religious concerns (fidelity to God; danger of idol worship) and social concerns (justice; care for the widow, the orphan, and the alien; etc.). Often their writings include warnings of disasters to befall the nation based on continued disobedience to God.

In times of distress, including the exile, their writings also included messages of hope and promises of restoration that would come at the

[7] On the ways in which each Gospel presents the parables in ways that align with their literary and theological purposes, see Hultgren, *Parables of Jesus*, 424–429.

50

Encountering the World and Words of Jesus

hand of God. The prophetic tradition of "the day of the Lord" represents the time when God would bring about justice for the oppressed and restoration for his people. Noted biblical scholar N. T. Wright refers to this as the time when God "would put all things right."[8] Dominic Crossan calls this "the great divine cleanup of the world."[9] It entailed themes such as the return of the exiles, the restoration of the people of God, renewed justice, peace and prosperity, authentic worship of God, and joyous celebration of the deliverance of God.

The Gospel writers make a point of showing that the life of Jesus is a fulfillment of many of the prophetic promises. For our purposes, the very fact that Jesus spoke in parables was itself considered a fulfillment of prophetic promises. Matthew, who points out many ways in which Jesus fulfills the expectations of the Jewish scriptures, explains Jesus's use of parables by citing the prophetic words of Psalm 78: "This was to fulfill what had been spoken through the prophet: 'I will open my mouth to speak in parables; I will proclaim what has been hidden from the foundation of the world'" (13:35). In other words, the parables themselves are a visible demonstration of fulfillment of God's promises. In his teaching Jesus is recorded as citing regularly from the prophets and referring to the prophets. In addition, the Gospels record that many people regarded Jesus himself as a prophet, seeing him in this long tradition of individuals calling the people and their rulers to faithfulness to God (see, for example, Mt 21:11, 46). Viewing Jesus in this way is not surprising since throughout the Jewish scriptures the use of parables and parabolic language is associated most closely with the prophets.[10]

Apocalyptic

A later element of the biblical writings which is reflected even more so in the literature of the Second Temple period is apocalyptic literature. This genre of writing became prominent in periods of exile and domination by foreign powers as people of faith sought to understand their dire situation in light of divine promises of blessing. Apocalyptic

---

[8] Wright, *Paul and the Faithfulness of God*, 128.

[9] Crossan, *Power of Parable*, 119.

[10] Klyne Snodgrass, *Stories with Intent: A Comprehensive Guide to the Parables of Jesus* (Grand Rapids: Eerdmans, 2018), 38–42.

Chapter 2

writings often used descriptions of heavenly visions and elaborate symbolic imagery to describe the events of the world within a larger context of God's work. In addition, similar to the prophetic writings, they described the coming decisive action by God to reverse the conditions of oppression that God's people were experiencing. In the Hebrew Bible the book of Daniel is an apocalyptic writing. The New Testament also contains an apocalypse in the Book of Revelation. Outside of the scriptures a number of early Jewish writings are apocalyptic in nature including works associated with Enoch, Ezra, and Baruch. Jesus's familiarity with the themes and elements of apocalyptic writings can be seen his teaching. In particular the synoptic gospel writers include an apocalyptic sermon on the mouth of Jesus—infused with the language of Daniel (see Matthew 24–25, Mark 13, and Luke 21).

Additional Motifs: Wisdom, Justice, Kingship

There are other important motifs woven through the Jewish scriptures and that provide important religious and historical context for the parables. Of particular importance for the teaching of Jesus is the wisdom tradition. Linked to the famous King Solomon who was thought to have authored the biblical books of Proverbs, Ecclesiastes, and Song of Songs, the wisdom tradition emphasized practical insights, the fear of the Lord, and often used insights from the created world to illustrate ethical and spiritual truths. Not only parables, but riddles, aphorisms, proverbs and other elements of folk wisdom within the teaching of Jesus can be best understood as connecting with this tradition of instruction.[11]

There is also a very strong tradition of social justice within the Jewish scriptures. From the Law of Moses to the prophets to the Psalms, it is clear that God is on the side of the oppressed and the poor, to deliver them from their bondage. In Ps 81 God is pictured as the judge of all the earth. His judgement is on the nations for their unjust treatment of the poor, orphans, and the needy. In a similar vein the prophet Isaiah calls the people to "seek justice, rescue the oppressed, defend the orphan, plead for the widow" (1:17). The prophet Micah famously declares that

---

[11] Hultgren, *Parables of Jesus*, 129–130.

Encountering the World and Words of Jesus

what God desires of God's people is "to do justice, and to love mercy, and to walk humbly with your God" (6:8).[12]

In addition to explicit commands to care for those in need, the prophets often condemned the rulers of Israel for their greed and neglect of the poor. On the other hand, in the Jewish literature of the Second Temple period, individuals with extreme wealth such as Abraham and Job were lauded for their generosity. God's care for the poor and the human obligation to do the same found expression in Jewish teaching about almsgiving. By the time of Jesus a tradition that was later recorded in the Mishna indicates that the giving of alms and actions of mercy was seen as one of three elements on which the foundation of the world stood. Not surprisingly in light of our review above, the other two were the Torah and worship (see *m. 'Abot* 1:2).

Another important motif is the heritage of King David. In fact, among the most famous biblical characters are the Jewish kings, David and Solomon the son of David. God's covenant described above came to include the Davidic line, a lineage of rulers who would be blessed by God as they lead the people of Israel with fidelity to the covenant. Jesus himself refers to David a handful of times, and others use the appellation "Son of David" with reference to Jesus. Likewise, Jesus is recorded as referring to Solomon a couple of key times as well (cf. Matt. 6:29; 12:42; Lk 11:31; 12:27). The reputation of Solomon as a wise and wealthy king is somewhat mixed given that he failed as a king and did not fulfill the obligation to care for the people. Yet, in writings of the Second Temple period, an ideal king, a new Solomon was expected who would do just that. A first-century collection of psalms called *Psalms of Solomon* is an important text from this era that describes the coming ruler's commitment to social justice—a motif that was central to the life and teaching of Jesus.

Even a quick overview of elements of Judaism in the time of Jesus makes it clear that Judaism was not simply a religious tradition. It involved a national identity and political realities such as the Davidic line versus domination by foreign rulers such as Rome. It involved

---

[12] Summarized well in Brooks Harrington and John C. Holbert, *No Mercy, No Justice: The Dominant Narrative of America Versus the Counter-Narrative of Jesus' Parables* (Eugene, OR: Cascade Books, 2019). See Chapter 2, "The Justice and Mercy of God?" for an overview of the biblical message of justice and mercy as together part of the character of God and the expectation for God's people (10–16).

Chapter 2

economic realities such as the support of the temple and its personnel which was accomplished through a tax system and the system of sacrificial offering. It involved social realities such as caring for the poor of the land as well as ways of engaging with non-Jews. And how one engaged with the religious, political, economic, and social aspects of Judaism was certainly determined to a large extent by where one stood within society, both geographically relative to Jerusalem and on the social ladder of wealth and power or lack thereof. Given that in the time of Jesus Jerusalem was under the control of the Roman Empire, all of these various dimensions included an aspect of living under foreign domination.

Sociopolitical Context: An Advanced Agrarian Society within the Roman Empire

Since the parables are based in familiar situations from the world of Jesus and the lives of listeners, it is important to understand some of the elements of that first-century world which may not be readily apparent to readers today. Two important dimensions of that first-century world relate to economic and political realities that are quite different from today. First, in terms of the means of production and subsistence the world of Jesus was what sociologists call an advanced agrarian society. Second, in terms of its political structure it was part of an aristocratic empire, namely, the Roman Empire. We'll discuss each of these briefly and tease out some implications for our understanding of the parables.[13]

Socio-Economics of an Advanced Agrarian Society

To say that the world in which Jesus lived was an advanced agrarian society is to take up a type of classification system used by sociologists to describe how societies produce their food, and what this means in terms of social order. Among pre-industrial societies, the most basic

[13] The portrayal that follows is indebted to Herzog, *Parables as Subversive Speech*. See especially Chapter 4, "The World of Agrarian Societies and Traditional Aristocratic Empires," (pp. 53–73) where Herzog attends carefully to sociological models which can illuminate. See also Chapters 3–5 in Anthony J. Saldarini, *Pharisees, Scribes, and Sadducees in Palestinian Society: A Sociological Approach* (Grand Rapids, MI: W.B. Eerdmans, 2001).

54

Encountering the World and Words of Jesus

has been called the hunting and gathering society, with advances in horticulture leading to agrarian societies up to advanced agrarian societies with iron tools and weapons. While no two cultures and contexts are identical, there are enough similar features of advanced agrarian societies that, even without knowing too many specific details about a particular time and place, it is possible to understand some of the sociological dynamics and typical societal structures that enable such a society to function. Advanced agrarian societies typically support a ruler and a ruling class, the top tier of the society, which make up only a small percentage of the population. The majority of the population consists of a large lower tier comprising peasants, artisans, merchants, as well as the lowest classes of the "unclean" and the "expendables." Cities play an increasingly prominent role in advanced agrarian societies with the development of specialized bureaucratic systems to ensure necessary functions are carried out. The bureaucracies that support advanced agrarian societies typically include a financial hierarchy, a military one, and a priestly entity. Each of these entities can be seen to play a role in maintaining the society but also in supporting the ruling class and securing wealth for the elite at the expense of the peasants. At the margin of the ruling class are what are called "retainers:" individuals in functional roles who enact the policies and practices that maintain order and see that the wealth produced by the lower classes is appropriately taxed, collected, and utilized.

Interestingly, within the top tier the elites and retainers who serve the ruler are often themselves in competition for resources and better positions. Such a climate produces conflict and struggle. As Herzog notes, "The conflict over wealth, status, and power never ceased; agrarian societies were agonistic societies. Elites struggled with each other and with the ruler, always trying to advance their position at the expense of their peers and, once this had been done, to secure their gains."[14] Rulers were not ignorant of such struggles but rather took advantage of this dynamic to secure loyalty. Elites and retainers thus used their positions in service of the ruler, but also to attempt to advance their own careers, all the while being careful not to be perceived as a threat to their superiors.

[14] Herzog, *Parables as Subversive Speech*, 59.

Chapter 2

The financial, military, and priestly bureaucracies played an important role in supporting the ruler. However, the increasing influence of any of these always carried a potential risk of their becoming too powerful or being at odds with the ruler. The obvious example would be the military, which played a vital role in maintaining control for the ruler, but also was a threat in the event of a coup. Similarly the priestly class legitimated the ruler, and could benefit from a privileged place within the hierarchy, accumulating their own wealth and power. But they could also play an adversarial role, taking a prophetic stance of denouncing the ruler from the standpoint of religious values. So there was potential for tension there as well.[15]

A small portion of the population that made up the merchant class benefited from providing luxury goods and items to the wealthy.[16] By far, however, the largest portion of society were the bottom 70% of the population who were the peasants, living in villages, living on limited means, but also generating the wealth to be enjoyed by the ruling class. As Herzog explains, "Peasants provided the labor which generated the wealth on which agrarian societies were based."[17] Not only so but "they labored for the urban-based aristocracy who controlled the land and its usufruct."[18] Because the whole system was based on exacting as much as possible from the land for the benefit of the ruler, peasants had barely enough to survive. For their survival and well-being, they found support in their village networks and family networks.

From what we know of the world of Greco-Roman antiquity, these dynamics of advanced agrarian societies were all certainly at play in ancient Galilee during the time of Jesus. The wealthy included the high-priestly clans who profited from the temple system; the landowning Jewish aristocracy who were somehow able to maintain their lands despite the abuses of the governing powers; the appointed ruling family of Herod the Great and his successors; and select merchants who rose to power and wealth and controlled significant aspects of the economic life of the region.[19] The poor included the mass of everyone else,

[15] Herzog, *Parables as Subversive Speech*, 59–63.

[16] Herzog, *Parables as Subversive Speech*, 63.

[17] Herzog, *Parables as Subversive Speech*, 63.

[18] Herzog, *Parables as Subversive Speech*, 64.

[19] See "Rich and Poor" in Joel B. Green, *Dictionary of Jesus and the Gospels* (Downers Grove, IL: IVP Academic, 2013), 702.

Encountering the World and Words of Jesus

often generically called the "people of the land." Yet even the masses were differentiated as different groups whether being owners of their own small lands, or tenant farmers, or hired laborers, or beggars, each with their own challenges for survival. The "characters" in Jesus's parables can be seen to fit broadly into certain social roles, so that Jesus's listeners would have quite a bit of cultural knowledge about a merchant, for example. The same holds for other cultural figures in the parables whether a landowner, a farmer, a woman with ten coins, a shepherd with one hundred sheep, a day laborer, or a small family farm. Those occupations and settings would all carry with them a sense of social order and obligation, as well as stereotypes and emotional associations, whether negative or positive. Part of increasing our appreciation of the parables will depend on paying attention to these economic and social dynamics in the characters, as well as among Jesus's original listeners who themselves were largely rural peasants in this context. Herzog explains this: "Because the parables are full of typifications, their seemingly unique scenes and individual characters actually imply a social construction of reality in which people interact in typical ways. Even the characters found in the parables are not individuals but socially recognizable types who stand in for larger social groups."[20] Thus we need to attend to "the social construction of reality that the parables imply."[21]

This concept of an implied social construction of reality is an important one for readers trying to understand the parables two-thousand years after they were written. It means that as we read a specific parable, we are not just learning about the specific situation of that parable; we are also getting an indirect glimpse at a whole social order and set of assumptions that sit invisibly "behind the scenes" as it were. Yet because these assumptions about the social order were shared by Jesus and his listeners they did not need to be stated or explained. In a similar way, many of the religious beliefs and assumptions of Jesus and his audience are also taken for granted in the parables. In our study, we will thus need to attune our ears not only to the words of the parable but to the implied understanding of existence in which the parable works.[22]

---

[20] Herzog, *Parables as Subversive Speech*, 54.
[21] Herzog, *Parables as Subversive Speech*, 54.
[22] See Via, *Parables*.

Chapter 2

In addition to the characters in the parables, Jesus's listeners and Jesus himself held positions within that same social structure. Scholars debate the extent to which Jesus himself was a rural peasant or from a family of more substantial means. Many scholars today understand the clues in the Gospels to suggest that Jesus came from a family of modest means and that, with his father identified as a carpenter (Matt. 13:55), he would not necessarily have been considered a part of the peasant class.[23] Even so, he was a part of that social world and could understand its structuring and engage its values.

The Roman Empire

As we have seen, the broad brush strokes that tell us about advanced agrarian societies from a sociological point of view give us some important insights into the world of Jesus. That Jesus lived in an advanced agrarian society sheds important light on his teaching, particularly the parables which are set in that very context. In a similar vein, understanding the dynamics of aristocratic empires will allow us further insight into the context in which Jesus lived and taught. The world in which Jesus lived was a world governed by the Roman Empire, through client kings and others forms of provincial administration, as well as by a temple bureaucracy whose power was based on its ability to cooperate with the ruler. It is to the Roman Empire that we now turn.

The Roman Empire was well established by the time of Jesus and was ruled by the Roman emperors—first, Augustus, then Tiberius, Caligula and Claudius. Each offering their own unique spin on the role, they played a critical part in expanding and maintaining the influence and power of Rome. In part to consolidate power and to inspire fear and awe, the emperor was portrayed in symbols, coins, art, architecture, rituals, and ceremony as a divine figure—a "son of the gods" who was a gift of the gods to humanity. Not merely an authoritarian, the emperor was portrayed as a benefactor who was responsible for all of the blessings the inhabitants of the empire enjoyed. He was also portrayed as a

---

[23] See the views in Craig A. Evans, "Context, Family and Formation," in *The Cambridge Companion to Jesus* (ed. Bockmuehl; *Cambridge Companions to Religion*; Cambridge: Cambridge University 2001). Evans suggests that Jesus was from "an artisan family of modest but adequate means."

Encountering the World and Words of Jesus

father and the empire as his household. All of this can readily be seen in the case of Augustus who, as the son of the deified Julius Caesar, could literally be honored as son of a god, and who was the subject of inscriptions, honors, declarations, statues and many other forms of honor throughout the reach of the empire.[24]

Galilee, where Jesus grew up, was in Palestine, a region far from the center of Roman power. But this did not spare the region and its inhabitants from far-reaching changes brought about by Rome. In fact, this was one region that went through quite a bit of political turmoil in the first century, particularly after the death of Herod the Great, client king under Caesar Augustus.[25] As for who the ruler was—whether a client king, or the temple aristocracy, or some other arrangement—this was actually not as important for the lower classes because, as Herzog explains, "Roman imperium, imperial province, client kingdom, and temple hegemony had much in common."[26] As a result, changes in rulers had little impact on the poor since their situation was largely unchanged—they remained at the bottom of a very challenging economic order regardless of who wielded power or under what banner.

Jewish responses to the unwelcome imposition of Roman rule filled a wide spectrum from outright rejection to wholesale embrace, with many positions in between. From the review of central Jewish themes above, it is not difficult to see that on a conceptual level there is a major conflict between the notion of God as king who has specially chosen the people of Israel and given them their land, and the notion of the Roman Emperor as a divine ruler who, through his armies, has colonized the land of Israel and established his rule there. How could the covenant promises of God (which surely cannot fail) be reconciled with the reality of foreign domination by an individual claiming to be divine? And on a practical note, to what extent could Jewish people honor the divine Roman emperor and still remain true to their obligation to worship the one true God and serve God alone?

Violent rebellions in Palestine and the appearance of a number of messiah figures suggest that this was not an era of peaceful acceptance

---

[24] See for example Frederick W. Danker, *Benefactor: Epigraphic Study of a Graeco-Roman and New Testament Semantic Field* (St. Louis, MO: Clayton Publishing House, 1982).

[25] Herzog, *Parables as Subversive Speech*, 55.

[26] Herzog, *Parables as Subversive Speech*, 55.

Chapter 2

of the inevitability of Rome's power.[27] The ultimate destruction of the temple in 70 CE by Roman forces demonstrates the extent to which the Romans felt the need to put a forceful end to Jewish rebellion and resistance. Evidence of further instances of armed resistance even after that traumatic event show the extent to which many Jews were unwilling to accept Rome's claims of absolute power.

With these realities in view we can note that Jesus was raised in a Jewish context fraught with conflict with Roman Imperial dominion, and in which religion, economics, social standing, and political might were intertwined. In such a context, as simple a statement as "Render unto Caesar what is Caesar's; and unto God what is God's" (Matt. 22:21) would carry profound implications and also run the risk of crossing the lines of acceptability for one group or another. How much more when we turn to parables about kings, lords, and others in power.

4. The Words of Jesus

Based on our brief overview above, we can see that the Judaism of the first century CE was unavoidably entangled within a complex social, economic, and political context. Within the broad spectrum of Jewish responses to the challenges of first-century life in the land of Judah, where did the message of Jesus fit? What ultimately was the message of Jesus? In this section we begin with a foundation for understanding the words of Jesus, and then examine some examples and then some themes around which the teaching of Jesus coheres.

Our primary historical source for the words of Jesus is the New Testament which contains the four Gospels: Matthew, Mark, Luke, and John. Rather than fitting the strict genre of biography as we understand it today—with an expected attention to historical accuracy, chronology, and including every phase of a person's life—the Gospels can be considered more along the lines of "theological history." While grounded in actual events their purposes appear not to be primarily to answer historical questions about Jesus and his life but rather to provide a theological explanation of his message and his significance as the Messiah,

---

[27] Evans, "Context," 13.

Encountering the World and Words of Jesus

the son of God. Accordingly, the Gospels are historical witnesses to how the early followers of Jesus remembered him, particularly in light of their understanding that he had risen from the dead.

The goal of such writings, therefore, was to promote faith in Jesus as God's agent of salvation with the result that readers would embrace the message themselves and become followers of Jesus. This much is clear from the words of the gospel writers themselves. Mark began his gospel calling it "the good news about Jesus Christ, the Son of God." With his claim that the subject of the book is "Christ" (meaning the anointed one, the Messiah) and "the Son of God," it is clear that Mark intended to address more than just verifiable facts of his subject's life. This is a message of good news about a person who bears titles of divinity. Similarly at the end of John's Gospel, John explained that his account was written "so that you may come to believe that Jesus is the Messiah, the Son of God, and that through believing you may have life in his name" (John 20:31). With these explicit statements from within the texts themselves, it is fair to say that the Gospels tell about Jesus to enable readers to adopt a particular view of Jesus, and to respond in faith. At the same time, they are also among our earliest primary sources in revealing details about the life and message of Jesus.

The fact that we have four books called Gospels in the New Testament is noteworthy in that it allows us to learn about Jesus from four different perspectives. It is very clear that each author has written their work with a specific audience in view, and with specific aspects of the message and life of Jesus which are important to them. Furthermore, three of the Gospels share a significant amount of material (causing them to be known collectively as the Synoptic Gospels), but also each have material that is unique. Even so, it is also clear that there is much that they write that is consistent with each other, pointing to the reality that the authors were not just making things up about Jesus out of whole cloth. Rather they were at the very least passing on what was understood and accepted within the community of followers of Jesus, albeit in a narrative framework that suited the needs of their particular community.

From the witness of the Gospels we can identify some important themes which permeate the teaching of Jesus. Each of the Synoptic Gospels includes summary statements about the message of Jesus which provide a helpful starting point for us:

Chapter 2

> Jesus came to Galilee, proclaiming the good news of God, and saying, "The time is fulfilled, and the kingdom of God has come near; repent, and believe in the good news." (Mark 1:14–15)

> Jesus went throughout Galilee, teaching in their synagogues and proclaiming the good news of the kingdom and curing every disease and every sickness among the people. (Matthew 4:23)

> Soon afterwards he went on through cities and villages, proclaiming and bringing the good news of the kingdom of God. (Luke 8:1)

These summaries, while not providing detail about what this good news of the kingdom of God entailed, indicate clearly that the acts of teaching, proclaiming, and bringing a message are understood to have been a critical part of what Jesus was about.

As we examine the words of Jesus in more detail we will be able to identify important elements that the summary statements hint at. The following four elements offer a good starting point:

Jesus proclaimed a message of good news.
It was a message of good news specifically to the poor and oppressed.
It was a message of good news about the kingdom of God rooted in Jewish belief and tradition.
It was a message of good news delivered in a context of Roman imperial domination.

Given what we saw above about the interaction of Jewish belief and Roman occupation, these elements combine to create a captivating and dangerous dynamic—one that is reflected in many ways in the parables.

Good News

Luke's Gospel provides a fascinating account of one specific instance of teaching in which Jesus elaborated on what he meant by the message of good news of the kingdom of God. In a synagogue setting Jesus utilized the Jewish scriptures to fill out the nature of this kingdom message. The passage is worth quoting at length here:

> When he came to Nazareth, where he had been brought up, he went to the synagogue on the sabbath day, as was his custom. He stood up to read,

Encountering the World and Words of Jesus

and the scroll of the prophet Isaiah was given to him. He unrolled the scroll and found the place where it was written:

"The Spirit of the Lord is upon me,
   because he has anointed me
      to bring good news to the poor.
He has sent me to proclaim release to the captives
   and recovery of sight to the blind,
      to let the oppressed go free,
to proclaim the year of the Lord's favor."

And he rolled up the scroll, gave it back to the attendant, and sat down. The eyes of all in the synagogue were fixed on him. Then he began to say to them, "Today this scripture has been fulfilled in your hearing." (Luke 4:16–21)

It is very significant that Jesus here identifies his ministry among his people as a fulfillment of Jewish scriptures. What Mark and Matthew describe as the good news, the good news of God, and the good news of the kingdom, Luke makes concrete in connecting it directly and explicitly with the prophecy of Isaiah. In such a way Jesus is indicating that the very activities which he was undertaking among them (teaching, healing, proclaiming a message of good news and liberation) were a direct fulfillment of the prophetic promises of restoration from Isaiah. In other words, the time of the great divine cleanup had begun— through Jesus!

The "good news" proclaimed by Jesus is a central term to understand. In the Greek the term *euangelion* (from which we get words like evangelism and which is also translated as "gospel") quite literally means a "favorable announcement." But obviously it is the content of this favorable announcement that is what is important. Stephen C. Barton explains that it is shorthand for the "message of salvation and judgment proclaimed by Jesus" and "an announcement of hope and warning in view of the drawing near of God."[28] Peter Tomson

---

[28] Stephen C. Barton, "Many Gospels, One Jesus?" in *The Cambridge Companion to Jesus* (ed. Bockmuehl; *Cambridge Companions to Religion*; Cambridge: Cambridge University 2001), 178.

Chapter 2

summarizes that this good news is "a message of liberation" and points out that the phrase "gospel of God" connects to "a wider movement in Israel's history in which Jesus came to play a crucial role."[29] But even these explanations leave open a wide range of meanings. For example, what is the "salvation" that Jesus proclaimed supposed to be saving people from? Is it salvation for an individual person from their sins? Saving them from an eternity in torment? Or is it saving the people of God from the harsh rule of the Romans and other oppressors? Or something else? The "good news" of salvation could potentially be understood as a spiritual salvation or a very real earthly kind of rescue. Recognizing that this message fits into a wider movement in Israel's history is helpful in determining a starting point for understanding what "good news" might mean, but given the variety of ways in which Jews in the Second Temple period understood the expected deliverance of God, the context only takes us so far. Thus, we need to continue to explore the content and themes of the message of Jesus if we wish to really get a handle on the good news.

Kingdom of God

As suggested in the summary statements of Matthew, Mark, and Luke, the concept of the kingdom of God was a primary subject for Jesus; it was also the subject of the good news. In some ways it can be considered a shorthand expression for the overall message Jesus brought. But what does it mean?

This concept connects deeply to a prominent theme of the Hebrew Bible: the notion that God is king, and reigns over all things. Such a theme figures prominently in many of the biblical psalms as well as in the prophets.[30] The kingly reign of God can be seen to be of increasing importance in the Second Temple period as seen in, for example, the *Psalms of Solomon*. We can notice also that kingdom language is

[29] Peter J. Tomson, "Jesus and His Judaism," in *The Cambridge Companion to Jesus* (ed. Bockmuehl; *Cambridge Companions to Religion*; Cambridge: Cambridge University 2001), 29.
[30] See for example Psalms 93–99. Norman K. Gottwald, "Kingship in the Book of Psalms," in *The Oxford Handbook of the Psalms*, Oxford Handbooks (ed. William P. Brown, 2014; online edn, New York: Oxford Academic, 1 July 2014), 437–444.

Encountering the World and Words of Jesus

suggestive of the Davidic line which God established. There is also an implicit comparison and contrast to the kingdoms of this world.

Letting us know that we are on the right track with this cluster of associations, it is not just Jesus who speaks of the kingdom in Luke's Gospel. The angel Gabriel's message to Mary included these words: "He will be great, and will be called the Son of the Most High, and the Lord God will give to him the throne of his ancestor David. He will reign over the house of Jacob forever, and of his kingdom there will be no end" (Luke 1:32–33). The angelic announcement makes it clear that Jesus himself will be a king, with his own unending kingdom along the lines of David. By contrast, when Jesus is tempted in the wilderness, the tempter offers him all the authority of the kingdoms of the world (Luke 4:5–6). Jesus, of course, refuses and readers are invited to understand a deep contrast between the kingdom of God and the kingdoms of this world.

Giving us another hint as to the meaning of the kingdom of God, the miracles of Jesus attest to the presence of the kingdom of God through his ministry and life. These miracles include actions of healing as well as casting out of demons. In Luke's Gospel, when opponents suggest that Jesus's power comes from the devil Jesus explains, "But if it is by the finger of God that I cast out the demons, then the kingdom of God has come to you" (Luke 11:20).

Parables scholar Dominic Crossan suggests that the particular message of Jesus about the kingdom represented a paradigm shift in the context of first-century Judaism.[31] To explain this as it relates to the kingdom of God concept, Crossan starts with the book of Daniel to illustrate the accepted paradigm. Daniel is part of the apocalyptic tradition containing striking symbolism and in Daniel 7 we encounter a vision of successive earthly empires from the Babylonians to the Syrians. At the time of its writing in the second century BCE the Jews were under the tyrannical dominion of a Syrian ruler, and Daniel's vision described history to this point, but also included the coming

---

[31] See Crossan, *Power of Parable*, 113–137. He finds that the Christian portrayal of Jesus as Messiah is "atypical with the common consensus on that [Messiah] figure in its contemporary environment. That is a *paradigm shift*, a revolutionary change, a swerve within the Jewish popular consensus of its time and place" (Crossan 115).

65

Chapter 2

intervention of God's kingdom. In Daniel's vision the kingdom is prepared in heaven, then kept there in waiting, then comes down to earth.[32] This vision rests on the notion of the covenant that we explored above, the idea that God had created the earth and chosen Israel as a restorative presence and locus of God's blessing in the earth. At the same time, the experience of Israel of oppression and suffering raised serious questions about that covenantal understanding. One way of resolving this was through a growing expectation that God would intervene in the future to put an end to injustice, violence, and war in a renewed earth. This is the great divine cleanup we mentioned earlier. Theologians refer to this as the *eschaton* ("the end"), a time period which would mark the end of the reign of earthly kingdoms and the beginning of the reign of God.[33]

As we saw above, this idea is reflected in early Jewish texts outside of the New Testament. John the Baptist, Jesus's cousin and predecessor, seems to reflect this widespread paradigm of the coming kingdom of God within first-century Judaism. John's vision of the kingdom is that it is imminent (meaning that it could arrive any moment now), interventionist (meaning that a transcendent power will bring it about), and violent (it would entail the overthrow of Rome). With these descriptors it is not that John's message was one of human violence; rather because it necessitated divine intervention it included the expected divine judgment of an avenging God with punitive intent against powers of opposition. It was "imminent" in that it could be expected at any time. Such a vision can be supported by appeal to numerous Second Temple period texts which point to the expectation of a divinely appointed messiah who would intervene and set things right.[34]

By contrast, Crossan describes Jesus's kingdom vision as quite different relative to timing, level of divine action, and the nature of that action. In Jesus's view the kingdom is not imminent but already present, not interventionist but collaborationist, and not violent but rather

---

[32] Crossan, *Power of Parable*, 116–118.

[33] Crossan, *Power of Parable*, 119. Related, the term "apocalyptic eschatology" refers to how this great divine reversal will be revealed. Crossan calls this "Special Divine Revelation about the Great Divine Cleanup" (119).

[34] Crossan, *Power of Parable*, 120–123.

66

Encountering the World and Words of Jesus

non-violent.[35] That the kingdom is present, already here with the arrival of Jesus, is seen in direct statements by Jesus such as in Luke's Gospel. In one instance when asked by Pharisees about when the kingdom of God would arrive, Jesus answered: "The kingdom of God is not coming with things that can be observed; nor will they say, 'Look, here it is!' or 'There it is!' For, in fact, the kingdom of God is among you" (Luke 17:20–21). Similar expressions of the presence of the kingdom can be found in Luke 11:20; Mt 12:28; Mk 1:14b–15 and Mt 4:17.[36]

That the kingdom is collaborationist rather than interventionist means that it is not simply that God will intervene from outside of human affairs. Rather, God will work with humans in the context of their daily lives to bring about the transformation that the kingdom entails. Crossan explains, "God's kingdom is here, but only insofar as you accept it, enter it, live it, and thereby establish it."[37] In this way of thinking, Jesus announces a "collaborative eschatology" which means that "it is about a divine-and-human collaboration and not about a divine-only intervention."[38] In other words, "The Great Divine Cleanup will not happen without God, but neither will it happen without us."[39] Thus the teaching of Jesus invites listeners to participate with God in the work of the kingdom through their actions, including enacting a love ethic which we will see below.

That the kingdom view of Jesus was nonviolent can be seen in several ways, but most pointedly by comparing his movement with other violent movements of resistance to Rome from the first century CE.[40] Instead of taking up arms, Jesus proposed another way. And it is not simply that he will leave the violence to God. Rather, the model for human non-violence is divine non-violence. In the teaching of Jesus God is a heavenly father who is kind even to the ungrateful and the wicked.[41] This view also puts Jesus's death on the cross in perspective,

---

[35] Crossan, *Power of Parable*, 120 and 125–131.

[36] Crossan notes also the connection between Jesus and the title "Son of Man" which linked to Daniel, who brings the kingdom, means the kingdom is already here (125–126).

[37] Crossan, *Power of Parable*, 127.

[38] Crossan, *Power of Parable*, 127.

[39] Crossan, *Power of Parable*, 127.

[40] Crossan, *Power of Parable*, 128–129.

[41] Luke 6:27–28, 35. Crossan, *Power of Parable*, 129–131.

Chapter 2

as he does not fight the brutal Roman tool of oppression, but willingly endures it thereby overcoming it.

With this understanding of the kingdom of God as rooted in a biblical perspective on God as ruler of all, a God who has plans to set the world right, and a role for all of God's children, it becomes clear that in the setting of the Roman Empire such a message could certainly be considered anti-imperial. And it certainly was. Jesus was not put to death by his Jewish contemporaries but by the only ones who had the authority to do so: the Roman authorities who judged him to be a threat. Jewish leaders of the time also regarded his popularity as a threat—but it seems likely that it was not so much that Jesus was a threat to their influence or popularity among the masses, but rather with regard to the stability of their region in the eyes of Rome. A popular messiah proclaiming the arrival of a new kingdom had the potential to bring down the force of Rome upon the Jews in ways that would devastate them and their ability to continue to worship with what little autonomy they had left. If that was the concern of some of Jesus's Jewish adversaries, they were not mistaken as the destruction of the temple by the Romans in 70 CE shows.

When we get to the point of exploring the concept of the kingdom as it relates to particular parables, we will need to attend to one other important element of interpretation. It has to do with the idea that the term "kingdom" functions as a *symbol* as opposed to being a *concept*. As a symbol the term evokes a whole network of associations with the biblical myth (i.e., guiding narrative) of God as king; and only to the extent that those associations are operative in the listener's thinking can Jesus's use of the term be understood. In other words, God's kingdom needs to be understood and interpreted in the same way that parables are interpreted: as metaphor. A symbol works and metaphors work to the extent that listeners share the cultural significance of the symbol. With real earthly kingdoms in view, and heavenly kingdoms as a metaphor, this can get a little tricky as readers move back and forth between an earthly reality and a symbolic meaning. For contemporary readers for whom the term kingdom is not part of our lived experience—with the myth of God as king even further removed—the viability of the symbol becomes even more challenging.[42]

[42] On this see Perrin, *Jesus and the Language of the Kingdom*, 196–200.

Encountering the World and Words of Jesus

In a similar vein, Crossan suggests that "kingdom" is a word that is both archaic and patriarchal.[43] To get at its significance in the teaching of Jesus, which was egalitarian and non-hierarchical, Crossan suggests we might understand that it really means something along the lines of a ruling style. The concept of the kingdom of God is really then a metaphor that "ponders how this world would be if God were actually seated down here ruling—as it were—from a human throne. How would the 'ruling style' of God differ from that of a human emperor?"[44]

One final important observation comes from Herzog who suggests that Jesus's message of the kingdom was not based solely on his grasp of Jewish scriptures. It also came from his perceptions about the realities unfolding in his lifetime. Herzog explains, "Jesus' proclamation of the reign of God, including its attendant theology and ethics, grew out of his social analysis."[45] And it seems the social analysis of Jesus included special attention to the lived experiences of people in need, who ended up being the recipients of his message of good news.

The Poor, Oppressed, and Social Justice

From the account in Luke of Jesus's first teaching in the synagogue it is explicit that the poor and oppressed of society are of particular focus for Jesus. The scripture passage from Isaiah specifically mentioned bringing "good news to the poor," along with "release to the captives," "recovery of sight to the blind," and the setting free of the oppressed. Thus, the good news of the kingdom of God is particularly intended for those on the margins of society.

When John the Baptist, Jesus's predecessor sent his followers to Jesus to find out if he was the messiah, Jesus's response focused on these very areas:

> And he answered them, "Go and tell John what you have seen and heard: the blind receive their sight, the lame walk, the lepers are cleansed, the deaf hear, the dead are raised, the poor have good news brought to them." (Luke 7:22)

[43] Crossan, *Power of Parable*, 119.
[44] Crossan, *Power of Parable*, 119.
[45] Herzog, *Parables as Subversive Speech*, 264.

Chapter 2

Recognizing from the social context that perhaps 70% of the population were among the peasant class and thus poor and with little prospect of financial security, Jesus's focus on good news for the poor is significant. Drawing from the teaching of the Jewish tradition, Jesus's teaching includes warnings of the dangers of wealth (e.g., Mk 10:25), emphasis on giving to those in need (e.g., Lk 12:33), and an assumption that such giving contributes to a heavenly treasury of merit with reward in the life to come (e.g., Lk 14:14).[46] In addition, the teaching of Jesus highlights the special place that the poor have in God's eyes. In Luke 6:20 Jesus says, "Blessed are you who are poor, for yours is the kingdom of God." He continues that those who are hungry and who weep are also blessed. There is a special place in God's heart for those who suffer in this world. Accordingly, both poor and wealthy can look to God for their provision (Mt 6:33; cf. Lk 12:22–31). In particular, Jesus taught that those blessings could be experienced within the renewed community of followers of God. Eminent theologian James Cone grasps this element of Jesus's teaching exceptionally well and explains: "It seems clear that the overwhelming weight of biblical teaching, especially the prophetic tradition in which Jesus stood unambiguously, is upon God's unqualified identification with the poor precisely because they are poor. The kingdom of God is for the helpless, because they have no security in this world."[47]

With this scriptural and theological foundation in mind, Cone can claim that "Jesus' proclamation of the kingdom is an announcement of God's decision about oppressed humankind."[48] Cone can also identify that "Jesus' teaching about the kingdom is the most radical, revolutionary aspect of his message. It involves the totality of a person's existence in the world and what that means in an oppressive society. To repent is to affirm the reality of the kingdom by refusing to live on the basis of any definition except according to the kingdom."[49]

---

[46] On the treasury of merit see Gary A. Anderson, *Charity: The Place of the Poor in the Biblical Tradition* (New Haven: Yale University, 2013).

[47] James H. Cone, *A Black Theology of Liberation* (Maryknoll, NY: Orbis Books, 1990), 117.

[48] Cone, *Black Theology*, 116.

[49] Cone, *Black Theology*, 117. Cone continues that "The kingdom, then, is the rule of God breaking in like a ray of light, usurping the powers that enslave human lives. That is why exorcisms are so prominent in Jesus' ministry. They are a visible manifestation of the presence of the kingdom." Here Cone cites Luke 11:20.

Encountering the World and Words of Jesus

It is important to note that the message of Jesus was not only that God cares for the poor and oppressed. It also included the idea of God's identification with and solidarity with them. This can be seen in the Christian concept of the incarnation of Jesus. Cone, again, notes, "Jesus is the Oppressed One whose work is that of liberating humanity from inhumanity. Through him the oppressed are set free to be what they are."[50]

These social perspectives and ethical considerations, rooted in an understanding of God's love for all persons, especially the poor, link back to Jesus's foundational understanding of God in the image of father. While the concept is a deeply Jewish one, the emphasis on God as father is found in the teaching of Jesus more so than in other Jewish writings of the time. Marianne Meye Thompson finds Jesus's more pervasive use of the term to be reflective of a prophetic theme in Jer 3:17–19, a text that speaks to the coming time of Israel's restoration and the expectation that people would call God their father in that day. Elements of the fatherhood of God include the concepts of God's mercy and God's justice. God's mercy is manifested in healing, deliverance, redemption, release from oppression, and so on.[51] At the same time, God's justice was expected to set things to right. Thompson explains that Jesus "also shared a common hope that God's sovereignty would be manifested to injustice and unrighteousness, that God's kingly rule over the earth would someday be fully manifested and bring about his reign of justice and peace."[52] There is a lot packed into that last statement and we can see that it aligns closely with what we cited from James Cone above. Love and justice are thus integrally linked. A God who loves the oppressed will not leave the oppressors unaddressed.

Jesus's teaching about God as father is consistent with God's concern for the poor. The concept of the parenthood of God included a recognition that every person was a child of God, and thereby a beneficiary of God's kindness. But if it is the case that God particularly cares for the poor, and it is not the case that earthly wealth is a sign of God's favor, then the reversal of a common human perspective on poverty is in order. Reflecting on the teaching of Jesus, ethicist Lisa Sowle Cahill explains,

---

[50] Cone, *Black Theology*, 117.

[51] Marianne Meye Thompson, "Jesus and His God," in *The Cambridge Companion to Jesus* (ed. Bockmuehl; *Cambridge Companions to Religion*; Cambridge: Cambridge University 2001), 49.

[52] Thompson, "Context," 49.

Chapter 2

God's presence to the poor precedes financial security and is not dependent on it; but if the privileged want to share in the kingdom with the poor, their attitudes and actions must change in ways that will necessarily have far-reaching social effects. Sincere conviction and consistent action would produce quite a different politics of inclusion and redistribution.[53]

With this recognition comes the understanding that the social order might look different if the priorities of Jesus guided the workings of society, even in the time of Jesus.[54]

Along these lines Cahill notes that Jesus's teaching was subversive enough to attract the hostility of both the Jewish leaders and Roman rulers. "Since enacting the good news of the kingdom for and with the poor obviously figured high on his agenda, it is logical to surmise that it posed a substantial threat to those with wealth and power."[55] At the same time, it seems that Jesus was not necessarily advocating political change as we might understand it today. Cahill explains this in a way that is worth quoting at length:

Jesus was not a political or economic reformer in today's sense. He was not a 'community organizer,' he did not make glorious proposals about a just economic system, and he did not preach universal community of property or complete economic equality. He did call people to relate with active compassion to human deprivation, a stance that if taken seriously would change the economic and political institutions standard in most societies. Jesus also backed his position with reference to the traditional Israelite idea that the poor are a part of God's covenant people and are entitled to share in the nation's prosperity.[56]

Taking a slightly different approach is Herzog. Herzog in his powerful, *Parables as Subversive Speech*, explains: "Jesus' ministry was concerned with political and economic issues. Matters of justice were not peripheral to a spiritual gospel but were at the heart of his proclamation and

---

[53] Cahill, *Global Justice*, 102.

[54] bell hooks makes a similar observation for today noting the economic and political changes which would result from "relating with active compassion to human deprivation." See bell hooks, *All about Love: New Visions* (New York: William Morrow, 2000).

[55] Cahill, *Global Justice*, 102–103.

[56] Cahill, *Global Justice*, 102.

Encountering the World and Words of Jesus

practice."[57] Thus, for Herzog, it is not an exaggeration to claim that "Justice was at the center of Jesus' spirituality."[58]

So was the kingdom message of Jesus a message of good news about spiritual salvation or good news about earthly salvation? Or perhaps better, to what extent does Jesus's message about the kingdom engage spiritual realities, and to what extent does it engage conditions and realities here on earth? Our answer to these questions has to be that the spirituality of Jesus's message was deeply intertwined with a life lived in concrete earthly realities. And the realities in which Jesus lived included social, economic, and political realities—some of which supported human flourishing, and others which crushed the human spirit through their oppressive impact that worked against human well-being. If the message of Jesus is good news to the poor, freedom to the captives, and so on, then it is ultimately a message of human flourishing. It includes a vision of people living in loving and supportive community and reaching their potential as they enjoy the freedom to live their lives exercising essential human rights. Where that is not being experienced as present reality, there is injustice. And Jesus's words and actions were such that it is fair to say that justice was a critical component of his message. In light of that understanding we cannot simply spiritualize the social critique that is inherent in the parables; we must reckon with it as potentially impacting life in the here and now on a practical level. We will have opportunity to test these claims as we encounter the various parables in our study.

5. Words about Jesus

While we have focused above on words spoken by Jesus and recorded in the Gospels, the New Testament also contains much more that is said about Jesus. It tells us about his interactions with all kinds of different people, Jewish and non-Jewish, male and female, young and old, powerful and powerless. It tells us about his actions including healings, miracles, and exorcisms. It also tells us about his last days on earth including his very intentional final journey to Jerusalem,

[57] Herzog, *Parables as Subversive Speech*, 264.
[58] Herzog, *Parables as Subversive Speech*, 264.

Chapter 2

his arrest, trial, crucifixion, and resurrection. The parables of Jesus find their place within this context as well.

The Actions and Example of Jesus

In addition to his words, Jesus taught through his actions. He was remembered not only as a teacher but as a healer, a miracle-worker, and, shockingly to modern sensibilities, an exorcist. He was also remembered for his compassion and concern for others, whether parents of young children wanting their children to be blessed by Jesus, or a blind beggar by the road, or a Samaritan woman at a well, or an unscrupulous tax collector, Zacchaeus, who wanted to see Jesus. In each of these instances, actions by Jesus accompanied by words add to an understanding of his message. Jesus demonstrated compassion and concern for all, and the gospel writers show us that he was especially attentive to those others may have dismissed.

One element we will see referenced in the parables is Jesus's practice of eating with a wide range of people. In particular, Jesus draws criticism for eating with "tax collectors and sinners." Several of Jesus's parables are a response to such criticism. Yet Jesus's action is meaningful in and of itself, as it shows that all are welcome at the divine banquet that God is preparing. Cone explains, "Jesus' messiahship means that he is one of the humiliated and the abused, even in his birth. His eating with tax collectors and sinners, therefore, was not an accident and neither was it a later invention of the early church; rather it is an expression of the very being of God and thus a part of Jesus' purpose for being born."[59]

Exorcisms—the casting out of demons—are a significant part of Jesus's actions as well. These figure in similarly to reinforce the liberating message and work of the kingdom of God: "The kingdom, then, is the rule of God breaking in like a ray of light, usurping the powers that enslave human lives. That is why exorcisms are so prominent in Jesus' ministry. They are a visible manifestation of the presence of the kingdom."[60] Here Cone cites Luke 11:20 where Jesus tells his critics, "If I drive out demons by the finger of God, then the kingdom of God has come upon you."

---

[59] Cone, *Black Theology*, 115.
[60] Cone, *Black Theology*, 117.

Encountering the World and Words of Jesus

Healing and other miracles also play a role in the activities for which Jesus was known. In every case, it can be argued that the act of healing contributed to a person's ability to re-integrate and connect meaningfully with their community. Thus, while healing miracles show that Jesus is interested in alleviating the suffering of those who are afflicted, it also embodies his larger purpose to promote communities of well-being where all can be included and all can thrive.

Death and Resurrection

While we have focused thus far on the words of Jesus and some of his actions, there are two elements of the Jesus story that we have not touched on: his death and resurrection. As remembered by the gospel writers, each of these is critical to understanding Jesus and his message. We may be tempted initially to consider that these events came only at the end of the teaching ministry of Jesus, and that they ended the production of parables. While that may be true, the significance of each helps to shed light retrospectively on the message of Jesus, including the message of the parables.

We know that crucifixion was a form of death utilized by the Romans. Its purpose was to inspire fear and enable them to control populations under their power through putting on public display an incredibly painful and shameful end. That Jesus was crucified tells us a few things about how he was perceived by the Romans. It also became a symbol for Christians of the extent of Jesus's love for humanity, and his willingness to surrender his rights for others.

Kelly Douglas Brown expresses this powerfully: "In Jesus's first-century world, crucifixion was the brutal tool of social-political power. It was reserved for slaves, enemy soldiers, and those held in the highest contempt and lowest regard in society. To be crucified was, for the most part, an indication of how worthless and devalued an individual was in the eyes of established power. At the same time, it indicated how much of a threat that person was believed to pose to society."[61] Brown goes on to explain that Jesus's willing acceptance of the cross demonstrates his solidarity with all of the devalued, oppressed, and crucified people of

---

[61] Brown, "Anglican Theology and the Crucifixion," 28.

Chapter 2

his day. While theologians often interpret the crucifixion of Jesus as God's graciously sending God's beloved son from heaven to die on the cross (a divine perspective, viewing the crucifixion "from above"), there is another perspective that can be considered. Viewing the crucifixion "from below" gives attention to the perspective of those at the bottom of society, rather than from a divine being outside of and above it all. Those at the bottom of society Brown refers to as the "crucified class" of people—the marginalized, oppressed, and disinherited. According to Brown, Jesus's crucifixion embodies his identification with the crucified peoples:

> Jesus's crucifixion revealed his absolute solidarity with the crucified class. To approach the crucifixion from above as simply a divine salvific sacrifice is to miss what it meant for the historical Jesus to empty himself of privilege in order to identity with the crucified people. Jesus fully divested himself of all pretensions to power and privilege, not only in terms of his divinity, but also in terms of who he was as a Jewish male. In doing so, he refused to save himself from crucifixion. It is in recognizing Jesus's divestment of privilege that the salvation/atonement signified on the cross is about more than what God did through Jesus. Rather, Christians are challenged "to take up their cross and follow Jesus" by divesting themselves of any pretensions to privilege that thwart utter solidarity with the crucified class of people in their own day.[62]

Brown is here drawing attention to the idea that Jesus willingly entered into the crucifixion, a tradition that is conveyed in each of the Gospels. Jesus is shown to have known what was coming, and his disciples were either ignorant, or sought to dissuade him from this path. But by willingly walking this path, Jesus demonstrated solidarity with other oppressed persons and also victory over the tools of Roman domination. Such a model challenges Jesus's followers in all generations to divest themselves of whatever privilege and power they may enjoy, following the example of Jesus in identifying with those who are oppressed.

In this light, the message of the resurrection of Jesus takes on new meaning as well. Not only was it vindication that Jesus was the son of

---

[62] Brown, "Anglican Theology and the Crucifixion," 28.

Encountering the World and Words of Jesus

God; it was rather a visible demonstration of the power of God to overcome human oppression not by force but by surrendering privilege and power. Cone explains,

> *The finality of Jesus lies in the totality of his existence in complete freedom as the Oppressed One who reveals in his death and resurrection that God is present in all dimensions of human liberation.* His death is the revelation of the freedom of God, taking upon himself the totality of human oppression; his resurrection is the disclosure that God is not defeated by oppression but transforms it into the possibility of freedom.[63]

This then becomes the paradigm for what it means to be fully human: it is to live in the freedom of God, and like God, to use that freedom to join with the oppressed in the work of liberation from their oppression.

Further, this perspective on Jesus's death and resurrection fits within the broad sweep of Jewish theology as the sign of the arrival of the new age. Cahill also notes that Jesus's death and resurrection relate to various titles and figures expected in early Judaism. The suffering was appropriate as "eschatological prophet" which Jesus saw himself as. Jesus "considered himself an eschatological prophet, one with special agency in the drama of God's decisive victory."[64] Jesus's resurrection and his followers' continuing experience of Jesus as risen allowed his followers to rework the traditional categories and also invoke new titles. This reassessment of Jesus after his death and resurrection was "in continuity with the remembered Jesus of history, but locating that life against a greatly changed horizon."[65] The early Christian message of the kingdom and its values is thus understood to be in direct continuity with the message of Jesus about the kingdom. And as the gospel writers include the parables of Jesus in their compositions, they do so looking back at Jesus's teaching through the lens of the crucifixion and resurrection and all that those signify.

---

[63] Cone, *Black Theology*, 117, italics original.
[64] Cahill, *Global Justice*, 120.
[65] Cahill, *Global Justice*, 120.

Chapter 2

6. Postscript: Jesus and Crucified Peoples Today

As we saw above, the message, actions, death, and resurrection of Jesus all point to a unique focus on the poor, the oppressed, and the cast-down as special recipients of the favor of God. What Brown spoke of as a solidarity with the crucified class of people is an important thread of the Christian message which has sometimes been obscured by a focus on other elements. That this thread has been overlooked at times is certainly concerning. But what if it is the case that Jesus's identification with oppressed peoples is not merely one thread but the actual heart of the Christian message? If so, then Jesus's solidarity with the poor and marginalized as the embodiment of God's concern for the oppressed *is* the good news. And theological systems or religious institutions that overlook this central element cannot really be considered authentically "Christian" if they are disconnected from the central feature of the life and teaching of the one they claim to believe and follow.

Linking with some of our discussion of the kingdom of God and social justice above, James Cone put it this way:

> There can be no Christian theology that is not identified unreservedly with those who are humiliated and abused. In fact, theology ceases to be a theology of the gospel when it fails to arise out of the community of the oppressed. For it is impossible to speak of the God of Israelite history, who is the God revealed in Jesus Christ, without recognizing that God is the God *of* and *for* those who labor and are over laden.[66]

Cone went on from this claim to show that it is the case in both Israelite history and in the person of Jesus that liberation is the focal point of God's activity in the world. He explains, "By electing Israelite slaves as the people of God and by becoming the Oppressed One in Jesus Christ, the human race is made to understand that God is known where human beings experience humiliation and suffering."[67] With this understanding

[66] Cone, *Black Theology*, 1.

[67] Cone, *Black Theology*, 63–64. Similarly, Cone writes, "God's election of Israel and incarnation in Christ reveal that the liberation of the oppressed is part of the innermost nature of God. Liberation is not an afterthought but the essence of divine activity" (64).

78

Encountering the World and Words of Jesus

in view, the question for any generation is the extent to which people are standing with the suffering, the oppressed, the humiliated, as a key indicator of the extent to which they have truly understood the good news of God. Given the situation of African Americans in 1970 when Cone was writing, he argued that:

> Those who want to know who God is and what God is doing must know who black persons are and what they are doing. This does not mean lending a helping hand to the poor and unfortunate blacks of society.... Knowing God means being on the side of the oppressed, becoming *one* with them, and participating in the goal of liberation.[68]

Particularity becomes important in this context, meaning the particular experiences of suffering peoples. In this vein Cone argues that the idea of universal humanity (thinking about humanity collectively as a whole) in practice actually supports the perspective of the oppressor. Cone's emphasis on particularity helps address this concern: "God did not become a universal human being but an oppressed Jew, thereby disclosing to us that both human nature and divine nature are inseparable from oppression and liberation."[69]

Writing a generation earlier than James Cone, Howard Thurman made very similar claims about the extent to which the message of Jesus was one for the oppressed. In his *Jesus and the Disinherited* he explained, "It seems clear that Jesus understood the anatomy of the relationship between his people and the Romans, and he interpreted that relationship against the background of the profoundest ethical insight of his own religious faith as he has found it in the heart of the prophets of Israel."[70]

We can already see some of the truth of Thurman's claim simply from the connections between the teachings of Jesus and the prophetic tradition in light of the economic and social situation of the first century CE. But Thurman also generalizes the solution that Jesus found and shows how it can apply to oppressed peoples of all times and places:

[68] Cone, *Black Theology*, 65.
[69] Cone, *Black Theology*, 85.
[70] Thurman, *Jesus and the Disinherited*, 18.

Chapter 2

> The solution which Jesus found for himself and for Israel, as they faced the hostility of the Greco-Roman world, becomes the word and work of redemption for all the cast-down people in every generation and in every age.... Wherever his spirit appears, the oppressed gather fresh courage; for he announced the good news that fear, hypocrisy, and hatred, the three hounds of hell that track the trail of the disinherited, need have no dominion over them.[71]

Rather than responding to social situations of marginalization with fear, deception, and hatred, Jesus was able to call his followers to embody a "love-ethic" which was counter-cultural and ultimately cost him his life.[72] Such an ethic of love required as a starting point a "common sharing of a sense of mutual worth and value" grounded in authentic human to human exchange.[73] It also required a deep and difficult recognition of the humanity of both the oppressed and the oppressor.

Jon Sobrino, who we met in Chapter 1, also draws attention to the crucified peoples explicitly, linking the experiences of the poor and suffering today with the person of Jesus as the crucified one. Sobrino explains the sad reality, invisible to many of us in the affluent West, that "this world is one gigantic cross for millions of innocent people who die at the hands of executioners."[74] In light of this reality, Sobrino argues, "To react with mercy, then, means to do everything we possibly can to bring them down from the cross. This means working for justice—which is the name love acquires when it comes to entire majorities of people unjustly oppressed."[75] What Sobrino, Cone, and Thurman have in common is their ability to offer contemporary readers of the words of Jesus an important corrective. While the parables of Jesus are indeed offered as the message of good news for all peoples (see Luke 2:10–11), they are also especially a message of good news for the oppressed. At the same time, given the message of divine reversal and "the great divine clean up" that Jesus brought, his words also need to

---

[71] Thurman, *Jesus and the Disinherited*, 18–19.

[72] Thurman, *Jesus and the Disinherited*, 79.

[73] Thurman, *Jesus and the Disinherited*, 90.

[74] Sobrino, *Principle of Mercy*, 4.

[75] Sobrino, *Principle of Mercy*, 10.

Encountering the World and Words of Jesus

be carefully considered as a warning to those who are doing the oppressing. Reading the parables with a lens of social justice and an awareness of contemporary implications invites all of us to consider what the message of Jesus will have to say to us in our particular positions—wherever we may see ourselves on the human spectrum of power and privilege, and of suffering and struggle.

Works Cited in Chapter 2

Anderson, Gary A. *Charity: The Place of the Poor in the Biblical Tradition*. New Haven: Yale University, 2013.

Barton, Stephen C. "Many Gospels, One Jesus?" Pages 170–183 in *The Cambridge Companion to Jesus*. Edited by Markus N. A. Bockmuehl. of *Cambridge Companions to Religion*. Cambridge: Cambridge University, 2001.

Brantmeier, Edward J. and Noorie K. Brantmeier. *Culturally Competent Engagement: A Mindful Approach*. Charlotte, NC: IAP, Information Age Publishing, Inc., 2020.

Cahill, Lisa Sowle. *Global Justice, Christology and Christian Ethics*. New Studies in Christian Ethics. New York: Cambridge University, 2013.

Cone, James H. *A Black Theology of Liberation*. 20th anniversary ed. Maryknoll, NY: Orbis Books, 1990.

Crossan, John Dominic. *The Power of Parable: How Fiction by Jesus Became Fiction about Jesus*. New York: HarperOne, 2012.

Danker, Frederick W. *Benefactor: Epigraphic Study of a Graeco-Roman and New Testament Semantic Field*. St. Louis, MO: Clayton Publishing House, 1982.

Evans, Craig A. "Context, Family and Formation," Pages 11–24 in *The Cambridge Companion to Jesus*. Edited by Markus N. A. Bockmuehl. of *Cambridge Companions to Religion*. Cambridge: Cambridge University, 2001.

Green, Joel B. *Dictionary of Jesus and the Gospels*. Second ed. Downers Grove, IL: IVP Academic, 2013.

Harrington, Brooks and John C. Holbert. *No Mercy, No Justice: The Dominant Narrative of America Versus the Counter-Narrative of Jesus' Parables*. Eugene, OR: Cascade Books, 2019.

Herzog, William R. *Parables as Subversive Speech: Jesus as Pedagogue of the Oppressed*. Louisville, KY: Westminster/John Knox, 1994.

hooks, bell. *All about Love: New Visions*. First ed. New York: William Morrow, 2000.

Hultgren, Arland J. *The Parables of Jesus: A Commentary*. The Bible in its World. Grand Rapids: Eerdmans, 2000.

Chapter 2

Kelley, Shawn. *Racializing Jesus: Race, Ideology, and the Formation of Modern Biblical Scholarship.* Biblical Limits. New York: Routledge, 2002.

Levine, Lee I. *The Ancient Synagogue: The First Thousand Years.* Second ed. New Haven: Yale University Press, 2005.

Levine, Lee I. "Temple, Jerusalem," Pages 1281–1291 in *The Eerdmans Dictionary of Early Judaism.* Edited by John J. Collins and Daniel C. Harlow. Grand Rapids: Eerdmans, 2010.

Perrin, Norman. *Jesus and the Language of the Kingdom: Symbol and Metaphor in New Testament Interpretation.* Philadelphia: Fortress, 1976.

Saldarini, Anthony J. *Pharisees, Scribes, and Sadducees in Palestinian Society: A Sociological Approach.* Grand Rapids, MI: W.B. Eerdmans, 2001.

Snodgrass, Klyne. *Stories with Intent: A Comprehensive Guide to the Parables of Jesus.* Second ed. Grand Rapids: Eerdmans, 2018.

Sobrino, Jon. *The Principle of Mercy: Taking the Crucified People from the Cross.* Maryknoll, NY: Orbis Books, 1994.

Thompson, Marianne Meye. "Jesus and His God," Pages 41–55 in *The Cambridge Companion to Jesus.* Edited by Markus N. A. Bockmuehl. of *Cambridge Companions to Religion.* Cambridge: Cambridge University, 2001.

Thurman, Howard. *Jesus and the Disinherited.* Boston, MA: Beacon Press, 1996.

Tomson, Peter J. "Jesus and His Judaism," Pages 25–40 in *The Cambridge Companion to Jesus.* Edited by Markus N. A. Bockmuehl. of *Cambridge Companions to Religion.* Cambridge: Cambridge University 2001.

VanderKam, James C. *An Introduction to Early Judaism.* Second ed. Grand Rapids: Eerdmans, 2003.

VanderKam, James C. "Judaism in the Land of Israel," Pages 57–76 in *The Eerdmans Dictionary of Early Judaism.* Edited by John J. Collins and Daniel C. Harlow. Grand Rapids: Eerdmans, 2010.

Via, Dan Otto. *The Parables: Their Literary and Existential Dimension.* Philadelphia: Fortress, 1967.

Wright, N. T. *Paul and the Faithfulness of God.* Minneapolis: Fortress, 2013.

3

The Parable of the Good Samaritan (Luke 10:25–37)

"The world is a dangerous place, not because of those who do evil, but because of those who look on and do nothing." Albert Einstein

"Do not stand idly by." Elie Wiesel

1. Introduction

The first parable we will examine is perhaps the most well-known of all of Jesus's parables. As such, it is a parable that is both disarmingly simple and deeply challenging. The simplicity of this parable comes in the fact that it has been considered an "exemplary narrative" parable, meaning that the parable is a story that gives an illustration of the kinds of actions we all should take. The Samaritan shows mercy to the wounded man and readers of the parable should, as Jesus indicates after telling it, "Go and do likewise." Simple enough, right? But with that simplicity comes some surprising levels of complexity.[1]

---

[1] As an entry point to the issues in interpreting this parable, see the discussions in Hultgren, *Parables of Jesus*, 92–103; Snodgrass, *Stories with Intent*, 338–362; Levine, *Short Stories*, 77–116. For a recent book-length study geared toward contemporary implications, see Emerson B. Powery, *The Good Samaritan: Luke 10 for the Life of the Church* (Touchstone Texts; Grand Rapids, MI: Baker Academic, 2022).

Social Justice in the Stories of Jesus: The Ethical Challenge of the Parables, First Edition. Matthew E. Gordley.
© 2024 John Wiley & Sons Ltd. Published 2024 by John Wiley & Sons Ltd.

Chapter 3

A major part of the complexity of this parable comes in the fact that the characters in this story—the priest, the Levite, and the Samaritan—are either unfamiliar to contemporary readers or come to us with stereotypes that may not have been shared by the first listeners to this parable. So that means we have to do a bit of work to understand the significance of the characters in the story in order to appreciate the emotional impact of the story on its original audience. When we can read this parable in its context (i.e., in the cultural setting in which it was originally told), we will discover that this story was not *only* an example to be followed. It also offered a challenge to readers to the way things are. As we saw in chapter one, the point of parables is often to surprise and incite us and get us to interrogate our own values and actions. They "shatter and probe, disturb and challenge," getting us to question the way things are and imagine the way things ought to be.[2] In this chapter, we will embark on an interpretive journey to enable us to hear the disturbing message that Jesus intended in the parable of the Good Samaritan.

To enable a more appreciative reading of this parable we will work through the process of interpretation we outlined in the introduction. We will give a little more attention to the process in this chapter than in future chapters, simply to make the connection between the process and what we are learning about how parables work. We will begin with grasping the details of the story and then move on to ask some probing questions to see how we might understand the parable more fully. Those questions will lead us to spot the twist—that moment in the parable when the story defies readers' expectations and disorients us. From there we will consider the metaphor more fully with the goal of being able to articulate the challenge, and then ultimately consider implications for our own lives and our own communities. We will see that the principle of mercy that undergirds this parable invites us to be predisposed toward mercy. It challenges us to embrace a kind of mercy that is embodied in a prior commitment to see the suffering of others, to be moved with compassion, and to take action to alleviate that suffering.

[2] Perrin, *Jesus and the Language of the Kingdom*, 200.

84

The Parable of the Good Samaritan (Luke 10:25–37)

2. The Text: Parable of the Good Samaritan (Luke 10:25–37)

Just then a lawyer stood up to test Jesus. "Teacher," he said, "what must I do to inherit eternal life?" He said to him, "What is written in the law? What do you read there?" He answered, "You shall love the Lord your God with all your heart, and with all your soul, and with all your strength, and with all your mind; and your neighbor as yourself." And he said to him, "You have given the right answer; do this, and you will live."

But wanting to justify himself, he asked Jesus, "And who is my neighbor?" Jesus replied, "A man was going down from Jerusalem to Jericho, and fell into the hands of robbers, who stripped him, beat him, and went away, leaving him half dead. Now by chance a priest was going down that road; and when he saw him, he passed by on the other side. So likewise a Levite, when he came to the place and saw him, passed by on the other side. But a Samaritan while traveling came near him; and when he saw him, he was moved with pity. He went to him and bandaged his wounds, having poured oil and wine on them. Then he put him on his own animal, brought him to an inn, and took care of him. The next day he took out two denarii, gave them to the innkeeper, and said, 'Take care of him; and when I come back, I will repay you whatever more you spend.'

Which of these three, do you think, was a neighbor to the man who fell into the hands of the robbers?" He said, "The one who showed him mercy." Jesus said to him, "Go and do likewise." (Luke 10:25–37 NRSV[3])

3. Our First Step: Grasp the Story

The narrative of this parable is easy to grasp. The parable itself is in six verses (vv. 30–35) embedded in the middle of this passage. An unnamed man on his way to Jericho for an unspecified reason is robbed, beaten, and left for dead. Three different individuals come upon the wounded man. Unlike the wounded man about whom little information is

---

[3] Unless otherwise noted, translations of the biblical texts are from the NRSV.

Chapter 3

provided, a key detail is provided about the identity of each of the individuals who come upon him: the first is a priest, the second a Levite, and the third a Samaritan. The first two see the man but, for reasons that are not provided, keep their distance and pass by him on the other side of the road. The third is "moved with pity" and goes to the man and cares for his needs. Not only does he care for his immediate needs, but he also takes him to an inn, stays with him overnight, and then provides funds for the innkeeper to take care of him into the near future until he returns.

Surrounding this simple story is the narrative context of Luke's Gospel (vv. 25–29). Not every parable Jesus tells is closely or carefully linked with preceding dialogue, but this one certainly is. With Luke's narrative framing we are to understand that this parable originated when an expert in the law approached Jesus to challenge him (v. 25). In the society of Jesus's day to "test someone" like this was a type of verbal sparring and an attempt to bolster one's own standing at the expense of dishonoring the one being tested. When Jesus cleverly turned the tables on the lawyer by putting his own question back to him (vv. 26–28), the lawyer asked Jesus a further question as a means of preserving his honor (v. 29). The question was, "Who is my neighbor?" What we refer to as "The Parable of the Good Samaritan" is the story that Jesus told in response to that question. And then *after* telling this parable, Jesus again turned the question back on the lawyer when he asked in v. 36: "Which of these three, do you think, was a neighbor to the man who fell into the hands of the robbers?" The lawyer correctly identified the neighbor as "the one who showed mercy," and Jesus enjoined him and presumably all of his listeners to "go and do likewise." In other words, be a neighbor to those who are in need.

Luke's presentation of this parable as embedded within a verbal exchange between a lawyer and Jesus gives us a lot to work with both in terms of the parable itself and how the context may help shape our interpretation. One thing that is important for us to note is that this parable and its context together allude to many of the key themes we noted in our chapter on the world in which Jesus lived and taught. First, there is the lawyer asking about inheriting eternal life, which we may take to be a question about hopes for an afterlife—a contested theological issue in Judaism of the first century CE. Second, Jesus makes this into a discussion about the Jewish scriptures when he asks, "What is written in

The Parable of the Good Samaritan (Luke 10:25–37)

the law? What do you read there?" Whether or not this was just a tactical move by Jesus to turn the tables on the lawyer, with this move Jesus draws attention to the importance of the scriptures for understanding issues such as this. Third, with the lawyer's answer we come face to face with the greatest commandment, to the love the Lord your God (the *Shema*), and the commandment to love one's neighbor. In this case, these commands are not the unique teaching of Jesus, but they are biblical commands cited by the lawyer and whose importance is presumably widely understood by Jews of this period. Fourth, Jesus affirms the lawyer's biblical answer but again shifts the focus from "eternal life" in the future to something else: the present moment. Jesus says, "Do this and you will live," suggesting that these commands are essential not only for eternal life but to live a true and genuine life in the present. Finally, we should be aware of the long list of characters from the first-century world that we encounter throughout the passage: lawyer, teacher (the lawyer refers to Jesus as "teacher"), man, robbers, priest, Levite, Samaritan, innkeeper, and even an animal—the Samaritan's donkey. With these characters are also mentions of key elements of Judaism (the law; the *Shema*; Jerusalem) and elements of material culture (oil and wine; inn; denarius—a Roman silver coin, lest we forget that Rome is at all times in the background) all things which mark the time and place of this parable and give it particular meaning. Each detail may vary in its overall significance, but for our purposes at least being aware of the details initially will enable us to move on to questions of meaning.

With a clear grasp of the basic unfolding of the story, we can now move on to ask a couple of questions that may help us better to understand some of the issues that follow in trying to interpret it today.

4. Our Second Step: Going Deeper through Asking Questions

What Can We Know about the Characters?

For the nearly two thousand years that this parable has been told and read, it has been clear that the first two characters are the negative ones, and the third is the good one. That is how this parable works, using the common

Chapter 3

motif of a series of three. The first two fail to show mercy, but the third one, the model character, does show mercy. It happens that the first two characters are a priest and a Levite—Jewish religious leaders. We know they are bad because they pass by the wounded man and do not stop to help him. The third character, the Samaritan, is the one who has mercy. He stops and cares for the wounded man. He is the "good guy" in the parable.

It is surely significant that Jesus gave specific designations to each of the people in this parable—priest, Levite, Samaritan—rather than having them be simply three unidentified individuals. When we think about it, if this this parable were merely an example to be followed it would work just fine if it were just a series of three unidentified people coming upon the man. The point would still hold: we should follow the example of the third one. So why the descriptors of each character? One of the first questions that we as contemporary readers of this parable must look at is the way in which the different types of characters in the parable are portrayed and what the first hearers would have understood about those characters. What did it mean to them that two Jewish religious leaders were the negative examples?

We can start with some basic information about each of these characters. Priests and Levites were two groups of people who were associated with the religious and worship practices of early Judaism. Reaching back to early Israelite history and the twelve tribes of Israel, the descendants of Aaron were the priests and the descendants of Levi assisted the priests in service roles relating to worship.[4] For Jesus's audience the associations would likely have been positive. In Luke's Gospel, priests are mentioned only four other times, the first of which is the very positive inclusion of the priest Zechariah in the birth narrative as the father of John the Baptist, Jesus's cousin and forerunner (Luke 1:5). The "chief priests," on the other hand were the religious leaders of the Jews in Jerusalem and they have a decidedly more negative portrayal in Luke's Gospel, opposing Jesus and seeking to find a way to put him to death. Levites are not mentioned again in Luke's Gospel and appear only two other times in the New Testament. In Luke's other major writing, the Acts of the Apostles, we learn that one of the leaders of the early church,

---

[4] For additional details see the entries by Robert A. Kugler, "Priests," and Joachim Schaper, "Levites," in *The Eerdmans Dictionary of Early Judaism* (eds. Collins and Harlow; Grand Rapids: Eerdmans, 2010).

The Parable of the Good Samaritan (Luke 10:25–37)

Barnabas, was a Levite (Acts 4:36). In the Jewish scriptures, priests and Levites are commonly mentioned together with a third group being "all Israel." For example, Nehemiah 11:3 refers to various groups of people living in the towns of Judah as "Israel, the priests, the Levites."[5] Priests, Levites, and Israelites would seem to capture the whole collection of the people of God, with the first two having a designated role in religious worship, and the latter being everyone else.

With this in mind, what expectation does this story set up for the third character? If the priest and the Levite do not help the man, then surely the next up would be the third member of the traditional grouping, the true Israelite, and that person would help. If the true Israelite were the third on the scene, the point would have been that it is the common person, not necessarily a religious leader, who can demonstrate compassion and thereby show themselves to be a person of true devotion to God. The shock, however, comes in the fact that the third character is not a Jew at all. The third character is a Samaritan.

Samaritans, like Levites, are mentioned infrequently in the New Testament. However, when they are mentioned their appearance is significant. This is because between Jews and Samaritans there was significant historical animosity going back many generations before the time of Jesus.[6] For those with some background in reading the Bible, it is often portrayed that Jews viewed Samaritans as "less than" since their connection to the twelve tribes of Israel is in question due to historical events that led to inter-marrying with non-Jews. In that sense they are not "true" Israelites. But there is more to their troubled history than just the question of who claims the legitimate connection to Father Abraham. Jews listening to Jesus tell this parable would have been raised in a culture in which they were socialized to see Samaritans as their enemies. Jewish New Testament scholar Amy-Jill Levine explains, "To understand the parable as did its original audience, we need to think of Samaritans less as oppressed but benevolent figures and more as the enemy, as those who do the oppressing."[7] Viewing a Samaritan as their neighbor, much less as the "good guy" in a story about a Jew in need, would be the last thing they would expect.

---

[5] Levine, *Short Stories*, 98–103.

[6] Levine, *Short Stories*, 103–112.

[7] Levine, *Short Stories*, 104.

Chapter 3

This way of understanding the characters in the parable highlights two things. First, based on the characters, the first two would be the types of people the listener would expect to help, while the Samaritan would be the one least likely to help. Second, aside from these descriptors the key distinguishing feature between these characters is not their lineage, ethnicity, or occupation but rather their action. Namely, the action of "having compassion." We will look more closely at this aspect of the story in a moment. But first we need to ask another set of questions.

Good Samaritan ... and Bad Jews?

With some basic understanding of the original audience's expectations about these characters, it becomes clear that the retelling of this popular parable throughout two thousand years of subsequent history may put us at risk of missing the point or at least misconstruing it. Today a "good Samaritan" is someone who helps others. So in a parable about a good Samaritan we expect that person to be the helpful one. By contrast, given the influence of some of the currents of anti-Jewish interpretation that we touched on in chapter one, we expect very little of the priest and the Levite. In fact, we might expect them to be legalistic, uncaring, and unwilling to put themselves at risk to help someone in need. We expect them to be over-concerned with rigid following of purity regulations and under-concerned about the well-being of their fellow human. But such understandings do not come from the story itself; there is no mention of the thoughts, motivations, or rationalizations of the first two characters. These negative views of the priest and Levite also do not align with what Jewish listeners in the first century would have had in mind. How did we get here?

Throughout history the fact that the characters who pass by on the other side and do not show mercy are Jewish religious leaders, has given rise to anti-Jewish readings of the parable. In this context anti-Judaism takes shape in an interpretation which, whether intentionally or unintentionally, promotes Christianity as superior and Judaism as inferior.[8] A standard anti-Jewish view of this parable assumes that Judaism is legalistic and heartless and that the priest and the Levite

---

[8] For a good overview of anti-Jewish interpretation of the parables, Levine, *Short Stories*, 23–25.

The Parable of the Good Samaritan (Luke 10:25–37)

choose to observe Jewish Law rather than help a fellow human being. This is unfortunate since there is nothing in the parable about the Jewish law or the reason the first two did not help. Interpreters who make those connections have imported that information into the story based on erroneous assumptions. Also in this anti-Jewish interpretation, Christianity (understood as equated with the merciful actions of the Samaritan) focuses on love and compassion and this parable shows that Jesus came to introduce a message of compassion which is, if not foreign to Jewish thought, at least only minimally present in it. The logic seems to be: the priest and Levite are bad; the Samaritan is good. The extension of that logic has become, for some: Judaism is bad; Christianity is good.

There are several flaws in this line of thinking. To begin with, we may rightly wonder if Jesus intended to create "us" and "them" dichotomies through his parables. As we will see later, it may very well be that the choice to teach in parables (rather than in some other form) actually itself tells something of Jesus's intention to draw people into community together rather than dividing them.[9] The act of hearing a story and talking about it together is far more egalitarian than hearing a lecture or sermon and being expected to accept the propositional truths as delivered. We will consider this in more depth when we look at the parable of the Pharisee and the Tax Collector which is all about prejudging one or the other character.

But the "us" versus "them" approach aside, one other major flaw in this line of interpretation is that Jesus was not introducing a new teaching from outside of Judaism at all. Rather, he was drawing attention to what Judaism already taught: the obligation to have compassion on one's neighbor and someone in need. The Hebrew scriptures are rich with teaching about God's concern for the poor, the widow, the orphan, the alien, and of the obligation of God's people to care for them.[10] Even the legal traditions found in the book of Leviticus—as strange as some of those may sound to modern ears—speak to the importance of caring for one's fellow human. The quote at the beginning of this chapter from Holocaust survivor, writer, and activist Elie Wiesel is his paraphrase of Lev 19:16: "Thou shalt not stand idly by." Jesus, as a Jew speaking to

---

[9] This is a key insight of both Dominic Crossan and William Herzog, as we will see.

[10] Levine, *Short Stories*, 101–102.

Chapter 3

Jews, was not denouncing Judaism with his parables, but reminding Jewish listeners of truths they already knew.

Another flaw in this line of interpretation is that there was no "Christianity" in the time when Jesus first told this parable. So to imagine that Jesus was denouncing one entire religious tradition in favor of another one that did not yet exist is, at best, problematic, and at worst, highly anachronistic. More significantly, such an approach runs the risk of also missing the actual point that Jesus was trying to make. Further complicating things, to equate the Samaritan's actions with Christians (or Gentiles who become Christians) is also not at all present in the text. The Samaritan is emphatically not a Christian or a Gentile, but a Samaritan. There is nothing in the parable to suggest that the Samaritan was a follower of Jesus or should represent followers of Jesus. Rather, the implication is that, like the Samaritan, all human beings should respond with compassion when seeing a fellow human being in need.

Whether or not it is intentional, anti-Jewish readings distort the message and short-circuit responsible interpretation. Interpretation in the twenty-first century requires that we be aware of the subtle ways in which anti-Judaism has influenced biblical interpretation and may continue to influence it. As we noted in the introduction, from anti-Jewish biblical interpretation to destructive action is not a big step. John Dominic Crossan's observation is sobering: "The trajectory of human violence escalates almost inevitably from the ideological through the rhetorical to the physical."[11] Interpreting the parables in anti-Jewish or other ways that dehumanize, whether intentionally or unintentionally, is a first step on this trajectory of human violence. It is incumbent on anyone who wishes to interpret the parables of Jesus to be mindful of this reality.

5. Our Third Step: Spot the Twist

Our explorations thus far have made it clear that Jesus was not introducing a new teaching, nor was he touting the superiority of Christianity over Judaism. So where do we find the twist in this parable? We find the twist, as expected, in the third person to come upon the wounded

---

[11] Crossan, *Power of Parable*, 247.

The Parable of the Good Samaritan (Luke 10:25–37)

man: the Samaritan. And as noted already, we needed to do a little work to understand the social world of the first century in order to be able to grasp the significance of this detail. In this case, to understand the challenge of the parable requires an understanding of the significance of the Samaritans in the Jewish culture of Jesus's day. Historical research helps us understand the degree of "ethnic, political, and religious animosity within the land of Israel" that the Samaritan represents.[12] In this parable, the hated person (the other) is the one who is the source of the suffering man's rescue.

When we approach this parable with this information in mind we can see just how radical the parable is. And we can begin to get a sense for the challenge that it offers us today. This parable may provide an opportunity for all of us to explore our own biases and preconceived ideas about groups of people with whom we may have some natural, historical, or cultural enmity. The early 2020s have witnessed significant social division in the United States particularly around race and the continuing effects of racist policies and practices throughout the country's history. Black and brown bodies were literally being killed in the streets by white police officers, and in 2020–2021 arguably the largest protest movement in the history of the United States occurred coming in response to the murder of George Floyd. Sadly, rather than coming together as a nation to face the evil of racism and its continued impacts, many political leaders, including then-president Donald Trump, refused to acknowledge or engage the issue, focusing instead on "law and order."[13] Trump supporters chanting things like "white power!" at protesters were publicly praised by the former president. In a similar vein, crimes against Asian Americans have increased to an all-time high seemingly enabled and empowered by racist political rhetoric related to COVID-19. Threats and attacks on Jewish communities are also on the rise, as are attacks on LGBTQ and transgender persons.[14] Legislation in

---

[12] Crossan, *Power of Parable*, 60–61. See the details in Levine, *Short Stories*, 104–111.

[13] More than half a century ago James Cone (writing in 1970) was able to clearly articulate that "law and order" was code for maintaining the status quo of white supremacy and structures of oppression. See Cone, *Black Theology*, 16, 37.

[14] Data and current trends related to hate crimes in the United States can be found at https://www.justice.gov/crs/highlights/2021-hate-crime-statistics (accessed May 18, 2023).

Chapter 3

some states also now seeks to limit the rights and protections of transgender persons or physicians who care for them.[15] In such a context the deep animosities between first-century Jews and Samaritans do not seem that far removed from what is happening in our own country today. What would it mean to be a neighbor in this context?

And there may be another "twist" in this story. As the story begins we expect that the neighbor is the man lying on the side of the road. This is the person who needs help. A neighbor is therefore anyone in need. While that may be true, another twist in the parable is that the person identified as the neighbor is not the man lying in the road, but the man who shows mercy: the Samaritan.[16] And if we note that the command that sets up this parable is to "love your neighbor as yourself" (v. 27), then it is clear in this parable that the Jewish listener is being taught to love his or her enemy, the Samaritan. Again, as we ponder how we might translate such a message into our own context, we can see that there is a deep and sobering challenge emerging from this parable.

6. Our Fourth Step: Consider the Metaphor

Our process of interpretation thus far has enabled us to grasp the story itself, to ask key questions to increase our understanding, and then to spot the twist. The next step in our process is to consider the metaphor. As Barbara Green reminds us, "A parable is a narrative metaphor—a metaphor in motion—that by the peculiar working of its juxtaposed elements startles the mind into fresh awareness."[17] As a metaphor in motion we want to ensure that we attend to what elements are being compared, and

[15] On this legislation and the ways in which its proponents believe it to be "biblical" see David Crary, *Wave of Anti-Transgender Bills in Republican-Led States Divides U.S. Faith Leaders* (May 12, 2023 [Accessed May 21, 2023]); available from https://www.pbs.org/newshour/nation/wave-of-anti-transgender-bills-in-republican-led-states-divides-u-s-faith-leaders. Crary explains the scope of this legislation: "By the latest count, at least 20 states have imposed bans or limits on transgender athletes' sports participation at the K-12 or collegiate level. And at least 18 states have adopted laws or policies—including some blocked by courts—barring gender-affirming medical care, such as puberty blockers, hormone therapy and surgery for minors."

[16] Keenan, *Works of Mercy*, 4.

[17] Green, *Like a Tree Planted*, 10.

The Parable of the Good Samaritan (Luke 10:25–37)

then consider how that comparison functions. In a narrative metaphor like this involving multiple characters one impulse that is almost automatic is for the preconscious mind to look for a character with which to identify. Knowing this is a "story with intent" readers look for the character that corresponds with them in the story, so that they can make the connections that the metaphor implies but does not state directly. Along these lines, readers might then bring that impulse into conscious consideration with questions: In what ways am I like the characters who saw someone in need but passed by, apparently unmoved by suffering? In what ways am I like the Samaritan who sees, feels, and acts on behalf of another? In what ways am I like the wounded man on the side of the road who is dependent on the mercy of another for restoration and healing?

We have been examining this parable as an exemplary narrative, meaning that the story itself provides an example to be followed. Given that the positive example is the Samaritan, we may ask specifically what it would mean for us to embody that approach to others in our own lives. Thus far we have noted that the example has to do with caring for a person in need. If the primary image is that of a wounded man on the road, it is a small step to consider that such an image might represent a whole host of people in need that we encounter: victims of the oppressive actions of others, people who are suffering, and people in dire situations of distress. The implied question of this parable then is will we be a neighbor to those people?

One important element of the story as narrative metaphor is the sequence of actions: seeing, feeling, and acting to restore the humanity of the suffering person. The first action in that sequence, "seeing," as simple as it is, cannot be overlooked as essential to mercy. According to Anne Curtis, RSM, the choice to really see the wounded man was critical to all that followed in the parable:

> The Samaritan notices, sees the person lying by the side of the road. This is no small thing. There is a choice made to either see or not notice. To see, really see stirs or evokes something, a sense of compassion that draws one in and connects. In this case, the Samaritan connects with the person lying at the side of the road.[18]

---

[18] Anne Curtis, RSM, "The Good Samaritan," 2019. See her complete reflection in Appendix 1.

Chapter 3

The choice to see, to notice, leads to connection and compassion. The parable tells us that the priest and the Levite "saw the man" but passed by. The wounded man came into their field of vision briefly, but for whatever reason they did not choose to really see, perceive, all that was at stake for this fellow human being in need. As a metaphor with implications for today, contemporary readers might wonder if they are people who choose to see or choose not to notice what is happening in situations of need in the world around them.

Aside from the wounded man as a primary image, another key image is that of the Samaritan being the unexpected helper. The readers of this parable are challenged to see an enemy as a fellow human being, a neighbor, who has dignity and may be more compassionate than they expect. With this image we might think about people in our sphere from a group which we tend to paint negatively based on our own experiences or the way in which we are socialized within our culture. Are we open to the common traits of our humanity which connect us, rather than those biases which divide us? The imagery in the story engages the mind to extend the connections and invites us to transfer the meaning to our own lives. These considerations of the metaphor will inform our consideration of both the challenge of the parable and the implications for today in the following sections.

But as a parable, it is important to note that there are other ways this story has been interpreted. Here we can briefly consider the rich array of allegorical interpretations of the basic imagery of the story. In an allegorical interpretation it is not so much the overall image that carries the message but the symbolic meaning of each of the individual elements.[19] For example, the elements of this parable have famously been interpreted by as influential a theologian as Augustine as telling the story of salvation through Jesus Christ. If the wounded man is viewed as the biblical figure of Adam, the first human who is ensnared by sin, the priest and the Levite in this line of reasoning could be seen to be the Jewish tradition and the Jewish Law which, according to Augustine, are unable to help the lost sinner (note: we can already see how such an approach is pressing deeply into anti-Judaism). The Samaritan could be

---

[19] For discussion of this approach to the parable of the Good Samaritan, and parables in general, see Craig L. Blomberg, *Interpreting the Parables* (Downers Grove, IL: IVP Academic, 2012), 33–40.

96

The Parable of the Good Samaritan (Luke 10:25–37)

viewed as representing Jesus, who rescues the sinner, saving him, and bringing him into the Church (the inn), until he returns, and leaving him in the hands of the Apostle Paul (the innkeeper).[20] Bonaventure, a theologian of the Middle Ages who wrote a massive commentary on Luke, demonstrates the lasting influence of Augustine's allegorical approach to this parable. Yet while including discussion of the allegorical meaning, Bonaventure also attends to the literal meaning as demonstrating that anyone in need, or who can show mercy to one in need, is indeed their neighbor.[21] While the literal sense of the parable may have a lesson, some interpreters hold that the deeper "spiritual sense" is made accessible through the allegorical reading.

Depending on our background such an interpretation may make a lot of sense, or it may leave us scratching our heads. In favor of such an approach, we have already seen that the parable enjoins compassion on those in need. It is not out of line to suggest that that kind of compassion represented in the parable can be favorably compared to the compassion that God has on fallen humanity. Further, the biblical understanding is that the compassion that humans show to one another is rooted in the compassion that God has for God's creation. And the incarnation of Jesus and his death on the cross is the ultimate embodiment of that compassion. So if we wish to see ourselves as the wounded people, and Jesus as our rescuer who has compassion on us, that would seem to align very well with both the parable and with broader biblical teaching.

However, there are some aspects of this allegorical approach which should give us pause. In the more elaborate allegories key elements of early Judaism come out looking very bad indeed, symbolized (in this kind of reading) by the priest and the Levite. We have already given some attention above to the importance of reading this parable with a fair assessment of early Judaism rather than with stereotypes that pit a "superior" Christian religion against an "inferior" Jewish religion. This allegorical approach reinscribes such negative stereotypes as it seeks to show the superiority of Jesus over a supposedly inferior Jewish Law. As we will see in other parables, however, Jesus himself has a very positive

---

[20] On Augustine's approach see David B. Gowler, *The Parables after Jesus: Their Imaginative Receptions across Two Millennia* (Grand Rapids: Baker Academic, 2017), 40–44.
[21] Gowler, *Parables after Jesus*, 95–98.

Chapter 3

view of the Jewish Law. He was not seeking to undermine Judaism at all but rather to remind his Jewish hearers of what was already contained within the tradition. So a negative portrayal of Judaism in these kinds of allegorical interpretations is not something that is inherent in the text itself but is rather imported from the world of the interpreter.

In light of the subtle ways in which anti-Judaism makes its way into allegory, our recommendation here is to proceed with caution when it comes to allegorical interpretations of the parables, and to begin instead with understanding the story *as a story* where the overall meaning is found in the picture as a whole. If a parable is to be read as an allegory, then we will caution that we should do so with attention to whether such an interpretation does violence to the story itself or contradicts other clear teaching of Jesus or the tradition.

7. Our Fifth Step: Articulate the Challenge

Having asked good questions, spotted the twist, and considered the metaphor more fully, we are now in a position to articulate the challenge of this parable. We approach this step recognizing that this is essentially a process of translation: translating the meaning from a narrative story to a set of propositional statements. With that process of translation of ideas, there is a risk of losing some of the emotional and affective impact of the way a metaphorical story works. With that awareness, we move forward cautiously and always with a willingness to revisit our conclusion in light of our own experience of the parable as a story.

To help us articulate the challenge of this parable we turn to the writings of theologian Jon Sobrino, one of our social justice conversation partners we encountered in chapter one. Sobrino's assessment of this parable is simple: the Samaritan embodies mercy which is the *natural response to another human being who is suffering*. For Sobrino it is the dynamic combination of being moved internally and acting to alleviate that suffering that defines mercy. Mercy is thus both "an activity of love" and "a re-action to someone else's suffering, now interiorized within oneself."[22] We can see this clearly in the text of the parable where the Samaritan is literally "moved with pity" (v. 33). This internal reaction

[22] Sobrino, *Principle of Mercy*, 16.

The Parable of the Good Samaritan (Luke 10:25–37)

produced a result in action. With this clue from the text we recognize that the Samaritan did not take action because it was the right thing to do or because he was committed to putting his beliefs into action. Rather, he acted because he was moved with compassion for a fellow human who was suffering. This is an important concept for Sobrino who points out specifically that "this activity, in action, is motivated *only* by that suffering."[23] Sobrino explains, "The interiorized suffering of another is the first principle and foundation of the reaction of mercy."[24] This notion of the "interiorized suffering of another" helps us understand how mercy operates. As we consider the range of possible responses to the suffering of another human, mercy may be seen not as a response that is conjured up artificially, but one that erupts naturally from an open human heart.

With these observations about the nature of mercy and compassion, Sobrino goes a step further to derive from this parable what he calls the "principle of mercy." This principle of mercy is what the Good Samaritan embodies:

> By the principle of mercy, we understand here a specific love, which, while standing at the origin of a process, also remains present and active throughout the process, endowing it with a particular direction and shaping the various elements that compose it. We hold that this principle of mercy is the basic principle of the activity of God and Jesus, and therefore ought to be that of the activity of the church.[25]

In the observation above, we can see that the parable of the Good Samaritan reflects both what Jesus desires from one human to another, but also the disposition of God toward God's creation. The Samaritan embodies this principle of mercy both in his initial act and in his ongoing efforts on behalf of the wounded man. In this way, the Samaritan and his parable become paradigmatic for the mercy that God shows to humanity, and the mercy which God expects God's children to display as well.

Along these lines, other writers do an excellent job of reflecting on the nature of mercy. Margaret Farley, a Sister of Mercy who taught for many years at Yale University, identifies a response of mercy with a

[23] Sobrino, *Principle of Mercy*, 16.
[24] Sobrino, *Principle of Mercy*, 16.
[25] Sobrino, *Principle of Mercy*, 16.

99

Chapter 3

response of love but "with the added notion of 'suffering with.'"[26] In a similar vein, James Keenan, a Jesuit at Boston College, defines mercy as "a willingness to enter into the chaos of another."[27] What both of these individuals pick up on with their phrases of "suffering with" and "entering into" is the importance of drawing near to the one in need with an openness and a willingness to be present as a fellow human being. The precondition for the natural human response of mercy is an openness to see and to feel.

With these perspectives from different vantage points within Roman Catholicism, Jon Sobrino, Margaret Farley, and James Keenan, have introduced us to an important element of what is called Catholic Social Teaching. As a recent embodiment of this long tradition of reflection on societal concerns, Pope Francis's 2020 encyclical provides an excellent place for us to pause. In *On Social Friendship* the Pope himself engages deeply with the parable of the Good Samaritan and its implications. He recognizes the timeless challenge of this parable calling it "a story constantly retold," not in its narrative sense but in the fact that the realities of the story are lived out every day—people ignoring and passing by those in need, but with an opportunity to respond with compassion. Through his analysis he points to the importance of what he calls a "culture of encounter," in which the privileged and wealthy respond with compassion to the poor and wounded because they recognize the interconnection of all people. He writes,

> Jesus' parable summons us to rediscover our vocation as citizens of our respective nations and of the entire world, builders of a new social bond. This summons is ever new, yet it is grounded in a fundamental law of our being: we are called to direct society to the pursuit of the common good and, with this purpose in mind, to persevere in consolidating its political and social order, its fabric of relations, its human goals. By his actions, the Good Samaritan showed that the existence of each and every individual is deeply tied to that of others: life is not simply time that passes; life is a time for interactions.[28]

[26] Margaret A. Farley, "Wisdom, Dignity, and Justice: Higher Education as a Work of Mercy," *The MAST Journal* 16 (2006): 8.

[27] Keenan, *Works of Mercy*, 5.

[28] Pope Francis, *Lettera enciclica Fratelli tutti del Santo Padre Francesco sulla fraternità e l'amicizia sociale* (Città del Vaticano: Libreria editrice vaticana, 2020), par. 66.

The Parable of the Good Samaritan (Luke 10:25–37)

With these words Pope Francis introduces us to a key concept within Catholic Social Teaching and ethical theory, namely, the "common good." A concept that can be traced back to Thomas Aquinas, the idea of the common good has both ethical and political considerations with regard to the ordering of society and achieving the flourishing of all its members. In fact, the common good can be encapsulated as "nothing less than the fulfillment of all human persons and communities."[29]

In light of his analysis of the contemporary state of disintegration and discord on a global scale, Francis invites his readers to use the parable as a guidepost for considering what a just society would look like. For him, it certainly includes bringing the voices of those from the wounded and marginalized into the center, so that everyone has a place at the table. With regard to policies and projects to create better human conditions he explains how this might work: "The decision to include or exclude those lying wounded along the roadside can serve as a criterion for judging every economic, political, social and religious project. Each day we have to decide whether to be Good Samaritans or indifferent bystanders."[30] And for Francis, the line between indifferent bystanders and complicity with the robbers is a narrow one. He writes, "'Robbers' usually find secret allies in those who 'pass by and look the other way'. There is a certain interplay between those who manipulate and cheat society, and those who, while claiming to be detached and impartial critics, live off that system and its benefits."[31] In other words, a corrupt social system can benefit even those who do not see themselves as perpetrators of injustice. This is because whether they agree with it or not in principle, the system works on behalf of privileged peoples in certain ways while it works against the oppressed at the same time. While it is beyond the scope of this chapter, the widely studied concept of "white privilege" is just one example of benefits that accrue to people of light skin color in the North American context,

---

[29] According to Finnis, for Aquinas "the common good that is the ultimate concern of political philosophy, and thus of the reasonable person, is nothing less than the fulfillment of all human persons and communities." See John Finnis, "Aquinas' Moral, Political, and Legal Philosophy," *The Stanford Encyclopedia of Philosophy* (ed. Zalta; Stanford University: Metaphysics Research Lab, 2021), https://plato.stanford.edu/archives/spr2021/entries/aquinas-moral-political.

[30] Francis, *Fratelli tutti*, par. 69.

[31] Francis, *Fratelli tutti*, par. 75.

Chapter 3

whether they hold racist beliefs or not. That is how a racist system works, regardless of a person's individual belief.[32] In this way Catholic Social Teaching looks not only at individual situations of need but at larger systems that perpetuate or create the situations of need. With this kind of move from principle to practical implications we see the kind of social analysis that can be possible when we engage the parable with imaginations attuned to issues of justice for all persons.

While the parable is obviously pointing to the value of showing mercy to others, social analysis makes it clear that there are other negative forces at work beyond just that of not showing mercy. Similar to Pope Francis, Sobrino draws attention to the idea that there is "anti-mercy" at work in the world. In the parable this "anti-mercy" can be seen in the actions of the robbers (v. 30) and potentially even in the economic and social systems that have led those individuals to take those desperate and inhumane actions. Those are realities that today's "Good Samaritans" need to acknowledge and address. In Sobrino's view, those working for the liberation and healing of the wounded people lying along the road today must not only promote mercy but actively resist anti-mercy if their work is to have lasting impact.[33]

With this first parable we have begun to wrestle with what mercy means and begun to articulate an understanding of mercy as more than just a feeling, and more than just a single kind act. It is a quintessential human response to the suffering of another. Mercy requires, among other things, seeing the suffering of the other. In short, the Good Samaritan shows us that, for Jesus, mercy is a characteristic of the ideal human being. The principle of mercy, then, involves a commitment to see, a commitment to feel, and a predisposition to react to the suffering of another, and then to take action toward relieving that suffering.

8. Our Final Step: Consider Implications

With the help of theologians like Jon Sobrino, Margaret Farley, and Pope Francis, we have been able to articulate the challenge of this parable. Our final move is to consider the implications of this parable in

[32] Bryan N. Massingale, *Racial Justice and the Catholic Church* (Maryknoll, NY: Orbis Books, 2010), 36–37.

[33] Sobrino, *Principle of Mercy*, 19, 24.

The Parable of the Good Samaritan (Luke 10:25–37)

our own current contexts. Having "interrogated" the parable, we now allow the parable to interrogate us as we consider what implications it may have in the here and now of our lives. As simple a question as "who are the wounded persons by the side of the road today?" can open up many avenues for productive thinking. Here we will consider three areas of implications: the corporal works of Mercy; the natural world; and the humanity of our enemies.

Physical Care for Those in Need: The Corporal Works of Mercy

The "corporal works of mercy" is a concept that has been discussed throughout church history as the embodiment of mercy in its physical form. Delineated as seven specific works derived from the teachings of Jesus in the Gospels, they are: to visit the prisoner, shelter the homeless, feed the hungry, give drink to the thirsty, bury the dead, visit the sick, and clothe the naked. Just from the list, we can see that the parable of the Good Samaritan touches directly on at least a couple of these, and tangentially on a couple of others. James Keenan, SJ, provides an insightful overview of the works of mercy, including their development throughout the history of the church and their application today. In each case Christians, often religious orders, organized themselves to address tangible needs in the society around them. For each need, however, Keenan shows that there is not just the addressing of the need itself; just as importantly there is also attention to the root causes of the need and how these can be addressed. Accordingly, each area has implications today not just for addressing human suffering but also for alleviating it and preventing it. Interestingly, Keenan also makes this connection to the parable of the Good Samaritan noting that it "serves as the foundational explanation of Jesus's commandment to love."[34]

Here we will only be able to skim the surface of how the works of mercy operate and draw our attention to contemporary concerns that invite a response of loving compassion. With regard to the work of "sheltering the homeless," depending on one's exposure to homelessness one may envision that this would be about individuals living on the streets of a major city, and the need to address that as either an

[34] Keenan, *Works of Mercy*, 5.

Chapter 3

individual or a societal problem. However, Keenan draws attention to a much wider view of this work of mercy to include the refugee crises, displaced families, immigrants (and the link to globalization and its impacts), and victims of domestic abuse. Each of these scenarios involves humans, all of whom need and deserve shelter and whose challenges point to complex global issues that need to be addressed. With the refugee crisis alone, Keenan notes that women and children make up 80% of refugees out of 65 million refugees and displaced persons worldwide.[35] In this line of thinking, the metaphorical "wounded man" by the side of the road is more likely to be a woman or a child fleeing from a life-threatening situation of suffering. So we may ask ourselves about the extent to which we even see the need, and if seeing, whether we perceive to the point that we are moved with compassion.

In a similar vein the work of "feeding the hungry" can be seen as much more than just helping those in need in our community (as valuable as that is). The work of feeding the hungry is closely connected with the larger idea of the inclusion of all persons in the world's bounty, and is therefore tied up with major issues like climate change, globalization, volatile markets, and food wastage, all of which play a part in exacerbating the problem of hunger. "Giving drink to the thirsty" likewise raises issues of availability of clean water, sustainable industrial and agricultural practices, and the commodification of water, calling attention to our own lifestyles and how they impact the environment and our neighbors. Burying the dead, visiting the sick, and clothing the naked likewise all speak to matters of human dignity, recognizing the sacred in our human bodies (sacramentality), and working toward the health and well-being of all persons.

In each of the above instances, it is not difficult to note that it is primarily the poor who bear the indignities and who are impacted disproportionately as they suffer physically in these ways. Thus, attention to each of the works of mercy is an invitation to all people to see, feel, and respond to the suffering of others, especially those who are poor. For example, "The call to give drink to the thirsty is itself the call to develop an attitude that respects the needs of those who are poor and that appreciates the gifts of the earth."[36] While this is important as far as it

[35] Keenan, *Works of Mercy*, 27.
[36] Keenan, *Works of Mercy*, 39.

The Parable of the Good Samaritan (Luke 10:25–37)

goes, there is more. Keenan rightly notes that issues of injustice are never isolated, but have an impact on everyone: "The web of life requires a harmonious estimation of both ourselves and our planet: Where we harm our planet, we eventually harm ourselves. Inevitably, justice affects us all."[37] Keenan's insights about our planet bring us to another implication of this parable: care for the natural world in which we all must live.

The Natural World

Anne Curtis, RSM, explores another implication of this parable along the lines of Keenan. She suggests that included within the scope of this seeing, feeling, and acting is also an implied concern for "the other-than-human neighbor." By this she refers to our interconnectedness with the created world. Curtis explains,

> What does that then portend if creation, Earth, is my neighbor? The ecological crisis we are experiencing calls me to notice and understand a new way of being neighbor. This inclusive view invites me to see not just humans, but also animals, trees and rocks, sunshine and sea, the stars and insects (yes, even mosquitoes!) as neighbor. To be neighbor calls me to see cosmically as well as locally.[38]

Theologically, this extension of mercy beyond application to our fellow humans is important because we encounter God and experience God's presence to us not only in the incarnation (in Jesus, as a person) but also in the world God created. Curtis explains, "Thus I see the face of the divine in my neighbor and in all of creation. Love for my neighbor cannot be separated from love for the planet. We are all made of the same stuff. All of life is intricately interrelated." She cites the wisdom of Native American leader Chief Seattle, who said, "Humankind has not woven the web of life. We are but one thread within it. Whatever we do to the web, we do to ourselves. All things are bound together. All things connect." If we truly are inter-connected with the entire web of life,

---

[37] Keenan, *Works of Mercy*, 39.
[38] Curtis, "Good Samaritan."

Chapter 3

then we can agree with Curtis's summary: "The urgent call to 'do mercy' comes now with not only a social but also an ecological ring."[39]

In thinking about our obligations to care for the world around us, having compassion on both our fellow humans and the world in which we all live, it may seem like we have come a long way from a simple act of caring for a wounded man by the side of the road. However, it is important to recognize two realities. First, today's ecological crises and environmental challenges have a much more significant impact on the poor, oppressed, and marginalized than they do on the wealthy, privileged, and powerful. Thus, to care for our fellow human requires attending to the environment. Second, as we will see, in his parables Jesus himself drew attention to the importance of the created world as a locus for the presence of God's kingdom. The interconnectedness of all things is a thread we will also see when we turn in Chapter 6 to a nature parable in which these realities are brought explicitly into view: the parable of the mustard seed (Mark 4:30–32; Matthew 13:31–32; Luke 13:18–19).

The Humanity of Our Enemies

Having worked through our process to this point, we now have a clear picture of the message of this parable and of practical areas where we are invited to apply the principle of mercy today. While readers may rightly see this, as Luke does, as an example to be followed (i.e., "Go and do likewise," Luke 10:37b) it is also important to see this story as a challenge to the way we see the world. The key fact that the exemplary character is a Samaritan while the less-than-helpful characters are the ones who would have been expected to be the "good guys" suggests the nature of the challenge. As parables scholar Dominic Crossan observes, rather than simply offering a moral lesson "it is better understood as a challenge parable, a story that challenges listeners to think long and hard about their social prejudices, their cultural presumptions, and, yes, even their most sacred religious traditions."[40] In our contemporary world with its divisive rhetoric and propensity for demonizing of those whose views do not agree with ours, this parable offers a timely opportunity for reflection on how we think of others who are different from us.

[39] Curtis, "Good Samaritan."
[40] Crossan, *Power of Parable*, 62.

106

The Parable of the Good Samaritan (Luke 10:25–37)

Howard Thurman found that this parable invites us to view the concept of neighbor as qualitative rather than geographical.[41] We are called to be neighbor not only to those who are near us, similar to us, or positively regarded by us. The call goes far beyond proximity and includes much more than positive regard for other people. We are called to see, feel, and respond as part of what it means to be fully human, and to support others in their "being-fully-humanness." Even our enemies.

This notion brings us back around to the idea of how parables "work." This story in which we wonder where we can see ourselves, invites us to imagine a world in which our enemy is our neighbor; and maybe even is a better person than we are. This would be hard to convince someone of through reasoned discourse; that is why it is more effectively done through the work of a parable, inviting readers to see themselves within a disarmingly simple story. The preconscious work of parables helps that to happen before readers can even put their guards up.

Ultimately, as Pope Francis suggests, this parable presents a powerful challenge as it outlines the responsibility that humans bear for one another. He concludes: "All of us have a responsibility for the wounded, those of our own people and all the peoples of the earth. Let us care for the needs of every man and woman, young and old, with the same fraternal spirit of care and closeness that marked the Good Samaritan."[42]

Works Cited in Chapter 3

Blomberg, Craig L. *Interpreting the Parables*. Second ed. Downers Grove, IL: IVP Academic, 2012.

Cone, James H. *A Black Theology of Liberation*. 20th anniversary ed. Maryknoll, NY: Orbis Books, 1990.

Crary, David. *Wave of Anti-Transgender Bills in Republican-Led States Divides U.S. Faith Leaders*. May 12, 2023 [Accessed May 21, 2023]. Available from https://www.pbs.org/newshour/nation/wave-of-anti-transgender-bills-in-republican-led-states-divides-u-s-faith-leaders.

---

[41] "Neighborliness is nonspatial; it is qualitative." Thurman, *Jesus and the Disinherited*, 79.

[42] Francis, *Fratelli tutti*, par. 79.

Chapter 3

Crossan, John Dominic. *The Power of Parable: How Fiction by Jesus Became Fiction about Jesus*. New York: HarperOne, 2012.

Curtis, Anne, RSM. "*The Good Samaritan.*" 2019.

Farley, Margaret A. "Wisdom, Dignity, and Justice: Higher Education as a Work of Mercy." *The MAST Journal* 16 (2006): 3–8.

Finnis, John. "Aquinas' Moral, Political, and Legal Philosophy." in *The Stanford Encyclopedia of Philosophy*. Edited by Edward N. Zalta. Stanford University: Metaphysics Research Lab, 2021. https://plato.stanford.edu/archives/spr2021/entries/aquinas-moral-political.

Francis, Pope. *Lettera enciclica Fratelli tutti del Santo Padre Francesco sulla fraternità e l'amicizia sociale*. Città del Vaticano: Libreria editrice vaticana, 2020.

Gowler, David B. *The Parables after Jesus: Their Imaginative Receptions across Two Millennia*. Grand Rapids: Baker Academic, 2017.

Green, Barbara. *Like a Tree Planted: An Exploration of Psalms and Parables through Metaphor*. Collegeville, MN: Liturgical Press, 1997.

Hultgren, Arland J. *The Parables of Jesus: A Commentary*. The Bible in its World. Grand Rapids: Eerdmans, 2000.

Keenan, James F. *The Works of Mercy: The Heart of Catholicism*. Third ed. Lanham: Rowman & Littlefield, 2017.

Levine, Amy-Jill. *Short Stories by Jesus: The Enigmatic Parables of a Controversial Rabbi*. New York: HarperOne, 2014.

Massingale, Bryan N. *Racial Justice and the Catholic Church*. Maryknoll, NY: Orbis Books, 2010.

Perrin, Norman. *Jesus and the Language of the Kingdom: Symbol and Metaphor in New Testament Interpretation*. Philadelphia: Fortress, 1976.

Powery, Emerson B. *The Good Samaritan: Luke 10 for the Life of the Church*. Touchstone Texts. Grand Rapids, MI: Baker Academic, 2022.

Schaper, Joachim. "Levites," Pages 885–887 in *The Eerdmans Dictionary of Early Judaism*. Edited by John J. Collins and Daniel C. Harlow. Grand Rapids: Eerdmans, 2010.

Snodgrass, Klyne. *Stories with Intent: A Comprehensive Guide to the Parables of Jesus*. Second ed. Grand Rapids: Eerdmans, 2018.

Sobrino, Jon. *The Principle of Mercy: Taking the Crucified People from the Cross*. Maryknoll, NY: Orbis Books, 1994.

Thurman, Howard. *Jesus and the Disinherited*. Boston, MA: Beacon Press, 1996.

4

Lost Sheep, Lost Coin (Luke 15:4–10)

1. Introduction

From a scene of highway robbery we turn next to two vignettes from the rural environment in which Jesus lived and taught. One is a situation in which a shepherd notices that he has lost one of his hundred sheep. In the other, a woman loses one of ten coins. They both engage in a series of actions to find their lost items and both respond similarly—and somewhat surprisingly—when they find it, inviting their friends and neighbors to celebrate with them. As simple, concrete, and grounded in this world as these stories are, in both instances we come to understand that these actions actually have something to say to us about the joy that is experienced in heaven when a sinner repents. As we read these two parables our curiosity is already engaged and we may also be left scratching our heads a bit. How are sheep and coins connected with sinners and heaven? And what are we to make of this in our world today where most of us will probably only ever see sheep at the petting zoo and coins, well, hardly ever. As we work through our process of interpretation to understand these parables in their original world, and then consider their meaning in our own time and place, we will see that the notion of being lost and being found has the potential to engage us just as it did Jesus's original listeners.

Social Justice in the Stories of Jesus: The Ethical Challenge of the Parables, First Edition. Matthew E. Gordley.
© 2024 John Wiley & Sons Ltd. Published 2024 by John Wiley & Sons Ltd.

Chapter 4

2. The Text: Lost Sheep, Lost Coin (Luke 15:4–10)

Now all the tax collectors and sinners were coming near to listen to him. And the Pharisees and the scribes were grumbling and saying, "This fellow welcomes sinners and eats with them." So he told them this parable: (Luke 15:1–3 NRSV)

> "Which one of you, having a hundred sheep and losing one of them, does not leave the ninety-nine in the wilderness and go after the one that is lost until he finds it? When he has found it, he lays it on his shoulders and rejoices. And when he comes home, he calls together his friends and neighbors, saying to them, 'Rejoice with me, for I have found my sheep that was lost.' Just so, I tell you, there will be more joy in heaven over one sinner who repents than over ninety-nine righteous persons who need no repentance." (Luke 15:4–7 NRSV)

> "Or what woman having ten silver coins, if she loses one of them, does not light a lamp, sweep the house, and search carefully until she finds it? When she has found it, she calls together her friends and neighbors, saying, 'Rejoice with me, for I have found the coin that I had lost.' Just so, I tell you, there is joy in the presence of the angels of God over one sinner who repents." (Luke 15:8–10 NRSV)

3. Our First Step: Grasp the Stories

As we are considering two parables rather than just one, it is important to notice that both follow a very similar pattern and many words are repeated verbatim. Essentially, these parables can be considered twins. The narrative development of each of these parables is very similar. They begin with a question, making them interrogative parables. They both include the identification of a main character, something of value that is lost, a process of searching for it, finding it, and calling neighbors together to rejoice over the finding of the valuable item which was lost. In addition, there is a concluding application statement linking the joy in the parable to joy in the divine realm over the repentance of one sinner.[1]

---

[1] For analysis of these parables and their interconnections, see Hultgren, *Parables of Jesus*, 46–70; Snodgrass, *Stories with Intent*, 93–117.

110

Lost Sheep, Lost Coin (Luke 15:4–10)

With the parable of the lost sheep (vv. 4–7), the main character is a person, using the most general term for person in Greek (*anthropos* from which we get our terms like anthropology), which is generally translated with the generic "man" since the rest of the parable uses Greek masculine endings to describe him. Jesus introduces this man in a very general way in the form of a question, "which person among you." The full description is actually a person "having a hundred sheep and losing one" (v. 4). By this we are to understand that the character is a shepherd. We can note that Jesus introduces the character and the action in the form of a question in the form of "which person among you ... in such and such a situation... would not do X, Y, and Z?" It is a rhetorical question because, of course, if one were a shepherd, one would not simply abandon a lost sheep, but would go get it. Then Jesus says that this man leaves the rest of the sheep, goes after the lost sheep, until he finds it. That is what shepherds do. From the rhetorical question which sets up the parable, Jesus then goes on to describe what happens once the shepherd finds the lost sheep. He puts it on his shoulders and rejoices. With these actions the sheep is brought back, and the stress of having a lost sheep is resolved into rejoicing (v. 5). From there, the shepherd takes another interesting step: he calls his friends and neighbors together to rejoice with him (v. 6). It's party time at the shepherd's house! And the shepherd recounts to his friends what has happened: "I have found my sheep that was lost." At this, the parable ends and a statement of application follows. The application is that one sinner who repents (presumably like the lost sheep that is found?) is a cause of more rejoicing in heaven than ninety-nine righteous persons who do not need to repent (presumably like the ninety-nine sheep who do not get lost?).

As we turn to the parable of the lost coin (vv. 8–10), the main character is a woman. More specifically it is a woman "having ten coins and losing one of them" (v. 8). As with the parable of the lost sheep, Jesus here introduces the character and her actions with a rhetorical question: "what woman ... in such and such a situation ... would not do X, Y, and Z?" In this parable the actions are lighting a lamp, sweeping the floor, and searching for the coin with the ultimate action of finding it. As with the previous parable, the act of finding is not the end. What follows is an invitation to her female friends and neighbors to come together and rejoice with her (v. 9). It's party time at the woman's

Chapter 4

house, as she recounts to her friends what has happened. Again the celebration scene is followed by an application statement about joy over a sinner who repents. This time it is in the presence of the angels of God, and presumably the sinner who repents is analogous to the coin that is found.

While we are grasping the story, it is also important to note the narrative context in which Jesus tells these twin parables. According to Luke 15:1–2, they are told in a moment in which certain Pharisees and scribes were grumbling about the way in which Jesus welcomed tax collectors and sinners. Not only did he welcome them but he went so far as to share meals with them. Through sharing a meal with them his actions embodied an acknowledgement of their fellow humanity and an acceptance of them as worthy. For some of the Pharisees and scribes that Luke has in mind, such actions were not considered appropriate for someone who was supposed to be a teacher, healer, or prophet. His actions toward sinners communicated a strong message which challenged some of these religious leaders' attitudes toward and method of dealing with those whom they judged to be far from God. In the context of such a conflict, these two parables and a third which we will discuss in a separate chapter (the parable of the lost sons) offer a challenge to religious leaders and to all readers to reconsider their views about "sinners," and to rethink their attitudes and actions toward them.[2]

4. Our Second Step: Ask Questions to Gain Understanding

As brief snapshots of experiences set in the rural, agrarian context of Jesus and his listeners, we can begin thinking of a number of questions both about the details and the overall meaning of each. On a larger level, we may wonder if these parables were originally about joy over sinners repenting (as the summary statements indicate), or if that is simply one particular application of these parables which Luke makes

---

[2] For help in understanding the place of these parables in the larger context of the section of Luke's Gospel known as the travel narrative, see Snodgrass, *Stories with Intent*, 93–95.

Lost Sheep, Lost Coin (Luke 15:4–10)

in his recounting of the parables? For example, we can observe that the sheep and the coin do not repent (they aren't capable of doing anything to repent of!), so that might cause us to consider if these are parables primarily about repentance, or if they are about something else as well? We may also wonder were the characters in the stories responsible or irresponsible? For example, while the shepherd goes after the one sheep, has he abandoned the ninety-nine in the process? And what was the value of one sheep to the shepherd, or the one drachma to the woman? And what significance might there be to having a woman as the main character in a parable in a first-century context? What social dynamics are in play here? Are we to understand these characters as rich or poor or somewhere in between? And in interpreting these parables, should we see the main characters as representative of God in some way? If so, who are the sheep or the coins? Who are the friends and neighbors?

While all of the above questions can give us added insight, some fruitful lines of inquiry to start with relate to the social and economic realities reflected in the parable, as well as the symbolic field of meaning of the images. Asking questions about these areas can help us get to the link between story and social justice, as well as give us insight to answer some of the questions above.

What Glimpse Does Each Parable Give Us into Economic Realities in the First Century?

Understanding the social location and economic situation of a shepherd gives us added insight into two important features of the parable: the joy of finding and the communal celebration. The shepherd with one hundred sheep suggests the context of a rural, family farm. In that environment every sheep mattered so that the finding of the lost sheep was indeed important to the family. The one "having a hundred sheep" could be the owner of the sheep or may have been a member of the extended family given charge of the hundred sheep. Either way, in a rural context, this shepherd would likely have been connected by familial ties to the owner of the sheep, and so the community as a whole had a vested interest in the well-being of the sheep. In addition, despite a few notable shepherds in Jewish history (Moses and David were

113

Chapter 4

shepherds!) shepherds were apparently considered very low on the social ladder in terms of their status.[3] By selecting a shepherd and a sheep Jesus points to realities familiar to his listeners. While his audience was surely not all shepherds, this verbal picture reflects the realities of the daily struggle for survival in their rural context.[4]

Likewise, the woman and the coins invite consideration of money and economic realities for women in the ancient world. Whether married or single, the story may suggest that this was basically all that she had, and that this money was what she depended on in this rural economy for her daily survival. One coin (here, a *drachma*, the equivalent of a day's wage) for her would likely have provided food for about two days. On the other hand, in a rural economy where trade for the commodities of daily life was the norm rather than cash purchasing, coins may have been considered much more rare, making the loss of one all the more significant.[5] By selecting a woman and hinting at her tenuous hold on the necessities for survival, Jesus again points to economic realities that were familiar to his audience.[6] Interestingly, in a patriarchal society such as first-century Palestine, such realities are rarely a focus of attention. Yet focusing on a woman's situation of loss and restoration adds perspective on the joy of finding and the communal celebration—there is recognition of the women's experience, as much as the men's experience. The joy of communal celebration and sharing with another's fortune is something common to male and female. We will return to the significance of such a female oriented story in a patriarchal context when we consider the challenge and the implications of this parable.

---

[3] For analysis of the cultural context of this parable see Kenneth E. Bailey, *Poet and Peasant, and Through Peasant Eyes: A Literary-Cultural Approach to the Parables in Luke* (2 vols.; Grand Rapids: Eerdmans, 1983), 147–150.

[4] More recently, connecting the economic realities of agrarian life in Jesus's day to those of our own, see the Gary Paul Nabhan, *Jesus for Farmers and Fishers: Justice for All Those Marginalized by Our Food System* (Minneapolis, MN: Broadleaf Books, 2021).

[5] See Bailey, *Poet and Peasant*, 157–158. Bailey is overconfident on the extent to which negative attitudes toward shepherds and women were a feature of the Pharisees whom Jesus was addressing in these parables. Such assertions can contribute to anti-Jewish interpretations which we intend to be careful to avoid.

[6] Nabhan, *Jesus for Farmers*, 145–147.

Lost Sheep, Lost Coin (Luke 15:4–10)

What was the significance of celebratory gatherings of friends and neighbors? Such communal occasions were highly significant in the ancient Mediterranean context playing important roles in social formation. As connectivist, rather than individualistic, cultures such occasions served a number of functions. While enhancing the individual's sense of belonging and security within the village, they also reinforce the interdependence of members of the community.[7] As we will see below, the action of rejoicing together also carried overtones for Luke's understanding of the ministry of Jesus in light of Jewish expectations about the coming age of renewal.

So there is a lot of meaning in the concrete realities themselves: how men and women survived in a particular economic situation; how community functioned to support well-being. We also have here a glimpse of the universal human experience of losing and finding, and the joy and relief which come with finding an item of value that was lost. In addition to these concrete realities, we can also consider the metaphorical significance of the imagery. We will reflect on the metaphors more fully below, but those with some knowledge of the Bible may already know that sheep and shepherd imagery has a long and rich tradition, as we will see. In addition, imagery of a celebratory feast has significance beyond just having a party. We will explore each of those in a moment, but next we want to spot the twist.

5. Our Third Step: Spot the Twist

As we have seen, both of these parables have the same pattern of actions: losing, searching, finding, calling together friends and neighbors, and inviting them to rejoice as they recount their story of losing and finding. Is there a surprise in any of these areas?

The searching is noteworthy in that in both cases it is described in a way that gives it some emphasis. It is not just that the shepherd goes and searches. Instead, it is pointed out that he literally abandons the ninety-nine. Of course, this action is not a reflection of value of the ninety-nine, rather a statement of the value of the one; in addition, one

---

[7] See Jerome Neyrey, "Meals, Food, and Table Fellowship," in *The Social Sciences and New Testament Interpretation* (ed. Rohrbaugh; Peabody, MA: Hendrickson, 1996).

Chapter 4

can assume they were well-cared for—their well-being just not a concern of this parable. Also, it is noted that he searches until he finds it. In the case of the woman, her searching is emphasized further with an even more protracted process of lighting a lamp, sweeping the house, and also searching "carefully." It is also noted that she searches until she finds it. So some emphasis is certainly given there. But in neither story does the searching seem to be represented as if it were in any way extreme; at least not extreme enough to be considered a twist. The story certainly hasn't gone off the rails, as it were. That the parables begin with the question along the lines of "which of you in this situation wouldn't do the same," suggests readers are in agreement to this point.

A more likely candidate for the unusual element in each story is the joyous communal celebration that follows the finding. In some ways, the experience of losing something of value is common, and that of finding it is certainly a happy occurrence. Contemporary readers can relate to that feeling. But at least in our day and age we do not generally hold a party for finding something we lost. It seems that the celebrations in these parables are disproportionate to the rest of the story. We can also see that the celebration is emphasized as much as or more than the seeking and finding. This is seen in the fact that the characters both speak at this point, and only at this point. And their words to their gathered friends and neighbors are "rejoice with me." It is an imperative, a command. In both cases it is the exact same Greek phrase, followed by the exact same Greek expression: "because I have found..."

With this request to "rejoice with" we seem to be on the right track to a central element of the meaning of these parables. This becomes clear when we recognize that rejoicing and joy are major themes of Luke's Gospel. In fact, the Greek words for rejoice and joy occur more in Luke than any other New Testament writer.[8] But more significant than the word count is the context and importance of rejoicing and what it means in Luke's account of the good news about Jesus. The significance for Luke is linked directly to the theme of joy in the Jewish scriptures. Rejoicing is a major theme of the prophetic writings about the coming day of the Lord and the restoration of Israel in the new age. It was

---

[8] The term "rejoice" occurs 11 times in Luke, but only 6 times in Matthew and only twice in Mark. The term "joy" itself occurs 8 times in Luke, 6 times in Matthew, and only once in Mark.

Lost Sheep, Lost Coin (Luke 15:4–10)

expected to be a sign of arrival of the new age. Such a focus on rejoicing is a sign not just that people are happy and content but that the new age has arrived.[9] Certainly that is what Luke would have his readers understand when joy and rejoicing explicitly accompany key moments, including the angelic annunciation of the birth of Jesus which is good news of "great joy" (Luke 2:10).[10]

In our parables here though, there is an interesting compound verb that is rarely used: "rejoice with." This idea of "rejoicing with" is used very infrequently in the New Testament as well as in the Jewish scriptures. But when it occurs, it is quite significant. Luke's only other use is in 1:58 when Elizabeth's neighbors rejoice with her in the birth of John (who would later be known as John the Baptist, the forerunner of Jesus). This usage is noteworthy in that it links to the only occurrence of this verb in the Septuagint (the Greek translation of the Jewish scriptures also referred to as the LXX). In Gen. 1:26 LXX this verb occurs at the birth of Isaac when Sarah, the wife of Abraham and mother of Isaac, says that everyone who hears "will rejoice with me." It seems that to "rejoice with" carries important connotations of recognizing the beneficence of God's provision in the context of new life. It also has strong associations with the birth of major figures in the liberating work of God in history.

For these two parables, then, this notion of "rejoicing with" carries significant overtones, for both Luke and the Jewish tradition more broadly. It appears that this is where Luke would have readers feel that the parable grabs their attention.

Interestingly, there is also rejoicing in the version of the parable of the lost sheep in Matthew's Gospel (Mt 18:12–14; Matthew does not have the parable of the lost coin). However, in Matthew's version we only ever learn of the individual shepherd rejoicing over the one sheep that was found. The communal gathering of celebration and the call for others to rejoice is not part of Matthew's telling. It does not mean that this detail is Luke's creation, although it could be. What we can be

---

[9] See for example Jer 38:12–13; Bar 4:36–37 which specifically includes the joy of the lost returning; Bar 5:5–6.

[10] For an analysis of this theme, see Kindalee Pfremmer De Long, *Surprised by God: Praise Responses in the Narrative of Luke-Acts* (Beihefte zur Zeitschrift für die neutestamentliche Wissenschaft; vol. 166; Berlin: Walter de Gruyter, 2009).

Chapter 4

more sure of is that Luke includes this detail to ensure the reader can make this connection with the larger tradition. Matthew, for some reason, did not.

All of these considerations suggest that the "twist" and therefore the focal point of these twin parables is in the collective rejoicing in the whole process of the lost being found, and what was not whole being made whole.

6. Our Fourth Step: Consider the Metaphor

Having reached this point we can now give some focused attention to the metaphors that are in play in this parable. But which ones are the most important ones here?

Shepherd and sheep seem promising since the images of a shepherd and sheep are rich ones in the biblical tradition. We noted above that Moses and David were shepherds. According to the Gospels, Jesus used this image of sheep in other places to describe the people of Israel, and potentially even for the Gentiles (see John 10:16). Shepherd imagery was also used to describe Jesus. In John Jesus refers to himself as "the good shepherd" (see John 10:11, 14).[11]

Of the Gospel writers, Luke actually seems to be the *least* interested in the sheep and shepherd metaphor to describe the people of God and the messiah. For Matthew, Mark, and John, the imagery is important in understanding the identity of Jesus in line with prophecies from the Jewish scriptures. For Luke, however, that particular image is not prominent. Luke's only two shepherd references are to actual shepherds: the shepherds in the nativity narrative to whom the angelic messenger announces good news (Luke 2:8); and here in this parable. And as if to highlight that the focus is not on the sheep/shepherd analogy, Jesus tells the lost sheep parable along with the parable about the woman and the ten coins—a parable which seems to have the same point. Such a move seems to take the focus off of the sheep and shepherd and puts it squarely onto those elements that are common to both: the activity of searching, finding, and celebrating.

[11] Nabhan, *Jesus for Farmers*, 135–139.

118

Lost Sheep, Lost Coin (Luke 15:4–10)

Even though sheep and shepherd imagery was not a major focal point for Luke, Jesus's listeners (and Luke's readers) would still share the rich associations with the sheep and shepherd imagery. The famous and powerful Psalm 23 looks to God as shepherd of one's life: "The Lord is my shepherd" it begins. The Psalms are rich with sheep and shepherd imagery, including the psalmist claiming to be a lost sheep and asking God to seek him out (Ps 118:176 LXX). Elsewhere the psalmist declares, "He is our God, and we are the people of his pasture" (Ps 95:7; cf. Ps 100:3).

But it is not only in the imagery of the Psalms that we encounter a shepherd and sheep. The prophets also develop this shepherd and sheep imagery. Isaiah compares the people to sheep who have gone astray (Is 53:6–7 is a key passage for early Christian views of Jesus). The prophet Micah describes the return from exile of the remnant of Israel using sheep imagery. Zechariah has more ominous imagery about bad shepherds (Zech 10:2–3). Yet he also includes some positive uses of the imagery including Zech 9:16 about God's tending God's people as a flock. Jeremiah also uses this imagery (Jer 27:6 notes that God's people are like lost sheep), and Jeremiah 31 is clearly about God's rescuing the people as a shepherd rescues lost sheep. From the perspective of exile, Jer 31:10–13 indicates that God will bring the people back as a shepherd, and the result will be great rejoicing. These are intriguing elements of a long tradition on which Jesus was drawing as he selected a sheep and a shepherd as the focus of this parable.

The words of the prophet Ezekiel are most instructive in this context. In Ezekiel 34:12 (but also see the whole passage) the prophet notes that the bad shepherds harmed the sheep, but that God himself will seek out the lost sheep. Jesus uses the same verbs in his own parable. Ezekiel goes on to explain that God will raise up a shepherd. Given that this imagery is applied directly to Jesus in John's Gospel, it seems that at least in the context of sinners returning to God, these biblical passages would be in the background. This close connection to Ezek 34 suggests two things. First, with this story and subject matter Jesus may be offering an implicit critique of the current religious authorities for not seeking the lost. Second, it strongly suggests that Jesus may have seen himself in connection with the prophecies of Ezek 34 on some level.[12]

---

[12] Snodgrass, *Stories with Intent*, 105–107. Whether Ezek 34 specifically is in view or not, the parable is unquestionably connected to the imagery and ideas from the Jewish scriptures.

Chapter 4

Given that Luke does not focus elsewhere on shepherds, and that the only time he does has these strong messianic overtones, we can posit a very strong link here with the work of Jesus in welcoming sinners as an affirmation of Jesus's work being in line with the restorative activity of God for God's people. The flip side is that the Pharisees who complained about Jesus's welcoming sinners find themselves in the position of those bad shepherds whom the prophets critiqued for their lack of concern for the lost. Of course, given that Jesus was speaking in parables, such critiques would only be implicit. But to the careful listener able to make the connections with the Jewish religious traditions and their current social context, such a critique would likely have come through clearly enough.

The metaphor of a woman searching for a lost coin moves us in some different directions. While it is not a metaphor that can be traced to a particular earlier tradition, that does not limit its significance in this context. Rather, it means that we need to ask more pointedly about its specific importance here. To begin with, we can note that female imagery is used of God throughout the Jewish scriptures. While not as extensive as the shepherd metaphor, a female metaphor is used in several important areas.[13]

When it comes to the Gospels, scholars regularly note that Luke is most attentive to the inclusivity and universal applicability of the good news about Jesus. Women play a more significant role in Luke than in any of the other Gospels. So it is not surprising that Luke would have a female lead character in some of the parables he recounts.[14] We may note too that this stands out in that the majority of parables of Jesus are focused on male characters and engage male activities. Despite our assumption of their applicability to all persons, for a female-identifying reader to enter into the imaginal world of male-centric parables she must at least temporarily identify with a male character or a male experience. From there she needs to consider its import in her experience as a female. Such a process of putting oneself into a male mindset has been

---

[13] See, for example, Deut 32:11–12, 18; Isa 66:13, and Hosea 11:3–4. For more, see Rosemary Radford Ruether, "The Female Nature of God," in *Exploring the Philosophy of Religion* (ed. Stewart; Upper Saddle River, NJ: Pearson Prentice Hall, 2007), 298–304.

[14] Snodgrass, *Stories with Intent*, 112–115.

Lost Sheep, Lost Coin (Luke 15:4–10)

referred to as immasculation.[15] Feminist scholars help contemporary readers appreciate these dynamics without anachronistically reading modern sensibilities into the first-century world. At the very least, having a parable that centers the experience of a woman in losing and finding is noteworthy in that it steps outside of those assumptions that story and narrative reality is first and foremost a male-centered experience.

Having touched on the complexities of having a female lead character in a parable, we should note here that scholars draw different conclusions about the significance of a parable about a woman. Some see the fact that Jesus would tell a parable about a woman as counter-cultural in and of itself, claiming that Jewish male listeners would even take offense. Levine helps us understand that such an assumption about early Jewish views of women, and Jesus's subversion of those, is misguided. Debunking the thought that to have a woman as a main character would be out of the bounds of acceptability in the Jewish tradition, she teasingly wonders what Deborah, Esther, or Judith would have to say about that. As strong female characters in their own or larger narratives, their presence in the Jewish scriptures helps us limit the extent to which we might claim that Jesus's use of a female character was pushing any boundaries. Instead, we might recognize that this is a place where anti-Judaism once again can creep into our interpretations. It requires an ugly picture of early Jewish views of women to argue that Jesus's views are progressive and a much better alternative.

This is not to say that there is no significance to this imagery. Louise Schottroff provides insightful analysis of the significance of this imagery without resorting to anti-Jewish stereotypes. First, she finds that by setting a parable with a female character alongside a parable with a male character, the significance may be to recognize that women's work in the context of the household is validated along with men's work. "The fact that women's work is presented as having equal status with men's work is really remarkable in a social context that notoriously makes

---

[15] Barbara E. Reid and Shelly Matthews, *Luke 10–24* (Wisdom Commentary; vol. 43B; Collegeville, MN: Liturgical Press, 2021), 443–445.

Chapter 4

women's work invisible."[16] Second, with the desperate search for one coin she sees the context as one of economic challenge that reflects the lives of poor people in rural Judaea. She explains, "The parable shines a spotlight on a rural situation in which people have no land of their own and are dependent on money and on being able to buy their food. The woman needs the money to survive, even more than the shepherd needs his hundredth sheep."[17] And third, she sees the inclusion of the woman's celebration with her neighbors as metaphor for divine joy to be highly instructive: "The devaluation of women's community and women's chatting and laughing together in patriarchal societies makes this parable noteworthy. It uses happy neighbor women to paint a picture of God. If you want to see the angels' happiness, look at happy women."[18] Thus, for Schottroff this parable elevates women's work in a context of economic difficulty as it uses a female experience of joyous community as a metaphor for divine joy.

As for the lost coin, the connections are different still. Jesus himself speaks of money at different times, and some of his other parables deal with money. In the parables we are exploring: The man by the road is robbed (presumably of his money) and the Samaritan gives the innkeeper coins; the contrast of the wealth of the rich man and the poverty of Lazarus is noted;[19] and a vineyard owner pays wages to his workers.[20] Further, a Pharisee praying in the temple mentions his philanthropic giving; a prodigal son asks for his portion of the inheritance and then runs out of money; and a merchant seeking pearls sells all and buys one amazing pearl. Money is thus a common topic for the

---

[16] Luise Schottroff, *The Parables of Jesus* (Minneapolis: Fortress, 2006), 153. In addition, Reid and Matthews note in connection with the parable of prodigal son, the third in the trio: "Domestic work and household management have not always been held in as high esteem as work outside the home. If all three parables are meant to convey the same message, then the sheep owner, the woman, and the father have equally important roles that ensure the economic well-being of the family, whether it be the management and operation of the farm and the livestock, the daily oversight of the household finances, or the distribution of the inheritance." Reid and Matthews, *Luke 10–24*, 447.

[17] Schottroff, *Parables*, 154.

[18] Schottroff, *Parables*, 154–155.

[19] The parable of the rich man and Lazarus is found in Luke 16:19–31. See the extended analysis in chapter nine below.

[20] The parable of the laborers in the vineyard is in Matthew 20:1–16. See chapter eight below.

Lost Sheep, Lost Coin (Luke 15:4–10)

parables. Here, though, it is about losing and finding that money. But how significant was one of ten drachmas? The coin brings us back to the economic context in which the woman lived, and which is in the background in all of Jesus's teachings. It is hard to find any explicit critique here of the economic system in which the woman finds herself. Instead, we simply find acknowledgment of the reality that for this woman, the retrieval of the lost coin was critical to her survival. She had lost something on which her life depended. How hard she searches for it suggests how difficult it would have been to replace.

If the characters and lost items themselves provide some linkages to the wider cultural and social world of metaphors, the specific actions of the characters do as well.

Lost and Found

The activity of searching and finding is one with important connections outside of this parable. In another parable, the pearl of great price (Matthew 13:45–46) Jesus tells of a merchant who seeks out pearls and finds one of great beauty. That angle is a little different than what we find in the present parables in that the merchant had not lost anything, although he is actively searching. The image in the present parable of something lost then found brings into view a different emotional element. Here there is a redemption component that comes into play because of the recognition of the possibility of being lost. We are invited into the story as listeners because we can imagine what it would be like to have lost a sheep or to have lost a coin or to have lost something of value. This is because loss is a part of the human experience. Though the emotion associated with loss is not described, it is implicit in both of these parables. We can see it through the actions of the man and the woman. Their devoting of their full attention and energy to finding the lost sheep and coin, until it is found, lets us know that this item is of great value to them. And readers can relate.

As listeners, we may also relate to the feeling of being lost. The sheep's perspective is not the focus, but certainly there is an emotional element to being the one who is lost. This is especially clear in the application of this parable in Luke's Gospel which makes an explicit analogy between the lost item that is found and one sinner who repents. In Luke's application statement, then, we are to imagine humans who are metaphorically

Chapter 4

lost and found, and heavenly rejoicing at this restoration of a person to a place in the community of which they had been a part.

Communal Rejoicing

Finding what was lost brings us to the ultimate imagery of these parables which is that action of rejoicing together: Calling people together to celebrate the return of what was lost. We noted the significance of the invitation to "rejoice with me" above, in that it taps into some important themes in the Jewish tradition. Rejoicing in itself is a characteristic of the age of renewal—the anticipated great divine cleanup. Rejoicing *together* is as well. And with these parables we see hints at an important aspect of the restoration of all things: the messianic banquet.[21]

The messianic banquet is the expression used to describe the celebration that will occur when the people of God are freed from their oppressors, and those in exile return to the land God gave them. It is hinted at in places like the prophet Isaiah who describes a rich feast that God will host, which will include the elimination of sorrow, despair, and death as God wipes away the tears of his people, they experience salvation, and they are glad and rejoice together (Isa 25:6–9). In Isaiah 62:1–9, the imagery is that of a wedding banquet, and of eating and drinking while giving praise to God. In 2 Esdras 2:33–41 we read Ezra's announcement of coming deliverance. Here the prophet uses imagery of a shepherd who will come at the end of the age to give everlasting rest. This is followed by rewards of perpetual light and great joy and thanks, including imagery of a great banquet. These prophetic examples show us that the hoped for messianic banquet was the celebration that would occur when God's messiah gathers the lost from exile, restores the people of God, and delivers them from their suffering. It is what would happen when the kingdom of God arrived in its fullness.

This imagery of the banquet at the day of God's deliverance is picked up in the New Testament in a number of places. It is explicitly described as a wedding feast in Rev 19:7–9. Jesus speaks explicitly of the messianic banquet in Luke 13:29 as he describes people coming from all corners of

---

[21] Schottroff reads the celebrations in all three of the parables in Luke 15 as reflecting the "great messianic feast of God's joy" which will occur "when the people of Israel and all nations have found the way to life" (156). See Schottroff, *Parables*, 138–156.

Lost Sheep, Lost Coin (Luke 15:4–10)

the earth to "eat in the kingdom of God" along with the great people of faith from the Jewish tradition. He also uses the imagery of a banquet in several parables aside from the ones we explore here. Luke includes the parable of the great banquet (14:16–24) and Matthew includes a similar parable of a wedding feast (22:1–14). These both include their own interpretive challenges. For our purposes here, it is important to note the prevalence of banquet imagery as indicating the arrival of the kingdom of God.

In the ministry of Jesus his inclusive table fellowship seems to have been understood as an anticipatory practice related to the messianic banquet. In his final days with his disciples he memorialized eating and drinking as a sign of the kingdom through the institution of what is now called the Eucharist, communion, or the Lord's supper, depending on one's tradition. With the initiation of this "new covenant" Jesus was tapping into central themes of Jewish belief. The apostle Paul would recount that through this memorial meal followers of Jesus proclaimed the message about Jesus's death "until he comes"—meaning in anticipation of the return of Jesus and the great banquet that would ensue.

The preceding discussion is not to argue that these are parables directly about the messianic banquet. Rather, it is to invite us to notice that language of losing and finding, and of joyful communal celebrating of a return to wholeness, does not come out of nowhere. This language and imagery fits within the larger pattern of the message of Jesus about the kingdom, which itself fits into a rich landscape of Jewish belief about what it would look like and what it would mean when God's agent, the messiah, inaugurated the age of renewal.

Taken together, these images suggest a restoration of a whole that was broken, the completion of a set, the value of one element and its restoration to its rightful place, and the affirmation of that value through celebration of it by the community to whom it mattered. The imagery of sheep and coins and celebrating is the stuff of daily human life and not explicitly religious in any way. Yet as metaphors and in the context of the teaching of Jesus and first-century Jewish expectations of an awaited deliverer, these images become a window into understanding spiritual realities as well.[22]

---

[22] Schottroff explains the relationship between the true-to-life experiences in the parable and the ultimate hope of divine restoration this way: "The little party of happy neighbor women is a foretaste, promise, and assurance of the great healing." Schottroff, *Parables*, 156.

125

Chapter 4

7. Our Fifth Step: Articulate the Challenge

As we move to articulate the challenge of these parables, we are reminded of the difficulty of translation from one genre to another. Parables are stories and their impact is through the power of the story, and the thoughts, feelings, and questions that stories provoke in the mind of the listener. Seeking to distill such a multivalent impact into a descriptive sentence or two runs the risk of missing the point, or focusing on just one point within a larger constellation of meaning. It also runs the risk of taking the emotional element out altogether, in favor of outlining "the moral of the story" in a detached, analytical way. Particularly with short and simple parables like these, our pages and pages of analysis could easily be removing us farther and farther from the gut-level impact of Jesus's stories. As we articulate the challenge, then, we do so being mindful of the risks. We will also move on to considering implications as we reflect on where the parable takes on meaning in our context today.

For these two parables, we may be wondering if these are about God. Is God like the shepherd? Is God like the woman? Howard Thurman approaches these parables as answering in some ways the question "What is God like?" Since parables are comparisons, Thurman's question offers one fruitful way of considering these parables and their challenge. The challenge will be to come to grips with what God is like, and also to consider whether we find ourselves aligned with God's character or out of sync with it.

Of course, on a very concrete level these parables do not mention God at all; they are stories about a shepherd and a woman. How do we map them onto a possible understanding of what God is like? One way to answer the question is suggested by the way analogies work. Snodgrass suggests that these parables work on the level of a "how much more" argument. The shepherd in the story is not God. But if this is how a shepherd responds to a lost sheep, *how much more* will God seek out and rejoice in the finding of lost people? The woman in the story is not God. But if this is how a woman responds to a lost coin, *how much more* will God seek out and rejoice at the finding of "sinners"? Sister Cynthia Serjak, RSM, puts it like this:

> God's mercy is always searching for us, even when we think we are forgotten, even when we get distracted or lose track of ourselves. God's

126

Lost Sheep, Lost Coin (Luke 15:4–10)

mercy goes beyond a quick look around for a little lost sheep. It is abundant and exceedingly generous, going as far and wide as need be to find a lost soul. There is an intensity in God's love for us that breaks through even our strongest defenses; this intensity opens the path for mercy to flow into us, even when we were not expecting it.[23]

With this approach, we do come to understand something of what God is like from the characters in the parables. But there is another implication. When a person is found and is a part of that process of joyous reconnection, there is a desire to share that joy inducing reality with others:

Because of your joy in being found, you become an instrument of this divine impulse as you begin to find others who are suffering and looking for connection and you help them come back. We become the Mercy of God by seeking out the one on the margins, the one who is looking to see if anyone cares, the one whose heart is so waiting and wanting to be found.[24]

In addition, since the presenting problem at the beginning of Luke 15 was that the Pharisees were grumbling about Jesus's welcoming sinners and eating with them, the implication is that it is Jesus's activity aligns with the character of God.[25] Snodgrass explains, "By his reception and eating with such people he demonstrated the presence of the kingdom and the forgiveness available to all. Indirectly this is a kingdom parable, for with this parable Jesus asserts that the promised activity of God to shepherd his own people was taking place."[26] Furthermore, the parables suggest that "those complaining about the actions of Jesus are out of line with God's desires." And through such parables Jesus "invites them to join in the kingdom celebration of the forgiveness being dispensed."[27]

---

[23] Cynthia Serjak, RSM, "The Lost Coin, the Lost Sheep," 2019. See her complete reflection in Appendix 1.

[24] Serjak, "Lost Coin."

[25] Snodgrass, *Stories with Intent*, 107–109. Snodgrass calls it an "analogical 'how much more argument'" (107). "The shepherd is not God, Jesus, or anyone else, and the sheep is not a person or group" (107) but the images do have resonances and bring to mind the traditional use of these images. "At least with respect to Luke, the analogy of the shepherds refers to both the character of God and the activity of Jesus… It portrays an analogy to the attitudes and actions of God" (107–108).

[26] Snodgrass, *Stories with Intent*, 109.

[27] Snodgrass, *Stories with Intent*, 109.

Chapter 4

In this way we can see that the challenge of these parables is complex and multifaceted, linking the stories to Jesus's own context, and peoples' perceptions of his actions toward "sinners." Given our interest to connect the parables with social justice, we can consider the themes here that support an understanding of the dignity of every person. Through such a lens we can articulate the challenge as recognizing the following: To follow Jesus's love ethic is to recognize the inherent worth of each person—if sheep and coins have worth, how much more do people. More so, to follow Jesus's love ethic is also to recognize the inherent worth of each person, even and especially those who are in some sense lost.

Howard Thurman especially notes that the essential movement of God and creation is toward harmony, and thereby stresses the corresponding pain of God at the lostness of any of God's creation. This recognition also leads to understanding the joy of God at the lost being found. Thus, those who have become disconnected from the community are worthy of special attention. Being found (that is, being saved) is a return to a place of connection with one's community. Thurman puts it this way: If to be lost is to be out of touch with the community that sustains a person, then "salvation is reestablishing one's sense of belonging."[28] Reconnecting the marginalized to a full participation in the human community is a work of God that should be celebrated. To celebrate that work is to align oneself with the joy and rejoicing of God.

From these recognitions come implications. For Jesus it was the practical welcoming of "sinners" and eating with them. What might it be today? Like other parables, this one does not tell us how, but there are hints. First, there is the activity of seeking and searching: the actions of the shepherd and the woman, somehow reflective of the action of God, are at the same time suggestive of important human actions. Second, there is the work of restoring someone or something to a place in line with its created purpose: sheep back into the fold; coin back into the purse; and on the human dimension? Perhaps this could be a person brought back into community, given the freedom to live and thrive; and to share their unique genius and gifts with the community. Thurman points to activities of non-religious workers such as counselors, social workers, and medical professionals who engage in practices that heal, restore, and reconnect people to life and to their community. Though

[28] Thurman, *Sermons on the Parables*, 24.

128

Lost Sheep, Lost Coin (Luke 15:4–10)

their work may be outside of the church and not explicitly religious in any way, Thurman points out that it is well aligned with the restoring work of God. And third, there is the celebration aspect of these parables, with the thought of welcoming all to the banquet table. These considerations give us some angles to consider as we think about implications of these parables today.

8. Our Sixth Step: Consider Implications

In the previous section we started down a path that was suggestive of implications for today. In this section we continue on that path as we seek to engage creatively the imagery, challenge, and message of these parables in the realities of our current context. If Jesus's parables offered a challenging message of transformation for the disinherited, what are some implications for those who are on the margins (and those in the center) today?

As we think about implications of these two parables, a place to start is to ask ourselves whether these parables were intended for individuals and their personal actions or for a community and its collective activity. On the individual side, we can see that the protagonist is an individual in each parable: a shepherd who seeks and finds; a woman who seeks and finds. There is also one lost individual item that needs to be found. Focusing on these elements draws our attention metaphorically to individuals who are "lost" in our day and need to be "found." Or individuals who seek and find them. These are certainly fruitful areas for consideration. But we can also note that a focus on the individual is not the only element of these stories. On the communal side, both parables begin with an individual item that was part of a group. They also both end with an out-of-proportion joyous group celebration of the finding of the lost, reminding us of the critical importance of being connected in community—particularly so for Jesus's original listeners in their rural agrarian economy under an exploitive imperial power. Focusing on this element draws our attention to the societal dimension of community networks of support that can hold together in times of difficulty and rejoice together when the community includes all of its members. It seems that a case can be made for both levels of focus, individual and communal.

Chapter 4

If we step back from this parable and include the larger context of the teaching of Jesus in other parables, we can gain some further clarity on these interpretive options. The implicit vision of embracing one's full humanity in the teaching of Jesus certainly includes taking responsibility for one's individual actions. The parables describe individual characters making life-altering choices for good or for ill. Within the frame of each individual parable, those choices either embody the values of the kingdom or deny them. That the parables focus on activities of daily rural life make it clear that individual choices in listeners' daily lives are the decisive moments. The "eschatological moment of decisiveness" (to use a phrase from parables scholar Dan Otto Via) is not a future coming judgment but the individual's choice in each daily event. At the same time, in Jesus's vision living into one's full humanity requires doing so as an individual within community. The decision moments of the parables, while made by individuals, are almost always directly connected to communal concerns. So the decision points pertain not to an isolated, autonomous self, but to ways that individuals relate to one another in a community that embodies (or denies) the values of the kingdom.

This discussion may seem easily resolved by simply noting that the individual versus communal interpretations are not mutually exclusive; both are elements of Jesus's teaching. While that is true, there is a deeper complication. If both elements are inherent in the teaching of Jesus, the history of interpretation has not always embraced both. Our Western ears, socialized to embrace the autonomy of the self and rugged individualism, readily hear the individual component but also effortlessly and unconsciously screen out the communal component.

Emilie Townes helps shine a light on ways that Enlightenment notions of autonomy have led to a wholesale focus on individualism to the near exclusion of what it means to be part of a healthy society which supports all of its members.[29] She argues that this focus on individualism has a consequence of diverting energy and attention away from structural evil and systemic injustice. If the central issue is understood as individual choice, and protecting individual freedom is the highest goal, there is less interest in attending to structural and systemic issues that perpetuate injustice and actually (though invisibly) limit the

---

[29] Emilie Maureen Townes, *Womanist Ethics and the Cultural Production of Evil* (Black Religion, Womanist Thought, Social Justice; New York: Palgrave Macmillan, 2006).

Lost Sheep, Lost Coin (Luke 15:4–10)

individual freedoms and choices available to some members of a society, particularly those marginalized in some way.

While this may seem a theological or theoretical debate, it turns out to be demonstrably the case that this focus on individualism to the exclusion of communal action impacts public policy. Townes explains, "Far too much of our current public policy debates concentrate on individual morality and focus our attention on pieces of the social structure rather than the structure in its entirety."[30] This focus on individuals and away from social structure allow the structures to remain unchanged, while laws and policies focus on individual behavior. Salient examples in her 2006 study include the 1996 welfare reform as one illustration, and the infamous "War on Drugs" as another. Townes explains,

> The religious values that are at the core of these policies—an appeal to the person as an independent unit; the autonomous, selfdetermining ego; stress on personal responsibility; and the abhorrence of dependency— belie a basic inability or unwillingness to recognize structural evil and/or inequities that require public policies that move beyond the notion that government must work through individuals who care about themselves first and foremost, if not exclusively.[31]

This focus on the individual to the near exclusion of the collective is not an inherent element of Christian faith or of the teaching of Jesus. But in contemporary North American context it is an accepted and revered principle that is rarely even acknowledged let alone examined. It might be something we need to reconsider in the light of Jesus's parables with their prominent communal dimensions.

As we consider the teaching of Jesus in the parables, we arguably can see the individual and the community in balance. Townes uses the concepts of justice and the common good to explain how this works. Justice, according to Townes, "is relational, not autonomous, and leads to a sense of caring that is actualized in accessible and affordable health care and childcare, and to the development of a federal and rural development policy that is systemic rather than episodic. It recognizes the

---

[30] Townes, *Womanist Ethics*, 124.
[31] Townes, *Womanist Ethics*, 124.

Chapter 4

interdependence in which we all actually live."[32] Townes thus advocates for policies rooted in a culture of care with a recognition of the realities of human interdependence rather than independence.

Public policies oriented around justice and that benefit everyone are clearly linked to the common good. This notion of the common good is one we will have the opportunity to explore further in relation to other parables. For now, Townes helps us understand it in this way: "Perhaps the simplest way to think about the common good is in terms of having the social structures on which all depend work so that they benefit all people as we strive to create a genuinely inclusive and democratic social and moral order."[33] In focusing on the common good and social structures, however, Townes is not downplaying the importance of individual choices. Rather, she is bringing the collective element into conversation with the individual element. She ultimately suggests that it is not an either/or situation of choosing individual responsibility or public responsibility for addressing social issues. Rather, she advocates that we "find a healthier ground that crafts a creative, progressive, and inclusive space for everyone. This space would demand the best from us as individuals; this space would expect nothing less than corporate attempts to create a just society."[34] While this is an attractive vision, Townes suggests, however, that it is the wealthy and powerful who are often against such approaches. This is likely the case, she claims, since the status quo benefits them. Thus, why change?

While Townes suggests that these individualist approaches are in the interest of the wealthy and powerful, Vivek Murthy suggests it is less out of intention and more out of benign neglect that contemporary society has veered from collective to individual. His diagnosis:

> We've emphasized freedom of individual expression without also ensuring the underpinnings of community are protected and strengthened. Now we need to recapture our investment in the collective elements that matter—our relationships, our community organizations, our neighborhoods, our social and cultural institutions—and we must do this while continuing to protect individual expression.[35]

[32] Townes, *Womanist Ethics*, 135.
[33] Townes, *Womanist Ethics*, 137.
[34] Townes, *Womanist Ethics*, 138.
[35] Vivek H. Murthy, *Together: The Healing Power of Human Connection in a Sometimes Lonely World* (New York, NY: Harper Wave, an imprint of HarperCollins, 2020), 96.

132

Lost Sheep, Lost Coin (Luke 15:4–10)

Murthy's recommendation is not to prioritize one over the other, but to ensure that we support individual autonomy along with our collective responsibility to care for one another.

With these understandings in view, one implication of these twin parables for today is related to the importance of true community. When community is restored, when the lost are found, when "sinners" repent and reconnect with their community, God rejoices. In our society today we are deeply divided. Perhaps we can to reconsider the value of connected community for all of our well-being. Can we set aside our unquestioned commitment to individualism and learn how to think collectively and to think communally?

Bryan Massingale's explorations of racism within the Catholic Church are highly relevant here. First, he shows how racism has functioned culturally, dividing Christians and creating a class of people who are marginalized. Looking at this phenomenon from an individualistic frame of reference, we might think it is sufficient to educate and train people to overcome their biases and reject racist tendencies. By this logic, if fewer people are racist then things will improve. However, this approach overlooks the ways that racism is embedded in systems that will not change unless specifically addressed at a wider societal level. Interestingly, while aspects of the Christian tradition support individualism, there is much within Christian belief and practice that supports the kind of communal perspective that Jesus promotes in the parables. Central to all streams of Christian tradition are the practices of conversion, baptism, and the Eucharist. Massingale shows how these shared practices, if practiced intentionally, each have the potential to reinforce values that are essential to addressing injustice. Specifically, these Christian practices can promote equality, transformative love, and solidarity—the kinds of values and beliefs that support collective action for the common good and not just an individualist perspective. Regarding the Eucharist, for example: "Jesus' meal ministry and his practice of table fellowship seems a deliberate strategy by which he symbolized and made real his vision of radical human equality before God."[36] In addition, as we see even in these parables, "Jesus' table fellowship thus stretches our social imaginations, and challenges the

---

[36] Massingale, *Racial Justice*, 125.

Chapter 4

boundaries we give to our inclusion and acceptance."[37] Such communal practices have the potential to challenge white privilege and help form a counter-identity based in solidarity and community. But Massingale is careful to note that this potential can only be realized if Christians recognize and elevate the values that have always been there embedded within those practices.

What is God like? God is in some ways like the shepherd who seeks the lost sheep; and God is in some ways like the woman who seeks the lost coin. And God is in some ways like them as they call their friends to celebrate the restoration of what was lost. We might even say that God's highest joy is in seeing the fullness of the human community. God seeks, saves, and restores to community. In other words, God is a God of mercy. If the Samaritan in the parable of the good Samaritan showed mercy to the man on the side of the road that he came upon, and restored his dignity and human well-being, the shepherd in this parable embodies mercy in restoring the place and wholeness of the lost sheep.

What is our level of sensitivity to the lost, the estranged, the marginalized, the outcast? If we recognize the heart of God for lost persons, and the joy of God in their being restored, we can also join in that work of restoration. Actions to restore the lost to a place of dignity, and thereby restore the community to wholeness, are actions that embody the mercy of God and enhance the joy in the world. Cynthia Serjak, RSM, explains that those who experience the relief and joy of being found can also then,

> Imagine God's divine joy in doing the finding. And then think about how each time one of us is found, God's mercy is released even more widely into the world. Because of your joy in being found, you become an instrument of this divine impulse as you begin to find others who are suffering and looking for connection and you help them come back.[38]

In this way, joining in the work of finding the lost, "We become the Mercy of God by seeking out the one on the margins, the one who is looking to see if anyone cares, the one whose heart is so waiting and wanting to be found."[39] Sheep and coins may not be part of our daily

---

[37] Massingale, *Racial Justice*, 125.

[38] Serjak, "Lost Coin."

[39] Serjak, "Lost Coin."

Lost Sheep, Lost Coin (Luke 15:4–10)

lives in contemporary North America, but fostering a sensitivity to the experiences of lostness and marginalization of others, and of the joy of their restoration, is a practice that is as needed today as it was in the days of Jesus.

Works Cited in Chapter 4

Bailey, Kenneth E. *Poet and Peasant, and Through Peasant Eyes: A Literary-Cultural Approach to the Parables in Luke.* Combined ed. 2 vols. Grand Rapids: Eerdmans, 1983.

De Long, Kindalee Pfremmer. *Surprised by God: Praise Responses in the Narrative of Luke-Acts.* Vol. 166, Beihefte zur Zeitschrift für die neutestamentliche Wissenschaft. Berlin: Walter de Gruyter, 2009.

Hultgren, Arland J. *The Parables of Jesus: A Commentary.* The Bible in its World. Grand Rapids: Eerdmans, 2000.

Massingale, Bryan N. *Racial Justice and the Catholic Church.* Maryknoll, NY: Orbis Books, 2010.

Murthy, Vivek H. *Together: The Healing Power of Human Connection in a Sometimes Lonely World.* New York, NY: Harper Wave, an imprint of HarperCollins, 2020.

Nabhan, Gary Paul. *Jesus for Farmers and Fishers: Justice for All Those Marginalized by Our Food System.* Minneapolis, MN: Broadleaf Books, 2021.

Neyrey, Jerome. "Meals, Food, and Table Fellowship," Pages 159–182 in *The Social Sciences and New Testament Interpretation.* Edited by Richard L. Rohrbaugh. Peabody, MA: Hendrickson, 1996.

Reid, Barbara E. and Shelly Matthews. *Luke 10–24.* Vol. 43B, Wisdom Commentary. Collegeville, MN: Liturgical Press, 2021.

Ruether, Rosemary Radford. "The Female Nature of God," Pages 298–304 in *Exploring the Philosophy of Religion.* Edited by David Stewart. Upper Saddle River, NJ: Pearson Prentice Hall, 2007.

Schottroff, Luise. *The Parables of Jesus.* Minneapolis: Fortress, 2006.

Serjak, Cynthia, RSM. *"The Lost Coin, the Lost Sheep."* 2019.

Snodgrass, Klyne. *Stories with Intent: A Comprehensive Guide to the Parables of Jesus.* Second ed. Grand Rapids: Eerdmans, 2018.

Thurman, Howard. *Sermons on the Parables.* Maryknoll, NY: Orbis Books, 2018.

Townes, Emilie Maureen. *Womanist Ethics and the Cultural Production of Evil.* Black religion, womanist thought, social justice. New York: Palgrave Macmillan, 2006.

5

The Lost Sons (Luke 15:11–32)

1. Introduction

Following immediately after the parables of the lost sheep and the lost coin is one of the most well-known of all of Jesus's parables. The parable of the lost sons (commonly referred to as the parable of the prodigal son, focusing on the younger son who leaves and returns) is the longest and, arguably, one of the most dramatic of Jesus's parables. For these reasons there is a rich tradition of interpretation and a lot for us to work with as we consider this parable and its message in our own day.[1]

2. The Text: The Lost Sons (Luke 15:11–32)

Then Jesus said, "There was a man who had two sons. The younger of them said to his father, 'Father, give me the share of the property that will belong to me.' So he divided his property between them. A few days later the younger son gathered all he had and traveled to a distant country, and there he squandered his property in dissolute living. When he had spent

---

[1] The literature on this parable is vast. The commentaries and studies we have been working with on earlier parables also provide a good entry point to the issues: Hultgren, *Parables of Jesus*, 70–91; Snodgrass, *Stories with Intent*, 117–144; Blomberg, *Interpreting the Parables*, 198–211.

Social Justice in the Stories of Jesus: The Ethical Challenge of the Parables, First Edition.
Matthew E. Gordley.
© 2024 John Wiley & Sons Ltd. Published 2024 by John Wiley & Sons Ltd.

The Lost Sons (Luke 15:11–32)

everything, a severe famine took place throughout that country, and he began to be in need. So he went and hired himself out to one of the citizens of that country, who sent him to his fields to feed the pigs. He would gladly have filled himself with the pods that the pigs were eating; and no one gave him anything. But when he came to himself he said, 'How many of my father's hired hands have bread enough and to spare, but here I am dying of hunger! I will get up and go to my father, and I will say to him, "Father, I have sinned against heaven and before you; I am no longer worthy to be called your son; treat me like one of your hired hands."' So he set off and went to his father. But while he was still far off, his father saw him and was filled with compassion; he ran and put his arms around him and kissed him. Then the son said to him, 'Father, I have sinned against heaven and before you; I am no longer worthy to be called your son.' But the father said to his slaves, 'Quickly, bring out a robe—the best one—and put it on him; put a ring on his finger and sandals on his feet. And get the fatted calf and kill it, and let us eat and celebrate; for this son of mine was dead and is alive again; he was lost and is found!' And they began to celebrate.

"Now his elder son was in the field; and when he came and approached the house, he heard music and dancing. He called one of the slaves and asked what was going on. He replied, 'Your brother has come, and your father has killed the fatted calf, because he has got him back safe and sound.' Then he became angry and refused to go in. His father came out and began to plead with him. But he answered his father, 'Listen! For all these years I have been working like a slave for you, and I have never disobeyed your command; yet you have never given me even a young goat so that I might celebrate with my friends. But when this son of yours came back, who has devoured your property with prostitutes, you killed the fatted calf for him!' Then the father said to him, 'Son, you are always with me, and all that is mine is yours. But we had to celebrate and rejoice, because this brother of yours was dead and has come to life; he was lost and has been found.'" (Luke 15:11–32 NRSV)

3. Our First Step: Grasp the Story

While commonly referred to as the parable of the prodigal son— suggesting that it focuses on this one character—this powerful story is about much more than a younger brother who leaves home, bottoms

Chapter 5

out, and returns to a lavish welcome. Those events are critical to the parable and can certainly stand on their own with their emotive impact on the reader and metaphorical power to demonstrate the compassion of God for God's children. Nevertheless, the welcoming back of the prodigal son sets the stage for another crucial moment: the older son's indignant speech and the father's patient reply. As we have noted often, the force of a parable is often in the whole, rather than the parts. Here again we will see that each part lends an important dimension to the overall message which would be otherwise incomplete without each part. Keeping this larger framework of the story in view, we will follow our process and take a moment to ensure a grasp of each element of this captivating parable.

As the longest of Jesus's parables and one of the most dramatic, our effort to grasp the story can be aided by some attention to how this story reflects features of ancient literary art. As a brief but powerful work of narrative fiction this parable is illuminated by attending to its linkages to the patterns of tragedy and comedy, as well as to the social world it assumes. These are features we can note as we walk through the story and attend to each element.

The parable begins with a simple introduction of three unnamed characters: a man and two sons (v. 11). Even with such a simple beginning the reader's mind is teased into thinking about related scenarios and traditions, and where this might lead. Is this going to be a happy story or a sad one? In the Jewish tradition the reader might instinctively think of Isaac and his sons, Jacob and Esau. Or Adam and his sons, Cain and Abel. Even if we discover that this parable does not allude to those traditions directly, we are at least prompted to imagine a contrast that might unfold, especially knowing the importance of birth order and birth right in ancient society and the tension that sometimes resulted. We might also imagine a contrast being set up as tales of two sons often reflect two very different lives. This is even true in the parables of Jesus in another parable about two sons (see Matt. 21:28–32). At any rate, with the opening lines, even without knowing where the story will go, the emotions and feelings are already anticipating a story of significance.

With these precognitive stirrings in mind, we next learn that the younger son asked the father for his share of the inheritance prior to his father's death (v. 12). As the first action in this narrative and the first

138

The Lost Sons (Luke 15:11–32)

instance of direct speech this suggests to us that the younger son is likely the protagonist—the character around whom the story will focus. We might wonder what this action tells us about the younger son as we consider how common such a request was, what kind of disrespect it may have conveyed for the father, or what kind of conflict it may set up with the father or the older brother. But no time to worry about that: we immediately learn that the father granted the son's request. Whether it was a socially acceptable request or not, and whether it was a wise decision by the father or not, the result is the dividing of the inheritance. Thus far Jesus is still setting the stage for what will follow, but we have some early hints that all may not be well with this family.

Next the younger son used his share to finance an escape from his father's household and essentially blew all his money on having a good time (v. 13). Without knowing much else from the story we get the idea here from terms like "squandering" that this young son was foolish. This confirms the reader's earlier initial impulse that the son's asking for the inheritance might have been problematic and disrespectful. Taken together this behavior would certainly bring dishonor to the family, reflecting poorly not only on the son but on the father as well. The son's being in "a far country" also taps into themes of exile and is suggestive of the story of Joseph, a youngest son in the Jewish scriptures who was sold into slavery in Egypt. While the thematic echoes help to reinforce the significance of the story and heighten the reader's expectation that something important will occur, this tale develops in its own ways.

The younger son's story took a few turns for the worse as he ran out of money and found himself in a severe famine and in need (v. 14). He then hired himself out and was sent to the fields to feed pigs (v. 15). A powerful low point in the parable is where the son longs to eat even the food of the pigs, but no one gave him anything (v. 16). The verb for "to give" here is the same as that in v. 12 where the son asked his father to give him his inheritance. The son has gone from a situation of living in the home of a giving father to a place in which no one would give him anything. By this one can see how far the son's condition has deteriorated: from son to hired hand; from wealthy to in need; from being in his own home and homeland to working in the fields in a far country. The protagonist's story thus far has been a downward movement from well-being to a very desperate situation. In terms of ancient dramatic

Chapter 5

fiction, depending where things go from here this story may yet be a tragedy or a comedy.

A turning point occurs when the son "came to himself" (v. 17). This is an important phrase that is followed by the son's dialogue with himself (the second instance of direct speech in the story) about how much better it is back at home, even for the hired hands. This revelation of the son's thoughts to the reader also includes his resolution to return home and make a speech to his father (vv. 18–19). His planned speech acknowledges that he has sinned, which in this context is likely understood to encompass all of his actions thus far which have dishonored his father and brought shame to the family, in addition to squandering the resources he had received. His speech also reveals his plan to ask to be treated like one of the hired hands—which according to his memory is far better than his current experience. With that he simply set off and returned to his father (v. 20).

Thus far in the parable Jesus has been setting the stage for the engagements that will follow which are where we find the surprises. The first surprise is the father's reaction to the son's return. Someone who has never heard the parable would not know what to expect, or whether the son's plan to be able to come back as a hired hand would be successful. But before the son even arrives the father sees him, is filled with compassion and welcomes him lavishly: running to him, embracing him, and kissing him (v. 20). Not only so, but after the son delivers only part of his planned speech the father interrupts him and orders the servants to bring the best robe, a ring, and sandals, all of which together show the father's restoration of the son as a son, not a servant (v. 22). That these are the first spoken words of the father in the parable is also noteworthy. This exchange is followed by the killing of the fatted calf and a celebration based on the father's declaration that the son was dead and is now alive, was lost and is now found (vv. 23–24).

We can pause here momentarily to consider the father's being filled with compassion. Interestingly, this is the same verb used to describe the response of the Samaritan to the wounded man by the road in Luke 10:33. In the Gospels its only other usage is to describe the compassion of Jesus whether for crowds of people or for an individual seeking the help of Jesus (see Matt. 9:36; Mk 1:41; Luke 7:31). In reference to the father's compassion Sister Judy Schubert, RSM, reminds us: "Compassion ranks as one of the primary elements of Mercy.

140

The Lost Sons (Luke 15:11–32)

A compassionate person demonstrates great wisdom and patience, as this caring parent does."[2] She goes on to point out, "Through these unexpected and generous actions, the father presents a complete demonstration of love. He has overlooked entirely the insulting disrespect and demands that his younger son originally made years ago. In a spirit of authentic mercy, the compassionate father has forgiven the unforgiveable and restored his broken son to his former status."[3] If the parable had concluded here it would clearly be seen as a powerful expression of the love of a father for a lost son—much like the joy in the previous two parables of finding the lost sheep and the lost coin. However, the parable does not end here but continues; and in the continuation we encounter some additional family dynamics that are not reflected in the parables of the sheep and coin. What happens next is thus highly significant for understanding the point of this parable.

The older son, who has not been mentioned since the opening verses, was in the field—apparently laboring diligently for the small family farm—and only learned of these happenings when he came to the house and heard the sounds of the celebration (v. 25). Since he had not been summoned to the celebration (had the father forgotten him altogether?) he inquired of a servant what was going on (vv. 26–27). On learning the details, his response was one of anger rather than joy at the return of his brother, and he refused to go into the party. With that the father came out and spoke to him, urging him to come in (v. 28).

The dialogue of the father and oldest son is fascinating in its own right. In it we learn that the older brother was angry that the father had never showed him this kind of lavish treatment, despite the fact that he had labored for the father and obeyed him for "all these years" (v. 29). Rather than referring to his brother as a brother he referred to him as "this son of yours." And he referenced the son's misdeeds that have brought dishonor to the family in contrast to his own actions which have benefited the family (v. 30). By way of response the father (in his second direct speech of the parable) did not dispute the facts but in the end simply reaffirmed the older son's place in the family ("Son, you are always with me, and all that is mine is yours," v. 31) along with insisting on the importance of celebrating the return to life of the

---

[2] Judy Schubert, RSM, "The Lost Sons," 2019. See her complete reflection in Appendix 1.
[3] Schubert, "Lost Sons."

Chapter 5

younger son (v. 32). The father's speech concludes the parable and in the end it is not revealed whether the father has convinced the older brother or not.

As this brief overview makes clear, this is a parable with multiple snapshots and focal points. Initially it is the father with two sons. Next it is the younger son making a request of his father and the father granting the request. Then we see the younger son on his own and learn of his actions, interactions with others, thoughts, and plans. Next, we see the father and son reunite. Then we see the older son with his actions and thoughts and interactions with others. Finally, we see the father and older son together. As Hultgren points out, this is essentially a story about a father who is "trying to restore a family that has fallen apart."[4] This story raises a lot of questions, to which we now turn.

4. Our Second Step: Ask Questions to Gain Understanding

As the longest of Jesus's parables, and one of the most dramatic, an important question we might ask is how this parable functions as a literary composition. Dan Otto Via is a biblical scholar who helps us think about how stories like these function as works of art or, as he calls them, "aesthetic objects." His way of approaching a parable as an aesthetic object can help us appreciate the literary art of this parable and also guide us to some new questions that can help sharpen our understanding. Before we turn to these new questions it will be helpful to understand some the key elements of his literary approach.

A first key insight is that the process of encountering a literary work is a complex one because of the nature of literature and of artistic products more generally. To help with this Via introduces two concepts that relate to encountering an aesthetic object: focal awareness and subsidiary awareness. Focal awareness refers to what the viewer (or reader, in our case) is conscious of and paying primary attention to at a given moment. In reading literary fiction, the focal awareness is primarily on what is happening in the story: the plot, the characters, the actions, and

---

[4] Hultgren, *Parables of Jesus*, 81.

The Lost Sons (Luke 15:11–32)

so on. These are things that are internal to world of the text. Taken together these elements combine to create what Via calls the "in meaning" of the story, because it is primarily oriented around what is happening in the text in the story. Subsidiary awareness, by comparison, is less conscious and can even be unconscious. In the act of reading literature this subsidiary awareness is related to things like how the story connects to the reader's experience or to the external world in general. While not the primary focus in reading or hearing a story, questions like "What does this story mean in terms of the real world?" "How does this artistic product connect to my experiences?" and "Where do I see myself in the story?" are often formulating in the back of the reader's mind, even if not fully articulated as explicit questions. Bringing attention to these elements allows one to get at the "through meaning," the way literature enables readers to see their world in a new way through the medium of the story.

Essentially then, in first experiencing an aesthetic object (in our case, hearing a story parable), the focal awareness is initially primarily on the object and its world. Subsidiary awareness is on its affective impact and potential connections to the reader's world. And this affective dimension and impact on the person may not even be grasped consciously. Via explains, "In aesthetic experience the focal attention is non-referentially grasped, and the *whole* self is moved in ways of which the beholder or reader is not fully aware."[5] This is one way of understanding how it is that parables have such a powerful hold on the imagination and impact a reader on a deeper level than if one were just reading propositional statements. While a person may be focusing primary awareness on the story, their subsidiary awareness is seeking to make connections between the story and their own experiences of the world.

A second key element of this literary approach is the recognition that behind the actions and events of narrative fiction lies an "implied understanding of existence." With this phrase Via refers to the worldview that is presupposed by the author and reinforced or reimagined in the telling of the story. This implied understanding of existence (also referred to as the "existential understanding") is not necessarily spelled out directly but it is nonetheless present as it is infused throughout the narrative. The relationships of the characters to one another, and the

[5] Via, *Parables*, 94.

143

Chapter 5

outcomes of their decisions let us gain insight into the worldview behind the story. A process of analysis and interpretation can help bring to light this implied understanding of existence and enable readers to gain a deeper appreciation of the meaning of a text from a different culture, time, or place.[6]

Third, in light of how focal and subsidiary awareness work, it is important to recognize that the act of interpretation (e.g., analyzing and understanding a story, as opposed to reading it and experiencing it) brings with it a change in the interpreter's focal awareness. Rather than experiencing the world of the text (the in-meaning), the process of interpretation has the potential to bring into focus the elements that are implicit in the work—its implied understanding of existence, worldview, social construction of reality, and other elements that are present but not the focal point when experiencing the story as a story. In the process of interpretation focal awareness shifts intentionally to include both the in-meaning *and* the through-meaning. This broader scope can facilitate a fuller cognitive grasp of the meaning of the story. However, this more complete grasp carries a trade-off: in the process of explaining the meaning by putting complex dynamics of narrative into descriptive language or propositional statements, it becomes difficult if not impossible to adequately convey the affective, precognitive dimension that was in operation in the initial experience of the story. This dynamic reminds us that we need to translate the meaning of a parable not only from one language to another, but from one medium (narrative) to another (propositional statements). This dynamic also links back to what we have discussed previously about metaphor and how it works: its power lies in engaging the mind and emotions in ways that direct speech often cannot. This is not to downplay the importance of direct speech for articulating understanding. Here we call to mind the contrast of a butterfly in flight versus a butterfly preserved for study in a case: both together can enable a renewed appreciation for the beauty of the object being encountered. This same dynamic is at play with

---

[6] This is not dissimilar from our efforts to understand the social construction of reality also represented by the text, noted in Chapter 2. While the social construction of reality refers to the relational and social dynamics at play in the social context, the existential understanding of reality is broader and includes religious and other beliefs as part of a larger worldview.

The Lost Sons (Luke 15:11–32)

literary artistry and the narrative of parables. The process of interpretation, as important as it is, runs the risk of limiting the sense of wonder and emotive impact.

If we follow Via's literary approach and apply it to parables, some very interesting implications and questions emerge. Here we outline three implications. First, because parables are stories, it seems highly likely that in the act of speaking in parables, Jesus was inviting his listeners to focus on the story, at least initially, rather than applying it directly and immediately to any specific reality in their world. Parables, as literary art, bring primary focus to the story itself with subsidiary attention to the implied understanding of existence or metaphorical links to actual events in the ministry of Jesus. Via explains:

> When Jesus told the parables, the story itself probably did engage the hearers' attention focally while the pointing of certain aspects in the story to aspects of Jesus' ministry evoked only subsidiary attention. When the meaning of a parable as a whole is grasped, however, it is a window through which we may see the world anew.[7]

To grasp the meaning of the parable as a whole requires one first to come to grips with the story itself. From there attention can be more focally directed to its linkage to the hearer's world so that the parable becomes a window to see our own world in a new way.

Second, because the initial focus is on the story and its characters, access to the message of the parable's teaching about God, or spiritual realities more broadly, is largely indirect. Teaching about God is rarely spelled out propositionally, but we get at it by attending first to the relational and interactional dynamics within the parable. To a large extent the understanding of the divine in any parable is part of the implied understanding of existence, an aspect of the parable which is present but of which the reader may only have a subsidiary awareness at first. This is not to say that the message about God is not important within the parables. It is of great importance. But the message of the parables about God is an indirect one: the story itself is primary and must first be understood along with its implied understanding of existence. From an understanding of the story and its implied

[7] Via, *Parables*, 88.

Chapter 5

understanding of reality one can then apply it to the divine-human relationship. Via puts it this way:

> The parables do not teach directly or focally about God; therefore the first task is to work out the existential implications of the human interrelationships *within* the parable. But this existential understanding is then to be applied to the divine-human relationship as a definition of faith or unfaith.[8]

Thus an important step for moving to understanding the challenge and implications of a literary parable is to ensure a firm grasp of what is occurring in the human relationships within the parable. It is in the dynamics of these relationships that much of the raw material for extending the meaning to instruction about God and God's kingdom can be found.

A third implication is that by using human interactions based in everyday reality as the medium and focal point for his teaching, Jesus demonstrated something very important: the value of daily human existence as the place in which humans encounter the divine. Via explains,

> The impingement of the divine upon the human is indicated not only by the fact that Jesus compared the kingdom of God to ordinary happenings, but—even more importantly for our purposes—by the way everyday reality is dealt with in the parables themselves.[9]

Jesus's depiction of everyday reality as primary subject matter "suggests that everyday existence is crossed by the problematical, contingent, and unpredictable."[10] The result is: "The parables' existential understanding is that existence is gained or lost in the midst of ordinary life, that the eschatological occurs within the everyday."[11] This recognition that everyday life is where one encounters moments of decision with eschatological significance is not explicitly stated by Jesus, but is clearly part of the implied understanding of existence that

---

[8] Via, *Parables*, 95.
[9] Via, *Parables*, 105.
[10] Via, *Parables*, 106.
[11] Via, *Parables*, 106.

146

The Lost Sons (Luke 15:11–32)

the act of telling parables like this assumes.[12] In this way the parables strike a note of great urgency and infuse all of present reality with meaning and significance.

These implications of the ways in which a parable functions as literature shed light on how this particular parable works. As we begin by focusing first on the story as a story, we can begin to grasp its in-meaning. We can also attend to the implied understanding of existence as a way of getting to the parable's through-meaning and its teaching about God, which is indirect. Part of the implied understanding of existence in the parables of Jesus is an understanding that interactions in everyday reality are the pivotal moments of decision. With those implications in mind, what decision is this parable of the two sons inviting readers to make in their everyday lives?

To answer this question we can recall that we have already begun this chapter by grasping the story as story. In so doing, we have given primary focus to the events and actions within the parable. Via's approach invites us next to explore the implied understanding of existence which undergirds and infuses the parable. We can do so both with information from within the parable and by considering cultural and contextual information from the first-century Jewish and Greco-Roman world in which the parable was originally told. What can we learn about this story's implied understanding of existence?

From the story itself, we can see features which help us. Repetition of key terms and ideas, the dramatic turning point, the surprising actions, and critical dialogue moments give us good indicators. Among other things, these elements suggest to us that familial relationships, with all their strains and their successes, are vital for well-being. More broadly even than family, we can note the critical importance of connection to a supportive community for one's well-being. To be separated from sustaining community is to be lost and, even worse, dead. Death was a real possibility for the younger son, and death imagery pervades the parable. To be connected to one's community is to be found and is to be alive.

---

[12] As Via explains, "The parables ... indicate the eschatological crossing of the everyday" (188), and "The parables pull the ultimate loss of existence implied in the final judgement into a pattern of happening human existence so that the final judgment, the unrecoverable loss of existence, becomes an event in the midst of history" (188).

Chapter 5

A second aspect of the implied understanding of existence is the importance of each member of the community for a healthy community, and the recognition that members of the community can be lost and cut off in multiple ways. For example, the older son is lost but in a different way than the younger son was lost. Though he never left the father's household, we learn that he nevertheless did not experience the fullest enjoyment of the relationship. As he described it he felt that he had been "working like a slave" for his father (v. 29). A closely related aspect to the possibility of being cut off from the community is the prospect of being restored to the community and gaining a new place within it. In the teaching of the parable such restored connections are worth celebrating. The younger son's connection is largely restored through his return and his father's actions; but the parable leaves open the question of whether the older brother is convinced by the father. If he was, and if he chose to join the party and to genuinely and enthusiastically embrace his brother, we can imagine an even more meaningful celebration as all members of the family celebrate a newfound understanding of their interconnection with one another.

From outside the world of the story itself, an awareness of how narrative fiction worked in the ancient world in terms of comedy and tragedy also helps us. While dramatic tragedy featured disintegration of connections and ended in sorrow, this parable instead shows the indicators of ancient dramatic comedy.[13] In this case the initial downward movement of the protagonist from well-being to desperation gives way to an upward movement from a place of lostness to a place of restoration. This insight related to literary genre aligns with what we just observed from the internal indicators of the story which suggested that restoration of community is a critical element.

Another way we gain insight into the implied understanding of existence from outside of the story is from the broader context of the teaching of Jesus as well as his actions as recorded in the Gospels. This is where we consider the context of this parable as being told in relation to the responses of religious leaders to Jesus's activities of welcoming tax collectors and other "sinners" and eating with them (see Luke 15:1–2). Telling this parable (along with the parables of the lost sheep and the

[13] Via, *Parables*, 145–176.

148

The Lost Sons (Luke 15:11–32)

lost coin) in such a context invites the reader to make a connection between the world of the parable and the world in which Jesus was acting. This begins to help us understand the "through meaning" of the parable. Jesus's eating with tax collectors and sinners was a real-world embodiment of the parable's teaching about the importance of being connected to a community. Those individuals were, in a sense, lost sons and daughters returning home. Earlier in Luke, when directly questioned by the Pharisees why he "ate and drank with tax collectors and sinners" Jesus responded directly that he had come "not to call the righteous but sinners to repentance" (Luke 5:29–32). In this way we can see how the parable invited listeners to make a connection to what was happening in the daily activity of Jesus. We can also begin to see how the parable invites all readers to consider connections with the readers' own worlds—whether that was the world in which the Gospel of Luke was written or the twenty-first-century world of today's reader.

With the above considerations, we have begun to answer the question of how a story like this, told with such literary and aesthetic qualities, fits within the ancient world of story. And we have begun to consider what those connections enable us to see as the focal points and secondary elements of the story.[14]

Attuned as we are to interpretive bias related to anti-Judaism we can also ask about anti-Judaism in the interpretive process we are following. Starting with the internal coherence of the story, the "in-meaning," there is nothing in the parable linking it explicitly to uniquely Jewish beliefs or practices, whether positively or negatively. The implied understanding of existence that undergirds the story, a view of community and connection to community as central to life and well-being, reflects a Jewish worldview. That would seem to be a positive element. But the positive message of the parable, combined with the lack of any specific references to Judaism as a religion has not prevented this parable from being used to foster negative views of first-century Judaism.[15]

---

[14] We have merely scratched the surface of the insights that literary analysis can provide. For a recent literary analysis that attends to characterization and rhetorical features that reflect Greco-Roman fables and storytelling, see Amanda Brobst-Renaud, *Lukan Parables of Reckless Liberality* (New Testament Monographs; vol. 42; Sheffield: Sheffield Phoenix, 2021), 61–92.

[15] See the examples in Levine, *Short Stories*, esp 59–63, 70–71.

Chapter 5

This reality seems based, in part, on the context in Luke's Gospel of this and the other two parables.

Since this parable is spoken specifically in the context of Pharisees' grumbling about Jesus's welcoming sinners and tax collectors, the parable has been easily (though inappropriately) molded into a contrast between Judaism and Jesus. The logic is simple, though faulty: the grumbling Pharisees are taken to mean that all Pharisees are unwelcoming to sinners; the older son in the parable is taken to represent the Pharisees. The next step is that this generalized picture of Pharisees' not welcoming sinners is taken to be representative of Judaism of the first century as whole. Therefore, Judaism is like the older brother in the parable: cold, selfish, and unwilling to welcome the return of his younger brother. The corollary is: Jesus welcomes sinners, in contrast to the Jews who do not. Thus, in this way of reading the parable, negative Jewish values are contrasted with positive Christian ones. We have seen in other parables how such equations are actually flawed math; below we will use the concept of metaphor to understand another reason why this is problematic here.

For now, we can consider the through-meaning as the way in which the story invites listeners to connect with realities in their world in a way that does not need to denigrate Jewish beliefs and practices of the first century. In the ministry of Jesus as made clear by the context in Luke, Jesus's actions of welcoming sinners and eating with them was not well-received by certain religious leaders who were indeed Pharisees. These actions of Jesus embodied the reality that all persons find their greatest good in connection with others, in welcoming and supportive community—a belief deeply rooted in Judaism. Telling the parable of the lost sons in such a context would be a non-threatening way to bring such a teaching, and the values it entails, into view. Those who would grumble at sinners finding a place at the table of God's love could be challenged by the image of a rural farming family in crisis to reconsider their strong feelings of offense. In this way, the parable's through-meaning is rightly understood as a message for Jesus's opponents who were critical of his practice. His original listeners might well have made that connection. Readers of Luke's Gospel might have as well. Readers throughout history, however, are off-track to try to extend this parable and its original through-meaning to being a critique of Pharisees in general, or even worse, as a critique of Judaism as a whole.

The Lost Sons (Luke 15:11–32)

The significance of the parable to readers in new times and places is not to conclude that the Pharisees were bad and therefore readers ought to be like Jesus and not like the Pharisees. Instead, the significance is much more around inviting consideration of one's own understanding of community and of its vital importance for all persons, regardless of their position, status, or past. Such an approach can help us give due attention to the historical context of Jesus's original telling of the parable which involved Jewish persons (himself, his audience, including Pharisees), without taking this as a critique of first-century Judaism as a religious tradition. The parable's through-meaning is an opportunity for readers in any time and place to consider the extent to which they value reconnecting the lost in community, or instead let other values take a higher place than community health.

5. Our Third Step: Spot the Twist

Where in this parable do we meet a surprise? As we have noted, a first surprise is in the extravagant welcome home of the younger son. In and of itself, the idea that a loving father in any religious tradition or culture would welcome a lost son home is not surprising. But the extravagance of the welcome here is what is surprising.[16] The giving of a ring and the killing of the fatted calf are details that bring into focus the extent of the father's whole-hearted welcome and which might strike us as over the top. That these are extravagant is confirmed for us in the reaction of the older son later in the parable. For anyone who has been part of a family with sibling dynamics, the older son's reaction is not surprising. One can imagine a long history between the two. The latest episode of the younger son embarrassing the family, dishonoring the father, and so on would not be easily set aside by the older brother.

But in the literary context of Luke's Gospel the welcome and celebration are not really all that surprising. The parables which immediately

---

[16] Brobst-Renaud points out the ways that Luke's portrayal of the father's "extravagant generosity" toward both undeserving sons went against the grain of contemporary literary figures. She notes that "Luke casts the Father's reckless liberality as a laudable trait, which departs from what one might expect" based on contemporaneous literature. Brobst-Renaud, *Lukan Parables*, 87.

151

Chapter 5

preceded this one, the parables of the lost sheep and the lost coin, set up some expectations for this third parable. Each parable has a lost item of value that is found, followed by an out of proportion celebration. A disproportionate celebration is odd, but no longer a surprise to us. So it may instead be in the *variation* from that pattern that we find the surprise.

That variation from the earlier pattern of the lost sheep and the lost coin can be seen in the angry reaction of the older brother and the father's need to go out and plead with him (vv. 28–32). The father's response to the older brother (vv. 31–32) is very instructive. In addition to a response of compassion and patience with the older son, the father also frames the younger son's return in stark terms: once dead, now alive; once lost, now found. The significance of the younger son's being included within the family community versus being removed from it (albeit by his own choice) is described as a matter of life and death. Disintegration of community connection was equated with death; reconnection of community ties brings life and with it cause for joyful celebration. This understanding places the older son in a precarious new light. At this point in the story we become aware of the reality that he is the one who is cut off from the community that is this small family farm. He was unaware of his brother's return and had to ask one of the servants what was going on. The servant was aware, but the older son was not. On learning of what was happening the older son became angry and refused to go in. Thus, he was literally on the outside looking in at a celebration but feeling anger, and perhaps a host of other feelings we can easily imagine: resentment, disappointment, but perhaps (maybe?) also a shred of relief that his brother was indeed still alive.

By going out to him the father imitates the shepherd and the woman from the previous parables who actively sought what was lost. Thus we see that the older son was indeed lost, and the father sought him out to restore him to the family and thereby restore the wholeness of that little community. The surprise then is that, younger son or older son, rebellious or obedient, prodigal or dependable, anyone can be lost.[17] To be separated from the life-giving connections of community, for whatever reason, is to be lost.

---

[17] See the similar considerations in Levine, *Short Stories*, 73–76.

152

The Lost Sons (Luke 15:11–32)

6. Our Fourth Step: Consider the Metaphor

From our exploration of metaphors thus far we know that metaphors work on multiple levels, both cognitive and affective. The overarching metaphor here is one of a family farm where the familial relationships are strained to the point that not even social convention can hold them together. This is family drama at its highest. Within this metaphorical family in the parable the characters themselves use metaphorical language, so that we have metaphors within a metaphor! For example, images of being lost and found or dead and alive are not literal, but figurative. Their use, however, highlights the urgency and importance of each character's decisions. From the perspective of each character, these are issues of life and death.

Looking at the metaphor of death, we note that an inheritance—which is the first thing we learn about from the mouth of the younger son as he requests it from his very much alive father (v. 12)—is associated with death, as it is normally received upon the death of the parent. The younger son, after his money runs out recognizes that he is, in his own words, "dying of hunger" (v. 17). In his plan to return he recognizes he cannot return as a son but asks to return as a servant; in essence, his identity has died. Later in the parable the older son complains about the younger son's bad behavior that he literally, in the Greek expression, "devoured the father's life" (v. 30). There is more death though—the son's return results in the killing of the fatted calf (v. 23). Showing the significance of that death-dealing action, the killing of the calf is mentioned three times (vv. 23, 27, 30). The father's view that the son was once dead is also repeated (vv. 24, 32). All told there are six explicit mentions of death or killing, with a seventh implied by the notion of the inheritance. Without our necessarily recognizing it, death is a dark thread woven throughout this parable.

Perhaps just as important as the death references are the references to life and returning to life. Though not as numerous, the explanation of the son's return to life is also repeated three times. First, the father gives it as the rationale for the extravagant welcome and the killing of the fatted calf: "for this son of mine was dead and is alive again; he was lost and is found!" (v. 24). Second, the servant explains to the older son that the father received his son back "safe and sound" (literally, in good

Chapter 5

health, as opposed to sick or dying) (v. 27). Third, the father explains to the older son that his younger brother was dead and is alive, was lost and is found (v. 32).

One way of understanding these multiple references to death and threefold reference to health and wholeness is to recognize that they bring a serious tone to the whole. The choices that each character makes are choices that have life and death consequences. And on the way toward death or life, we see the pathway of the younger son as one of descent, disconnection from his community, and potential death. Viewed as the literary form of comedy as opposed to tragedy, we note that the younger brother's position is indeed precarious. However, following the arc of dramatic comedy he moves upward from his low point in this story toward a place of well-being, reconnection, and re-integration into the community. This change of direction is facilitated in a moment of recognition as he "came to himself" (v. 17). His change of direction is also publicly acknowledged in a scene of celebration—the banquet. So we have a character in the younger son who can be compared to the protagonist in a comedy.[18]

Within ancient comedy are also "blocking characters" who thwart the movement of the protagonist toward well-being. In some instances, the protagonist's own traits can be blocking characters, and in this case perhaps the younger son's desire for independence or his quest for pleasure could play this role. Those are overcome in his moment of recognition. We can also see that the older brother is in some ways a blocking character. Though not appearing until the end of the narrative, his refusal to welcome home the younger brother and integrate him back into the family stands in the way of a full return and inclusion in society. Will the older brother come around and welcome the protagonist's return?

Moving on to other metaphors within the parable, there are also a number of concrete references related to money and labor. Inheritance begins and ends the parable. There is reference to hired hands, slaves, and prostitutes. It is a complex metaphorical social world with

---

[18] Via, *Parables*, 165–166. Via notes that many of the parables function as dramatic comedy "in the broad sense of a plot that moves upward toward the well-being of the protagonist and his inclusion in a desirable society" (145). In fact, he argues that this is the arc of biblical narrative.

154

The Lost Sons (Luke 15:11–32)

complicated relational dynamics. Jesus does not seem to shy away from any of these either in this parable or in his other teaching. As with other parables, the medium is part of the message: readers are reminded that the kingdom of God is experienced *in such earthly activities as these*, not apart from these in some abstract way.

References to slavery are a part of this metaphorical world. At his lowest point the younger brother longs to be a slave in his father's family (vv. 17–19)—this, after taking his share of the inheritance. By contrast, the older brother uses a metaphor of slavery to describe his own experience in the family for all these years (v. 29). While the older brother's experience was figurative, the dire situation of the younger brother was real. Contemporary readers might consider whether the kingdom of God could be experienced similarly today in the experiences of individuals who find themselves in dire circumstances: immigrants, unprotected workers, sex workers, victims of human trafficking, exploited workers, child laborers, and so on. This parable is not "about" those issues specifically, but the reality of human life which includes such scenarios where individuals are lost, disconnected from healthy community, and subject to death, both metaphorical and real, are the locus of where the kingdom of God can be seen and experienced. The implied understanding of existence that we encounter in this parable and in its metaphors is that humans live in a world in which life is found in connection with others in genuine community. And movement toward or away from healthy community is an ever-present possibility that is enacted in our daily actions and the thoughts and feelings that generate those actions.

In entering into this narrative metaphorical world, it is almost second nature for readers to make a connection with one or more of the characters. This leads to the question of whether there is an example to be followed here. The younger son is not exemplary in his dissolute living, although his repentance and return is perhaps a model to follow. The older son, whose obedient behavior might be considered exemplary, is problematic with his anger and resentment. His honest expression of emotion may be a starting point on the path toward a future reconciliation—but the story does not take us that far. The father may be considered an example, as he warmly welcomes his one son, and also goes out to bring back his older son. On the other hand, perhaps the father was not so great—he was permissive and then extravagant with the younger

Chapter 5

son, and at the same time never noticed the older son's disconnection, forgetting even to tell him that his brother had returned. Is the permissive, extravagant, oblivious father the example? If metaphors function indirectly and serve as a way of getting at a delicate situation without going in headfirst, then this is less about finding the right example in one particular character and more about seeing different sides and understanding the dynamics as a whole. Each of these three main characters in the story needs a broader perspective if the family is to survive.

One final note on the metaphor of this narrative is that it is one that to a large extent reinforces an ancient patriarchal perspective, whether intentionally or unintentionally. In ancient Roman culture the father was the *paterfamilias*, the head of the household who had absolute authority over the household and all who lived within it. While some elements of Luke's Gospel do challenge ancient notions of patriarchy and are suggestive of the inclusive nature of the message of Jesus, Schottroff points out that the "critical consciousness" of this particular parable is very limited. The father in the parable, Schottroff explains, "governs male and female slaves, male and female laborers, his wife, his daughters, and the other female members of the household, who are so unimportant in the mind of the narrator that, insofar as they are female, they remain invisible."[19] Accordingly, "The parable of the lost son remains within the horizon of patriarchy."[20] Such an observation is not necessarily surprising, as it is essentially a reflection of the culture in which the gospels were written. We observed in Chapter 4 that even having a female character as the protagonist in the parable of the lost coin was noteworthy.[21] But this particular parable's patriarchal focus has had the (perhaps unintended) result within the history of interpretation of, in effect, a "divinizing of the patriarchal father and the romanticizing of the patriarchal household."[22] In our contemporary world that still struggles with patriarchal systems and misogyny, and in which

[19] Schottroff, *Parables*, 139.
[20] Schottroff, *Parables*, 144. Further, "The text sees no problem in maintaining silence about the presence of women and female slaves in the household" (143)
[21] Feminist readings of the parables can open our eyes to the reality that the parables are largely androcentric. For example, of 108 main characters in the parables, 99 are male. Reid and Matthews, *Luke 10–24*, 443 n. 10.
[22] Schottroff, *Parables*, 150.

The Lost Sons (Luke 15:11–32)

women's struggles for equality continue, such implied messages within a biblical context can serve to reinforce negative cultural patterns. In light of that, feminist-theological readings offer new ways of reading, whether reading "against the grain," or at least in ways that name and challenge the dominant male perspective.[23] While the approach taken in this chapter is a literary analysis that seeks to understand the social context of the narratival-metaphorical world of the parable, this approach should not be taken to preclude the value of other more critical approaches that could be used.

7. Our Fifth Step: Articulate the Challenge

Our exploration of this complex parable seems to point to numerous ways in which this parable might challenge a reader. The variety of ways of expressing the challenge relate to which character is seen as a focal point or with which character the reader identifies most closely. Is the challenge to consider what it means to come to one's senses and return home, like the younger son? Is it to welcome the lost with extravagant love like the father? Is it to interrogate our unwillingness to extend mercy to others, like the older brother? Or is it something else?

Each of these angles could be valid points of consideration. However, if we consider the path we have traveled in our process of interpretation, we can use not only the characters in the story, but also our awareness of both its genre and its implied understanding of existence to help us articulate its message. Approached like this, there is a way of capturing the challenge in this parable that includes each of the above elements and others.

In broadest strokes the challenge of this parable is to embrace the central importance of community and to value healthy connection within community as among the highest of human priorities. While the actions of each individual are important, if we can resist our tendency toward individualistic interpretation we can notice the communal dimensions

---

[23] One imaginative strategy is to identify characters on the fringe of the narrative and explore the parable from their perspective, with attention to the social dynamics of the first-century world (e.g., the hired hands, slaves, or prostitutes mentioned in this parable). Reid and Matthews, *Luke 10–24*, 442–444.

Chapter 5

which the overall story strongly suggests. This is somewhat similar to what we saw with the lost sheep and lost coin, which were not only about an individual who is lost or found but a community which attains its highest joy when all members are included. In the same way the parable of the lost sons points to individuals in community as its guiding vision.

Howard Thurman wrestled deeply with both the individual and communal aspects of this parable and his insights can help us grasp this challenge.[24] For Thurman this parable expresses a profound reality that what it means to be fully human is to recognize that my individual well-being is linked to your individual well-being, and our greatest well-being is found when we all are free to thrive in community. The linkage of each person's well-being to that of every other person is simply a result of the way that life, designed by the creator of life, works. Such a realization has profound implications for community building and especially for social justice.

To understand this approach it is important to understand Thurman's logic which is much more than drawing abstract principles from this one parable. Five insights will enable us to walk this path with Thurman. He begins first with the value of each person: every person has inherent worth as a child of God. This value is independent of social location, economic status, gender, race or any other markers. For Thurman, this sense of identity as a child of God is crucial to a proper perspective on one's place in the larger world. This of course is not a unique view of Thurman's but is a deeply rooted Christian and Jewish belief that is reflected throughout the scriptures beginning with the understanding that humans are in some sense created in the image of God (Gen. 1:27). It can be traced throughout the various scriptural traditions and also finds a prominent place in the teaching of Jesus, including within the parables. Thurman would go so far as to say that this inherent worth connects to the reality that every creation of God—human and non-human—is infused with God's purpose. And this conviction seals the value of each person without any doubt.

---

[24] Thurman's insights on the parables are now readily available in Thurman, *Sermons on the Parables.* For insights into Thurman's theological perspective see his Howard Thurman, *With Head and Heart: The Autobiography of Howard Thurman* (New York: Harcourt Brace Jovanovich, 1979). Also helpful is the book-length study: Luther E. Smith, *Howard Thurman: The Mystic as Prophet* (Richmond, IN: Friends United Press, 1992).

The Lost Sons (Luke 15:11–32)

Second, this recognition of the inherent value of each person leads Thurman to a see that a primary condition for human vitality is freedom to self-actualize: to grow, to live, to become what one was created to be, to live fully out of the center of who one is. One widely shared quote of Thurman's is: "Don't ask what the world needs. Ask what makes you come alive and go do that, because what the world needs is people who have come alive."[25] To come alive is to connect with what is most genuine about oneself and to live out of that reality. Thurman identifies this theme in the parable of the lost sons with the notion of the younger son "coming to himself" (Luke 15:17). "Coming to oneself" is to connect to what is deepest within oneself, which is the divine presence and also the urge to align in harmony with the rest of creation. Of the lost son, Thurman explains, "Jesus says that he came to himself. He discovered that which was deepest in him, that which he most fundamentally desired over all else, now that the shouting and tumult had died [and this] was precisely what God wanted. I am my father's son, and my father is my father. When he became aware of this, salvation became operative."[26] Salvation for the younger son was literally to be saved from his dire circumstances. To "come to himself" in this sense was to return to the divine, and thereby return to community. This understanding has implications for a spirituality of contemplation and quiet that enables one to "center down" and get in touch with what is at the heart of one's being.[27]

Third, God created the world and humans to be part of community. This can be expressed in a number of ways but essentially Thurman asserts that a movement toward growth and harmonious relationships is inherent in everything that God created. All life is an expression of the creative activity of God which has a purpose. And in Thurman's view "the divine purpose is that there shall be increasingly, in all creation, community, a sense of ingatheredness, a sense of wholeness, a sense of integration."[28] These notions of wholeness, ingatheredness,

[25] Cited now in Lerita Coleman Brown, *What Makes You Come Alive: A Spiritual Walk with Howard Thurman* (Minneapolis: Broadleaf Books, 2023).
[26] Thurman, *Sermons on the Parables*, 84.
[27] In this thinking Thurman acknowledges his indebtedness to Quaker spirituality, in particular the writings of Rufus Jones.
[28] Thurman, *Sermons on the Parables*, 81.

Chapter 5

and integration are ways of talking about community where each life has a part. The human connection within this web of life is intended to be one of alignment and harmony:

> Because God is the creator of life, God is the creator of all living things, God is our creator, there is within us the mark of his creation. This sensitive, palpitating, quivering divine dimension of us that is always seeking to align, to get into harmony, to complete the cycle between itself and God.[29]

Becoming aware of our divine dimension as God's creation means we become aware of a part of us that seeks to be in harmony with the rest of the world that God created. To be attuned to that dimension of ourselves will naturally lead us to move toward community. Thus, movement toward community is our own individual work and, at the same time, the work of God.

With those three foundational elements—the worth of each individual; the goal of individual life to self-actualize; and the notion that life moves toward connection—a fourth insight emerges which reconnects us to this parable. It relates to the notion of being lost and found. What it means to be "lost" is to be separated from the vitality of community. Thurman explains, "Now a man is lost when he is out of community, when he has a sense of being isolated, cut off from his immediate direct conscious involvement in the collective destiny of life."[30] To be found is thus to be reconnected; restored to one's place as a free and developing person. And this is the highest joy for God. The impromptu banquet that the father throws for the younger son is an expression of the joy that ensues when a person is restored to community. Thurman generalizes this suggesting, for example, that when a person is able to "enter into a dimension of community with another soul" and recognize their worth, it is then that God rejoices. He writes, "The morning stars sing together, and the sons of God shout for joy, and the loneliness of God because one of his creatures is out of community is broken."[31] This is life achieving its purpose.

[29] Thurman, *Sermons on the Parables*, 84.
[30] Thurman, *Sermons on the Parables*, 81–82.
[31] Thurman, *Sermons on the Parables*, 85.

160

The Lost Sons (Luke 15:11–32)

Finally, if others are out of community or cut off from their purpose of thriving in community, that reality impacts not only that individual but also the community. That disconnection of another impacts all of us, including God. The opposite of angels rejoicing in heaven suggests the intense divine sorrow over one who is lost, and over the community which is diminished because of it.[32] So the implication of all of this is that all of us have an inherent obligation to work toward community both for the benefit of those who are not currently experiencing this life-giving connection, and for our own well-being. Thurman explains:

> For better or for worse, God and I, God and you, are bound together, and I cannot be what it is that I must be if between you and me, between you and God, there is no community.
>
> I must work out my salvation by seeking in every way to further communion between myself and all living things and myself and God. Who am I that with my life and my limitations, my sins, my bigotry, who am I that I should hold up the work of salvation in the world and beyond?[33]

In other words, whether we like it or not, our ability to engage in loving community with others has a profound impact on ourselves and others.

With Thurman's insights in mind we can reaffirm one way of expressing the challenge of this parable: to embrace the central importance of community and to value healthy connection within community as among the highest of human priorities. The implied understanding of existence in the parable is that of community as linked to life and well-being, and separation from community as indicative of death. The arc of the narrative moves from separation and disconnection in a far-off land to reconnection in the home of the father, a restoration of life for the younger son, and joy for the father. But it also reminds us through the angry older son that one can be a part of the community without fully experiencing or fully understanding the nature of true community.

---

[32] Thurman expresses this in striking language: "The redemption of the whole creation rests upon the redemption of a single human being. God cannot be happy in his heaven if any man is in hell" (85).

[33] Thurman, *Sermons on the Parables*, 85.

161

Chapter 5

To distill the focus of this parable to the life-promoting power of community in contrast to the possibility of death that becomes operative through disconnection is not simply an ancient figurative notion. Dr. Vivek Murthy, former surgeon general of the United States gets at, from a medical and research perspective, what Thurman gets at from a theological perspective. In his book *Together: The Healing Power of Human Connection in a Sometimes Lonely World*, Murthy summarizes lines of research demonstrating this very reality.[34] Of interest here he cites the work of Dr. Julianne Holt-Lunstad whose analysis of 148 studies "showed that people with strong social relationships are 50 percent less likely to die prematurely than people with weak social relationships."[35] In other words, people who are connected to a community are demonstrably likely to live longer. By contrast Murthy explains, "The impact of lacking social connection on reducing lifespan is equal to the risk of smoking fifteen cigarettes a day."[36] In addition, "Weak social connections can be a significant danger to our health" given that there is proven to be a "higher risk of early death among the lonely" as it is linked to numerous disease risks including coronary heart disease, high blood pressure, stroke, anxiety, dementia and others.[37] Thus, the need for connection is not simply a nice image in a parable, or a good thing to hope for; it is literally linked to well-being. Murthy explains that loneliness is then an indicator for us of the way things work: "Loneliness is a built-in reminder that we are stronger together, not just as clans or tribes or family and friends, but also as caring communities that form the foundation of a healthy culture."[38] The goal of Murthy's subsequent work has become to find ways to foster genuine and authentic community.

Returning to the metaphor of the father, we can see that some of the father's actions and traits are ones that help support the possibility of community. Brobst-Renaud finds that the father's "reckless liberality" and "extravagant generosity" in welcoming the younger son home and inviting the older son in are the kinds of traits that Luke wanted readers

---

[34] See especially pp. 12–14 of Murthy, *Together*.

[35] Murthy, *Together*, 13.

[36] Murthy, *Together*, 13.

[37] Murthy, *Together*, 13–14.

[38] Murthy, *Together*, 52.

The Lost Sons (Luke 15:11–32)

of his gospel to embody toward one another.[39] It is possible to see in the father indications of the embodiment of compassion that invites, welcomes, and restores unity. Sister Schubert, RSM, captures this well:

> While the eldest son protests with bitterness, the father responds in loving forgiveness. Truly, the father, who has experienced two lost sons, remains openly compassionate to both of them. He overlooks bad behavior in their demands as well as complaints or shameful remarks made to him. Through his superb listening skills, his eagerness to unite his family, as well as his patient waiting, the Father's behavior signals acceptance, an invitation to celebrate and rejoice with unwavering compassion. In essence, the Father models the boundless mercy of God![40]

The kingdom of God that Jesus proclaimed could be defined broadly as the conceptual space in this world where God's highest values are enacted in human lives. And in light of this parable, we can now say that the kingdom of God can be seen as enactment of and participation in loving community. So we can see that this parable is a challenge to embrace this view of the importance of community, and to see ourselves as individuals-in-community with an inseparable link to others that will impact all of us one way or another, whether promoting our communal life or potential death, metaphorically and in reality.

8.   Our Sixth Step: Consider implications

As we move to consider implications of this parable for today we can readily see that the challenge of this parable as articulated by Howard Thurman faces some serious obstacles in the real world of the twenty-first century. Thus one implication in our quest for community is to consider what embracing this vision would look like in our current divisive political and social climate.

The election of Donald Trump as president of the United States in 2016 introduced new levels of vitriol into public and political discourse while at the same time empowering white supremacist groups and

---

[39]   Brobst-Renaud, *Lukan Parables*, 92.

[40]   Schubert, "Lost Sons."

Chapter 5

white supremacist behaviors.[41] Nowhere was this more evident than in the attempted insurrection of January 6, 2021, when racist symbols were proudly on display among the rioters who were encouraged in their efforts by the president himself. The agenda of those who empowered and continued to support the former president is still being carried out at multiple levels, and it is clear that it will continue in the work of his successors and in initiatives like voter suppression bills based on the former president's outright lies about voter fraud in the 2020 election. The agenda also continues in the work of the now conservative Supreme Court to which the former president appointed three justices. June 27, 2022, saw the overturning of *Roe v Wade*, and the first time that a constitutionally protected right has been taken away from American citizens, in this case women. Abortion, of course, has long been a highly polarized issue, but in an instant half a century of legal precedent was overturned by raw political power. The Supreme Court's decisions and explicit statements that followed indicate that more conservative rulings related to current rights of American citizens are certainly on the way.

In this highly polarized environment where it seems that basic human rights are at issue there does not seem to be a lot of promise for building community across difference. In fact, the rhetoric around the possibility of a future civil war continues to draw attention.[42] But even if civil war seems unlikely, "civil breakdown" can now be seen to be a major threat to the continued well-being of the United States.[43] Is there

---

[41] For discussion of the former president's support of white nationalism, promotion of xenophobia, spreading of lies, and undermining of democracy as being religious, moral, and human rights issues rather than *political* ones, see Wallis, *Christ in Crisis*, 79, 82, 84, 85, 95, 101, 103, 106, 107, 110, 112, and 130–134, for examples.

[42] Recent examples include Nicholas Golberg, "Worried about Another American Civil War? It's Not Imminent, But ...," *Los Angeles Times*, December 9, 2022, accessed on May 19, 2023 at https://www.latimes.com/opinion/story/2022-12-09/new-american-civil-war. See also Stephen Marche, "With the end of Roe, the US edges closer and closer to civil war," *The Guardian*, June 26, 2022, accessed on May 19, 2023 at https://www.theguardian.com/commentisfree/2022/jun/26/second-civil-war-us-abortion.

[43] See Steven Simon and Jonathan Steven, "The Threat of Civil Breakdown Is Real: National Security Officials Are Still Not Prepared for a Far-Right Revolt," *Politico*, April 21, 2023, accessed on May 19, 2023 at https://www.politico.com/news/magazine/2023/04/21/political-violence-2024-magazine-00093028.

The Lost Sons (Luke 15:11–32)

any place for creating community in such a climate? What place does enactment of and participation in loving community have in today's challenging environment? It seems like such an approach is at best, unrealistic, and at worst, a waste of one's energy which might be better spent in self-protection and isolation.

While despair and lack of hope are natural responses for many, a different set of answers is suggested in the book, *Taking it to the Streets: Public Theologies of Activism and Resistance.*[44] In it Jennifer Baldwin and her contributors suggest that there are many possibilities for responses to the current moment: responses that are guided by Christian values and a commitment to justice, equality, and the possibility of human flourishing for all. As Baldwin explains, "Public theologies and practices of activism and resistance are ultimately about participating in the crafting of God's vision for creation in our shared global world."[45] The scholars and practitioners in this volume challenge all of us to "harness our innate capacities for compassion, courage, just anger, clarity, and curiosity to support those in need, cultivate the honor of desiring 'enough' rather than 'all,' and foster resiliency and balanced flourishing."[46] Rather than eschew the political dimension, Baldwin and her fellow authors remind readers that there are things that can and should be done to bring about real societal change: "Protest, activism, and resistance to the structures, policies, and systems of oppression, opportunism, domination, and harm are, at times, necessary actions and are worthy of theological reflection and support."[47] Here we consider a couple of examples with a particular focus on prospects for bridging the social divide and moving toward community, even in small ways. These examples suggest a constellation of activities that might help us re-establish community, rehumanize our adversaries, and create conditions that promote inclusive human flourishing.

Womanist scholar Linda Thomas reflects on the role pastors can play in supporting their congregations during such a time of crisis. Among her recommendations she counsels pastors to pay attention to the most

---

[44] Jennifer Baldwin, *Taking It to the Streets: Public Theologies of Activism and Resistance* (Lanham, MD: Lexington Books, 2019).
[45] Baldwin, *Taking It to the Streets*, xiii.
[46] Baldwin, *Taking It to the Streets*, xiii.
[47] Baldwin, *Taking It to the Streets*, xiii.

Chapter 5

vulnerable, listen to their experiences, offer hope in the midst of distress and defeat, and reflect with intentionality on one's own responses to current events. These are practices anyone can engage in, regardless of their position. But while these are all important, Thomas's strongest recommendation is a surprising one: to listen to and understand the experiences and views of *those on the other side*. She explains,

> To hear the perspectives from others who thought or voted differently than others as myself, we must develop the ability to take seriously the experiences and understand their positions. That takes some real work. Work that so many don't want to bother doing. It's easier to blame someone else for your challenges rather than working to understand the cause of the present situation, as well as actively endeavoring to grasp the perspectives of others that are different from our own.[48]

With this emphasis Thomas challenges readers that in addition to pursuing justice, we are also called to "adapt one's mindset and behavior to bridge across differences" citing the IDI Intercultural Development Plan.[49] This idea of taking responsibility for one's mindset and actions in terms of bridging across differences is a difficult one, especially for those who feel threatened by the views, policies, and perceived destructive intentions of their political and cultural opponents. It is important, also, that this call to adapt not be heard as a call to silence or tamp down the voices of the marginalized who are rightly crying out. Instead, coming from Linda Thomas, herself a woman of color who attends deeply to the daily experiences of those in vulnerable positions, this is a recognition that there is an unavoidable interpersonal dimension to these intractable problems. It is also a recognition that they will not be solved without all of us creating within ourselves the capacity for genuine engagement with others who see the world very differently than we do.

Thomas is not the only one to call out the importance of listening, understanding, and building bridges with those on the other side of

---

[48] Linda Thomas, "A Womanist Perspective on the Election of Donald Trump: What Pastors are Called to Do," in *Taking It to the Streets: Public Theologies of Activism and Resistance* (ed. Baldwin; Lanham, MD: Lexington Books, 2019), 22.

[49] Thomas, "Womanist Perspective," 22. On the Intercultural Development Inventory (IDI) see https://idiinventory.com.

166

The Lost Sons (Luke 15:11–32)

issues. The practice of "compassion-based activism" is a holistic model that includes this same emphasis.[50] It includes eight principles of practice, many of which are relevant for our consideration. Three of these are "universal inclusion," "love of one's adversary," and "openness to the other's truth." These are stances which require action toward the fostering of understanding and that can help create the potential for genuine community. It is important to note also that these three principles stand in creative tension with three other principles: "firm limits around violation," "empowered personal dignity," and "grounded non-reactive presence." Empowered personal dignity, for example, means that one "boldly stands up for one's personal dignity" and "speaks truth to power, refuses to be ashamed, and asserts one's worth before those who are dismissive or condescending."[51] As for the importance of setting firm limits around violation, "compassion-based activism extends love and dignity to all human beings, [but] it does not allow violation to go unchecked."[52] Grounded non-reactive presence is a powerful tool and one that is illustrated most famously by black students at the lunch counter sit-ins of the 1960s who endured abuse of all kinds, but did not react to it. These principles of practice, taken together, empower an activism for social change that arguably aligns with the message of Jesus around the interconnectedness of all of God's children.

The activist approaches discussed above are not simply theoretical frameworks for an ideal world. Rather, they have been put into practice around the world in the work known as peacebuilding. Peacebuilding is a framework for action which has been used in situations of deep division and deadly conflict in some of the most challenging places in the world. A slow but effective activity, its key components include fostering community, trust, and learning about the adversary.[53] Lisa Sowle

---

[50] Frank Rogers, "Warriors of Compassion: Coordinates on the Compass of Compassion-Based Activism," in *Taking It to the Streets: Public Theologies of Activism and Resistance* (ed. Baldwin; Lanham, MD: Lexington Books, 2019).

[51] Rogers, "Warriors of Compassion," 32.

[52] Rogers, "Warriors of Compassion," 35.

[53] For an explanation of the principles of the peacebuilding process (PB), see Mohammed Abu-Nimer, "Building Peace in the Pursuit of Justice," in *The Wiley-Blackwell Companion to Religion and Social Justice* (eds. Palmer and Burgess; Malden, MA: Wiley-Blackwell, 2012).

Chapter 5

Cahill explains it as "a practical commitment to restore or build conditions of peace by working for structural justice and reconciliation at the grassroots level; by involving interreligious partners; and by seeking networked reinforcement of conditions of peace among local, national, regional, transnational, and international organizations, both civic and governmental."[54] With this description we can see that peacebuilding, with its emphasis on restoring peace and promoting reconciliation, is a concrete embodiment of the challenge of the parable of the lost sons.

Cahill points to the practice of peacebuilding as being a special kind of advocacy: "advocacy for inclusive human flourishing."[55] Rather than an idealistic process, it is also a realistic one that fully recognizes the reality of the persistence of evil, suffering, and conflict, but moves forward with hope for change. Interestingly, Cahill draws on a theological tradition that links action with the fostering of hope. Citing theologians from Aquinas to Pope Benedict to Kwok Pui-Lan, she explains that "the theological virtue of hope is born in action for change."[56] In other words, hope is not a feeling one can manufacture out of thin air or through internal mental processes. Hope does not develop on its own but rather grows out of action. She elaborates, "Hope takes root in actual work to change conditions, work in which we find solidarity with others, experience successes as well as discouragements and failures, and develop the fellowship and the courage that enable us to go on working toward the better future we envision."[57] She considers it a way that Christians live out their belief in the reality of the resurrection despite impossible odds.[58] As a concrete example, Cahill reports the heartbreaking and inspiring work in Liberia led by Leymah Gbowee, who helped to unite Muslim and Christian women in 2003 in response to the terror and suffering unleashed by Charles Taylor.[59]

---

[54] Cahill, *Global Justice*, 294.

[55] Cahill, *Global Justice*, 290. See Chapter 8 "Hope," 290–303 in which she refers to peacebuilding as a "Christian expression of the politics of salvation" (290).

[56] Cahill, *Global Justice*, 292.

[57] Cahill, *Global Justice*, 292–293.

[58] Referring to what third world and indigenous women offer the Western world, she calls it "a rare gift—hope abundant." (cited in Cahill, 292). We can note here the linkage to Sobrino's notion of the gifts the poor which we will encounter in the parable of the rich man and Lazarus.

[59] See Cahill, *Global Justice*, 295–302.

The Lost Sons (Luke 15:11–32)

As it works out in reality on the ground in places across the world, peacebuilding is a complex and messy process that is ongoing and seldom a straight path to permanent change. However, its practitioners see it less as implementing hard and fast rules of justice and peace and more as an ongoing commitment to "finding very practical ways to discover and create opportunities to reduce violence and strategize for better social conditions" for all.[60] Reconciliation and forgiveness are part of that, but also in tension with the need for justice and reparation, linked to accountability. And while Cahill highlights the Christian theological foundations of peacebuilding, she is clear that the work is the work of peoples from all traditions, and is best carried on with an appreciation of and respect for difference:

> Peacebuilders are respectful of distinctive identities that lead to different worldviews, practices, and priorities. Yet they are also convinced that people everywhere value basic respect, access to the essential conditions of a dignified life, political participation, and social organization that facilitates peaceful coexistence.[61]

Thus she begins with Christian faith but joins it with the experience of God in other traditions to articulate a vision of human dignity embodied in peaceful coexistence.

Demonstrating that it is not only those in religious traditions that recognize the power of peacebuilding, Vivek Murthy also brings international peacebuilding work into view in his book. Murthy connects the health crisis of loneliness and disconnection with the current combative social and political context. "One more change stoking the current trends of loneliness is the politicized climate of distrust and division that hangs over much of the world."[62] Murthy sees social disconnection as a root cause of the distrust and tendency to vilify those who disagree with us on certain topics. It is this reality that suggests that the practices associated with peacebuilding could become effective tools in addressing our current social crises. Among the principles undergirding the work of the peacebuilders Murthy engages are

---

[60] Cahill, *Global Justice*, 294–295.
[61] Cahill, *Global Justice*, 303.
[62] Murthy, *Together*, 134.

Chapter 5

important assumptions about the dignity and humanity of every person—principles not unlike those we saw articulated by Howard Thurman. This assumption of the humanity of all persons leads to an understanding of the need to "rehumanize" one's opponents, recognizing the shared needs of all people. Murthy explains, "Humanization is the beginning of belonging, and when we share space together we promote a *mutual* sense of belonging."[63] Murthy highlights that peacebuilding addresses the need to "promote a mutual sense of belonging" and to develop "collective empathy—you see the world from how they perceive and live it" among all those impacted by traumatic events.[64] The tools of this complex work can be very simple: even as simple as showing up, having a conversation, and listening to the experiences of others. Such actions are about "rehumanizing a situation that has lost that connection at a very deep level."[65]

If Murthy shows us clearly how isolation can be deadly he argues even more strongly that connection is an indispensable element for promoting human flourishing. What does this suggest for an ethic of love, mercy, and justice? Three elements link directly to our discussion here. First is the transformative power of human kindness, which Murthy illustrates through the example of an unusual mayor, Tom Tait, who faces each challenge by asking what a kind community would do. Second is the empirically verified reality that practices of giving, serving, and helping others benefit both the one who is helped and the one who helps. And third, the reality that isolation from different others is increasingly impossible, and actually "costs us" more than it protects us.[66] There is both an "emotional tax" on us in vilifying others, and a loss of valuable knowledge, insight, and perspective when we close ourselves off to people of other beliefs, cultures, and backgrounds. Murthy helps us see that embracing our full humanity means to recognize our own need for others and their need of us. Genuine love for one's neighbor includes the recognition of all peoples' need for connection.

We conclude this chapter with mention of one final practice that Margaret Farley, ethicist and Sister of Mercy, identifies as one of the

---

[63] Murthy, *Together*, 137.

[64] Murthy, *Together*, 136.

[65] Murthy, *Together*, 137.

[66] Murthy, *Together*, 96.

The Lost Sons (Luke 15:11–32)

most critical for rebuilding relationships and restoring connection with others. It is one of the seven spiritual works of mercy which in the Christian tradition stand alongside the seven physical works of mercy. It is to forgive all injuries. In a climate of divisiveness where real harms have been done, intended, or not prevented by our opponents, forgiveness is a very real challenge. Much has been written about the healing power of forgiveness to release both parties from the bonds of anger and resentment. Yet the full enactment of this practice faces a significant obstacle: forgiveness and reconciliation in its fullest sense is not possible when the offending party has not come to the point of acknowledging the harm caused or of seeking forgiveness. In such a situation, how can a person who was harmed by another even begin to move toward forgiveness, let alone reconciliation? Should the offended party simply ignore the offence in favor of rebuilding a relationship? How could such a relationship be grounded in reality if the offending party is unwilling to see it? In such cases Farley advocates for what she calls "anticipatory forgiveness."[67] By this she means a way of perceiving the offender that recognizes their humanity and their need of mercy. The idea is essentially to create a space where one is willing to offer full forgiveness when the offender recognizes their harm, ceases to harm, and seeks forgiveness. This brings us back to several of the principles of compassion-based activism above, especially "love of one's adversary" and "openness to the other's truth." If one can regard the offending party in this light, one can at least begin to see that they have a dire need for mercy and forgiveness, even if they do not see it. It is important also to restate the principles of "firm limits around violation" and "empowered personal dignity." These must be foregrounded to ensure that anticipatory or actual forgiveness does not allow harm or abuse to continue.

This line of thought invites us to consider whether we can (and whether we want to) find ways to promote the flourishing community where all may thrive and all play a part—even those with whom we vigorously disagree. Returning to the parable of the lost sons, the father was ready and willing to welcome the son back. The older brother was not. Not only so, but he was angry with his father for his eagerness to

---

[67] Margaret A. Farley, "Mercy and Its Works: If Things Fall Apart, Can They Be Put Right?" *Proceedings of the Catholic Theological Society of America* 71 (2016).

Chapter 5

welcome the son back into the family. The father invites the older son to change his view of the situation, to see the humanity of the younger son and to recognize his own place in the father's household. But will the older son accept that father's invitation to a renewed perspective? Would we? Will we?

Works Cited in Chapter 5

Abu-Nimer, Mohammed. "Building Peace in the Pursuit of Justice," Pages 620–632 in *The Wiley-Blackwell Companion to Religion and Social Justice*. Edited by Michael D. Palmer and Stanley M. Burgess. Malden, MA: Wiley-Blackwell, 2012.

Baldwin, Jennifer. *Taking It to the Streets: Public Theologies of Activism and Resistance*. Lanham, MD: Lexington Books, 2019.

Blomberg, Craig L. *Interpreting the Parables*. Second ed. Downers Grove, IL: IVP Academic, 2012.

Brobst-Renaud, Amanda. *Lukan Parables of Reckless Liberality*. Vol. 42, New Testament Monographs. Sheffield: Sheffield Phoenix, 2021.

Brown, Lerita Coleman. *What Makes You Come Alive: A Spiritual Walk with Howard Thurman*. Minneapolis: Broadleaf Books, 2023.

Cahill, Lisa Sowle. *Global Justice, Christology and Christian Ethics*. New Studies in Christian Ethics. New York: Cambridge University 2013.

Farley, Margaret A. "Mercy and Its Works: If Things Fall Apart, Can They Be Put Right?" *Proceedings of the Catholic Theological Society of America* 71 (2016): 33–40.

Hultgren, Arland J. *The Parables of Jesus: A Commentary*. The Bible in its World. Grand Rapids: Eerdmans, 2000.

Levine, Amy-Jill. *Short Stories by Jesus: The Enigmatic Parables of a Controversial Rabbi*. New York: HarperOne, 2014.

Murthy, Vivek H. *Together: The Healing Power of Human Connection in a Sometimes Lonely World*. New York, NY: Harper Wave, an imprint of HarperCollins, 2020.

Reid, Barbara E. and Shelly Matthews. *Luke 10–24*. Vol. 43B, Wisdom Commentary. Collegeville, MN: Liturgical Press, 2021.

Rogers, Frank. "Warriors of Compassion: Coordinates on the Compass of Compassion-Based Activism," Pages 25–41 in *Taking It to the Streets: Public Theologies of Activism and Resistance*. Edited by Jennifer Baldwin. Lanham, MD: Lexington Books, 2019.

Schottroff, Luise. *The Parables of Jesus*. Minneapolis: Fortress, 2006.

The Lost Sons (Luke 15:11–32)

Schubert, Judy, RSM. *"The Lost Sons."* 2019.

Smith, Luther E. *Howard Thurman: The Mystic as Prophet.* Revised ed. Richmond, IN: Friends United Press, 1992.

Snodgrass, Klyne. *Stories with Intent: A Comprehensive Guide to the Parables of Jesus.* Second ed. Grand Rapids: Eerdmans, 2018.

Thomas, Linda. "A Womanist Perspective on the Election of Donald Trump: What Pastors are Called to Do," Pages 15–23 in *Taking It to the Streets: Public Theologies of Activism and Resistance.* Edited by Jennifer Baldwin. Lanham, MD: Lexington Books, 2019.

Thurman, Howard. *With Head and Heart: The Autobiography of Howard Thurman.* First ed. New York: Harcourt Brace Jovanovich, 1979.

Thurman, Howard. *Sermons on the Parables.* Maryknoll, NY: Orbis Books, 2018.

Via, Dan Otto. *The Parables: Their Literary and Existential Dimension.* Philadelphia: Fortress, 1967.

Wallis, Jim. *Christ in Crisis? Why We Need to Reclaim Jesus.* First ed. San Francisco: HarperOne, 2019.

6

The Parable of the Mustard Seed (Mark 4:30–32)

1. Introduction

The parable of the mustard seed brings into view a fascinating element of Jesus's teaching: the natural world as a source for insight into the meaning of human existence. In this chapter we explore the parable of the mustard seed with an eye toward appreciating the role of nature in Jesus's teaching, as well as what it reveals about his understanding of the interaction of the divine and human. Recognizing that parables are comparisons, we can consider ways in which the kingdom of God is similar to and different from the phenomenon in view here.[1]

The parable of the mustard seed is one of many parables Jesus told that focus on aspects of the natural world. Seeds and fields are found several times in the teaching of Jesus, with the parable of the soils, the parable of the growing seed, and the parable of the wheat and the weeds.[2] Beyond seeds we encounter other natural elements within parables such as fish, sheep, dogs, a pearl, a tree, yeast, and storms.[3] Vines

---

[1] For key cultural background and discussion of interpretive issues with an eye toward contemporary application, see Hultgren, *Parables of Jesus*, 392–403; Snodgrass, *Stories with Intent*, 216–228.

[2] Parable of the soils (Mark 4:3–20; cf. Mt and Luke); parable of the growing seed (Mark 4:26–29); parable of the wheat and the weeds (Matthew 13:24–30).

[3] Fish (Matt. 13:47–50); sheep (Luke 15:3–7); dogs (Luke 16:21); pearl (Matt. 13:45–46); tree (Luke 13:6–9); yeast (Matt. 13:33); storms (Matt. 7:24–27).

Social Justice in the Stories of Jesus: The Ethical Challenge of the Parables, First Edition.
Matthew E. Gordley.
© 2024 John Wiley & Sons Ltd. Published 2024 by John Wiley & Sons Ltd.

The Parable of the Mustard Seed (Mark 4:30–32)

and vineyards also find a place.[4] And we even have the Samaritan's donkey.[5] Within these kinds of parables it is not only aspects of the natural world which are on display but also elements of the agrarian economy of first-century Palestine. With such familiar images many of Jesus's stories were of things that could be seen in the world around or of scenes similar to what his listeners would encounter in their daily lives. Such scenes remind us that through the parables we have a window onto a time and place that is very different from our own.[6]

In addition to being a nature parable this is also explicitly a kingdom parable, one in which Jesus seeks to explain something about the kingdom of God to his listeners. The kingdom of God is a focal point of Jesus's teaching. As we saw in Chapter 2, the kingdom is a metaphorical expression, a way of talking about God's influence in the world, and ultimately, of imagining what it would be like if God were the one ruling here on earth. The arrival of the kingdom was closely associated with God's setting things right—the great divine cleanup. There was great debate in the first century as to what it would mean for the kingdom of God, the age of the messiah, to arrive. This parable is one of a number of kingdom parables through which Jesus both taught and challenged his hearers about the kingdom. These parables explicitly bring the kingdom of God into comparison with some earthly phenomenon or experience. This is important for us so that as we are exploring the parable and beginning with its in-meaning, we know that we are also being invited to consider God's kingdom and in what ways it is like the object of comparison. Thus we are invited to consider its through-meaning and how this image becomes a window through which we can see the world anew in view of the kingdom's arrival.

---

[4] For parables that reference vineyards see Matt. 20:1–16 and Luke 20:9–19, Matt. 21:33–46, and Mark 12:1–12.

[5] Luke 10:34.

[6] For a reading of the parables through an agrarian lens, see Nabhan, *Jesus for Farmers*. Nabhan invites readers to consider the "rural social dynamics, the agro-ecological context, as well as the richness of culinary symbolism and the sacramental dimensions of farming, fishing, and food in his place and time" (28–29).

Chapter 6

Hinting at the through-meaning, Sister Sheila Carney, RSM, finds the parable of the mustard seed to be one that reflects "humility, interdependence, and hospitality."[7] As we work through our interpretive process with this short parable, we can do so with an eye toward these qualities. And if it is these traits that are brought to mind through this image, we might also consider opportunities for these to be operative in our world today.

2. The Text: The Parable of the Mustard Seed (Mark 4:30–32)

> He also said, "With what can we compare the kingdom of God, or what parable will we use for it? It is like a mustard seed, which, when sown upon the ground, is the smallest of all the seeds on earth; yet when it is sown it grows up and becomes the greatest of all shrubs, and puts forth large branches, so that the birds of the air can make nests in its shade." (Mark 4:30–32 NRSV)

3. Our First Step: Grasp the Story

This brief parable is introduced by Jesus with a double question: "With what can we compare the kingdom of God, or what parable will we use for it?" These questions remind us that what we are looking at is a comparison. We have already seen Jesus using questions in several parables including the lead up to and the conclusion of the parable of the Good Samaritan. The parables of the lost sheep and lost coin also both begin with questions. Jesus also uses double questions in a number of places, including several times in Mark 4.[8] Questions appear to have been a key feature of Jesus's teaching style.

---

[7] Sheila Carney, RSM, "The Mustard Seed," 2019. See her complete reflection in Appendix 1.

[8] See Mark 4:13 where Jesus asks, "Do you not understand this parable? Then how will you understand all the parables?" and Mark 4:40 where he asks, "Why are you afraid? Have you still no faith?"

The Parable of the Mustard Seed (Mark 4:30–32)

The parable develops by bringing into direct focus a mustard seed: "It is like a mustard seed." We first observe that there is no action initially. The kingdom is not compared at first to a growing seed. Simply, "like a mustard seed." At this simple beginning, as readers our minds may already be engaging, asking ourselves in what way the kingdom could be like a mustard seed, anticipating what will come next. Being a master storyteller and communicator who attracted huge crowds, one can imagine Jesus taking a dramatic pause at this point before going on to clarify exactly what it is about a mustard seed that compares with the kingdom of God. What aspect of a mustard seed has any connection to the kingdom of God, that conceptual space in which God's highest values are enacted in human community? Rather than making direct claims about the kingdom the parable immediately moves on to descriptions of a mustard seed's size, growth, and ultimate transformation.

We next learn that "when it is sown upon the earth, it is the smallest of all the seeds on the earth." Jesus draws attention to size, in particular its small size, relative to other seeds. Here we have an initial impression that this is not necessarily being called out as a good thing; and the small size suggests insignificance. This may suggest a measure of humility which is something we can consider later. We can also observe that the reference is to the size when it is sown. And while there is a reference to its being sown, there is no reference to any person doing the sowing. In most parables and even in other nature parables, there are humans who play a role; but here the human element is passed over with a simple passive verb. The focus is on the seed itself with no mention of a sower.

One way that a writer draws attention to key ideas and concepts is through repetition. That this parable is focused on the earth and its produce is supported by the repeated use of the Greek word for earth (*ge*). Not only is it repeated in this parable, it occurs five times in this chapter in Mark. With this repeated term, we may consider whether "the earth" should play a significant role in our interpretation. At the very least the repetition of earth here grounds this parable in the realities of the natural world.

Jesus next introduces the idea that "when it is sown it grows up and becomes" something else. The mustard seed's being sown (passive voice) is referenced a second time. And then growth ensues. The result of the growth is that it becomes "the greatest of all the shrubs and

Chapter 6

makes large branches." So the progression in this parable is starting exceptionally small, then when sown growing up and becoming the greatest of its class. We may wonder at the significance of this particular class of item. "Greatest shrub of all time" does not necessarily seem like a title to be all that proud of (no offence, shrubs). Its acquired greatness is a reference to its size which involves large branches under which birds are able to find shade and make their nests.

This parable concludes with the expression "such that under its shade the birds of the heavens are able to dwell." In other words, the transformation of the mustard seed results in the creation of a hospitable habitat for others of God's creatures. This observation brings into view the notions of hospitality and interdependence. The seed is dependent on being sown, and dependent upon the earth for its growth. The birds are dependent on the growth of the seed into a mature plant for the provision of shelter. Each element of the image does its part to create the idyllic scene which Jesus invites his listeners to imagine as somehow comparable to the kingdom.

The development of this parable is simple enough. And as we can see, this parable is not even really a story as much as a verbal picture of a scene within nature. How are we to move from the simplicity of this word-picture to connecting it with the kingdom of God? As we have seen earlier, one way to move deeper in our understanding is through the use of good questions. We next ask some questions about what first-century listeners would have brought to mind as they considered the elements of this verbal picture.

4. Our Second Step: Ask Good Questions

A good place to begin with our questions is with the mustard seed itself. What associations would the original hearers have had in mind when thinking about a mustard seed? References in literature from the ancient Mediterranean world make it clear that a mustard seed was proverbial for something very small in size. This is seen in both Jewish and Greco-Roman writings meaning that this was an image that extended across multiple cultures and places. This notion of incredibly small size is expressed elsewhere in the New Testament where Jesus famously talks about having faith as small as a mustard seed—meaning

The Parable of the Mustard Seed (Mark 4:30–32)

just about the smallest amount of faith possible.[9] Beyond the size associations, outside of the New Testament there are references to mustard as having some medicinal qualities, as well as to its being a weed.[10] These do not seem to be in line with this parable, which seems to have its focus on the growth and the corresponding contrast from being the smallest to becoming the greatest. For purposes of understanding this parable, we might also ask if the mustard seed itself is the focus, or if it is rather the whole picture. If the whole picture, then we will want to consider associations with the other elements of the parable.

A second question is what were the associations with agriculture in the time of Jesus? Or better, based on our concern for social analysis both then and now, is there any connection to this parable and the social structures of first-century daily life in Palestine? We have already noted that the agrarian economy within the context of the Roman Empire was based on a system of extraction of resources from the populace. To a large extent those who cultivated the land were at the mercy of those who owned the land and who collected the taxes and enforced the high margins needed to support their own lifestyles and the lifestyles of the wealthy ruling class. Tools such as dispossession and enslavement, along with severe debt, ensured the marginalization of hired workers and strengthened the position of the wealthy. Nevertheless, within this parable there is no explicit reference to any practices of oppression. There are actually no references to human struggle of any kind. Accordingly, it is possible to see this as an ideal picture of agrarian life, one that avoids any mention of the sufferings or trials of those who cultivate the land.[11] So while we are aware of the challenges that existed historically within such a context, this parable sets them aside with a positive focus entirely on the miraculous actions of natural growth. Rather than focusing on the human and social dimensions, this parable focuses exclusively on the natural world. It focuses on earth (*ge*) without reference to human institutions of any kind.[12]

---

[9] See Mt 17:20; Lk 17:6.

[10] Snodgrass, *Stories with Intent*, 220.

[11] Schottroff, *Parables*, 117.

[12] Nabhan takes a different approach, seeing in the image of rapid and uncontrolled growth of weeds the threat of a revolutionary movement that could grow quickly and threaten the stability of the Roman imperial control. Nabhan, *Jesus for Farmers*, 127–134.

Chapter 6

What are we to make of the size claims of the parable? Noting that mustard was proverbial for smallness, the claims for its extreme size when grown are also noteworthy. Mustard plants can grow to about ten feet in height and do have large branches which produce shade. Nevertheless, the language of the parable seems to be an exaggeration for effect, as the mustard seed is empirically not the smallest of all the seeds, nor is the grown mustard plant the greatest of all growing things. The intended effect seems to be to contrast extreme smallness with extreme flourishing.[13]

A late and somewhat surprising arrival into the parable are the birds which dwell in the shade of the mustard plant. What might they represent or what echoes of earlier traditions would a first-century Jewish audience have heard? It is noteworthy that the parable ends with a shift of focus from the seed and plant itself to introduce another natural phenomenon. The parable brings into view "the birds of the air" which are able to make their dwelling place within the shade of the plant. With this image the parable taps into a deeply rooted biblical metaphor that is found in a number of places in the Hebrew Bible. It is an image that has both literal and metaphorical uses. Some of the key passages include a psalm (Ps 104), a prophetic writing (Ezekiel 17:23; 31:6), and an apocalyptic writing (Daniel 4:12). While Jesus does not appear to be quoting directly from any one of these, the reference to large branches with shade in which the birds of the air are able to dwell is unmistakably part of this ancient tradition. To see just how close the connection is, it is useful to cite a few of these.

> By the streams the birds of the air have their habitation; they sing among the branches. (Ps 104:12, but see the whole Psalm for a view of nature and God's provision for all creatures)

> Its foliage was beautiful, its fruit abundant, and it provided food for all. The animals of the field found shade under it, the birds of the air nested in its branches, and from it all living beings were fed. (Dan 4:12)

> So it towered high above all the trees of the field; its boughs grew large and its branches long, from abundant water in its shoots.

[13] Levine, *Short Stories*, 170–171, 180–181.

The Parable of the Mustard Seed (Mark 4:30–32)

All the birds of the air made their nests in its boughs; under its branches all the animals of the field gave birth to their young; and in its shade all great nations lived.
It was beautiful in its greatness, in the length of its branches; for its roots went down to abundant water. (Ezek. 31: 5–7)[14]

On the mountain height of Israel I will plant it, in order that it may produce boughs and bear fruit, and become a noble cedar. Under it every kind of bird will live; in the shade of its branches will nest winged creatures of every kind. (Ezek. 17:23)

Interestingly, the psalm cited above is literal in that it is a reflection about nature itself. The other passages from apocalyptic and prophetic writings are clearly metaphors referring to the kingdoms of the world or the kingdom of God using imagery of trees and branches.

The above passages point to the possibility that Jesus was engaging with this tradition of metaphor as well. We will explore the metaphor further below, but for now we can also ask about the use of birds in the rest of Jesus's teaching. Not surprisingly, this is not the only place where Jesus spoke of birds. In line with the wisdom tradition in which Jesus's teaching can be placed, Jesus pointed to the "birds of the air" as offering a lesson for humanity in their dependence and trust in God for provision of their needs (Matt. 6:26). He also used them in reference to having a home in contrast to the Son of Man (a reference to Jesus himself) who had no home (Matt. 8:19; Luke 9:57). There are birds in the parable of the sower and the seeds as well (Matt. 13:4).

A final question we need to ask is: To what extent has anti-Judaism taken root in the interpretive tradition around this parable? Unlike the parable of the Good Samaritan there are no direct references to Jews or figures from within Judaism within the parable. There is nothing overtly Jewish or even religious about this parable at all. But that has not stopped interpreters who are steeped in anti-Judaism from finding ways for this parable to offer a critique by Jesus of the Judaism of his

---

[14] This passage from Ezekiel 31 is particularly interesting in that it refers to the kingdom of Assyria. The entire chapter elaborates on this imagery.

Chapter 6

day.[15] Thankfully, at least with this parable, many of those interpretations have not taken hold on the Western imagination.

Still, there are two strands of interpretation which do continue to pit Christianity against Judaism. These views commonly interpret the parable as referring to the growth of the Christian church, including the welcoming in of Gentiles (the birds being interpreted to refer to non-Jews) into the kingdom. Others envision Jesus promoting the transgressing of Jewish purity laws about weeds, again pitting a liberating Christian message against a legalistic Judaism. In each of these misguided approaches we see a false contrast that seeks to claim that Jesus was focused on grace and mercy and welcoming of all people while early Judaism as a whole was not. Those two strands of interpretation (the growth of the church; and an inclusive Christianity versus a supposedly exclusive Judaism obsessed with purity laws) seem unlikely to have been where this parable would have prompted Jesus's first listeners to go in their thoughts. In the first case, there was no church and no Christianity during the lifetime of Jesus. A parable about the growth of the church would have been meaningless to Jesus's hearers.[16] In the second case, the concept of non-Jews participating in the kingdom of God was, in fact, a part of Jewish expectation.[17] It was not a concept unique to Jesus or to his later followers like Paul. So this is a kingdom parable, yes. And it will indeed have something to say to those who count themselves among the followers of Jesus in the Christian church. But to imagine this as a parable about the church in contrast to Judaism is to import a much later issue. To introduce another agricultural metaphor, it might be appropriate to view an anti-Jewish interpretation of this parable as something akin to an invasive species. It is not original to the environment, and when it enters, it is harmful to the growth that

---

[15] See the examples interwoven into the discussion of this parable in Levine, *Short Stories*, 165–182.

[16] However, it may well have made more sense by the late first century and in decades in which the gospels were being composed. Thus an important "advanced" challenge for interpreters is to consider the message of the parable as originally delivered by Jesus along with the later interpretation of that parable in the context of a particular gospel.

[17] See J. R. C. Cousland, "Do 'the Birds of Heaven' in the Parable of the Mustard Seed Represent Gentiles?" *Catholic Biblical Quarterly* 85, no. 1 (2023): 53–74.

The Parable of the Mustard Seed (Mark 4:30–32)

was there. For our purposes, such interpretations are a reminder to us of the importance of being aware of our assumptions as we approach a parable. Ultimately, one can honor the teaching of Jesus most effectively by seeking to understand the parable on its own terms and letting it deliver its challenging message.

5.   Our Third Step: Spot the Twist

In our study of other parables we have noted that the twist is sometimes seen at the point where the story begins to diverge from expectations. It seems likely that the divergence here, which is almost comical, is in the mustard plant being ascribed the qualities of a great tree. This may be hinted at from the exaggerated language used about the mustard seed's size, both initially (smallest of all the seeds on the earth, which it is not), and after it grows (greatest of all the shrubs!). Could Jesus here be speaking tongue in cheek about the "mighty" mustard plant? That is a good possibility. On the other hand, one may certainly marvel at a mustard plant. It, like everything in nature, has its own beauty, serves its purpose, and (notably here) carries it out without human intervention.

Another twist in this parable may be that in a parable about the kingdom of God—a kingdom parable directed toward humans—there is really no mention of humanity at all. This is a parable about plants and animals period. That God's kingdom may be like a scene in which humans do not figure at all is perhaps somewhat striking. This imagery suggests that whether you or I are on board with it or not, the kingdom of God grows in its own way and in its own time—and reaches its intended effect.

Repeated phrases within the parable may also help us identify the twist: "when it is sown" is used twice; "upon the earth" is used twice. In fact, in Mark 4 the term for earth, *ge*, is mentioned five times. In light of this convergence of factors I propose that the twist here is the wholesale comparison of the kingdom to a phenomenon of the natural world which is transformational and which happens on its own once the process is initiated. And it is a phenomenon in which God's natural providing for God's creatures takes place.

Chapter 6

6. Our Fourth Step: Consider the Metaphor

With our minds attuned to the way this parable unfolds, we can pause now to look just at this image itself, without trying to assign meaning to each aspect of it. We can follow Louise Schottroff's lead and resist the impulse to apply this to the church, or even the ministry of Jesus. For while the early church certainly found significance in this parable for its own work, the parable clearly held its own meaning even prior to the beginning of the earliest Christian gatherings.

The essential metaphor is one of growth upon the earth and is suggestive of concepts of flourishing, thriving, and providing for the needs of other creatures. The mustard seed grows from small to great. The seed itself is also transformed in the process of growth from seed to shrub. A result of its miraculous transformation is its ability to provide shelter for others of God's creatures. Rosemary Radford Ruther writes of "communities of flourishing" and it may be that in this idyllic scene, we have a small ecosystem that flourishes and creates hospitable conditions for its members.

We should ask whether the birds are a key element or if, rather, they are included only to emphasize the size that the mustard plant obtains. If the latter, then their dwelling there is less important to the primary point. However, if the birds are a key element, perhaps the culminating moment of the parable, then understanding their place in the parable is critical. Either way, we need to engage with the birds.

We noted above the rich biblical tradition of imagery of trees and branches in which the birds could dwell. This tradition pictures an ancient empire as a tree, and as it flourishes it provides habitation for many creatures (see Ezek. 17:22–24). The image is used in the Jewish scriptures to describe oppressive human empires during their high points but also the coming divine realm of the reign of God. In poetry, in prophecy, and apocalyptic—three distinct genres—we encounter passages about the world tree. Notably in our parable, Jesus is not describing a tree at all, but a shrub. Does this mean that Jesus does not have this tradition in view as he tells the parable? Or does the mustard plant's being grafted into this tradition say something about the unexpected, overlooked, and surprising nature of the kingdom of God? I suspect the latter, since the references to branches, shade, and birds all

184

The Parable of the Mustard Seed (Mark 4:30–32)

very clearly echo the language of the earlier biblical texts. It seems that Jesus chose a mustard plant in contrast to a mighty oak or cedar which in human eyes would have been more suitable for comparison with a powerful kingdom. This choice of imagery suggests the element of humility which Sister Sheila Carney pointed to at the beginning of the chapter.

While it seems very clear that the image of the world tree is what is in view in this parable, the expression "birds of the air" does have other associations in the Bible outside of this tradition. Interestingly, it occurs more than 140 times in the Jewish scriptures. After the book of Genesis which includes birds of the air within the created order of things that are good (Gen. 1:20–22), the majority of references have to do with images of desolation and destruction. Often the references occur in scenes of dead bodies lying in the open as food for the birds of the air as a result of the devastation and carnage of warfare. "I will give your body to the birds of the air" is the taunt of the warrior Goliath to David, and from David right back at him.[18] It is an ominous visual expression of the destruction caused by armed conflict. This image of birds devouring the remains of dead warriors also becomes a theme in prophetic literature. It is powerful and haunting imagery. Prophetic writings use the birds of the air in the destruction and carnage sense of warfare above (Jer 7:32; Ezek. 29:5; 32:4). In an even more extreme usage the prophets also use birds to demonstrate utter desolation: the prophets can refer to a city destroyed to the extent that not even the birds of the air remain (Jer 4:25; 9:10; Zeph. 1:2). Birds can also be one of four "destroyers" that God sends in judgment upon his people (Jer 15:3). In each of these senses the birds are representative of destruction and judgment.

Less gruesome references do occur as well, for example in wisdom writings. One can even find birds on the lips of Jobs friend, who encourages Job to listen to the "birds of the air" so that he may gain wisdom. He exhorts:

> But ask the animals, and they will teach you; the birds of the air, and they will tell you; ask the plants of the earth, and they will teach you; and the fish of the sea will declare to you. (Job 12:7–8)

---

[18] See 1 Samuel 17:44 and 46.

185

Chapter 6

Linking the animal kingdom with lessons of wisdom is a feature of the Jewish wisdom tradition. And it is not unlike what we encounter in Jesus's own teaching.[19]

Imagery of birds of the air occurs in the beautiful nature psalm, Psalm 8. And in Ps 50 God declares:

> For every wild animal of the forest is mine,
>> the cattle on a thousand hills.
> I know all the birds of the air,
>> and all that moves in the field is mine. (vv. 10–11)

On this positive note, we can add that birds can be included in references to all of creation, including the covenant that God will make between God's people and all creatures (Hos 2:18)

With this rich background of metaphorical and literal imagery of birds in the Jewish scriptures, what are we to conclude about their inclusion in this parable? On the one hand, there is nothing negative or gloomy in the parable itself. The reference to birds certainly seems to be a positive usage here, as it is an idyllic scene. This seems to follow in the spirit of the wisdom tradition and the psalms. However, it may not be a stretch at least to consider whether there may be unfavorable overtones in the introduction of birds. Strengthening the possibility is the fact that the immediate context in Mark includes another seed and growth parable which culminates in the harvest and is also linked to prophetic warnings.[20] Could the birds be nesting as they prepare for the desolation and destruction to come? The gospel writers remember Jesus as pointedly predicting the coming destruction of the Jerusalem temple; an ominous arrival of birds would not be out of the question.[21]

We cannot import all of these associations into the teaching of Jesus. However, with an awareness that these possible references are in the background, we can be judicious about selecting a primary referent for our interpretation. We can try to notice the particular strand of the tradition that Jesus chooses to engage with. We can also be aware that

[19] See Matthew 6:25–34 for an example.
[20] See Mark 4:26–29.
[21] In the synoptic gospels, see Matthew 24:1–2; Mark 13:1–2; Luke 21:5–6. The allusion in John 2:19 is less direct.

The Parable of the Mustard Seed (Mark 4:30–32)

ambiguity may be a feature of this parable and its engagement with the bird tradition. Thus, it is likely that the birds here draw our attention to the health and vitality of the mustard plant in providing for the needs of others of God's creatures. They also bring to mind the prophetic and apocalyptic tradition of the world tree—with the surprising twist that this is no tree at all but a common mustard plant. Could God's kingdom be revealed in or through the ordinary and the everyday growth of common plants? At the same time, the presence of the birds creates a hint of doubt about what this scene may mean for humanity. There is the expectation of divine intervention against the oppressive kingdoms of the earth which, the tradition suggests, may bring with it destruction as a result.

7. Our Fifth Step: Articulate the Challenge

Pope Francis notes the parable of the mustard seed as indicative of the way in which Jesus was able "to invite to invite others to be attentive to the beauty that there is in the world because he himself was in constant touch with nature, lending it an attention full of fondness and wonder as he made his way throughout the land."[22] Nature parables in general can be seen as a "school for appreciating God's creation" which similarly invite us to reflect on nature; and through this reflection, come to understand something of the activity of God in the world.[23] If the parable of the mustard seed is a call to be attentive, to reflect and to understand, what is it we are called to understand here? One challenge of this parable might be expressed this way: To see in nature the divine action of God, causing growth and providing food and shelter, and to recognize that this is the same divine action of the kingdom of God. Furthermore, this action occurs without human involvement. And even further, this divine action of the kingdom exceeds the outcomes of human kingdoms, even as its activity is of a different order.

If such an understanding of God's activity in the world is at the heart of this parable, is there something that this parable calls

[22] *Laudato Si'*, 71.
[23] Schottroff, *Parables*, 122.

Chapter 6

listeners to do? Parables scholar Luise Schottroff articulates the challenge as an invitation to see. "Seeing" is something we have already encountered in other parables we have explored. The good Samaritan saw the man lying by the road and was moved with compassion. The father of the prodigal son saw the son from a long way off and ran to him. In another parable we will encounter a landowner who will see day laborers with no work and invite them to his vineyard. A willingness to see, to perceive the world around us, appears to be a critical aspect of Jesus's invitation to embrace our full humanity. What does the invitation to "see" nature mean in this parable? Seeing in the deepest sense of the word can include notions of looking, observing, and perceiving. It can also include the idea of wonder. If we are to take this challenge seriously and embrace the call to "see" the world around us, what would we see? This looking, observing, and being in awe of nature can lead to a deeper understanding of humanity's place in this world.

One important thing we would begin to see is to recognize and embrace the reality that we humans are not just "in" this world but are actually "part of" the natural world. Humans are interconnected with all other miraculous beings, each of which relates to God in their own ways. To honor God would then include the need to honor God's creation, human and nonhuman.[24] If there is a challenge in this parable for twenty-first-century listeners it is first to develop what can be called an ecological awareness. And it is an ecological awareness with a sensitivity to the hospitable provision of the needs of and space for all of God's creatures. Rourke explains that it is "ecological awareness, which helps us (humans) notice our interdependence on one another and on all of creation."[25]

By ecological awareness we refer to conscious reflection on our place within the world and our relationship to it. Such a perspective is not a novel view but is a tradition deeply rooted in the biblical narrative.

---

[24] Cahill, *Global Justice*. For a mystical and philosophical reflection on this concept from a Christian viewpoint, see Pierre Teilhard de Chardin, *Hymn of the Universe* (New York: Harper & Row, 1965).

[25] Nancy M. Rourke, "A Catholic Virtues Ecology," in *Just Sustainability: Technology, Ecology, and Resource Extraction* (ed. Peppard; vol. 3 of *Catholic Theological Ethics in the World Church*; Maryknoll, New York: Orbis Books, 2015), 194.

The Parable of the Mustard Seed (Mark 4:30–32)

Denis Edwards outlines "three interconnected and complimentary dimensions of the biblical/theological tradition" which are important features for our consideration.[26] These three strands are: "humans as called to serve and protect the wider creation; humans as called to cosmic humility before God and God's creation; humans as a part of the community of creation on Earth before God."[27] The creation narrative in Genesis prioritizes the importance of humanity's serving and protecting the created world. From the psalms and the enigmatic book of Job we encounter the need for humility in the face of the vastness of the mysteries of the natural world (cf. Job 38:4–7 and Ps 104). The psalms and apocalyptic writings also explicitly include humanity as a part of, not separate from, all that God has created (cf. Ps 148; Daniel).

A womanist theological perspective on creation highlights similar themes. Karen Baker-Fletcher finds that, "The creation account in Genesis 2 observes the fact that we humans, created from the dust of the earth and the breath of God, are deeply connected to the rest of creation."[28] In addition, Baker-Fletcher notes that God and creation are also interconnected and not entirely independent. She notes, "God and creation exist in responsible relationship.... In this understanding, God feels the suffering and joy of the land and its peoples."[29] Finally, while the irresistible ruling power of God as king and creator is a theme of the scriptures, it is also paradoxically the case that God grants freedom and choice to God's creation. "God *influences* creation, but God does not dominate and control creation. God persuades creation to participate in the infinite possibilities of creative becoming."[30] We can see this in the parable of the mustard seed. Birds nesting in the comfortable shade of wide branches are not there by force or command. The hospitable environment has attracted them. In a similar way, while the kingdoms of

---

[26] In this he follows biblical scholar Richard Bauckham. Denis Edwards, "Humans and Other Creatures: Creation, Original Grace, and Original Sin," in *Just Sustainability: Technology, Ecology, and Resource Extraction* (ed. Peppard; vol. 3 of *Catholic Theological Ethics in the World Church*; Maryknoll, New York: Orbis Books, 2015).

[27] Edwards, "Humans and Other Creatures," 161.

[28] Karen Baker-Fletcher, "How Women Relate to the Evils of Nature," in *Womanist Theological Ethics: A Reader* (eds. Cannon, et al.; *Library of Theological Ethics*; Louisville, KY: Westminster John Knox Press, 2011), 76.

[29] Baker-Fletcher, "How Women Relate," 68.

[30] Baker-Fletcher, "How Women Relate," 68.

Chapter 6

the world rely on domination to achieve their status, God's kingdom is marked by invitation, as seen in the created world.

These ways of seeing ourselves as part of creation rather than outside of it or over it align in many ways with the spirit of Saint Francis of Assisi. Francis, a Catholic mystic and monk born in the twelfth century, is well known as the founder of the Franciscan order and also, among other things, for his deep appreciation for nature. In this regard Francis saw himself and humans not as ruling over God's creation which existed only for the benefit and use of humanity, but saw humans rather as an integral part of the larger web of life that God had created. Humility was the appropriate response since creation was not centered on *humans* but rather centered on *life*, of which humans were one part.[31] In his understanding, the spiritual world and the physical world did not exist in isolation from one another but were linked. Because of this Francis saw himself in relationship to the rest of creation as brothers and sisters.[32]

In an important essay on the historical roots of our ecological crisis Lynn White suggested that Saint Francis provides an important corrective to modern assumptions about the natural world that have had increasingly negative impacts on how humans treat the environment. Rather than accepting the predominant view that the natural world existed for the benefit and use of humanity, Francis had a different approach. Calling him the "greatest spiritual revolutionary in Western history," White explains that Francis "proposed what he thought was an alternative Christian view of nature and man's relation to it; he tried to substitute the idea of the equality of all creatures, including man, for the idea of man's limitless rule of creation."[33] With such a view, White suggests that humility is a key to understanding Francis's approach to nature. White explains that Francis sought "to depose man from his monarchy over creation and set up a democracy of all God's creatures. With him the ant is no longer simply a homily for the lazy, flames a sign

---

[31] See Ilia Delio, *A Franciscan View of Creation: Learning to Live in a Sacramental World* (Franciscan heritage series; vol. 2; St. Bonaventure, NY: Franciscan Institute, St. Bonaventure University, 2003).

[32] See Francis's "Canticle of the Creatures" in which he recognizes the ways in which all elements of creation render praise to God through their individual works.

[33] Lynn White, "The Historical Roots of Our Ecological Crisis," *Science* 155 (1967): 1207.

The Parable of the Mustard Seed (Mark 4:30–32)

of the thrust of the soul toward union with God; now they are Brother Ant and Sister Fire, praising the Creator in their own ways as Brother Man does in his."[34] This perspective yields a much different approach to viewing the world than simply one of stewardship or responsibility for the natural world. The natural world is not then a resource, tool, or instrument for other "higher" purposes. It is not an external, expedient resource for human exploitation.[35] Humans rather are in familial relationship with all of creation. To recognize that carries with it a different paradigm of what it means to participate in and care for the created world.[36]

This line of thinking from the scriptural traditions through Saint Francis and into the modern world is highlighted by Pope Francis in his encyclical *Laudato Si': On Care for Our Common Home*.[37] In his assessment the stories in Genesis "bear witness to a conviction which we today share, that everything is interconnected, and that genuine care for our own lives and our relationships with nature is inseparable from fraternity, justice and faithfulness to others."[38] Pope Francis cites Saint Francis's "Canticle of the Creatures" with approval and invites us to recognize that "everything is related, and we human beings are united as brothers and sisters on a wonderful pilgrimage, woven together by the love God has for each of his creatures and which also unites us in fond affection with brother sun, sister moon, brother river and mother earth."[39] Such an awareness invites us to a "sense of fraternity" that "excludes nothing and no one."[40] It also leads to a consideration of what he calls integral ecology: a vision that takes into account the interconnectedness of all things, including the physical, environmental,

---

[34] White, "Historical Roots," 1206.

[35] See Dennis T. Gonzalez, "New Measures for Justice, Ecological Wisdom, and Integral Development," in *Just Sustainability: Technology, Ecology, and Resource Extraction* (ed. Peppard; vol. 3 of *Catholic Theological Ethics in the World Church*; Maryknoll, NY: Orbis Books, 2015), 74.

[36] For this reason, Lynn White proposed Saint Francis as the patron saint of ecologists.

[37] Pope Francis, *Laudato Si': On Care for Our Common Home* (Vatican City: Vatican Press, 2015).

[38] Francis, *Laudato Si'*, 52.

[39] Francis, *Laudato Si'*, 68.

[40] Francis, *Laudato Si'*, 67.

Chapter 6

economic, cultural, and social worlds in which humans live and in which we must pursue the common good.[41]

We can see that this perspective on the natural world is one that connects easily with the parable of the mustard seed with its focus on growth, unaided by humanity, and its image of hospitable welcoming of the birds among its branches. Describing this in a different way Rourke notes: "We are inextricably embedded within complex webs of interdependencies."[42] Ecological awareness, reflecting on what it means to be a responsible member of the community of life on this planet, leads us to consider our own practices in light of ecological virtues.

8. Our Sixth Step: Consider Implications

If we were to enhance our ecological awareness and consider the works of God in nature today, what might we see? Small seeds still grow; birds still perch on branches. We can observe the works of God with wonder and awe. Yet ecological awareness would also lead us to considerations of where our environment and our fellow creatures on this planet are suffering. Ecological awareness, seeing reality as it is, may lead us to consider issues of environmental justice. And as we have already considered, our planet earth is in trouble. Climate change is wreaking havoc as a result of human treatment of this world and its natural resources. Food supply is threatened by drought, over-fishing, and environmental disasters, and food insecurity affects many as a result. The health of our planet and environment becomes not only a matter of environmental justice (i.e., ensuring that our environment is protected from harm) but just as importantly, the provision of basic necessities of life for our fellow humans. And with regard to issues such as globalization, migration, and refugee crises (including climate refugees), it is the poor and those with limited resources who are disproportionately impacted. Very often, they are also not necessarily the ones directly responsible for using and misusing the world's resources, yet they are the ones most vulnerable.

[41] See Chapter 4 "Integral Ecology" in Francis, *Laudato Si'*. 103–120.
[42] Rourke, "Catholic Virtues Ecology," 194.

The Parable of the Mustard Seed (Mark 4:30–32)

Sister Sheila Carney, RSM, connects this parable with the call of Pope Francis to care for our common home. She explains:

> This same invitation to interdependence, humility, and hospitality is ours today as we respond to Pope Francis' call to care for our Common Home. Francis begins his encyclical Laudato Si with these words: "Our common home is like a sister with whom we share our life and a beautiful mother who opens her arms to embrace us" (Laudato Si, 1) – an image reminiscent of the mustard seed. A central message of the encyclical is the linkage created between the cry of the earth and the cry of the poor as we are reminded that those who suffer most from ecological degradation are those who live in poverty. Thus care for Earth becomes an issue of justice as we seek the rights of persons and of our planet as one indivisible cause.[43]

Recognizing this clear connection between the rights of the poor and the suffering of our planet, we can now turn to considerations of environmental justice and sustainability.

The concept of sustainability is a central one for contemporary consideration of integral ecology and environmental justice. Agriculture is one area in particular in which the technological advances have developed so rapidly that the impact on the environment has only recently begun to be assessed. It is now widely recognized that the environmental impact of industrial agriculture is not sustainable without dramatic changes.[44] Mark Graham refers to the "triumph of industrialized agriculture" in the last 100 years as "a momentous gamble upon which the lives of billions of people depend."[45] For Graham it is a gamble because: (1) historically, in the 10,000-year history of agriculture, industrialized agriculture is still in its infancy and already showing signs of "structural fragility"; (2) it is resource-intensive, requiring large amounts of land, water, and chemicals, all of which are finite resources; (3) further, the use of chemicals has led, and continues to lead, to harmful results (e.g., water pollution), and (4) patterns of food consumption and production are changing due to population, climate change, and other

---

[43] Carney, "Mustard Seed."

[44] See Mark Graham, "The Unsavory Gamble of Industrial Agriculture," in *Just Sustainability: Technology, Ecology, and Resource Extraction* (ed. Peppard; vol. 3 of *Catholic Theological Ethics in the World Church*; Maryknoll, NY: Orbis Books, 2015).

[45] Graham, "Unsavory Gamble," 106.

Chapter 6

factors. With these factors in mind, Graham points to research which shows that 25% of our planet's arable land is already "highly degraded." Further, economic development has led to significantly increased meat consumption which carries with it a much higher impact on the environment and is significantly more resource-intensive to support. The long-term impact of each of these factors is difficult to predict, but highly concerning if changes are not implemented.

In a similar vein, in *Just Water: Theology, Ethics, and Fresh Water Crises*, Christiana Z. Peppard provides an exceptional summary of the history of agriculture with a focus on the advances of the twentieth century. Technological advances including fertilizers, pesticides, fungicides; genetic manipulation and hybridization of seeds; innovations in agricultural machinery; water management including dams, irrigation, and water extraction technologies; monocultures and the decline of crop diversity; and consolidation of farm operations run as agribusiness have collectively enabled food production to increase significantly, along with economic profit for agribusiness and the industrial agricultural complex.[46] While the food production gains are arguably a wonderful result of the application of technology and industrial approaches to agriculture, there are also down sides to many of these advances. Synthetic fertilizers, pesticides, and fungicides have played a significant role in this agricultural output. Unfortunately, the environmental impact of the use of certain chemicals, particularly petroleum-based fertilizers, has been catastrophic particularly in watersheds, rivers, and even the oceans. As Peppard explains,

> Although crop yields have increased as a result of petrochemical applications, so too downstream bodies of water have become increasingly suffused with atrazine and other synthetic, agricultural petrochemicals. Ingestion of these compounds is not a choice for most individuals; rather it is a reality of bioaccumulation, such that most of the bodies of the planet's people—including the unborn—carry chemical composites ingested through food consumption, water supply, and even the air we breathe.[47]

[46] Christiana Z. Peppard, *Just Water: Theology, Ethics, and Fresh Water Crises* (Ecology and Justice, an Orbis Series on Integral Ecology; Maryknoll, NY: Orbis Books, 2018). See esp. Chapter 5, "The Agriculture/Water Nexus," pp. 86–117.
[47] Peppard, *Just Water*, 99.

The Parable of the Mustard Seed (Mark 4:30–32)

Peppard and Graham draw our attention to the urgent need for an increase in our ecological awareness, and the need to move toward practices which are sustainable and can ensure the health of our planet for future generations.

These considerations of ecological awareness have many potential implications for our lives in the twenty-first century. They invite us to a consideration of ecological virtues, environmental justice, and ecofeminism. Ecological virtues can enable us to live in the world with sensitivity and humility. Environmental justice seeks to address environmental challenges in ways that have lasting and positive impact and, rather than arrogant trust in science and technology, include a recognition of the realities of interdependence and interconnection along with the importance of humility. Ecofeminism challenges all of us to be attuned with greater clarity to the link between attitudes of oppression to women and to oppression and exploitation of the earth. If those are indeed connected, then in order to address the ecological crisis there is a need to address inequality of men and women.[48] Given the ways these topics are interrelated, we note here some of the virtues that can undergird meaningful action in our world today.

Ecological awareness calls us to practice virtues with an awareness of our contexts: social, physical, and environmental.[49] The virtues of integrity, wonder, temperance, and prudence all have an important role. In light of the parable of the mustard seed in which Jesus invites contemplation of a growing plant and its place in the environment, the ecological virtue of wonder is worth considering. Rourke counts wonder among the moral virtues, a set of virtues which are available to all persons who are willing to put in the work to cultivate them. Wonder, she suggests, can be cultivated through the simple practice of the study of nature. For example, the study of the incredible diversity of species can inspire wonder. Why does the study of nature promote wonder?

---

[48] Ann Marie Mealey, "Feminism and Ecology," in *Just Sustainability: Technology, Ecology, and Resource Extraction* (ed. Peppard; vol. 3 of *Catholic Theological Ethics in the World Church*; Maryknoll, New York: Orbis Books, 2015). Ecofeminism "seeks to relate the subjugation of women with that of the earth in order to create a dialogue that is based on equity, fairness, and justice in the fullest sense of the word—irrespective of, yet attentive to, the intricacies of social position, gender, class, and race" (188).

[49] See Rourke, "Catholic Virtues Ecology."

Chapter 6

Because, Rourke notes, "These lives and ecosystems are wondrous, generative examples of divine creativity."[50] In other words, wonder "is already infused into our environments." Objects of wonder are everywhere: "We have only to look, listen, pay attention and learn."[51] Such an approach to the world around us connects closely with Jesus's parables and other teaching which invite careful reflection on natural phenomena.

In addition, we can also consider that the sheltering impulse of God's work—the flourishing of nature that provides space and resources for God's creatures—is needed more than ever. It is needed for the humans who are displaced and without a home for the same reasons above: climate change, drought, food shortage. Some of this is due to civil war or armed conflict; some due to criminal activity; some due to the practices of multinational corporations and their greed, and policies which allow for it. Such a recognition calls to mind several of the corporal works of mercy: to shelter the homeless, to feed the hungry, to give drink to the thirsty.

With respect to giving drink to the thirsty, James Keenan links this work to the water crisis in our world. He explains, "The call to give drink to the thirsty is itself the call to develop an attitude that respects the needs of those who are poor and that appreciates the gifts of the earth."[52] Here we can again see the linkage between the cry of the poor and the cry of the earth. Keenan notes: "The web of life requires a harmonious estimation of both ourselves and our planet: Where we harm our planet, we eventually harm ourselves. Inevitably, justice affects us all."[53] The result is that this work of mercy "calls us to attend to developing a more environmentally sensitive form of spirituality."[54] This spirituality may be one that requires changes to our lifestyles, since "reflecting on the works of mercy not only asks us to consider what we need to do, but also asks us to examine matters about our own lifestyle as a person and as a people."[55]

---

[50] Rourke, "Catholic Virtues Ecology," 197.
[51] Rourke, "Catholic Virtues Ecology," 197.
[52] Keenan, *Works of Mercy*, 39.
[53] Keenan, *Works of Mercy*, 39.
[54] Keenan, *Works of Mercy*, 39.
[55] Keenan, *Works of Mercy*, 41.

The Parable of the Mustard Seed (Mark 4:30–32)

Returning to sheltering the homeless, this work at its core is really about hospitality and providing welcome to those in need. It also happens to be a paradigm and message of the Bible from Genesis through Revelation. In a brief survey Keenan notes the importance of hospitality and shelter for Adam and Eve, and also Ruth and Boaz; ultimately, hospitality and the welcoming of the stranger are critical for the historical memory of Israel, who themselves were refugees. From this rich biblical tradition has come a significant amount of church teaching on hospitality throughout the centuries. Moving to contemporary concerns where our commitment to hospitality is implicated, Keenan makes note of refugees (which are an aspect of globalization, with its many political, economic, health, safety, and environmental impacts), adolescent runaways (including human trafficking), and women whose need for shelter is directly related to domestic violence and abuse. Keenan cites the statistic that women and children make up 80% of refugees out of 65 million refugees and displaced persons worldwide.[56] Pope Francis reiterates that each refugee has "an inalienable right to live in peace and to aspire to a better future for their sons and daughters."[57] If our collective poor treatment of the earth limits the ability of others to live into their full humanity, or even to live and provide for their families, we have reached a critical moment where change is needed.

Sheila Carney explicitly links the parable of the mustard seed with this work of mercy through the sheltering of the birds. She explains,

> The word "shelter" appears in the Work of Mercy which urges us to make room. Shelter the homeless means more than put a roof over someone's head. The word is rich in meaning and challenge for it embodies a sense of protecting, safeguarding, wrapping, defending, shielding. To shelter is not an anonymous or impersonal gesture. It requires that one know and respond to the needs of the other, providing the resources and environment necessary for health and wholeness. The mustard seed doesn't simply tolerate a bird alighting on one of its limbs. It "puts out big branches so that the birds of the air can shelter in its shade." (Mark 4:32) It creates a place where the bird is kept safe from harmful conditions and predators.[58]

[56] Keenan, *Works of Mercy*, 27.
[57] Keenan, *Works of Mercy*, 27.
[58] Carney, "Mustard Seed."

Chapter 6

If the works of the reign of God relate to provision of food and shelter, then it follows that God's children, God's family, should be marked by provision of food and shelter as well. There are implications then for practices that support those who are impacted negatively by climate change whether they experience hunger, poor health, or displacement. There is also a call to take action to improve the condition of our planet so that the negative impacts on the poor are lessened and alleviated.

If to be about the kingdom is to stand in awe at the natural world, to foster growth, to shelter, to provide hospitality, is it also then to resist what kills, what rejects, what sends away empty? Jesus is not here giving us answers about what policies we should advocate for or what specific actions need to be taken. Instead he is, as always, engaging the imaginations of his listeners. He is inviting them to see the miracles around them, and consider what the kingdom is like.

What does this parable suggest about what it means to be fully human? To be human is to wonder at creation, to value the natural world for its own sake, to see oneself as part of that natural world, and to perceive the wonder and mystery of God's kingdom and how it operates. To find oneself as part of a larger, complex, whole which has meaning and value. It is also to grow and flourish as part of that whole, to a place where one's growth and one's community's growth benefit not just the individual or community, but a larger whole.

Feminist theologian Rosemary Radford-Reuther spoke about the call to "create communities of flourishing." Such a phrase captures well the image that is presented to us in the mustard seed which grows into the greatest of all shrubs. But what might this mean in practice? On the one hand we can consider how we might join in the divine activity of creating communities of flourishing, helping all to thrive. On the other hand, we might look at our lives, our society, and our social structures to consider where our practices are inconsistent with these values, or worse, working against them. Cultivating an ecological awareness, seeing ourselves as living in a dynamic relationship of interdependence with our environment, may bring us to a new awareness of how our way of life, and the structures we are part of, may be working against God's desires for the well-being of all. Following the divine impulse toward life and well-being we can reconsider our own actions and their impact. But rather than beating ourselves up about ways we have failed, womanist theologian Karen Baker-Fletcher writes of the possibility of participating

The Parable of the Mustard Seed (Mark 4:30–32)

with God in fostering hope: "Human beings look to blame, while God, whose aim is always the well-being of creation, forgives, and calls creation to participate in resurrection hope."[59]

The above considerations can potentially find a place in the approach of "integral ecology" outlined by Pope Francis, since it is closely connected with the common good. Francis notes the common good as "a central and unifying principle of social ethics" and describes it as "the sum of those conditions of social life which allow social groups and their individual members relatively thorough and ready access to their own fulfilment."[60] For Francis the common good is grounded in the belief in the dignity and worth of each human being, and their right to their own integral development. Yet the ways in which those rights are denied for many persons means that special attention is needed, particularly for the poor and marginalized. He explains, "In the present condition of global society, where injustices abound and growing numbers of people are deprived of basic human rights and considered expendable, the principle of the common good immediately becomes, logically and inevitably, a summons to solidarity and a preferential option for the poorest of our brothers and sisters."[61] We will take up these notions of solidarity and the preferential option for the poor in a future chapter. For now we simply note the inseparable linkage between the treatment of our environment and the treatment of those who suffer within it as a critical issue that is suggested from Jesus's teaching.

With this we can return to the notion that this is a parable that engages our imaginations around humility, interdependence, and hospitality. Sister Sheila Carney's reflection on this parable provides an apt summary for our considerations of the critical lessons from Jesus's school of nature:

> The mustard seed embraced its purpose and potential and stretched itself until it became a blessing. It lived interdependently within its environment and contributed what, in its nature, it could to the wellbeing of all. This parable offers an invitation to us to live in humility and interdependence and hospitality, attending, in how we choose to live our lives, to the cry of the earth and the cry of the poor.[62]

[59] Baker-Fletcher, "How Women Relate," 75.
[60] Francis, *Laudato Si'*, 116. Here he is citing the earlier *Gaudium et Spes*, 26.
[61] Francis, *Laudato Si'*, 117.
[62] Carney, "Mustard Seed."

Chapter 6

Works Cited in Chapter 6

Baker-Fletcher, Karen. "How Women Relate to the Evils of Nature," Pages 64–77 in *Womanist Theological Ethics: A Reader*. Edited by Katie G. Cannon, Emilie Maureen Townes, and Angela D. Sims. of *Library of Theological Ethics*. Louisville, KY: Westminster John Knox Press, 2011.

Cahill, Lisa Sowle. *Global Justice, Christology and Christian Ethics*. New Studies in Christian Ethics. New York: Cambridge University, 2013.

Carney, Sheila, RSM. "*The Mustard Seed*." 2019.

Cousland, J. R. C.. "Do "The Birds of Heaven" in the Parable of the Mustard Seed Represent Gentiles?" *Catholic Biblical Quarterly* 85, no. 1 (2023): 53–74.

Delio, Ilia. *A Franciscan View of Creation: Learning to Live in a Sacramental World*. Vol. 2, Franciscan heritage series. St. Bonaventure, NY: Franciscan Institute, St. Bonaventure University, 2003.

Edwards, Denis. "Humans and Other Creatures: Creation, Original Grace, and Original Sin," Pages 159–170 in *Just Sustainability: Technology, Ecology, and Resource Extraction*. Edited by Christiana Z. Peppard. Vol. 3 of *Catholic Theological Ethics in the World Church*. Maryknoll, New York: Orbis Books, 2015.

Francis, Pope. *Laudato Si': On Care for Our Common Home*. Vatican City: Vatican Press, 2015.

Gonzalez, Dennis T. "New Measures for Justice, Ecological Wisdom, and Integral Development," Pages 69–80 in *Just Sustainability: Technology, Ecology, and Resource Extraction*. Edited by Christiana Z. Peppard. Vol. 3 of *Catholic Theological Ethics in the World Church*. Maryknoll, NY: Orbis Books, 2015.

Graham, Mark. "The Unsavory Gamble of Industrial Agriculture," Pages 105–116 in *Just Sustainability: Technology, Ecology, and Resource Extraction*. Edited by Christiana Z. Peppard. Vol. 3 of *Catholic Theological Ethics in the World Church*. Maryknoll, NY: Orbis Books, 2015.

Hultgren, Arland J. *The Parables of Jesus: A Commentary*. The Bible in its World. Grand Rapids: Eerdmans, 2000.

Keenan, James F. *The Works of Mercy: The Heart of Catholicism*. Third ed. Lanham: Rowman & Littlefield, 2017.

Levine, Amy-Jill. *Short Stories by Jesus: The Enigmatic Parables of a Controversial Rabbi*. New York: HarperOne, 2014.

Mealey, Ann Marie. "Feminism and Ecology," Pages 182–193 in *Just Sustainability: Technology, Ecology, and Resource Extraction*. Edited by Christiana Z. Peppard. Vol. 3 of *Catholic Theological Ethics in the World Church*. Maryknoll, New York: Orbis Books, 2015.

The Parable of the Mustard Seed (Mark 4:30–32)

Nabhan, Gary Paul. *Jesus for Farmers and Fishers: Justice for All Those Marginalized by Our Food System*. Minneapolis, MN: Broadleaf Books, 2021.

Peppard, Christiana Z. *Just Water: Theology, Ethics, and Fresh Water Crises*. Revised ed., Ecology and Justice, an Orbis Series on Integral Ecology. Maryknoll, NY: Orbis Books, 2018.

Rourke, Nancy M. "A Catholic Virtues Ecology," Pages 194–204 in *Just Sustainability: Technology, Ecology, and Resource Extraction*. Edited by Christiana Z. Peppard. Vol. 3 of *Catholic Theological Ethics in the World Church*. Maryknoll, New York: Orbis Books, 2015.

Schottroff, Luise. *The Parables of Jesus*. Minneapolis: Fortress, 2006.

Snodgrass, Klyne. *Stories with Intent: A Comprehensive Guide to the Parables of Jesus*. Second ed. Grand Rapids: Eerdmans, 2018.

Teilhard de Chardin, Pierre. *Hymn of the Universe*. New York: Harper & Row, 1965.

White, Lynn. "The Historical Roots of Our Ecological Crisis." *Science* 155 (1967): 1203–1207.

7

The Pharisee and the Tax Collector (Luke 18:9–14)

1. Introduction

In this chapter we explore a parable that is both surprising and challenging. In the parable of the Pharisee and the tax collector, Jesus uses a popular style of ancient folk story to put forward a vision of reality that must have presented a quite challenge his original listeners. Through this parable of reversal listeners are invited to suspend their socially conditioned judgments of others, to consider the interconnectedness of all members of a community, and to embrace an understanding of the inclusive nature of community in which each member can receive mercy and also hold space for all others to receive the same mercy. How does this short story about a devout religious person (a Pharisee) and a person who had sold out to the Romans (a tax collector) lead us to these considerations? Let us follow our interpretive process and see.

Before summarizing the story, it will be especially helpful to raise an important question which we will need to answer. At its essence is this an example parable or a reversal parable?[1] If the former, then there is an

---

[1] For basic background and approaches to the issues in this parable, see Hultgren, *Parables of Jesus*, 118–128; Snodgrass, *Stories with Intent*, 462–476; Blomberg, *Interpreting the Parables*, 340–347. For an interpretation with careful attention to the intersection of social issues of related to class, religion, and empire in the first-century CE, see Herzog, *Parables as Subversive Speech*, 173–193.

Social Justice in the Stories of Jesus: The Ethical Challenge of the Parables, First Edition. Matthew E. Gordley.
© 2024 John Wiley & Sons Ltd. Published 2024 by John Wiley & Sons Ltd.

The Pharisee and the Tax Collector (Luke 18:9–14)

example here to be followed, and we can consider what it is that Jesus wanted his listeners to do. In this line of thinking it is probably that listeners should be humble like the tax collector and not proud like the Pharisee. If viewed as an example story, this parable is easy to understand, and also very safe (as writer Anthony Thiselton says we can cozy up to its moral message!). But if this is not an example parable but instead a parable of reversal, then it was told not to illustrate how one should act, but rather to *change the minds* of the listeners, as a proclamation and enactment of the arrival of the kingdom in and through Jesus. As a parable of reversal it would then offer a different kind of challenge to readers. This would be a twofold challenge, really: a challenge to how to interpret it, and then a challenge to accept its startling message. For now, let's put a pin in this question and see if we can first grasp the basics of the story.

2. The Text: The Pharisee and the Tax Collector (Luke 18:9–14)

> He also told this parable to some who trusted in themselves that they were righteous and regarded others with contempt: "Two men went up to the temple to pray, one a Pharisee and the other a tax collector. The Pharisee, standing by himself, was praying thus, 'God, I thank you that I am not like other people: thieves, rogues, adulterers, or even like this tax collector. I fast twice a week; I give a tenth of all my income.' But the tax collector, standing far off, would not even look up to heaven, but was beating his breast and saying, 'God, be merciful to me, a sinner!' I tell you, this man went down to his home justified rather than the other; for all who exalt themselves will be humbled, but all who humble themselves will be exalted." (Luke 18:9–14 NRSV)

3. Our First Step: Grasp the Story

While v. 9 introduces it, the actual parable itself begins in v. 10 where Jesus describes two men going up to the temple to pray. We are to understand this as the Jerusalem temple, and "going up" was the

203

Chapter 7

typical expression to describe such action (perhaps not unlike the way New Jerseyans say they are "going down the shore"). Their purpose is described with the simple verb "to pray." This verb does not really give us much of a clue of the type of prayer as it is the most general way to speak about the act of prayer. It is possible they were going to a set service of prayer (twice a day Tamid prayer), but just as likely they arrived at the same time for their own personal prayer.[2]

Next we learn something of the identity of each man. One was a Pharisee and one was a tax collector. As we already know, those identifiers are significant. We will explore them further later, but for now we can recall that Jesus's audience would most likely have had a very positive association with the Pharisee and a very negative association with the tax collector. Further, the combination of location (in the temple) and activity (prayer) are things that would align with the Pharisee's reputation; that combination might be a little bit out of sync with the tax collector's reputation.

We then learn about the physical position of the Pharisee and also about what he prayed. He stood off by himself, which gives the idea of some physical separation from the tax collector and from anyone else who was there. His prayer begins like many prayers do with an expression of thanks to God: "God, I thank you…" (v. 11). However, it quickly turns out that the focus of the prayer is on himself in contrast to the negative aspects of others, and with attention to the positive aspects of the Pharisee: "that I am not like other people: thieves, rogues, adulterers, or even like this tax collector. I fast twice a week; I give a tenth of all my income" (vv. 11–12). In contrast to those who steal, the Pharisee gives. In contrast to those who use their time seeking pleasure, the Pharisee maintains strict discipline and even denies himself.

We then learn about the tax collector's location and posture. He stood far off, looking down, and beating his chest. Each of these is a physical indicator of an inward sense of feeling unworthy or ashamed. And while his prayer begins like the Pharisee's by addressing God directly, it moves in a quite different direction from there both in length and content: "God, be merciful to me, a sinner" (v. 13). Of note, the tax collector in some ways shares the Pharisee's assessment of him. This is

---

[2] Snodgrass, *Stories with Intent*, 472–473.

The Pharisee and the Tax Collector (Luke 18:9–14)

likely the audience's assessment too. The tax collector is a sinner who stands in need of God's mercy. And just as importantly, and perhaps surprisingly, he asks for it.

Now that Jesus has set the scene for us, we are brought to the verdict. We cannot quite be sure what the original audience might have expected in terms of the Jesus's assessment of this scene. It is possible there were those in the audience who would have expected a favorable judgment toward the good Pharisee and a negative judgment toward the tax collector who, while he asked for mercy, likely did not deserve it and may not have been sincere. It is also possible there were those in the audience who might have expected a favorable judgment on both: the Pharisee for the same reasons above, and the tax collector with the assumption that he was genuinely repentant. But as we encounter the verdict of Jesus, we see something else entirely: "I tell you, this man [the tax collector!] went down to his home justified rather than the other" (v. 19). So it is the tax collector who is justified, but not the Pharisee. This is a surprising outcome indeed and a sharp reversal of the expectations of the audience. Whichever outcome the audience may have expected, by taking such an approach—setting a scene with two characters with a surprising, non-conventional judgment of them—this parable fits into an ancient category of story which helps us understand its impact.[3]

There is one complication here though. The Greek *para* (v. 14) which is translated here as "rather than," in the sense of a contrast, can actually be translated several different ways. It could be a comparative, "more than." It could also be "alongside." So depending on which way this phrase is interpreted, it could be that the tax collector is justified *and not* the Pharisee (the traditional reading), or the tax collector is justified *to a greater extent than* the Pharisee, or the tax collector is justified *along with* the Pharisee.[4] In any of these readings, the result is a surprise, a reversal of the audience's initial expectations. But which surprise ending are we to read here? Surely this is not a "choose your own ending"

---

[3] Robert Doran, "The Pharisee and the Tax Collector: An Agonistic Story," *Catholic Biblical Quarterly* 69, no. 2 (2007).

[4] Levine, *Short Stories*, 207–210. See further in Timothy A. Friedrichsen, "The Temple, a Pharisee, a Tax Collector, and the Kingdom of God: Rereading a Jesus Parable (Luke 18:10–14a)," *Journal of Biblical Literature* (2005): 116–117.

Chapter 7

scenario. We will need to consider these various translations below after we have done some more exploration.

Finally, it is important to notice that this parable has a particular context in Luke's Gospel. The words in v. 9 are not part of the parable proper, but are the narrative context that Luke provides the reader. This is undoubtedly intended as an important clue to help readers understand the parable. Jesus "also told this parable to some who trusted in themselves that they were righteous and regarded others with contempt" (v. 9). The setting is Jesus and unnamed individuals who had a certain way of perceiving themselves and of perceiving others. Who might these individuals be? While centuries of tradition predispose us to think these might be Pharisees, the wider context in Luke suggests another answer. Instead these were likely individuals among Jesus's own followers, as this parable is part of a group of parables that were addressed directly to his disciples (see Luke 17:22).[5] In this case, their criteria for self-evaluation and the evaluation of others was with regard to "being righteous." And we can certainly see a question forming here for our further consideration: What did it mean to "be righteous" in this context? Also, we can wonder whether this was a group of individuals doing this on an individual level or if this was a group perception. The summary statement at the end ("for all who exalt themselves will be humbled, but all who humble themselves will be exalted," v. 14) may have been Jesus's own ending line, or it may be Luke's summary that he added to highlight the particular application point that Luke wanted his readers to draw from this parable. Either way Luke's framing the parable with language about contempt and being humbled invites us to keep those concepts in mind as we consider the two characters.

In addition, we can wonder whether this parable was told directly to Pharisees and tax collectors, or whether it indirectly addresses a situation that Jesus was experiencing within his own followers. We have already noted in earlier chapters the power of parable and metaphor to address a specific situation indirectly. Rather than telling a story aimed directly at specific audience members it may rather be that a story about a Pharisee and tax collector in prayer is a metaphor with application to a different real world situation than what is portrayed in the parable.[6]

[5] Levine, *Short Stories*, 186.
[6] Doran, "Pharisee and Tax Collector," 269–270.

The Pharisee and the Tax Collector (Luke 18:9–14)

Once again, the fact that Luke places the parable as being addressed to Jesus's own disciples suggest that its application is not to Pharisees or tax collectors at all, but to his own followers.

4. Our Second Step: Ask Questions to Gain Understanding

This short parable raises a lot of questions for the careful reader. Given that the setting is prayer in the context of the Jerusalem temple, what do we need to know about the temple and Jewish prayer to better understand this parable? With two familiar character "types" mentioned, what do we need to know about Pharisees and tax collectors? Further, what social dynamics from the first century may be at play here that Jesus's original audience might have noticed but that we may overlook? What can social science and other critical approaches help us see?

The setting of this parable in the temple is a highly significant detail. As we saw in Chapter 2, the temple was a central focus of Jewish religious life. It was the locus of sacrifices, festivals, and other religious observances. It also figures significantly in the gospel portrayals of Jesus. Thus it was of significant cultural, religious, and symbolic importance within Judaism as well as in the memory of Jesus by the early Christians.

One of our key guides to the parables, Amy-Jill Levine, points to the temple as "a place of restoration, pilgrimage, worship, and inspiration."[7] In addition, she points out that while it is the place of sacrificial offerings to God associated with repentance, it was not the only place where a Jew could confess their sins or be reconciled to God. Jewish teaching held that God was omnipresent and God's presence could be encountered anywhere a person turned to God in repentance. Thus, Levine suggests that the parable's setting in the temple was intended to invoke positive associations with divine mercy, as opposed to any notions of exclusivity.[8]

Beyond sketching out these positive associations, Levine is also critical of New Testament interpreters who point to the temple system in a negative light. Refuting common interpretive tropes, she notes that the

[7] Levine, *Short Stories*, 197.
[8] Levine, *Short Stories*, 194–198.

Chapter 7

temple "was not a place known for overtaxing the population, exploiting the poor, in full collaboration with Rome, or profaning the covenant."[9] She goes on to note that the temple "did not function to suggest that people who worshipped elsewhere were precluded from receiving mercy."[10] She finds the idea that this parable is any way a critique of the temple or its functions within Judaism to be another instance of the kinds of anti-Judaism we have already encountered. These negative views also reflect interpreters' misunderstanding of some of Jesus's own statements about the temple. Levine explains, "From xenophobia to exploitation, commentators have developed a host of sins they perceived the Temple system as committing."[11] In each instance, she argues either that there is no primary historical source material for those claims, or that the sources that are being cited are not being used properly. Given our growing awareness of negative portrayals of Jewish belief and practice, these are warnings that we need to heed in this context as well.

While we can agree with Levine to an extent, it is also the case that there is a tradition of critique of the temple—one that actually comes from within Judaism itself. Such an approach does not reflect anti-Judaism at all as much as a perception by some first-century Jews that the priestly establishment was illegitimate and thereby compromised. In such a context, in addition to its religious and cultural significance, the role that the temple played in the economic and political life of Judea cannot be overlooked.[12] Nevertheless, for the purposes of what seems to be highlighted in this parable we can agree with Levine about the setting of the temple here. It is largely positive. She writes, "For both men in this parable the Temple is a place of prayer. It is a place where God is found; where fidelity can be celebrated and reconciliation found, without precluding other sites for such celebration and reconciliation; where Jewish distinction can be proclaimed over and against Roman insistence on assimilation."[13] Yet even her assertion suggests that the presence of Rome is a factor in understanding the significance of the temple in this context.

---

[9] Levine, *Short Stories*, 194.
[10] Levine, *Short Stories*, 194.
[11] Levine, *Short Stories*, 196.
[12] See the ways these intersect as described in Herzog, *Parables as Subversive Speech*, 173–193.
[13] Levine, *Short Stories*, 198.

The Pharisee and the Tax Collector (Luke 18:9–14)

As for the characters in this parable, a Pharisee and a tax collector make for a very interesting pairing. The whole parable is clearly setting up a contrast. In the parable we see the contrast of their posture, their location, and their words, and through those, their attitudes. It is difficult, though, for contemporary readers to appreciate the nature of the contrast based on the familiarity of the original audience with both character types. We have already met both the Pharisees and the tax collectors in our look at the parables of the lost sheep, the lost coin, and the lost sons. The Pharisees and scribes were grumbling about Jesus's welcoming attitude toward tax collectors and "sinners" (see Luke 15:1–2). Jesus offered those parables in part to defend his practices of hospitality to all, and in part to invite his listeners to see themselves and others in a new way. Here we can briefly describe features of each group that will help us better understand the dynamics of this parable.

As we have noted, Pharisees were one among several movements within early Judaism which sought to make sense of the covenant promises of God in light of their lived reality under the Roman Empire.[14] In contrast to the zealots, who sought to rise up against Rome through armed conflict, and in contrast to the Sadducees who, through their alignment with the temple sought to accommodate Rome and thereby seem to have benefited materially, the Pharisees found their place in this world through living in obedience to the Torah. They placed their confidence in God as their true king, sought to obey God's precepts as interpreted by the scribes, and trusted in God to keep the promises of the covenant. Contemporary sources indicate that at least some Pharisees understood their situation under Rome as one of God's discipline for the wickedness of the temple establishment, and trusted in God to send a deliverer, the Messiah. We learn a great deal from the *Psalms of Solomon*, a collection of psalms written in the first century BCE which give us a glimpse into their worldview. Interestingly, among their number was none other than the Apostle Paul, and so part of what we know about the movement we can know from his writings.

---

[14] Levine also provides a helpful overview and concise history of the Pharisees with attention to issues related to this parable: Levine, *Short Stories*, 188–194. For more comprehensive information on the Pharisees, see now the extensive new study by Kent L. Yinger and Craig A. Evans, *The Pharisees: Their History, Character, and New Testament Portrait* (Eugene, OR: Cascade Books, 2022). See also several of the essays in Joseph Sievers and Amy-Jill Levine, *The Pharisees* (Grand Rapids, MI: Eerdmans, 2021).

Chapter 7

We encounter the Pharisees multiple times throughout the Gospels where the portrayal of them is mixed. They seem to hold the respect of the people, and their focus on observance of the law is a key element. They are often linked with the scribes, who were the experts in interpreting the law. Some of them opposed and even challenged Jesus, while others were sympathetic to Jesus and his movement. Scholars discern that the earliest traditions preserved in the Gospels have the Pharisees outside of Jerusalem, and not directly involved in the plot to arrest and kill Jesus. The later elements of the gospel tradition connect certain Pharisees more directly with plans to arrest Jesus. Whether this reflects the actual Pharisees at the time of Jesus, or rather reflects the growing tension in the era in which the Gospels were written is a subject of historical debate. Either way, it is well established that the Pharisees were generally positively regarded as upright observers of the laws of God. This devotion to the Torah would explain the passion with which they debated with Jesus on its interpretation, as well as reflect the ways in which Paul describes his own background (see Phil 3:4–6 and Gal 1:13–14).

By contrast tax collectors were not nearly as well regarded in first-century society. Members of the merchant class, they were generally hired by higher ranking officials, often foreigners, who held contracts from Rome to extract a certain amount of wealth from the region.[15] The tax collectors themselves were generally from the local population, which contributed to resentment about their role. Levine captures this by referring to this tax collector as "an agent of Rome" who audiences would have "assumed to have been corrupt." This was because he was "a traitor to his people" who "has likely shown no mercy to others."[16] In literature outside the New Testament they are frequently condemned for their greed and unscrupulousness. They were not likely to have

---

[15] For a concise overview of tax collectors and their position in society, see Herzog, *Parables as Subversive Speech*, 187–189. Given the wide range of meaning of the Greek term, Herzog recognizes the individual in this parable as being a toll collector, "subsistence level wage employees used by the toll contractors and hated by nearly everyone else because of the way they were used to cheat and defraud the public" (188). Working for the toll contractors (a.k.a. tax collectors), the toll collector was thus "a visible yet low-level retainer who did the actual work of collecting for wealthier retainers who bid toll contracts and paid in advance. On the head of this class was heaped the scorn and hostility of the populace" (188).

[16] Levine, *Short Stories*, 188–189.

The Pharisee and the Tax Collector (Luke 18:9–14)

been wealthy themselves and were essentially low-level functionaries for the imperial bureaucracy. In the New Testament the prevailing negative view is reflected as they are frequently mentioned along with the more general term for "sinners." Of the twenty references to tax collectors in the Gospels, nine of these are paired the term with "sinners"— including this parable where the tax collector refers to himself as a sinner.[17] Two other references link tax collectors with prostitutes (Matt. 21:31) or Gentiles (Matt. 18:17). And the Pharisee in our present parable includes the tax collector in his list of unsavory people he is thankful that he is not like, which also includes thieves, rogues, and adulterers (Luke 18:11). As we have seen, some of the conflicts between Jesus and other religious groups were around the extent to which Jesus would welcome and eat with "tax collectors and sinners," thus including them in his sphere and demonstrating God's welcome of such people (see the parables of the lost sheep, lost coin, and lost sons).

When paired together and contrasted, it is difficult to know on which particular level the audience would see the sharpest contrast. One can certainly imagine the moral contrast between the two, with Pharisees known for their piety and tax collectors known for their greed. The Pharisee's grouping him in with other sinners is suggestive of a moral element. One can also imagine a religious contrast in terms of the Pharisee's strict observance of the law, and the tax collector's assumed neglect of some elements of it. Further, a class distinction may be in play as well as perhaps a stance toward the Roman occupiers: the tax collector making his living and even profiting from the taxes collected on behalf of Rome. By contrast the Pharisee reports that he gives a tenth of all he has to the temple. Economically, the giving of the Pharisee and the (commonly understood but not stated) taking of the tax collector could be seen as a very sharp point of contrast.[18]

In the end, the contrast between the two characters almost could not be greater. Yet they also share some important characteristics. What do they share? Both were Jews; both were practicing prayer; and both were

---

[17] Matt. 9:10; 11:19; Mark 2:15; Luke 5:30; 7:34; 15:1; and 18:13.

[18] For further analysis see Lawrence M. Willis, "Methodological Reflections on the Tax Collectors in the Gospels," in *When Judaism and Christianity Began: Essays in Memory of Anthony J. Saldarini* (eds. Saldarini, et al.; vol. 85 of *Supplements to the Journal for the Study of Judaism*; Leiden; Boston: Brill, 2004).

Chapter 7

doing so in the context of the temple; importantly, both were also living their lives out under the shadow of Rome.

In light of its importance in so many aspects of Jewish life, we can see that a Pharisee and a tax collector would each likely have a unique perspective on the temple. It could certainly include all of the positive associations outlined by Levine. But there could also be some ambivalence on the part of each. In the end, it is not a stretch to imagine that both characters appear on the scene at the mercy of larger social, economic, and political forces. The tax collector collecting unjust taxes on behalf of another, and clearly unsure about his place within the temple. The Pharisee part of a social movement that arose in response to corruption among the temple bureaucracy and a desire to see the blessing of God return to Jews as they live according to the Torah in such a context. In either case, there are dynamics of power at play—power over and under others. Tax collectors held the power to extract taxes; Pharisees held the social capital of the respect of the people and set high expectations for devotion among the people. Perhaps both could arguably be seen as oppressors on some level. But on another level, these individuals were both enmeshed in a system, caught in a web, which exerted significant influence over them, their actions, their sense of self, and their assessment of others.

With this recognition that there were multiple ways in which each character engaged forces of oppression, we can turn to an important insight from James Cone. Cone, seeking to articulate a theology specific to the situation of Black Americans in the 1960s, also identified larger themes that were applicable outside of the African American experience. One of these was what Cone calls the "universal note in black theology." For Cone this universal element is the conviction that "all human beings were created for freedom, and that God always sides with the oppressed against the oppressors."[19] In light of this insight we may wonder: whose side is God on in this parable? By Jesus's verdict at the end of the parable it would seem that God is on the side of the tax collector. This is indeed surprising, given the tax collector's complicity with Rome and actual work of cheating and defrauding the populace. In what sense was the tax collector "oppressed" as opposed to being the oppressor?

[19] Cone, *Black Theology*, 204 n.5.

The Pharisee and the Tax Collector (Luke 18:9–14)

We can begin to answer that question by noting that the Roman colonization of Judaea carried with it a significant amount of economic, political, social, and cultural implications. Whether benefiting from the Roman occupation or being harmed by it, all members of society had to adapt to it. In part, the Romans colonized not only the land of Israel but also the mindsets of the inhabitants. In this sense a tax collector must have bought in to the power of Rome and recognized that Rome's presence was something with which he had to reckon. At some level he had chosen to collaborate with, and thus benefit from, the power of Rome. Though Rome is not mentioned in this parable, the designation of one of the characters as a tax collector serves as a reminder of their presence: he is collecting taxes *for Rome*.[20]

Also unnamed here are the temple authorities under whose gaze both men are aware that they are praying. While living in a Roman occupied land, both men felt the need to understand their standing before God in terms of the temple system. The Pharisee can justify himself through looking at others who are somehow "less than" he is and through looking at his actions—both his ability to observe good religious practices and his financial commitment to the temple establishment. As inherently good as those things may have been, were they necessary for the Pharisee to enjoy a place within the community of God? It could have been that he felt the actions were essential to his being able to belong. In the parable, Jesus may be challenging those kinds of assumptions as well.

The tax collector, through his stance, his words, and his action in the story, shows that he feels he does not really belong there. As we saw, he has the same assessment of himself as the Pharisee! He recognizes that he is a sinner—he is in a system which exploits and diminishes community; and that all he can do is ask for God to be merciful to him. The Pharisee, despite his good actions (and likely even his good heart), does not quite recognize the way that the mercy of God is needed for this man. Or perhaps for himself as well.

Jesus's pronouncement at the end of the parable marks a clear reversal of the way the listeners assume things to be. In a similar way the summary expression provided at the end of the parable (that all who exalt themselves will be humbled) also strikes a note of reversal. These

[20] Herzog, *Parables as Subversive Speech*, 180.

Chapter 7

themes hearken back to the song of Mary who at the beginning of Luke's Gospel joyfully sang of the reversals that God initiates. She specifically celebrated the fact that God "has brought down the powerful from their thrones, and lifted up the lowly" (Luke 1:52).

Given the tendency of readers to spiritualize the message of the parables as "religious" teaching, we might be somewhat comfortable with expressing this as a spiritual reality. The Pharisee had the right external actions, but the wrong spirituality—the wrong internal attitude and assumptions about God. The tax collector—with the wrong external actions and lacking the outward signs of piety—had the better spirituality, one of humble reliance on God's mercy. But perhaps we can consider that the reversal in this parable is not only spiritual in nature but may also be political and social in nature. Mary's song certainly describes not only spiritual reversal but a political one as well, bringing down the powerful from their thrones. And if the assessment of God in this situation allows a political and social collaborator with Rome to be recognized as part of the community of God then this parable may reveal an unrecognized aspect of the reversals that the arrival of the messiah has enacted. In the end, justification may just be more complicated than we might think.

5. Our Third Step: Spot the Twist

In this parable, the twist is easy to spot—maybe. Two men going to the temple is not surprising. Especially that one of them is a Pharisee would not be surprising. Is the presence of the tax collector at the temple a twist? Whether it is a surprise or not, it is clearly setting up a comparison and potential contrast between the two that readers expect to see as the parable unfolds.

The actions of the Pharisee seem reasonable. Laudable, even. No twist here necessarily. His prayer, however, does show him as someone whose actions exceed the requirements of the law.[21] While not a twist, readers would begin to wonder about someone as uber-pious as this. His own actions were impressive, but what about his looking down on others?

---

[21] This is so both in his fasting and in his tithing, which go beyond what is required. See Herzog, *Parables as Subversive Speech*, 186–187; Levine, *Short Stories*, 203–204.

214

The Pharisee and the Tax Collector (Luke 18:9–14)

The prayer of the tax collector could potentially introduce the twist into this parable. It may be surprising to listeners that a tax collector would see himself as in need of God's mercy. Listeners may wonder if the tax collector was sincere on this point, or just audaciously (though in humble posture) seeking God's blessing.

While the development of each character is interesting, the twist seems to come at the end of the parable. It is in the assessment of Jesus of both individuals that this parable seems go off the rails. How can it possibly be that the sinful tax collector went away justified, while the righteous Pharisee did not? Surely, Jesus cannot be serious about this?

Levine captures it this way: "The Temple is the place that welcomes both the Pharisee and the tax collector, and it is the place where both find justification. How they both find justification is the surprise, and the challenge, of the parable."[22] With that sense of surprise and challenge, let us move on to consider the metaphor as presented in this parable.

6. Our Fourth Step: Consider the Metaphor

Consideration of the metaphor in this parable is more than a little tricky. As we have seen, parables deal in metaphor and comparison. They are stories that are about what they are about, and more besides. With a merchant seeking a pearl or a woman looking for her lost coin, we know that the image on display is not the only point—it is also the "more besides" which speaks of ultimate, divine realities by means of the concrete images. This is the distinction between Via's "in meaning" and "through meaning." How does that work in the case of a narrative like this? Is this parable simply an example of what to do and not do, or is there a "more besides" that takes us beyond these two men in prayer? If there is a "more besides" element, how do we get to that?

Seen in this way we can summarize the metaphorical reach of this parable in the following way. This is a parable about two characters who defy the stereotypical characteristics associated with their group; or at least who are outliers. As a parable it invites comparison with

---

[22] Levine, *Short Stories*, 171.

Chapter 7

other situations in which there is intergroup comparison, typecasting, and stereotyping, and where people draw boundaries without recognizing either the individuality of each person or the extent to which all persons are interconnected as beneficiaries of divine mercy.

In exploring the metaphor here it would be a mistake to expect that the parable is telling us something specific to Pharisees as a group or to tax collectors as a whole. In fact, with this parable we have the opposite challenge that we had with the parable of the mustard seed (see Chapter 6). In that parable, we needed to resist spiritualizing the parable and see that the kingdom was indeed very much like the mustard seed itself. Natural growth without human aid is an instance of the kingdom's expression in this world. The parable is about that concretely, and more besides, which is the spiritual element. In that case we needed to resist the impulse to jump to the extended spiritual meaning without really sitting with the concrete. In the case of the Pharisee and the tax collector, since it describes a human interaction, we are perhaps more content to sit with this concrete interaction and generalize it to Pharisees and tax collectors as a whole. But here our challenge is to recognize the metaphorical nature of parables and *not* generalize to Pharisees and tax collectors as a whole. Instead we are invited to let the metaphor do its work to tease our minds into considering analogous situations in our own context with similar dynamics.

Returning to the question we asked at the beginning of this chapter, we can now consider whether this is an example story or a reversal story. Parables scholar Dominic Crossan reads this parable as a parable of reversal, one that challenges the perspective of the listeners and lures them into thinking and reflecting. He points out that it sets up a scenario in which two characters are put on display, and a situation is set up in which the verdict is a surprise.[23] Doran explores this further noting the tradition of agonistic stories which compare two characters. Rather than an exclusive outcome, he suggests such a story calls for a comparative outcome, noting that "the story revolves around the question of who is more upright."[24] With this tradition of ancient story in

---

[23] Crossan, *Power of Parable*, 90–95. Crossan points out that in the context of speaking to a real audience, such "orally delivered challenges attempt to raise the consciousness of listeners by luring and leading them into thinking for themselves" (95). Such is the purpose of challenge parables as "participatory pedagogy," according to Crossan.

[24] Doran, "Pharisee and Tax Collector," here, 265.

216

The Pharisee and the Tax Collector (Luke 18:9–14)

view, and understanding it as a challenging reversal rather than an example, this parable could be seen in a different light.

If truly a metaphor, then it is necessary to consider this as more generally a case of one group compared to another group rather than specifically comparing Pharisees and tax collectors. Here, though, we may note once more the danger of anti-Judaism. For example, from Augustine on there has been a tradition of interpreting this parable allegorically with the Pharisee representing Jews and the tax collector representing Gentiles.[25] Certainly there was tension in the early Church between Jews and Gentiles who believed in Jesus as the messiah (see Acts 15 for example). But just as certainly, this tension was not even on the radar for Jesus or his original listeners—who were all Jewish. Such a meaning would have not been remotely possible. Even so, there is a legitimate way of applying this parable to inter-group relations, if we can determine the relative social positions and power of Pharisees and tax collectors, and then see where those similar dynamics are in play in a later context. That would be our final step of considering implications. But to understand this as a parable about Jewish legalism versus Gentile dependence on God's mercy in Christ is highly anachronistic at best, and conducive to anti-Judaism at worst.[26]

It seems clear that Luke did not want the reader to generalize this Pharisee to represent all of Judaism. Luke makes it clear that Jesus addressed this parable not to all Jews or even to all Pharisees but specifically to those who "who trusted in themselves that they were righteous and regarded others with contempt" (v. 9). Levine points out that by giving this context to this parable Luke was generalizing to any who fit that category and was explicitly not against "the Jews" or even "the Pharisees."[27] This is important to notice, since the history of interpretation has often drifted toward identification of this particular parabolic Pharisee with all Pharisees, and also with all Jews. Levine explains,

---

[25] Levine, *Short Stories*, 184–186; Schottroff, *Parables*, 9–11.

[26] Schottroff notes the ways in which the "us" versus "them" approach inscribed in such interpretations has legitimized hatred and violence. She notes that this kind of reading has "not only legitimized church dominance but, by its contrast of good and evil and the equation of the good with the 'we,' has achieved political significance. It contributes to the legitimation of violence in today's Western world. I consider overcoming this tradition of interpretation to be a necessity," Schottroff, *Parables*, 11.

[27] Levine, *Short Stories*, 187.

Chapter 7

> Here Luke helps us by having the parable addressed to disciples; thereby, Luke shows us that negatively judging others is not a trait that signals 'Jewish' values; it is, rather, a human trait, and one to which the followers of Jesus themselves may fall prey.[28]

Luke therefore makes it clear that this parable is told for all who trust in themselves and regard others with contempt.

As we continue to consider the metaphors here, we must also ask if this is a parable about justification—the theological concept of being declared righteous before God. Clearly, the word "justified" is used and it is critical to Jesus's verdict. But is this justification "by faith alone" in the sense we might find in Paul and in the theological writings of the Protestant Reformers? Or is it used here in some other sense? Is this a binary "justified or not," or is it about who is more comparably upright through their actions and attitudes? Recognizing that there are different ways to answer these questions, we may simply note here the danger of deducing doctrine from the parables. Parables are powerful instructional tools, but the move from narrative challenge to propositional statement about how things are is a challenging one.

In addition, as a metaphor a parable that speaks about justification may actually not be about justification at all but rather may be addressing another situation indirectly. Luke helps us understand this with his setting of the parable, and also with a concluding expression. In an us/them or an in/out context, we might do well to consider that the good are not completely good, the bad are not completely bad, and that it is God who justifies. Perhaps the good of the not completely good benefits the bad who are not completely bad.[29]

The treasury of merit is a concept within early Judaism and early Christianity that may help us advance our consideration of the metaphor of justification. Gary Anderson demonstrates the growth of this concept in Second Temple Jewish writings, including the New Testament.[30] It holds that a person's good works are stored in a divine treasury and can be called upon as needs arise. Jesus himself even referred to the concept as he encouraged his followers to store up

[28] Levine, *Short Stories*, 187.
[29] Levine, *Short Stories*, 209–212.
[30] Anderson, *Charity*.

The Pharisee and the Tax Collector (Luke 18:9–14)

treasures in heaven (Matt. 6:19) rather than on earth. Amy Jill Levine suggests that the treasury of merit is what lies behind the reasoning as to why the tax collector could be justified: the excess merit of the Pharisee reflected back onto the tax collector. And this was even against the will of the Pharisee! While I was initially skeptical that this concept had anything to do with this parable, I have since rethought my position. It certainly provides an explanation for the variety of possible interpretations of the Greek expression in v. 14 as "alongside" instead of "rather than."

In the end, with the Greek phrase "this one is justified alongside (*para*) that one," we are left with ambiguity. The phrase could be rendered justified and not justified; comparatively more justified; justified alongside the other; or justified on account of the righteousness of the other. What is the emotional impact and shock value of each? This plurality of possibility may be the genius of this parable. It, like others, does not give a simple answer, but sets up the reader to interrogate their own assumptions about themselves and others. As Crossan suggests, in this parable, as with all challenge parables, "The audience is lured, led, and provoked into reaction, response, and reflection. Challenge parables are participatory—because provocative—pedagogy."[31]

7. Our Fifth Step: Articulate the Challenge

In the process of moving from story to meaning Levine talks about "determining what the provocation is."[32] One way of expressing the challenge of this parable is to take the context of the parable, people who are sure of themselves and look down on others (Luke 18:9), as the starting point. The challenge is for those who think they are meeting God's expectations (in whatever way they may measure that), to consider whether they may actually be falling short with regard to the most important ones: respect for fellow humans and love for neighbor. To fall short in those areas is to fall short of God's expectations. Individuals like that need a wakeup call.[33] The flip side is to accept that true loyalty and devotion to God is best

---

[31] Crossan, *Power of Parable*, 95.
[32] Levine, *Short Stories*, 194.
[33] This is the view of Snodgrass, *Stories with Intent*.

Chapter 7

demonstrated by loving concern for one's neighbor. Or to put it even more pointedly, perhaps true devotion to God is demonstrated *only* by such loving concern for others.

If the treasury of merit is at all in view here, then the challenge relates to appreciating the interconnectedness of all in God's mercy. And it is also a back door into recognizing the value of our neighbor, whether one who does not live up to our criteria of goodness (how the Pharisee looks at the tax collector), or one who looks down on us (how the tax collector sees the Pharisee looking at him). For the former, the merit of one blesses many, even unintentionally. For the latter, as a member of the community, one is a beneficiary of mercy, which is for all.

Ultimately, this provocative parable seems to weave four threads together to create its challenge:

1) A thread of warning: Beware of looking down on others. Readers are challenged to watch their attitudes toward others; one cannot know God's judgment about another person in a given situation.
2) A thread of invitation: Seek God's mercy which is available to all. The mercy of God would seem to be accessible and offered to all who seek it genuinely, without limitation.
3) A thread of openness: Accept the surprises of the kingdom. Given that this parable offers a startling reversal, readers learn from it that just when they think they have the kingdom figured out, they may still be in for a surprise.
4) A thread of interconnectedness: Recognize anew that all are more closely interconnected to others than readers may realize.

With these four threads and others we could articulate, this parable brings with it an exciting multiplicity of applicability. Certainly there is no one simple point here. Rather this parable, like others, can be a "can opener for the mind" to quote Thurman. It is ultimately a brain teaser inviting readers to test their assumptions about God's perspective and how it aligns with or diverges from their own: how is it that the tax collector is more justified and the Pharisee is less so (or even justified along with)? As such it invites modern readers to think on a deeper level about challenging social dynamics, while at the same time recognizing that it applies to our contemporary situation only indirectly. It also reminds us of the need for each new generation and context to engage deeply with these ideas in light of their own social situations.

The Pharisee and the Tax Collector (Luke 18:9–14)

8. Our Sixth Step: Consider Implications

American society in the 2020s is fraught with division and us-versus-them thinking. Much of the division centers around human rights issues which have become politicized such as equality, racism, gender identity, women's rights, refugees, transgender rights, and so on. In every case it is often true that both sides believe they are "right" or the "righteous cause." For people seeking to follow Jesus and live according to an ethic of love, mercy, and justice that Jesus promoted, what does fully living into our humanity look like in relation to issues like these?

Certainly, as Luke encapsulates it in this parable, looking down on others, devaluing them, while at the same time being confident in our "rightness" is an indicator that we are off track. We all can examine our individual lives for that comparative impulse. We consider ways in which we measure ourselves and others against some standard that we have grabbed onto. And beyond just comparing ourselves, we can consider the extent to which our general approach to life may be one of competing with others. If competition and comparison is our approach then such dynamics are likely not only in play with those we are at odds with but also within our close friends and family relationships, at work, and in our community more generally. If we have in ourselves such feelings toward others, those feelings could serve as a clue that we might want to take a look at that approach to life and consider whether we may not have as firm a grasp on God's mercy as we thought. Or we may need to acknowledge that we accept it for ourselves but do not extend it as fully to others.

As a Sister of Mercy, Diane Guerin, RSM, has spent decades of her life not only serving others but actively working to improve structures and systems that impact the most vulnerable. She reflects honestly on this parable and her own struggle with her attitude toward others as she practices the works of mercy and advances these social justice issues. She explains,

> With over 40 years of ministry in justice, conflict resolution and race relations, it is easy for me to identify with the Pharisee. Indeed, the work focuses on righteousness and righteous indignation about inequities.

Chapter 7

> Experiences of opposition and adversity can spark self-righteousness. How can "they" not see this? What is wrong with "them?" Why are "they" so stubborn and unyielding?" Obviously, it is easy to fall into the trap that my view is the correct one.[34]

In the midst of such important social justice work, she sees the parable as a challenge and a reminder of the need of mercy that we all share. She also sees it as an invitation "to a deeper, more reflective stance and a realization of the universal need for mercy." In essence, to be open to learn from others with vastly different experiences and perspectives than ours. The Pharisee in the parable could benefit from being open to understanding the experience of the tax collector rather than dismissing him. He could also come to understand the degree to which they share a common humanity and both rely on God's mercy.

What actions are held up in this parable? Whether one reads this as an example story or a reversal story, it is likely that it serves both roles for Luke in his gospel. One scholar finds in Luke's parables in general patterns to imitate and patterns to avoid.[35] We can see both in this story. Acknowledgment of our shortcomings and our need for God's mercy are on display in the actions of the tax collector. Rather than clinging tightly to a notion that we can and do (or could and should) meet a standard that will justify us, we can let go of that and depend instead on the mercy of God. And we can do this right where we are at. The tax collector as a tax collector, both oppressed by the system and oppressing others, evidently received God's mercy in this scenario. Each of us, in our own social location, our multiple identities, oppressed, oppressing, even unaware of our complicity in oppressive systems, are candidates for divine mercy.

The above implications are centered on the individual—seeing ourselves individually in the two characters in this story. But as with the other parables there are also communal implications for those who embrace the love ethic of Jesus. On a group level sociologists have shown that humans have a natural bias toward "their" group and

---

[34] Diane Guerin, RSM, "The Pharisee and the Tax Collector," 2019. See her complete reflection in Appendix 1.
[35] Brobst-Renaud, *Lukan Parables*, 18.

The Pharisee and the Tax Collector (Luke 18:9–14)

against other groups. This is well documented and even shows up in experiments involving groups that are randomly assigned. How much more so might such a dynamic exist in groups with a history of division, conflict, or competition for resources. But how can we avoid falling into in-group and out-group dynamics? This parable with its surprise conclusion may at least suggest that as a starting point we should suspend judgment about groups of people, or types of people, that are different from us.

But this parable can take us a step further. If we go so far as to see the treasury of merit concept behind this parable, then we might once again reflect on the ways that our lives are truly interconnected. If the positive features of any one group can benefit the others in their areas of deficiency, then we could all recognize the extent to which we really do need each other for our collective well-being.

Emilie Townes gets at all of the above considerations in her important discussions of community and the common good. She writes,

> The common good calls us to think more deeply and strategically about our conceptions of community. Rather than see community as shaped solely by competition and domination, community can be a concrete site of strength and meaning making for engaged citizens. This understanding embraces individualism in the sense of encouraging self-definition and self-determination—but always in the context of the larger community as it joins other communities in defining and shaping the common good.[36]

Though not speaking specifically about this parable, it is clear that this parable is suggestive of each idea Townes presents. The parable supports revisiting our conception of community; eschewing competition in favor of connection; recognizing the value of each individual; and fostering a larger connection with other individuals in community for the benefit of all.

Dominic Crossan views parables as an ideal medium for communicating the paradigm shift that Jesus brought forward in his understanding of the kingdom of God. Townes likewise views the collaboration versus competition paradigm as a "conceptual shift," and what better

---

[36] Townes, *Womanist Ethics*, 137.

Chapter 7

way to get at such a shift than through a parable? With regard to this conceptual shift from competition to community Townes explains:

> Such an epistemological and conceptual shift requires that we recognize the ways in which each of us shifts from dominant to subordinate groups depending on time and circumstance. In doing so, we may then possibly see that from where we stand we have only a partial perspective on the world. As such, it is not for us to garner absolute truth, but to be in a process of radical engagement with each other as we participate, together, in constructing the common good.[37]

To apply this in relation to our parable, we might see that in the context of the parable both the Pharisee and the tax collector have only a partial perspective—one that they do not seem open to recognizing, although Jesus does. An alternative would be for them to recognize that reality, and to choose to engage with the other rather than judge from a distance, with the goal of helping to construct the common good—a more just and merciful world.

Sister Guerin gets at this concept by suggesting that honest reflection and communication are essential. She explains, "Failure to do so leads to escalating conflict, resulting in alienation and little or no mercy for opposing viewpoints. Perhaps, if these two men were able to speak with each other about their experiences, they would realize their commonalities." What would it take to enable them to make such a connection? Townes suggests that the ability to work together in this radical way on behalf of the common good requires "epistemological courage and theoethical fortitude."[38] The question is, do either or both in the parable have the courage and fortitude that Townes indicates is required for such a countercultural and counter-instinctual process? And today, do we? This approach defies the way in which the majority of us are socialized and enculturated to favor our own group, while dismissing others.

Former US surgeon general Vivek Murthy points to a fascinating concept that works against our ability to create a sense of belonging in which

---

[37] Townes, *Womanist Ethics*, 137.
[38] Townes, *Womanist Ethics*, 137.

The Pharisee and the Tax Collector (Luke 18:9–14)

we naturally accept and welcome people from groups other than out own. He explains that much of the contempt, anger, rage, and fear of those who disagree with us is "fueled by a cognitive bias called 'motive attribution asymmetry,' which tells us that our beliefs are grounded in love, while our opponents' are based on hatred."[39] This bias means that we attribute negative motives to our opponents when they choose a path or position that differs from ours. At the same time, we attribute positive intentions to the decisions and ideas of our own group. Apparently, this is only natural. To resist that impulse, however, takes courage along with intentionality. As for theoethical fortitude, the parables can be a resource that strengthens our commitment to the value of each person as a conviction that stems from an understanding of the divine and carries important ethical obligations. With such courage and fortitude, can we allow that the mercy of God extends to our cultural competitors just as we believe it extends to us? And can we then reorient our perspective to see that collectively we are stronger than individually?

We have noted racism as an issue that impacts human well-being and works against the kinds of connections in community that the kingdom of God promotes. Racism is one current challenge that seems to embody many of the dynamics we encounter in this parable, particularly the judging of others on the basis of external markers, and the inability to connect with them on a human level. Here we can turn to theologian and ethicist Bryan Massingale who helps readers think through the challenges inherent in overcoming the us-versus-them of racism and the lasting legacies of slavery. Massingale's understanding of racism and its impact can help us further consider how one group can be marginalized and discriminated against, and the negative effects of that evil. Massingale explains,

> The stain of racism in American society is our most perduring and intransigent social injustice. Further, one can argue that almost every major social question or phenomenon in the United States today—whether education, crime, health care, poverty—is entangled with, and/or exacerbated by, historic racial animus and present-day discrimination against people of color in general and African Americans in particular.[40]

---

[39] Murthy, *Together*, 139.
[40] Massingale, *Racial Justice*, 87.

Chapter 7

Massingale seeks to understand racism from a cultural framework, meaning that it is not simply one person's belief but rather a system that gives meaning and identity and that is often unconscious or preconscious. It is nonrational, in the sense that it operates at an emotional or visceral level, fostering positive and negative associations on the basis of skin color. Our parable of the Pharisee and the tax collector was not a parable about race or racism; but if we view racism through the lens of a cultural framework as Massingale does, then the link to our parable is not to the issue of race but the existence of a cultural framework that privileges some and excludes others.

In a North American context, racial injustice and systems that support racism (or grant or withhold social privileges on the basis of skin color) have the effect of creating whole communities who are not participating meaningfully or on equal footing within American society. In such a context, what can be done to undermine the lingering effects of this pernicious system—effects that continue even for those who believe wholeheartedly in equality, freedom, and justice as human rights for all persons?

Massingale points to racial reconciliation as one process that has the potential to get around the inherent animosity of whatever groups today embody the dynamics of prejudice and disdain. He explains,

> Racial reconciliation is not concerned with the elimination of racial differences, but rather the elimination of the stigma and privilege associated with race. Racial reconciliation, then, is the process of healing the estrangement, division, and hostility between racial groups by overturning or severing the linkage between race and social, cultural, and/or political subordination and dominance.[41]

This idea of healing the estrangement, overcoming the division, and eliminating the hostility is a powerful communal expression of seeking, finding, and restoring the lost. But overcoming the existing racial divides requires social transformation.[42]

Along these lines, in her book *The Sum of Us*, Heather McGhee looks at case study after case study where racist policies and practices harmed not only the people who were discriminated against, but also

---

[41] Massingale, *Racial Justice*, 93.
[42] Massingale, *Racial Justice*, 96.

226

The Pharisee and the Tax Collector (Luke 18:9–14)

the majority group.[43] Though not coming at the issue of racism and solidarity from an explicitly religious perspective, McGhee's illuminating analysis of the impacts of racism on both black and white Americans is very timely. Through careful analysis of key data points, interviews, and local investigation of both failures and successes in racial solidarity, McGhee shows three things. First, racism has negative impacts on more than just the victimized group; it also negatively impacts the majority white population as well, in demonstrable ways. One very poignant example is the community in St. Louis, Missouri, that chose to close its magnificent Fairground Park community pool rather than allow people of color to enjoy it. The decision negatively impacted residents of all races. This sad instance aligns with our understanding of the importance of attending to the interconnectedness of all things in this world. Second, she found that racism "works" in the United States through a flawed interpretation of reality she calls the "zero-sum" game. In this way of thinking, economic, social, and cultural resources are finite and when a racial group other than mine makes gains in their ability to access these resources, the "zero-sum" assumption is that it must have come at a loss to me and my group. McGhee shows that this is a way of thinking that is harmful, not true, and needs to be challenged by an alternate narrative. For our purposes, we may note that parables function in a similar way, to challenge an unrealized assumption through a story. Third, she proposes a better way for all which is based on multi-racial solidarity and results in what she calls the "solidarity dividend." This solidarity dividend is a benefit to all, and not at the expense of anyone. It is quite significant here that McGhee uses financial terms since those are the most directly measurable ways to show the impact of racism or the benefits of cross-racial solidarity movements. For our Pharisee and our tax collector, whose efforts both involve financial giving or receiving, as well as the metaphorical treasury of merit, the "solidarity dividend" is an interesting concept. In the metaphorical world of this parable the tax collector seems to have reaped such a benefit despite the Pharisee's intention to the contrary.

---

[43] Heather C. McGhee, *The Sum of Us: What Racism Costs Everyone and How We Can Prosper Together* (New York: One World, 2021).

Chapter 7

From different angles Massingale and McGhee both point to the benefit that could accrue to all members of society through racial reconciliation within communities that have suffered the negative impacts of racism and the zero-sum assumption. Yet the social transformation it requires is extremely complicated and fraught with difficulties. Massingale points to a model which involves four components, each of which is more difficult than the one before: recognition, responsibility, reconstruction, and reparation. Recognition stands first as it involves acknowledging the humanity of the other and the historical injustices that have occurred. Many Americans are wrestling with this component, and increasingly so since the murder of George Floyd in 2020 brought racism onto the screens of nearly every phone, tablet, TV, and computer in our country. Second, beyond recognition, responsibility entails understanding group agency for the harm, and taking on the obligation to address the harm. This is more challenging as systems of white supremacy include a wide range of tactics that enable white persons to claim they are not directly responsible for harms of the past, keeping them from seeing how complicity in systems of injustice is an ongoing manifestation of those harms. Third, along with recognition and responsibility, reconstruction is more challenging still as it moves toward processes that promote healing of the psychological and social wounds that have been inflicted. Fourth, reparation involves rectifying the material harms.[44]

In the above model with its four components, the first two can be grouped together under the broad category of "truth telling" and the second two under actions of "affirmative redress."[45] Truth telling, as simple as it sounds, is not just about acknowledging the past. It is also to acknowledge the truth of the impact of the past on the present: to acknowledge history along with its present-day consequences. For example, the intergenerational trauma and results of slavery for the black community are often simply unacknowledged by the majority white culture.[46] Yet, Massingale notes, "Facing history and ourselves, telling the truth of our situation, acknowledging our responsibility and our complicity, and declaring who profited and how from these

[44] Massingale, *Racial Justice*, 96–102.
[45] Massingale, *Racial Justice*, 97–102.
[46] See the extensive literature on the legacies of slavery at, for example, the CIC project: https://legaciesofslavery.net.

The Pharisee and the Tax Collector (Luke 18:9–14)

estrangements are essential to healing the wounds of racism."[47] Telling the truth has to do with being honest about who is lost—who is estranged, devalued, and disadvantaged by racist practices of the past which have continuing impact today—even if none of us think we hold racist beliefs. And while we may be firmly against antagonistic racism, we may be unknowingly benefiting from the privileges that come along with being white in a racist society. We may also be actively practicing a more subtle form of racism ourselves, whether it be "nice" racism or aversive racism which, while more subtle, fosters a preference for avoiding or limiting inter-racial engagement.

If the challenge of many of the parables is to recognize the inherent worth of every person, we have just discussed how racism and the legacies of systemic racism and systems of oppression work against the practical outworking of that belief in the lived experiences of people of color. If the vision of this and other parables is the recognition of the interconnectedness of all members of a society, with a goal of full restoration of human beings into rich, authentic community which fosters their growth toward self-actualization in line with their created purpose, we have seen that the legacies of racism work against that hope. What is needed is both a recognition of the inherent value of every person and collaborative and collective action to create conditions where every person is respected and valued and can become who they have the human potential to become.

The above analysis enables us to return to Jesus's message about the metaphorical kingdom of God—what it would be like if God were the one ruling. In addition to what we have already seen about the kingdom being present (it is to be enacted in the daily moments of our lives), collaborationist (we play a part, along with God), and nonviolent, this parable adds another: the kingdom is inclusive, not exclusive. The surprise assessment by Jesus of the tax collector as justified suggests that even a tax collector is not excluded from the vision of this kingdom. The kingdom is inclusive even of those who may seem like they are far from it. This is good news for those who for whatever reason have cause to feel far from valued by their community. It is also challenging news for those who feel they are included by virtue of their deserving it, in

---

[47] Massingale, *Racial Justice*, 100.

Chapter 7

contrast to their perceptions of others who should be excluded by virtue of their not deserving to be included.

Finally, salvation may be more complicated than we thought: so perhaps we should leave the judging to God. This would hold true also with respect to judging others we believe are racist or at least still complicit with racist systems. If I look down on you because you look down on others, well, I've fallen into the trap myself.

Works Cited in Chapter 7

Anderson, Gary A. *Charity: The Place of the Poor in the Biblical Tradition*. New Haven: Yale University, 2013.

Blomberg, Craig L. *Interpreting the Parables*. Second ed. Downers Grove, IL: IVP Academic, 2012.

Brobst-Renaud, Amanda. *Lukan Parables of Reckless Liberality*. Vol. 42, New Testament Monographs. Sheffield: Sheffield Phoenix, 2021.

Cone, James H. *A Black Theology of Liberation*. 20th anniversary ed. Maryknoll, NY: Orbis Books, 1990.

Crossan, John Dominic. *The Power of Parable: How Fiction by Jesus Became Fiction about Jesus*. New York: HarperOne, 2012.

Doran, Robert. "The Pharisee and the Tax Collector: An Agonistic Story." *Catholic Biblical Quarterly* 69, no. 2 (2007): 259–270.

Friedrichsen, Timothy A. "The Temple, a Pharisee, a Tax Collector, and the Kingdom of God: Rereading a Jesus Parable (Luke 18:10–14a)." *Journal of Biblical Literature* 124 (2005): 89–119.

Guerin, Diane, RSM. "The Pharisee and the Tax Collector." 2019.

Herzog, William R. *Parables as Subversive Speech: Jesus as Pedagogue of the Oppressed*. Louisville, KY: Westminster/John Knox, 1994.

Hultgren, Arland J. *The Parables of Jesus: A Commentary*. The Bible in its World. Grand Rapids: Eerdmans, 2000.

Levine, Amy-Jill. *Short Stories by Jesus: The Enigmatic Parables of a Controversial Rabbi*. New York: HarperOne, 2014.

Massingale, Bryan N. *Racial Justice and the Catholic Church*. Maryknoll, NY: Orbis Books, 2010.

McGhee, Heather C. *The Sum of Us: What Racism Costs Everyone and How We Can Prosper Together*. New York: One World, 2021.

Murthy, Vivek H. *Together: The Healing Power of Human Connection in a Sometimes Lonely World*. New York, NY: Harper Wave, an imprint of HarperCollins, 2020.

The Pharisee and the Tax Collector (Luke 18:9–14)

Schottroff, Luise. *The Parables of Jesus*. Minneapolis: Fortress, 2006.

Sievers, Joseph and Amy-Jill Levine. *The Pharisees*. Grand Rapids, MI: Eerdmans, 2021.

Snodgrass, Klyne. *Stories with Intent: A Comprehensive Guide to the Parables of Jesus*. Second ed. Grand Rapids: Eerdmans, 2018.

Townes, Emilie Maureen. *Womanist Ethics and the Cultural Production of Evil*. Black religion, womanist thought, social justice. New York: Palgrave Macmillan, 2006.

Willis, Lawrence M. . "Methodological Reflections on the Tax Collectors in the Gospels," Pages 251–268 in *When Judaism and Christianity Began: Essays in Memory of Anthony J. Saldarini*. Edited by Anthony J. Saldarini, Alan J. Avery-Peck, Daniel J. Harrington, and Jacob Neusner. Vol. 85 of *Supplements to the Journal for the Study of Judaism*. Leiden; Boston: Brill, 2004.

Yinger, Kent L. and Craig A. Evans. *The Pharisees: Their History, Character, and New Testament Portrait*. Eugene, OR: Cascade Books, 2022.

8

The Laborers in the Vineyard (Matthew 20:1–16)

1. Introduction

With the parable of the laborers in the vineyard we encounter yet another interesting facet of the agrarian economy of ancient Judaea. In this setting we will see day laborers who depend on being hired, and a landowner who is need of day laborers to bring in his harvest. We will also see what happens when some work the whole day and some only work part of the day. A twist occurs when it is time for them all to be paid, and the landowner takes a surprising approach to paying them. As a kingdom parable—one that explicitly uses an earthly narrative to disclose something about the kingdom of heaven—we are invited to consider how this short story reveals something about what it would be like if God were ruling here on earth.[1]

---

[1] For background information and commentary see Hultgren, *Parables of Jesus*, 33–46; Snodgrass, *Stories with Intent*, 362–379; Blomberg, *Interpreting the Parables*, 281–288; Herzog, *Parables as Subversive Speech*, 79–97; Levine, *Short Stories*, 213–237.

Social Justice in the Stories of Jesus: The Ethical Challenge of the Parables, First Edition. Matthew E. Gordley.
© 2024 John Wiley & Sons Ltd. Published 2024 by John Wiley & Sons Ltd.

The Laborers in the Vineyard (Matthew 20:1–16)

2. The Text: The Laborers in the Vineyard (Matthew 20:1–16)

"For the kingdom of heaven is like a landowner who went out early in the morning to hire laborers for his vineyard. After agreeing with the laborers for the usual daily wage, he sent them into his vineyard. When he went out about nine o'clock, he saw others standing idle in the marketplace; and he said to them, 'You also go into the vineyard, and I will pay you whatever is right.' So they went. When he went out again about noon and about three o'clock, he did the same. And about five o'clock he went out and found others standing around; and he said to them, 'Why are you standing here idle all day?' They said to him, 'Because no one has hired us.' He said to them, 'You also go into the vineyard.' When evening came, the owner of the vineyard said to his manager, 'Call the laborers and give them their pay, beginning with the last and then going to the first.' When those hired about five o'clock came, each of them received the usual daily wage. Now when the first came, they thought they would receive more; but each of them also received the usual daily wage. And when they received it, they grumbled against the landowner, saying, 'These last worked only one hour, and you have made them equal to us who have borne the burden of the day and the scorching heat.' But he replied to one of them, 'Friend, I am doing you no wrong; did you not agree with me for the usual daily wage? Take what belongs to you and go; I choose to give to this last the same as I give to you. Am I not allowed to do what I choose with what belongs to me? Or are you envious because I am generous?' So the last will be first, and the first will be last." (Matthew 20:1–16 NRSV)

3. Our First Step: Grasp the Story

For those familiar with this parable, this is one that can be difficult to hear with "fresh ears." Since it is a kingdom parable, beginning with "the kingdom of heaven is like," readers in the Christian tradition might automatically begin the process of replacing characters and concrete elements of the parable with spiritual realities associated with the kingdom. With an allegorical reading, for example, it is easy to assume

Chapter 8

that the landowner must represent God, the vineyard might represent God's kingdom, and the workers would represent people who come into the kingdom (i.e., become followers of God or followers of Jesus) at different times. If those identifications are correct then the day's wage would be the reward for serving in the kingdom; presumably, eternal life.[2] While the instinct to apply this in a spiritual way is not entirely wrong, and certainly not out of line with centuries of interpretation, it is also not entirely right. As we have seen, parables are generally metaphors, not allegories. For the metaphors to perform their creative work most effectively readers need first to understand the concrete reality of the parable as meaning what it actually says, and then something more. We have talked about this interpretive process in terms of grappling with the in-meaning and the through-meaning of aesthetic works including visual and literary art. In this case the concrete realities of the in-meaning are related to harvesting, wages, landowners, and laborers in a first-century agrarian economy. To really grasp the parable we need to sit with the concrete realities first. It is to the concrete details that we now turn.

This story is oriented around a landowner who hires laborers to work in his vineyard for the day. Five times during the day the landowner goes to the marketplace in town and finds laborers available to work. The group hired first agrees to work for "the usual daily wage"—a denarius—while the other groups hired later in the day agree to work for "whatever is right." Interestingly, the specific amount of their pay is not mentioned; it is only agreed that it will be *dikaios*, which means just, fair, or right. The last group, hired at five o'clock has a brief dialogue with the landowner who asks why they are standing there idle, and they explain that it is simply because no one has hired them. Then he sends them to work too. At the end of the day, when it is time for the wages to be paid, the landowner sets up an interesting scenario: he instructs the manager to pay first the ones hired last, apparently so that all may see. To the surprise of everyone, he pays those hired last not a fractional rate but a full day's wage. This is indeed a surprise since they

---

[2] Snodgrass, *Stories with Intent*, 370–371, 373; Levine, *Short Stories*, 216–218. See also Ernest Van Eck and John S. Kloppenborg, *The Parables of Jesus the Galilean: Stories of a Social Prophet* (Matrix–The Bible in Mediterranean Context; vol. 9; Eugene, OR: Cascade Books, 2016), 141–142.

The Laborers in the Vineyard (Matthew 20:1–16)

worked only part of the day and this was the amount he promised to those hired first. Seeing this generosity on the part of the landowner, those hired first then expect that, having worked longer, they will receive even more. Of course, they are deeply disappointed and even offended when they also receive only the same amount: the usual daily wage which they were originally promised—and no more.

The ones hired first and paid last grumble against the landowner, complaining that they worked the whole day while others worked only an hour. They claim it is unfair that, in essence, the owner has declared them all equal, while in reality the work they did was far from equal. In response the landowner explains to one of them his perspective. The owner's response is noteworthy since it ends the parable. First, he claims he is not doing any wrong to the worker. He asks rhetorically, did you not agree to the usual daily wage? With this he suggests, in effect, "We had a deal and I honored it." Second, he makes the point that he is allowed to do what he wants with his possessions; just as the workers are. Third, his response includes a turn to the laborer to examine the negative feelings that have arisen. He asks him, "Or are you envious because I am generous?" With this the landowner not only paints the worker in a negative light as envious, but he also paints himself in a positive light as generous, which is how he wants his action to be understood. And this is the final word of the dialogue (more of a monologue, really) as there is no response by the complaining laborer. The parable then ends with a parenthetical comment, perhaps by Jesus or perhaps added by the author of this gospel, giving Matthew's understanding of the point: So the last will be first, and the first will be last.

4. Our Second Step: Ask Questions to Gain Understanding

There are many directions we could go in asking questions of this provocative parable. As in other parables set in unfamiliar social scenes like this, we do well to ask about the social dynamics that are reflected here. We have noted numerous times the importance of understanding the social and power dynamics reflected in the relationships of the characters within the parables. As we have seen, the listening audience would be well familiar with these characters. They would recognize

Chapter 8

them as known "types" inhabiting a particular world—their world. Herzog notes, "Because the parables are full of typifications, their seemingly unique scenes and individual characters actually imply a social construction of reality in which people interact in typical ways. Even the characters found in the parables are not individuals but socially recognizable types who stand in for larger social groups."[3] We have also noted the stratification of ancient agrarian societies into a small elite class (consisting of the ruler, the bureaucrats, the retainers) and a large peasant class. So where do our landowner and laborers fit on this spectrum? What should we know in order to more fully appreciate the parable?

The landowner is an *anthropos oikodespotes*, Greek for master of the house, also translated as "householder." Later in 20:8 he is referred to as *o kurios tou ampelonos*, the lord of the vineyard. Such a general figure is common in the Gospels with ten of twelve references occurring in parables such as the weeds among the wheat (Matt. 13:24–30), treasures old and new (Matt. 13:51–53), and the wicked tenants (Matt. 21:33–46). In four instances, including here in Matthew 20, the householder is also referred to as a lord. The references are mostly positive or neutral; none seem to paint a householder in a particularly negative light.

Moving beyond the biblical references, from an historical and social lens we know that many landowners in this time were not part of the local community but lived far away and maintained these lands as part of their investments. They thus depended on local labor, including day laborers as well as stewards and managers, to generate the value they needed from their holdings. The landowner in our parable clearly has a manager who is presumably quite capable of facilitating the harvest and handling the finance. In this light it is somewhat surprising for the landowner to be so directly involved in the harvest, both in recruiting workers throughout the day and in directing the distribution of wages. His physical presence is suggestive of some level of anxiety about the whole operation. Furthermore, his recurring trips to the market for additional workers suggest that he has an extremely large harvest that even he was unable to estimate correctly. In this way, he could be a person of exceptional landholdings and exceptional wealth.[4] As we will see, his

[3] Herzog, *Parables as Subversive Speech*, 54.
[4] Herzog, *Parables as Subversive Speech*, 84–88.

The Laborers in the Vineyard (Matthew 20:1–16)

ultimate plan may indicate an intention to establish a more permanent relationship with some of these workers than simply a one-day job.[5]

The laborers are *ergates*, a general Greek term for anyone engaged in physical labor. This term can be used for any kind of physical labor but is prominent in reference to agricultural laborers. Like the master of the house this term does not have negative associations. Jesus used the term both literally and metaphorically, but almost always used the term in this sense of agricultural laborers. Other early Christian writers used the term this way as well, including James who explicitly noted the injustice toward laborers who were not being paid by the wealthy. James 5:4 is an exhortation for the wealthy to repent of their injustice: "Listen! The wages of the laborers who mowed your fields, which you kept back by fraud, cry out, and the cries of the harvesters have reached the ears of the Lord of hosts." This is not quite the same as the situation in the parable since the laborers in the parable do receive their wages, while the laborers in James are not even getting paid. What is common to both passages though is that James is pointing to a familiar dynamic in which laborers work in a manual labor role for the wealthy and have concerns about the receipt of their wages.

The position of laborers in the first-century economy was apparently a difficult one. Jesus himself said elsewhere that "laborers deserve their food" (Matt. 10:10) and "laborers deserve to be paid" (Lk 10:7). If payment of hired labor was *not* a concern, one wonders why he would even mention things of that nature. The Apostle Paul a generation later cites the same tradition Jesus used noting, "The laborer deserves to be paid" (1 Tim 5:18). Jewish writer Ben Sira, a century earlier, urged readers: "Do not abuse slaves who work faithfully, or hired laborers who devote themselves to their task" (Sir 7:20). The principle of just and timely wages is supported by appeal to the Jewish scriptures as well (cf. Num. 18:30–32).

The importance of laborers receiving their pay—and that it is sometimes withheld by the wealthy as an act of injustice—is indicative of the precarious position of day laborers within society. These were among the lowest classes, the "expendables," and the system did not enable them to build up large reserves or create social mobility.[6] The

---

[5] Van Eck and Kloppenborg, *Parables of Jesus*, 159.

[6] Herzog, *Parables as Subversive Speech*.

Chapter 8

parable of the lost coin also illustrates just how significant (and limited) cash reserves were in the rural agrarian economy. As we saw, finding one lost coin was cause for a communal celebration (Luke 15:8–9). Accordingly, we can see that the issue of the usual wage is a critical one.

The "usual daily wage" here, the denarius, is a Roman silver coin similar in value to the drachma which was the focus of the parable of the lost coin (Luke 15:8). The term occurs fifteen times in the Gospels, often in parables, but also in conversation with Jesus about taxes, about the ability of the disciples to buy food for a crowd, or the exorbitant cost of perfume used to anoint Jesus's feet that Judas argued could have been sold and the money given to the poor. Whether for landowners or workers, their denarii were important to them! Whether this "usual daily wage" was sufficient to sustain a family—or even a life—is debated. Given the uncertainty of daily work and the inability to build up reserves, the fact that a denarius would buy food for three to five days may not be sufficient. The result is that, in addition to the work of a male day-laborer, his wife and children (who, we may note, are not even on the horizon in this androcentric account) would also have to supplement that income through their own labor and resourcefulness.[7]

Finally, we should note the importance of this drama occurring in a vineyard. Vineyards are the setting of four different parables, one of which is found in each of the Synoptic Gospels (the parable of the wicked tenants, cf. Matt. 21:33–43). We will explore the vineyard concept further below when we engage more fully with the metaphor. Here we simply note it as indicative of a feature of the agrarian economy of ancient Judaea/Palestine.

5. Our Third Step: Spot the Twist

As we turn to consider the twist in this parable we can see there are a number of oddities. For example, the landowner seems very involved in the operation of his vineyard, much more than would be typical. He is wealthy enough to have a manager (who distributes the wages),

---

[7] On the possibility that the usual day's wage was exploitative, see Schottroff, *Parables*, 211–212; Herzog, *Parables as Subversive Speech*, 89–90.

The Laborers in the Vineyard (Matthew 20:1–16)

yet he is the one who continuously goes out to recruit laborers himself, even late into the afternoon. Further, he is there at the end of the day to direct the distribution of the wages as well as to engage with the disgruntled laborers afterward. Drawing on the documentary evidence about landowners and day laborers in antiquity, Van Eck points out that although these are odd behaviors for a landowner, they are not unrealistic in the sense that they could never happen.[8] Thus, Van Eck suggests, this parable includes "a combination of verisimilitude and unusual features" which is typical of the parables. Parables often include "a story that is realistic, if somewhat unusual, and deliberately invoke certain cultural scripts of beliefs about the world. Then it challenges or problematizes those scripts and beliefs through an unexpected narrative turn."[9]

In this case, these oddities also appear to be necessary to set up what is likely the ultimate twist in this parable which occurs at the end of the day when the manager pays the workers:

> When evening came, the owner of the vineyard said to his manager, 'Call the laborers and give them their pay, beginning with the last and then going to the first.' (v. 8)

We begin to be surprised in the order of the paying out, that those hired last would be paid first. Only in hindsight do we see that this was important so that those hired first could observe the pay of those hired last. But what is even more surprising is that those hired last received a full denarius, even though they worked only an hour.

> When those hired about five o'clock came, each of them received the usual daily wage. (v. 9)

This act of generosity sets up the final twist creating the expectation among those hired first that they would receive even more. The final surprise is that they only received the same amount: the amount originally agreed upon.

---

[8] Van Eck and Kloppenborg, *Parables of Jesus*, 146–152.
[9] Van Eck and Kloppenborg, *Parables of Jesus*, 152.

Chapter 8

> Now when the first came, they thought they would receive more; but each of them also received the usual daily wage. (v. 10)

This seems to be the crux of the matter and the surprise of the parable.

Nevertheless, the parable continues beyond this surprising moment. Verses 11–12 recount the grumbling of those hired first against the landowner. Verses 13–15 recount the landowner's response to one of them. And verse 16 provides a summary statement. As important as this dialogue is for understanding the parable, the twist seems to be in the amount paid to each group. The further dialogue serves to elucidate some of the dynamics that result from that moment of surprise—a surprise for both the characters in the narrative and the earliest listeners to the parable.

6. Our Fourth Step: Consider the Metaphor

As a parable explicitly about the kingdom it is easy to see a parable about a vineyard as delivering a spiritual message.[10] And spiritual interpretations have been the norm historically for this parable. As suggested above, such interpretations would see this parable as not ultimately about a landowner and laborers and wages but rather about salvation: The landowner (God) hires laborers (invites followers) into his vineyard (the kingdom); some come into the kingdom earlier, some later, but all receive the same full reward of a day's wage (perhaps eternal life or a place in heaven). This might make some people grumble (especially those who came into the kingdom earlier), but God is generous and has every right to be generous, even to those who may have spent long years outside the kingdom and only came in at the last hour. The simple, spiritual conclusion would be that all persons of faith should welcome others into the kingdom at any time, just as God does.

One not uncommon embodiment of this approach holds that those who were the first to be called represent the Jews, God's chosen people

---

[10] This section adapted from Matthew E. Gordley, "Parables and the Principle of Mercy: Reading Parables Alongside the Work of Jon Sobrino in a First-Year College Course," *Journal of Catholic Higher Education* 39 (2020): 15–36.

The Laborers in the Vineyard (Matthew 20:1–16)

who were chosen earlier in the history of salvation (i.e., the history of God's redemptive work in the world prior to Jesus). The first hired claim to have born the burden of the day which, in a spiritualizing interpretation is commonly equated with bearing the "burden" of the Jewish Law. Those hired later in the day are, possibly, the Gentiles (i.e., non-Jews) who in the historical experience of salvation through Jesus are late to the game in turning to the one true God but still receive all the benefits of being part of the kingdom. In this line of interpretation the ones who grumble are thus the Jews who are upset at the fact that Gentiles have been granted equal status to them in the kingdom. A similar but slightly different interpretation is that those bearing the burden of the day are the Pharisees of Jesus's day and those coming in late are the tax collectors and sinners. Those who have lived by the law grumble at the grace shown to those who have not worked for it as they have.[11]

The trouble with these spiritualizing interpretations is that there is very little basis in the parable itself for such interpretations. In fact, three observations make such spiritual interpretations unlikely. To begin with, when Jesus first told the parable there were no Gentiles coming into the kingdom, so telling a parable with that point would have made no sense to his listeners; if that was his point, it would have gone right over their heads. Second, there is nothing in the text to suggest any kind of moral deficiency in those hired later; nothing to connect them to the "tax collectors and sinners" referred to elsewhere in the gospels (cf. Luke 5:29–30). Nothing in the parable suggests that they were sleeping in after a late night of revelry or were too lazy to get to the square first thing in the morning. When the landowner asks why they are not working, they simply reply that no one has hired them yet (v. 7). Third, as happens with the Good Samaritan, these kinds of interpretations reflect an implicit (or explicit) anti-Judaism, assuming that Jesus is using the Judaism of his day as a negative contrast for a more generous, grace-filled, and superior Christianity. Levine rightly points out that such an anti-Jewish message is unlikely coming from Jesus to a Jewish audience: "Once Jewish Law becomes equated with 'bearing the burden of the day and the scorching heat,' we are no longer listening to

---

[11] Levine reviews these and similar interpretations in Levine, *Short Stories*, 216–218.

Chapter 8

the Jewish Jesus talking to fellow Jews. When Jewish practice or Jewish society becomes the negative foil to Jesus or the church, we do well to reread the parable."[12] Today more than ever, we all must recognize and resist such readings. On the one hand, they are a distortion of the reality of the first century when Jesus was teaching, and that can have dangerous consequences. On the other hand, if we do go down that interpretive path, then we are actually missing out on discovering the real challenge of the parable.[13]

Another option for interpretation is to take the metaphor itself as suggesting the way in which it may relate to the kingdom. If we take the metaphor seriously, we note that there are several relevant angles. First, there is the concrete reality of people making a living in the agrarian economy of ancient Judaea. The vineyard is part of a larger system which includes the land, the landowner, and the laborers who work the land, as well as the ruling authorities which require taxes from the land and its produce. Second, there is a rich scriptural background in which God's people are described using imagery of a vine which God planted and cultivated. Third, Jesus uses the image of a vineyard several times within his teaching, including in other parables. These threads weave together to generate the surprising impact of the use of vineyard imagery in this particular parable.

Of importance here is the clear emphasis on what is just, fair, equitable, and what is generous versus what is harmful. Interestingly, while the landowner paid a fair wage to all, and was generous to those who only started working late in the day, those who worked the whole day and received a fair wage experienced the generosity to others as harm—even though they had been treated fairly according to what had been agreed on. We can consider here that what the landowner perceived as generosity some of the laborers perceived as an injustice toward them.

One way of understanding this incongruity is to consider the positions of each of these individuals within the agrarian economy of the

---

[12] Levine, *Short Stories*, 228.

[13] We can add another problem with such a reading: The impulse to move immediately to an allegorical interpretation, where each item in the story symbolizes something else, actually misses out on the more challenging role of parables where it is often the whole story that makes the point.

The Laborers in the Vineyard (Matthew 20:1–16)

first century. First, while the usual daily wage is customary, it is difficult for us to be able to say that it was actually just; it was simply the common practice. But how much power did day laborers have to negotiate a better wage?[14]

Second, an important feature of ancient life in such a context was the patron–client relationship. In a society with few other forms of social security, a special relationship of reciprocal responsibility could be established whereby the patron provided benefactions to the client, and the client served the needs of the patron. Such a relationship was more than a contract for a day's work for a day's wage. It involved a more lasting set of obligations.[15] The act of paying more than was expected to those hired later in the day—an unexpected material kindness—was not only generous but could have been an indication that the landowner was acting as a patron to those individuals and establishing or confirming a special relationship with them. Such a relationship would be ongoing and entail the promise of future exchanges, something the landowner would need especially given his remote status. Van Eck explains, "One of the salient features of patron-client relationships was that it entailed a long-range social-interpersonal obligation, which included a strong element of solidarity that was sealed by exchange, couched in terms of interpersonal loyalty."[16] It may be this kind of relationship the landowner was establishing here.

Third, in the case of those who worked the full day and received the full wage, there would not necessarily be any special patron–client relationship being established. With a clear agreement to work one day for one day's wage, both parties fulfilled their obligation

---

[14] Herzog, *Parables as Subversive Speech*, 90.

[15] Elliott explains, "In general, the relationship is one of personal loyalty and commitment (*fides*) of some duration entered into voluntarily by two or more individuals of unequal status. It is based on differences in social roles and access to power, and involves the reciprocal exchange of different kinds of goods and services of value to each partner" (148). For a fuller description of the patron–client relationship in the Roman era see John H. Elliott, "Patronage and Clientage," in *The Social Sciences and New Testament Interpretation* (ed. Rohrbaugh; Peabody, MA: Hendrickson, 1996), 144–158.

[16] Van Eck and Kloppenborg, *Parables of Jesus*, 155. Similarly, Elliott explains that his kind of relationship entails "a strong element of solidarity linked to personal honor and obligations [that] is informed by the values of friendship, loyalty, and fidelity." Elliott, "Patronage," 149.

Chapter 8

and no more would be expected. So the grumbling of those who worked the full day may be not only that they did not receive more than those who worked a partial day, but also that they were not beneficiaries of the patron–client relationship that was established with the others.[17]

In such a setting, we can see that this parable presents some complex dynamics between a wealthy landowner and day laborers. The challenge then may not be about entering into a spiritual kingdom, but rather the relational dynamics related to social class, labor, and daily wages. Michael Cook expands on this thought: "The parable is a challenge to those who control the resources of society to give priority to fundamental human needs; but it is also a challenge to all of us, rich and poor alike, to overcome the competitiveness into which we have been socialized."[18] He adds, "In the kingdom of God, competitiveness and jealousy give way to concern for the basic needs of each one, and this most fundamentally on the level of simple economic need."[19]

Noting that the metaphor of a vineyard also relates to Israel in the collective imagination of first-century Jews gives us yet another angle for consideration. Within that metaphorical possibility this parable shows that attending to the needs of workers in the community is a practice that ought to be cultivated among God's chosen people. Rather than promoting abstract values for a future and other-worldly "kingdom of heaven," this parable is rooted in social relationships in an earthly context. If such a vineyard scene points in some way to God's rule on earth, then it is perhaps the values of reciprocity and solidarity on display that are where the metaphor joins its imaginary narrative to the real world.

As with the original hearers of this parable, few readers of the parables today are landowners in the first-century sense of the term. But today's readers can begin to ask in what aspects of their lives they may have the ability to influence others, to act in solidarity, to uphold human dignity and to challenge values of greed and competition. We today might ask where we are able to act with concern for those in need and

---

[17] Van Eck and Kloppenborg, *Parables of Jesus*, 155.

[18] Cook, "Jesus' Parables," 25–26.

[19] Cook, "Jesus' Parables," 26.

The Laborers in the Vineyard (Matthew 20:1–16)

support human dignity in our communities. And with questions like these we are in a position to move on to articulate the challenge of this parable.

7. Our Fifth Step: Articulate the Challenge

On a spiritual level, we can agree with those who articulate the challenge of this parable as recognizing that all are beneficiaries of God's generous mercy. God, like the landowner, is generous to all in the kingdom. And humans are challenged to accept that generous mercy for their estimation of themselves and of others. In this way, the generosity of the landowner illustrates the generosity of God to all.[20]

But if we take seriously the concrete circumstances of the parable as part of the meaning, we can articulate an additional challenge: to extend the generous mercy of God to others within the concrete reality of one's earthly sphere of influence. Thus, while interpreters are quick to point out that the landowner's action is not an economic prescription by Jesus about labor, we nevertheless do need to consider that it is one example of surprising and impactful generosity lived out in a particular social context. In this way, the parable is more than illustration to explain a heavenly reality; it is also an example of how the kingdom is enacted in concrete earthly circumstances.

Another way to put this is to say that if readers really embrace the generous mercy of God for themselves as a spiritual reality, they can recognize that Jesus invites them to also embody that generous mercy toward others. By acting with generous mercy (like the landowner did; like God does) one not only accepts the idea that God's mercy is for all, but also tangibly makes manifest that reality in the sphere of this life in which they have influence. For a landowner dependent on day laborers and cognizant of the challenges and limitations of their existence, a full day's wage paid to each laborer may be seen as a life sustaining act that defies expectation and goes above and beyond customary obligations. On the other hand, from our contemporary vantage point we may also wonder if this action had any real lasting impact on the social situation of these impoverished day laborers. If modern economic and social

---

[20] Hultgren, *Parables of Jesus*, 43.

245

Chapter 8

analysis regards the first-century agrarian economy as oppressive, then it was not individual acts of generosity that were needed but systemic change. Yet the reality is that the thought of overturning or even reforming such a system surely was not even a consideration for the landowner, let alone for the day laborers.[21] However, with this paying of a full day's wage to those who did not have the opportunity to work a full day, the landowner was taking at least one action that was available to him to support human dignity and the well-being of others.

But the parable also illuminates a problem with this kind of generosity. It elicits a negative response from some members of the community who grumble that those who worked less are considered equal with them in terms of their wage. And this conflict within the parable suggests an additional challenge: to embrace the counter-cultural value system of the kingdom. It turns out that this kingdom value system, as we have seen in other parables, may differ considerably from the competitive value system within which many of us are socialized and which often prevails. This insight leads to an important question: To what extent should a person's provision within the community be dependent on their contribution, or to what extent does their membership in the community give them an inherent right to sustaining resources?

Jon Sobrino and Ignacio Ellacuría

One way of exploring the values that Jesus is promoting with his metaphorical vision of the kingdom is to return to the work of Jon Sobrino. Sobrino borrows from his own mentor, Ignacio Ellacuría, the concept of a "civilization of poverty"—positively conceived—in contrast to a "civilization of wealth." The latter mindset arguably dominates the Western capitalist world and values individual achievement, competition, and the accumulation and enjoyment of wealth as the basis of the ideal life. By contrast the civilization of poverty rejects the individual possession and enjoyment of wealth as the basis of humanization and replaces those with "universal satisfaction of basic needs" and makes

---

[21] Van Eck points out that, while there was critique of individual wealth, greed, and exploitation, systemic critique did not necessarily exist in the first-century world: "the systemic critiques are absent because the conceptual frameworks to support such critiques were yet to be invented." Van Eck and Kloppenborg, *Parables of Jesus*, 143.

The Laborers in the Vineyard (Matthew 20:1–16)

"the growth of shared solidarity the basis of humanization."[22] Citing Ellacuría, Sobrino discusses how "strengthen[ing] 'shared solidarity [is] a fundamental characteristic of the civilization of poverty, in contrast to the closed and competitive individualism of the civilization of wealth.'"[23] In this way, Sobrino draws attention to the kind of spirit that informs a new civilization.

In a similar vein Brooks Harrington has pointed to a sharp contrast between the values of the United States and those embodied in the parables. From his years of experience as a criminal prosecutor as well as a victim's advocate he articulates what he calls the dominant narrative of our society regarding justice and mercy as contradictory of one another.[24] If justice relates to what one is due, then in America the focus has been on getting one's due with the assumption that if one works hard one can acquire possessions, prestige, and power. But the assumption does not hold for those born into poverty and oppression. Harrington explains, "The claim that anyone can make his or her way out of poverty today with hard work is a lie."[25] Harrington provides many heartbreaking stories of individuals for whom the system was literally working against them from day one. In contrast to the dominant narrative of justice and mercy being in contradiction to one another, Harrington suggests that the parables offer a counter-narrative of love, mercy, and justice as interconnected. This counter-narrative is one that involves supportive community and mutual commitment to the good of one another.

In the kingdom that Jesus proclaimed—the new age—values like these would inform human interaction. It is this spirit of generosity, of shared solidarity, that the landowner in our parable shows. His action is unexpected and does not necessarily make sense in a competitive society where some have more and many have much less. However, his action does allow everyone to work and have dignity while earning enough to support their families. His action may also ultimately create

---

[22] Jon Sobrino, *No Salvation Outside the Poor: Prophetic-Utopian Essays* (Maryknoll, N.Y.: Orbis Books, 2008), 14.

[23] Sobrino, *No Salvation Outside the Poor*, 14. Here, citing Ignacio Ellacuría, "El Reino de Dios y el Paro en el Tercer Mundo," *Concilium* 180 (1982): 595.

[24] See Chapter 5, "Justice and Mercy under the Narrative of America," 39–47 in Harrington and Holbert, *No Mercy, No Justice*.

[25] Harrington and Holbert, *No Mercy, No Justice*, 45. See also 46–47; 249–253.

Chapter 8

a better social climate for all concerned, including the landowner himself. What makes the parable so surprising is that it is unusual for a landowner to display this kind of generosity. For a landowner to display this kind of generosity requires a different value system, the spirit of the kingdom, which this landowner apparently has. Conversely, it is also this spirit that the grumbling and envious laborers struggle to embrace. They seemingly have internalized the values of competition and scarcity rather than the kingdom values of collaboration and solidarity.[26]

Helping us move further along these lines is Mary Kay Dobrovolny, RSM. She reads this parable as a challenge to see the needs of the community differently and also to rejoice with others' good fortune as they experience God's generosity.[27] In this way we can consider the values that are promoted by the parable.

With this turn to the values Jesus's parable promotes, the challenge is then threefold: accept the generous mercy of God toward all (including ourselves and others we think are "less deserving" for whatever reason); consider where we can extend that same generous mercy to others within our sphere of influence; examine our values relative to competition and collaboration in order to develop the spirit of the kingdom that will undergird our actions of generosity in this present world. For each of us in our lives, what kinds of generous mercy would become possible if we embraced a value structure more in line with the civilization of poverty than the civilization of wealth?

8. Our Sixth Step: Consider Implications

While all people can extend mercy in many areas to people around them, one important implication of this parable is related to the notion of solidarity with the poor. The economically poor are often those

---

[26] Here we can consider Gutiérrez's discussions of the threefold aspect of liberation: social, personal, and liberation from sin. The grumbling perhaps suggests that liberation is certainly needed in the personal dimension for the kingdom to be enacted. See Gustavo Gutiérrez, *A Theology of Liberation: History, Politics, and Salvation* (Maryknoll, N.Y.: Orbis Books, 1988), xxxviii.

[27] Mary Kay Dobrovolny, RSM, "The Laborers in the Vineyard," 2019. See her complete reflection in Appendix 1.

248

The Laborers in the Vineyard (Matthew 20:1–16)

whose human dignity and freedom to make a range of choices about their lives are compromised in significant ways by the circumstances of their birth (not of their choosing) or the explicit decisions of others with power (also not of their choosing).

Catholic Social Teaching includes a tradition of reflection on issues of economic injustice along with its roots. Pope Francis, in particular, has taken up this tradition and raised awareness of its implications in today's global economy. In *Mercy in Action: The Social Teaching of Pope Francis*, Thomas Massaro reviews the pope's teaching and finds a proposed solution to economic injustice: recognizing human dignity and basic human rights, promoting solidarity, and working for the common good. "The key principles at stake in our judgments about any economic reality relate to human dignity and the optimal way to protect it. All people should continue to enjoy the right to obtain and make good use of private property; citizens should retain the full range of civil liberties; families should continue to enjoy the ability to determine the course of their lives."[28] With this focus on human dignity and the well-being of each person, Massaro moves to focus on the common good as central: "The premier Christian theological principle that helps us sort out all our claims and judgments regarding equality and inequality is the notion of the common good."[29] The common good invites a focus on "the promotion of mutual gains and the fostering of favorable conditions for a shared life together that allows all to thrive."[30]

As a part of addressing economic inequities and injustices in the world, working for labor justice could be a major driving force. Massaro notes, "If Francis offers one top recommendation regarding the strengthening of that process [i.e. addressing the inequities in the global economy], it would be the development of solidarity across all lines of demography, religion, and profession."[31] But it is important to recognize that solidarity is not simply a feeling of camaraderie or goodwill that happens naturally. Massaro explains,

---

[28] Thomas Massaro, *Mercy in Action: The Social Teachings of Pope Francis* (Lanham: Rowman & Littlefield, 2018), 34.
[29] Massaro, *Mercy in Action*, 38.
[30] Massaro, *Mercy in Action*, 38.
[31] Massaro, *Mercy in Action*, 54.

Chapter 8

> Solidarity does not materialize out of thin air; this great virtue of fellow feeling and mutual support is the product of ongoing relationships that must be nurtured quite deliberately amid constructive projects of mutuality and genuine other-regard. By participating together in efforts to advance labor justice and forming coalitions to insist on respect for the rights of all workers, Francis is convinced, we will insure progress in the struggle for inclusion and human dignity.[32]

This idea of "participating together" in justice efforts as part of deliberately nurtured ongoing relationships of mutuality is both an opportunity and a challenge.

It may be a stretch to claim that our landowner fits the above understanding of solidarity or was somehow including the laborers in co-creating a solution to their circumstances. But it is fair to say that in this case the landowner's actions evolved in a way that at the very least respected and embraced the human dignity of each laborer. Our landowner was not starting a revolution or establishing new economic policies. But he was taking a small action that demonstrated solidarity with those unable to work the whole day. We might look at economic inequality in our own day.

Writing in an African context, Jean-Claude Loba-Mkolel provides an intercultural analysis of this parable in which he examines not only the world of the text but also gives attention to a particular tradition in which the text has been interpreted and to two contemporary cultures where the issues raised in the text have relevance. In this case, the tradition is that of Catholic Social Teaching, which we have encountered previously. The contemporary cultural situations are those of people living in extreme poverty in the Democratic Republic of Congo and in neighboring Rwanda. The intersection of these multiple worlds leads to some interesting conclusions about the parable's significance today. In looking at the world of the text, Loba-Mkolel considers the day-laborers as among the poorest members of society who had lost their land, and landowners as those who have a societal obligation to act as benefactors to the community. He also considers Catholic Social Teaching on just wages and on the

---

[32] Massaro, *Mercy in Action*, 54–55.

The Laborers in the Vineyard (Matthew 20:1–16)

broader obligations of employers to provide conditions in which their employees can cultivate a quality of life. In its original context, Mkolel finds that the parable "teaches another level of justice, namely that which consists of granting to someone more than what he or she deserves, caring for the labourer beyond just wage calculations."[33]

In turning to workers and wages in contemporary African contexts Loba-Mkolel provides an analysis of relative economic successes in Rwanda compared to DCR. Interestingly, he finds that these do not have to do only with fair wages but also government systems and societal structures which support the well-being of workers. Weaving these threads together he argues that just wages alone (or the generosity of one employer) cannot itself address poverty—there are other broader societal factors, both in the world of the parable and in the contemporary world that need to be tended to. Thus he calls this "a parable of justice beyond just wages."[34] With this approach he concludes, "the parable of Matt 20:1–16 does not prescribe just wages as the remedy for alleviating poverty; it rather provides grounds for promoting justice which goes beyond just wages."[35]

Solidarity as a practice figures importantly in working not only toward economic justice but also toward justice in other areas whether it be racial equity, health outcomes, educational attainment, or issues related to the environment. Each of these social justice issues invites and requires the engagement and support of those with greater power and privilege on behalf of those who suffer the injustices. Bryan Massingale understands solidarity as entailing "a constant effort to build a human community where every social group participates equitably in social life and contributes its genius for the good of all."[36] Massingale explains, "Solidarity is based on the deep-seated conviction that the concerns of the despised other are intimately bound up with our own, that we are, in the words of Martin Luther King Jr., 'bound together in a garment of mutual destiny.'"[37] With a focus on the

---

[33] Jean-Claude Loba-Mkolel, "Beyond Just Wages: An Intercultural Analysis of Matthew 20:1–16," *Journal of Early Christian History* 4, no. 1 (2014): 126.

[34] Loba-Mkolel, "Beyond Just Wages," 113.

[35] Loba-Mkolel, "Beyond Just Wages," 130.

[36] Massingale, *Racial Justice*, 117.

[37] Massingale, *Racial Justice*, 116.

Chapter 8

participation of every social group for the good of all, it is clear why solidarity would be critical for working toward social change for any marginalized group—whether due to race, or class, or other factors.

This notion of solidarity with the vulnerable has implications for many complex societal issues. We can briefly mention here the intractable issue of abortion as a case in point. The *Dobbs v. Jackson Women's Health Organization* Supreme Court decision in 2022, which reversed the long-standing *Roe v. Wade*, has returned decisions about abortion laws to state legislatures, leading to a wide range of restrictions on abortions in many states. While the media has focused on pro-life Christian groups and denominations as celebrating the *Dobbs* decision as a victory, it is fair to say that there actually is no singular "Christian" view on this issue. Christian denominations can be found with public positions on all sides of the issue and there is also divergence of views within denominations. In general, however, Catholics and evangelicals strongly oppose abortion, with notable exceptions within those traditions. Many mainline denominations such as the Episcopal Church and the United Church of Christ support the right of women to exercise their conscience on such a complex issue. Yet even those Christians who support the rights of women to make their own reproductive choices view the issue as "morally serious" since these choices involve early human life or potential life.[38]

While the division and sharp rhetoric around views about abortion runs deep, it may be possible to find some common ground in areas that directly impact abortion. A concern for the common good expressed through solidarity with the poor and marginalized could lead to support for policies which can help achieve improved community health outcomes—the kinds of outcomes that are among the shared goals of both reproductive rights advocates as well as "pro-life" groups.[39]

---

[38] For the range of views see Andrew Lustig, "Beginning of Life," in *The Wiley-Blackwell Companion to Religion and Social Justice* (eds. Palmer and Burgess; Malden, MA: Wiley-Blackwell, 2012), 550.

[39] Along these lines Jim Wallis challenges readers to consider how they could work "*together*, across ideological lines" and "agree to focus on significantly reducing both unwanted pregnancies and abortions in America, by directly and deeply addressing the circumstances that create such painful choices," Wallis, *Christ in Crisis*, 238.

The Laborers in the Vineyard (Matthew 20:1–16)

Ethicists, social analysts, policymakers, social workers, and theologians have demonstrated in a variety of ways that issues of economic justice, healthcare access, wage equality, paid maternity leave, and others directly impact a woman's ability to freely explore the full range of choices related to her potential for bearing a child.[40] While the focus in the courts, legislatures, and media has been on protecting abortion rights or enacting abortion restrictions, advocates for reproductive justice seek a much broader range of advances in our society—advances that would increase equality, improve health outcomes, and improve the lives of women, their children, and families.[41] If these and similar measures could be enacted on a broader scale we could expect not only improvements in the lives of women and their communities but also a decrease in the number of abortions.[42] The challenge appears to be the inability of even the best negotiators to gain agreement across political lines in the midst of competing efforts to galvanize voters around lightning rod issues. Regardless of where one falls on the issue of abortion itself, Jesus's ethic of love, mercy, and justice invites a recognition of shared, common humanity with those who find themselves facing the most serious of choices related to unwanted pregnancies. An ethic of love, mercy, and justice that embodies the values espoused in the parables might help to create flourishing communities where the conditions in which abortion is needed are addressed to a greater extent than at present. Addressing issues of poverty could go a long way, especially when we note that the majority of abortions are obtained by women who are already mothers; who are already living below the

---

[40] See the essays collected in Justin Murray, et al., *In Search of Common Ground on Abortion: From Culture War to Reproductive Justice* (Gender in Law, Culture, and Society; Burlington, VT: Ashgate, 2014).

[41] Rebecca Todd Peters, *Trust Women: A Progressive Christian Argument for Reproductive Justice* (Boston: Beacon Press, 2018).

[42] Wallis explains, "All the data shows that health care, nutrition, access to free or affordable contraception, and economic progress for low-income women does indeed actually reduce the number of abortions." Wallis, *Christ in Crisis*, 239. See also the research in Kristen Day, "Supporting Pregnant Women and Their Families to Reduce Abortion Rate," in *In Search of Common Ground on Abortion: From Culture War to Reproductive Justice* (eds. Murray, et al.; Burlington, VT: Ashgate, 2014), 143–158.

Chapter 8

poverty line; and who have obligations to their other children.[43] And for those concerned about protecting every life, an awareness of the experiences of women who suffer inequitable treatment under our society's current structures should be a call to all people of good will to work together to implement structural changes in line with Christian and family values.

We conclude this chapter returning to two of the critical social justice practices we have seen elsewhere for enacting social change. Massingale outlined these key practices as truth-telling (including acknowledging the harms experienced by others and taking responsibility for addressing their ongoing impacts even if "we" are not personally at fault in causing them); and affirmative redress, which is not only to take responsibility but to take action toward improving the situation. As critical as these kinds of actions are, Massingale suggests that in order for them to be truly transformative they must be grounded in love and compassion. Solidarity itself, he claims, must be *preceded by* compassion. In other words genuine other-concern is a necessary precondition to authentic solidarity, as compassion is what will enable a person to move from individual interest toward solidarity in pursuit of the good of others.[44] Massingale concludes, "Without the cultivation of such solidarity—rooted in lament, compassion, and transformative love—truth-telling and affirmative redress result in superficial palliatives that leave the deep roots of injustice undisturbed."[45] With this it may seem that we have moved a long way from the concrete situation of the laborers in the vineyard. Yet the implications we have considered here all share a grounding in the reality of mercy as seen in the parable: that we all are recipients of the mercy of God; and we all have an opportunity to enact that mercy in response to the concrete needs of the communities in which we find ourselves, using all of the resources we have at our disposal.

[43] See the statistics cited in Wallis, *Christ in Crisis*, 236–241.
[44] In Massingale's words, "Transformative love, or compassion, empowers them for authentic solidarity." Massingale, *Racial Justice*, 120.
[45] Massingale, *Racial Justice*, 120.

The Laborers in the Vineyard (Matthew 20:1–16)

Works Cited in Chapter 8

Blomberg, Craig L. *Interpreting the Parables*. Second ed. Downers Grove, IL: IVP Academic, 2012.

Cook, Michael L. "Jesus' Parables and the Faith that Does Justice." *Studies in the Spirituality of Jesuits* 24, no. 5 (1992): 1–35.

Day, Kristen. "Supporting Pregnant Women and Their Families to Reduce Abortion Rate," Pages 143–158 in *In Search of Common Ground on Abortion: From Culture War to Reproductive Justice*. Edited by Justin Murray, Meredith B. Esser, and Robin West. Burlington, VT: Ashgate, 2014.

Dobrovolny, Mary Kay, RSM. "*The Laborers in the Vineyard*." 2019.

Elliott, John H. "Patronage and Clientage," Pages 144–158 in *The Social Sciences and New Testament Interpretation*. Edited by Richard L. Rohrbaugh. Peabody, MA: Hendrickson, 1996.

Gordley, Matthew E. "Parables and the Principle of Mercy: Reading Parables Alongside the Work of Jon Sobrino in a First-Year College Course." *Journal of Catholic Higher Education* 39 (2020): 15–36.

Gutiérrez, Gustavo. *A Theology of Liberation: History, Politics, and Salvation.* Maryknoll, NY: Orbis Books, 1988.

Harrington, Brooks and John C. Holbert. *No Mercy, No Justice: The Dominant Narrative of America Versus the Counter-Narrative of Jesus' Parables*. Eugene, OR: Cascade Books, 2019.

Herzog, William R. *Parables as Subversive Speech: Jesus as Pedagogue of the Oppressed*. Louisville, KY: Westminster/John Knox, 1994.

Hultgren, Arland J. *The Parables of Jesus: A Commentary*. The Bible in its World. Grand Rapids: Eerdmans, 2000.

Levine, Amy-Jill. *Short Stories by Jesus: The Enigmatic Parables of a Controversial Rabbi*. New York: HarperOne, 2014.

Loba-Mkolel, Jean-Claude. "Beyond Just Wages: An Intercultural Analysis of Matthew 20:1–16." *Journal of Early Christian History* 4, no. 1 (2014): 112–134.

Lustig, Andrew. "Beginning of Life," Pages 547–560 in *The Wiley-Blackwell Companion to Religion and Social Justice*. Edited by Michael D. Palmer and Stanley M. Burgess. Malden, MA: Wiley-Blackwell, 2012.

Massaro, Thomas. *Mercy in Action: The Social Teachings of Pope Francis*. Lanham: Rowman & Littlefield, 2018.

Massingale, Bryan N. *Racial Justice and the Catholic Church*. Maryknoll, NY: Orbis Books, 2010.

Chapter 8

Murray, Justin, Meredith B. Esser, and Robin West. *In Search of Common Ground on Abortion: From Culture War to Reproductive Justice*. Gender in Law, Culture, and Society. Burlington, VT: Ashgate, 2014.

Peters, Rebecca Todd. *Trust Women: A Progressive Christian Argument for Reproductive Justice*. Boston: Beacon Press, 2018.

Schottroff, Luise. *The Parables of Jesus*. Minneapolis: Fortress, 2006.

Snodgrass, Klyne. *Stories with Intent: A Comprehensive Guide to the Parables of Jesus*. Second ed. Grand Rapids: Eerdmans, 2018.

Sobrino, Jon. *No Salvation Outside the Poor: Prophetic-Utopian Essays*. Maryknoll, NY: Orbis Books, 2008.

Van Eck, Ernest and John S. Kloppenborg. *The Parables of Jesus the Galilean: Stories of a Social Prophet*. Vol. 9, Matrix–The Bible in Mediterranean Context. Eugene, OR: Cascade Books, 2016.

Wallis, Jim. *Christ in Crisis? Why We Need to Reclaim Jesus*. San Francisco: HarperOne, 2019.

9

The Rich Man and Lazarus (Luke 16:19–31)

1. Introduction

The parable of the Rich Man and Lazarus is among the most elaborate and most memorable of Jesus's parables. It has a long-standing hold on the Western imagination being alluded to by everyone from Shakespeare to Melville, and from U2 to David Bowie.[1] The parable draws on a popular type of story about the fate of the rich and poor in the afterlife, which has connections with a number of other cultures in the ancient world. As such, it describes an unnamed man of incredible wealth and an incredibly poor man named Lazarus, who lay at the rich man's gate. In the afterlife their situations are significantly and strikingly reversed, and a dialogue ensues between the rich man and Father Abraham that sheds further insight on the dynamics of the men's earthly lives. Jesus used this popular motif to challenge his listeners regarding their views of wealth, poverty, and their obligations to the poor. While this is another parable about mercy, in contrast to the parable of the Good Samaritan where mercy is shown to a stranger far from home, this parable reflects on the dehumanizing and far-reaching impact of failing to show mercy to those in one's own community.

While it may be tempting to want to use this parable to draw some conclusions about the nature of life after death—the focus of this parable is on what unfolds in the afterlife—as a parable it is clearly a story

[1] Gowler, *Parables after Jesus*, 83.

Social Justice in the Stories of Jesus: The Ethical Challenge of the Parables, First Edition.
Matthew E. Gordley.
© 2024 John Wiley & Sons Ltd. Published 2024 by John Wiley & Sons Ltd.

Chapter 9

which is intended to challenge the listeners' actions in the here and now using a popular metaphor. The imagery that is drawn upon to do this, however, is imagery about the afterlife. Recognizing how the metaphorical imagination of parables work, this does raise some issues about the nature of Hades (the Greek term for the realm of the dead) and we will take a look at those. But as we will see, the challenge of the parable is less about the next life and much more about this one.[2]

Following our interpretive process, we will begin by taking a careful look at the elements of the story, asking some key questions, spotting the "twist" in the parable, considering the metaphor, and articulating the challenge. From there we reflect on the implications of this parable for our lives and the lives of our communities. In this process we will benefit from the wisdom of others who have walked this path before us.

2. The Text: The Rich Man and Lazarus (Luke 16:19–31)

There was a rich man who was dressed in purple and fine linen and who feasted sumptuously every day. And at his gate lay a poor man named Lazarus, covered with sores, who longed to satisfy his hunger with what fell from the rich man's table; even the dogs would come and lick his sores. The poor man died and was carried away by the angels to be with Abraham. The rich man also died and was buried. In Hades, where he was being tormented, he looked up and saw Abraham far away with Lazarus by his side. He called out, "Father Abraham, have mercy on me, and send Lazarus to dip the tip of his finger in water and cool my tongue; for I am in agony in these flames." But Abraham said, "Child, remember that during your lifetime you received your good things, and Lazarus in like manner evil things; but now he is comforted here, and you are in agony. Besides all this, between you and us a great chasm has been fixed, so that those who might want to pass from here to you cannot do so, and no one

---

[2] See the following commentaries and studies for important background information on the many issues raised by the parable: Hultgren, *Parables of Jesus*, 110–118; Snodgrass, *Stories with Intent*, 419–435; Blomberg, *Interpreting the Parables*, 254–262; Herzog, *Parables as Subversive Speech*, 114–130; Levine, *Short Stories*, 267–296.

258

The Rich Man and Lazarus (Luke 16:19–31)

can cross from there to us." He said, "Then, father, I beg you to send him to my father's house—for I have five brothers—that he may warn them, so that they will not also come into this place of torment." Abraham replied, "They have Moses and the prophets; they should listen to them." He said, "No, father Abraham; but if someone goes to them from the dead, they will repent." He said to him, "If they do not listen to Moses and the prophets, neither will they be convinced even if someone rises from the dead." (Luke 16:19–31 NRSV)

3. Our First Step: Grasp the Story

This parable consists of two acts. The first is a scene from the earthly life of the two main characters (vv. 19–22). The second is from the afterlife where a dramatic reversal has occurred (vv. 23–31). Act one begins with a rich man who is described in such a way that he is unimaginably wealthy—obscenely so.[3] In the ancient world purple linen and feasting were reserved for special occasions and events; but for this wealthy man, every day was like a feast. He was so affluent that he did not need to reserve his expensive clothes for special occasions. He wore them all the time. So not only was he exceptionally rich, but he enjoyed his wealth in such a way that it was on display for all to see. In our sketch of the world of Jesus and his original listeners, he would have been among the elite. Jesus's listeners would know that he was not "one of us." Amy-Jill Levine points out that the man is a caricature, like the Pharisee we read about in Luke 17: "He is too rich even to be recognized and outside any system of social responsibility."[4]

By contrast a poor man who lay at the rich man's gate, Lazarus, is described as being unimaginably poor. His suffering and his hunger are described in ways that show him to be as poor as the rich man is wealthy. As part of the class of expendables, he is poorer than the peasants and day laborers.[5] His is a sad case. That he has dogs licking his sores (v. 21) shows just how low his situation is. It is as if they are getting a meal from Lazarus, while Lazarus gets nothing. While some

---

[3] See Levine's analysis of his wealth in Greco-Roman and Jewish context: Levine, *Short Stories*, 271–274.

[4] Levine, *Short Stories*, 273.

[5] See Herzog, *Parables as Subversive Speech*, 118–120.

Chapter 9

translations refer to the man as a beggar, there is no indication in the parable that he even has the agency to beg or ask for anything. He never speaks at all. Amy-Jill Levine points out that the reader is unable to identify with either of these characters—we cannot imagine being that rich, and we cannot imagine being that destitute; the characters are extreme in every way to make Jesus's point.[6]

The name of the poor man is noteworthy. This is often noted by scholars as the only time in the parables of Jesus where a character is named (although we should also note that Abraham is named in this parable too). His name derives from the Hebrew which means "God is my help."[7] Clearly, it was the case that he was not receiving help from the rich man. So God truly was his only help. We might ask, in addition to the meaning of the name connecting with his situation, why did Jesus give a name to this particular character? The unfolding of the story gives us a clue. Though there was seemingly no interaction between the rich man and Lazarus in their earthly lives, in the afterlife we discover that the rich man actually knew Lazarus: he asks for him by name (v. 24). Though he apparently ignored him as he lay by his gate, it turns out that Lazarus was familiar to the rich man—he knew him by name.

Upon their deaths, we see a complete reversal. This is hinted at even with the way their deaths are described. Lazarus is "carried away by the angels to be with Abraham" while the rich man is simply "buried" (v. 22). This notion of "being with Abraham" is a traditional description of the afterlife of the righteous. Abraham is the father of the Jewish people as described in the Jewish scriptures, and well-known for his hospitality in welcoming in strangers (see, for example, Gen. 18:1–8). But just as in the first half of the parable, we see a sharp contrast: the rich man is described as in Hades, the generic Greek expression for the underworld. Not only so but he is in torment and agony (both terms being repeated to emphasize the fact), and his suffering sounds at least as bad as, but perhaps even greater than, that of Lazarus in his earthly suffering. At the same time, Lazarus is finally experiencing comfort.

The second half of the parable is then a dialogue between the rich man and father Abraham (vv. 23–31). The rich man makes three requests,

[6] Levine, *Short Stories*, 276.
[7] Herzog, *Parables as Subversive Speech*, 120.

The Rich Man and Lazarus (Luke 16:19–31)

each of which is denied. He asks for Abraham to send Lazarus to dip his finger in water to cool the rich man's tongue (v. 24). This is an ironic touch, since it was the tongues of the dogs who had licked Lazarus's wounds. The rich man, by contrast, had not lifted a finger to help Lazarus. Abraham refuses on the basis of what each had experienced in life and adds that it is not possible to cross the chasm between them.

The rich man next asks for Abraham to send Lazarus to his five brothers to warn them (vv. 27–28). It is clear that the rich man maintains his outlook on life which holds that others exist only to serve him. He has given no thought or acknowledgment to Lazarus as a person or as someone who suffered greatly; instead, he apparently sees Lazarus only as a means to achieve his own goals. Abraham's reply is that the brothers should listen to Moses and the prophets, a reference to the Jewish scriptures (v. 29) The implication is clear: that is what the rich man should have done as well.

Finally, the rich man insists that if someone came to his brothers from the dead, they would surely listen and repent (v. 30). Abraham's response is again negative: if they do not listen to the teaching that they have, they would not be convinced even if someone was raised from the dead (v. 31). And with that the parable ends.

4. Our Second Step: Going Deeper through Asking Questions

As with our exploration of other parables, asking good questions about key features of the parable can help to open up our understanding of the parable and its message. First and foremost, since this is a parable that raises issues of wealth and poverty it would help us to know more about the characters and the nature of their wealth or lack thereof. What can be known or assumed from the information provided in the parable? Second, given that the shocking reversal of the two characters happens in the afterlife, we might like to know to what extent this parable is intended to teach us about getting a good or a bad judgment in the hereafter. At the very least, what does this parable teach us about the afterlife? Third, since the parable suggests that the rich man and his brothers should listen to the Jewish scriptures, what specific teaching is in view there? Fourth, given our growing

Chapter 9

awareness of how parables have been used to reinforce negative stereotypes about early Judaism, we may ask whether this parable has lent itself to such interpretations.

The answers to these questions are closely interrelated, as the lens through which we look for answers to one question informs the others. For example, who were the wealthy in the time of Jesus? It could be that such a wealthy person was a Pharisee or Sadducee, perhaps a religious leader somehow linked to the wealthy ruling class and perhaps deriving his wealth through compromise with the Roman occupiers. In support of such a view, we can notice that just before telling this parable, Luke notes as an aside that the Pharisees were "lovers of wealth" (16:14). Luke's Gospel includes several parables which involve "a certain rich man" and warn about the folly of serving wealth rather than God. Luke also demonstrates concern for the poor with the motif of the reversal of the poor and wealthy occurring as early as the birth narrative and the song of Mary (Luke 1:46–55). In light of these contextual clues, the parable could possibly be taken as a pointed critique not just of the wealthy in general but of the callousness of the Jewish religious leaders who ignore the needs of their fellow Jews in this life and then face a reversal in the next. However, aside from the wealth of the rich man, there is no direct indication of his belonging to the Pharisees or Sadducees. And there were many other ways of being wealthy. The religious position or status of the rich man is nowhere in view, other than that he is able to refer to Abraham as "father" as well, indicating that we are in a Jewish setting.

Indeed it seems a stretch to try to make this parable a critique of any aspect of Judaism at all. Jesus's Jewish listeners would have been well aware that the rich man's ostentatious display of wealth and lack of concern for Lazarus at his gate were serious breaches of Jewish covenant responsibilities toward a fellow human being. Scriptural passages like Deut. 15:11 and Isaiah 58:7 make this abundantly clear. As for an assumption that Jews in the first century saw wealth as a sign of God's blessing, and suffering as a sign of God's judgment, the biblical book of Job helps problematize that claim. Against interpreters who think that Jesus's listeners would be surprised at the rich man's and poor man's reversals (because they believed that people must have deserved what they had in their earthly lives), Levine explains, "The scriptures of Israel repeatedly express God's concern for the poor, the widow, the

The Rich Man and Lazarus (Luke 16:19–31)

orphan, and the stranger—if they deserved their states, then the divine concern makes no sense."[8] Again, Jesus is not bringing forward a new teaching with this parable. To see this parable as a critique of a particular Jewish belief, value, or practice is to go against the evidence we have both in the parable itself and in the sources from the ancient world.

This leads to consideration of questions about views of the afterlife. Was Jesus seeking to make a point about what people should expect when they die?[9] Since we have touched above on the Pharisees and Sadducees with regard to wealth, we might be able to make a different connection with them in light of this issue. It is generally understood that a defining characteristic of the beliefs of the Sadducees was that they did not believe in a physical resurrection, while other Jewish groups did—including the Pharisees. Luke even addresses this later in his gospel when some Sadducees confront Jesus with a question about the nature of the afterlife (Luke 20:27–40). With such a pointed parable, it could be argued that Jesus was challenging the Sadducees' understanding of the nature of the afterlife. The simple act of telling a story that involved some version of an afterlife would potentially tap into some of this debate.

Should we take this parable then as a narrative that gives us a glimpse of what happens when we die, or at least as a parable that affirms a final judgment? Three factors suggest that teaching about the afterlife was not the point of this story. First, however one reads this, this is emphatically not a parable about the resurrection of the dead. Thus, the debate of the Sadducees and Pharisees on this point is irrelevant to this parable and its contents.

Second, this parable reflects a folktale motif—reversal of circumstances in the afterlife—which was commonplace in antiquity not only in Jewish but also Egyptian and Greco-Roman tales. Though Jesus is not necessarily borrowing from any one particular story, the motif was common enough that listeners would understand that a story like this has a point other than "this is how you get to heaven." Levine summarizes the features of these stories as disincentivizing selfish behavior; providing a sense of justice for those who suffer unjustly in this life; and

---

[8] Levine, *Short Stories*, 276.

[9] For a balanced discussion of the issues in light of the broader biblical and cultural context of the first century, see Snodgrass, *Stories with Intent*, 430–432.

263

Chapter 9

preventing the need for violent, social revolution to address the injustices in the present life. Such stories provide reassurance and a sense of justice that all will be sorted out.[10]

Third, recall that a parable is a comparison, a "laying alongside" of two different things to make a single point. The "point" of this parable is much more focused on the actions not taken in one's life. The elaborate situation in the afterlife, with its attendant dialogue, highlights not what the afterlife is like but the importance of one's actions in one's earthly life. So it seems most likely that this folkloric tale with a shocking reversal and descriptive elaboration of the rich man's after-death experience and dialogue is pointed in a direction other than telling us about the afterlife.[11]

Our next question relates to the phrase "Moses and the prophets" (v. 29). Where do they enter into this parable and why are they important? This phrase is shorthand for the totality of God's revelation through the scriptures. As we already saw through our discussion of the Good Samaritan, the Jewish scriptures are rich with teaching about God's concern for the poor, the widow, the orphan, the alien, and of the obligation of God's people to care for them (cf. Deut. 15:7; Isa 58:7). It is this heritage of teaching about the value of every human being that is in view here. Levine points out that in Jesus's teaching about the poor here and elsewhere "he is not being religiously innovative...he is reflecting his Jewish culture."[12] Jesus frequently drew upon the Jewish scriptures as he engaged with his opponents and their views about what it meant to be faithful to God in their context. Through this parable Jesus reinforces not only the rich tradition of Jewish teaching on caring for the poor and the oppressed, but also the continuing importance of the Jewish scriptures themselves for Jesus and for his followers.

Looking at each of these questions together, we can ask to what extent might anti-Judaism play into interpreting this parable? Given the possibility that the parable in its context in Luke can be seen as a critique of

---

[10] Levine, *Short Stories*, 286–287.

[11] This is in line with Snodgrass, who notes, "The use of folkloric themes and the fact that this is a parable with an intent other than teaching about the future life should warn against taking the picture too literally." Snodgrass, *Stories with Intent*, 430.

[12] Levine, *Short Stories*, 273.

The Rich Man and Lazarus (Luke 16:19–31)

the wealthy Pharisees or Sadducees, such a view can unwittingly be extended as a critique of Jewish belief and practice in general. Even further, with the possibility of an allusion to the resurrection of Jesus ("neither will they be convinced even if someone rises from the dead," v. 31), the parable could also be read as a critique of Jewish unbelief in the resurrection of Jesus. In other words, if we try to read the parable as "good Christian teaching" in contrast to "bad Jewish practice," then we would conclude that not only did first-century Jews not show compassion on those in need, they also rejected the message of Jesus, despite his being raised from the dead. Read in this way, the parable could be seen as denouncing Jewish unbelief, while showing that the marginalized poor (perhaps even identified with Gentiles who embrace the good news about Jesus) are the ones who enjoy God's pleasure in the afterlife.[13]

Such views are problematic on several fronts. First, as we have seen previously, anti-Judaism is a dangerous tendency that is easy to fall into without a grasp of the dynamics of first-century Judaism and the interplay between Judaism and Christianity. Yes, Jesus is shown in the gospels as being in conflict with some Jewish religious leaders. However, those narrative conflicts are a far cry from a portrayal of early Judaism as a whole standing in legalistic opposition to Jesus's teaching of love and compassion. Second, anti-Jewish reading of a parable like this, even inadvertent, opens the door to anti-Semitism and can be exploited by those who hold such ideological views. This concern is an important one particularly in our era when hate crimes and hate groups are experiencing a rise in activity and visibility. Responsible readers must stand against such misconstrual of what the biblical text is actually saying—which is anything but a message of ideological hate. Third, the biblical record itself, including the New Testament, confronts anti-Judaism directly since Christian faith places a very high view on Jewish faith, practice, and tradition. As we have already noted, in this very parable the importance of "Moses and the prophets" is explicitly upheld and reinforced (v. 29). It is difficult to find a more positive reference to Jewish tradition than this affirmation of the Jewish scriptures! Fourth, and most germane to our efforts to understand this parable, a reading that fosters anti-Judaism distracts from the real challenge and

---

[13] See examples noted in Snodgrass, *Stories with Intent*, 424–425.

Chapter 9

significance of the parable: the real punch is not against Jews (all of Jesus's listeners were Jewish, and so was he!) but against a value system that fosters the invisibility of and a lack of concern for the poor on the part of the wealthy.[14]

As we have seen, Jesus suggests that if anyone will not listen to the law (Moses) and the prophets—the divinely given Torah and the challenging words of the prophets calling the people back to the ways of God—a miracle will not make a difference in changing hearts. Ultimately, this parable brings into focus the inseparable connection of Christian faith with its Jewish beginnings. With answers to these questions in mind, we can now move to spot the twist in this parable. Where does the story go "off the rails" and surprise the listener?

5. Our Third Step: Spot the Twist

Identifying the twist in this parable seems simple enough. Lazarus is taken from intense earthly suffering to heavenly comfort; the rich man is taken from a life of luxury to an afterlife of agony. The stark reversal happens with no apparent explanation other than the characters' wealth or lack thereof in their earthly lives. No moral qualities are explicitly assigned to either character. As Schottroff notes, "The text does not speak of a devout poor man and a godless rich man."[15] No specific sinful actions are outlined. No particular religious belief or lack of belief is described. The reversal in the parable appears to be attributable only to what each experienced in their earthly lives. Father Abraham's explanation confirms this: "Child, remember that during your lifetime you received your good things, and Lazarus in like manner evil things; but now he is comforted here, and you are in agony" (v. 25).[16]

---

[14] Levine points to a number of other anti-Jewish ways of reading this parable aside from what is mentioned here. For a cautious reading of the parable with attention to implicit anti-Jewish overtones in the history of interpretation, see Levine, *Short Stories*, 267–296.

[15] Schottroff, *Parables*, 168.

[16] Along these lines Crossan points out, "Neither the rich man nor the poor man has done anything particularly moral or immoral. *They are simply described economically rather than appraised morally.*" Crossan, *Power of Parable*, 93.

The Rich Man and Lazarus (Luke 16:19–31)

This twist reflects a motif that is not uncommon in the parables or in ancient storytelling: a final assessment of two characters which defies the listeners' expectations. We have seen something similar before in the parable of the Pharisee and the tax collector (Luke 8:9–14) where the story culminates with an unexpected judgment passed in favor of one character over another. And this surprise judgment startles the listener and leads them to reflect as part of Jesus's "participatory pedagogy."[17]

Modern interpreters often point out that the reversal in this parable is potentially challenging to Christian theological sensibilities. This is particularly so for Protestants who emphasize justification not on the basis of good works done in this life but solely on God's grace through Jesus. All Christians, but particularly in those traditions, emphasize that salvation is a gift of grace and is by faith; one's actions cannot enable one to earn salvation. This parable would appear to challenge that, suggesting that Lazarus experiences salvation not as a result of faith but simply because he suffered, and that the rich man did not experience salvation, because of his wealth and perhaps based on actions he failed to take. Without resolving the tension between Christian theological belief about salvation and the implicit teaching of this parable, Greg Carey explains, "Let us simply consider the possibility that it matters what we do in this life—specifically, how we relate to the poor—and it matters more than we might be willing to appreciate."[18]

Another twist in this parable may be that the distance between the two men, symbolized by the gate in their earthly lives, continues in the afterlife. There is an incredibly vast socio-economic distance between the men in their earthly lives. The descriptors of both the rich man and Lazarus make that clear. That the distance also continues in the afterlife is surprising, as perhaps we may expect that both would be included in the benefits of God's eternal kingdom as children of Abraham. The fact that this distance remains is further emphasized in the dialogue with Father Abraham. Even if Lazarus was willing to bring water to the rich man, Abraham explains, the chasm between them would prevent him from doing so: "between you and us a great chasm has been fixed, so that those who might want to pass from here to you cannot do so, and

---

[17] Crossan, *Power of Parable*, 93–95.

[18] Carey, *Stories Jesus Told*, 93.

Chapter 9

no one can cross from there to us" (v. 26). This separation—the gate on earth and the chasm in the afterlife—is a powerful image which we can explore further. Can the space between the wealthy and the poor be bridged?

One final provocation of the parable may be that the parable continues on to a lengthy and longer second act after the initial life, death, and reversal sequence. This second act allows readers to understand the extent of the rich man's suffering: the Greek term for torment is repeated for emphasis (vv. 23 and 28); the Greek term for agony is repeated for emphasis (vv. 25 and 26); and the man himself begs for relief (v. 25). This second act also brings into view the finality of the decisions made during one's life. Finally, it allows the man's still-living brothers to come into the discussion. There is still hope for them to avoid the extreme torment and agony that the rich man experiences; but that hope is not in a supernatural messenger from the dead, but rather in their paying attention to "Moses and the prophets"—also explicitly mentioned twice for emphasis. And for readers who count themselves still among the living (all of us!), this may be the real provocation: to pay attention to the teaching we already have received.

6. Our Fourth Step: Consider the Metaphor

As we move on to consider this parable more deeply, we need to consider the question of what exactly is the metaphor we are working with here? Several images in this parable are particularly striking. One we have just noted is the chasm that separates the two men. Another is the vivid description of the extreme poverty of Lazarus. Another is the idea of a positive or negative judgment in the afterlife determined by one's actions or inactions in the present life. These visual images give us a lot to consider. If this parable serves as a warning, how do we work with these metaphors? In this section we explore further the significance of these images and how they may challenge us to see our world differently.

One aspect of this parable is the notion of the distance between the poor and the wealthy. In the first half of the parable this distance is made visible through the gate (v. 20). In the second half of the parable, the distance is maintained through the chasm separating the two men

The Rich Man and Lazarus (Luke 16:19–31)

(v. 26). These visible expressions of separation bring into view the multiple ways in which the distance between the two men kept them apart. Though Lazarus was near the rich man, the gate created distance, and enabled Lazarus to be out of sight while the rich man was in his home. Certainly the rich man would have had to see Lazarus when coming or going. But unlike in the case of the Samaritan seeing the wounded stranger on the side of the road, this seeing did not result in a sense of connection: the rich man was never "moved with compassion" (Luke 10:33). Furthermore, once in his grounds, the rich man could put Lazarus out of mind. In this sense he is like the priest and the Levite who encountered the wounded man but were able to put him out of mind as they simply continued on their own journeys (Luke 10:31–32). What is worse in this case, however, is that the rich man presumably would have encountered Lazarus day after day after day. This was not a one-time encounter. With the rich man, then, this was a pattern of ignoring someone in need; and someone who was part of his own community and not just a stranger on the road. In fact, some commentators suggest that the friends of Lazarus placed him at the rich man's gate precisely because he had the means to help.

This image brings to mind the ways that poverty is often made invisible to the wealthy and the mechanisms we use to distance ourselves from it today. The same may be said of many kinds of suffering including the suffering of workers in sweatshops, immigrant workers, or individuals and communities suffering harsh and unjust treatment at the hands of police officers. Contemporary society has mechanisms for insulating the wealthy and the dominant groups from having to wrestle with the suffering of their brothers and sisters of different races, nationalities, and circumstances. Many of those mechanisms have been put in place through policies and practices that ensure that wealthy white people seldom need to be confronted with poverty, homelessness, and other forms of human suffering.

But while the rich man was unmoved during his life it turns out that there was indeed an alternative which the rich man at least realizes in the afterlife. Accordingly he wants his brothers to be warned so that their fate will not be the same as his (vv. 27–31). From this dialogue we learn that the rich man himself could have acted differently; he could have listened to the teaching of the scriptures, to Moses and the prophets. Their message was to care for a neighbor in need and to look out for

269

Chapter 9

the needs of others, orienting oneself to the well-being of the community. Implied in the parable is that by doing so he would not only have saved Lazarus from his dire situation of suffering, but he would have received salvation from Lazarus as well. The parable could have had a very different ending: had the chasm been bridged in their earthly lives, it may not have continued into the hereafter.

A second image is that of a person in extreme poverty but who nevertheless enjoys God's favor. Such an image brings to mind a figure described in the Jewish scriptures and which, for the early Christians, came to be identified with Jesus. This figure is called the suffering servant. Isaiah 53:3 describes the servant as "despised and rejected by others" and "a man of suffering and acquainted with infirmity." It goes on to say that "as one from whom others hide their faces he was despised, and we held him of no account." People "accounted him stricken, struck down by God, and afflicted" (Isa. 53:4). But in the end, out of this darkness and suffering, the servant sees light, finds satisfaction through knowledge, and is allotted a place among the great (vv. 11–12). Jon Sobrino explains how this suffering servant is paradigmatic of the suffering poor throughout history.[19] There are many parallels he draws out that can illumine this specific parable. Isaiah describes the gifts that the suffering servant brings to humanity, two of which are light and salvation.[20] In the case of this parable, Lazarus offered the rich man both of these gifts.

First, the poor, oppressed, and marginalized offer the wealthy an invitation to see reality as it is. This is the light that the suffering servant brings: illumination. As Margaret Farley notes, mercy invites and requires people to see reality clearly: "Precisely because mercy involves beholding the value of others and suffering with them in their need, it opens reality to the beholder; it offers a way of 'seeing' that evokes a moral response—to alleviate pain, provide assistance in need, support in wellbeing. Mercy therefore illuminates justice and propels it to action."[21] The presence of Lazarus at the gate testified daily to a reality

[19] Sobrino, *Principle of Mercy*, 51–56.

[20] In outlining the salvation which the "crucified peoples" bring Sobrino includes such things as values that are not offered elsewhere, hope, love, forgiveness, solidarity, and faith. Sobrino, *Principle of Mercy*, 55–56.

[21] Farley, "Wisdom, Dignity, and Justice," here, 8. Here, p. 8.

The Rich Man and Lazarus (Luke 16:19–31)

that the rich man was unable, unwilling, or uninterested in facing. Lazarus's presence at the gate was a sign that something was wrong. Lazarus could have helped the rich man deal with reality. The reality on display was that a son of Abraham was in a deeply dehumanizing situation. The very presence of such a person in the rich man's life was (potentially) a gift of illumination: a wake-up call that priorities and values in his life were not in line and that his own place in the community was out of order.

Second, the poor offer the wealthy salvation in the form of an invitation to full humanity. As we saw with the parable of the good Samaritan, mercy and compassion are hallmarks of true humanity. Compassion is the natural human response to the suffering of another. Had the rich man had compassion for Lazarus, not only would Lazarus have been enabled to live in a more humane way, but the rich man would have been living into a fuller humanity than the insulated, closed, self-centered lifestyle in which he was fully immersed. Sobrino calls this kind of compassionate care "co-responsibility" and explains,

> This response to the suffering of the poor is an ethical demand, but it is also a practice that is salvific for those who enter into solidarity with the poor. Those who do so often recover in their own life the deep meaning they thought they had lost; they recover their human dignity by becoming integrated into the pain and suffering of the poor. From the poor they receive, in a way they hardly expected, new eyes for seeing the ultimate truth of things.[22]

Acting in solidarity with the poor thus benefits the poor and the wealthy alike. Sobrino puts this eloquently explaining that he holds on to "the hope that humanity will finally be healed, that there will be salvation for the poor, that we too will miraculously let ourselves be saved by them, and become truly a human family."[23] Day after day, Lazarus lay there offering both light and salvation to the rich man. He offered him the possibility of seeing reality, and the possibility of embodying human compassion which would have been to the benefit of both of them. The rich man did not care to see and did not care to be saved, to be

---

[22] Sobrino, *Principle of Mercy*, 150–151.

[23] Sobrino, *No Salvation Outside the Poor*, xii.

Chapter 9

humanized. Lazarus was in a horribly dehumanizing situation. By not seeing and not caring, the rich man was also in a deeply dehumanizing situation, but one of his own choosing. He was unwilling to receive the gifts that Lazarus held out to him.

Here we may note the way this concept is expressed within the Catholic tradition under the broad umbrella of Catholic social teaching. Drawing on the rich theological resources of Jewish tradition and the teachings of Jesus, Catholic social teaching includes an emphasis on what has been called "the preferential option for the poor." In his 1965 encyclical *Gaudium et Spes*, Pope John Paul II highlighted the importance of the sufferings of the poor in the very first line: "The joys and the hopes, the griefs and the anxieties of the men of this age, *especially those who are poor or in any way afflicted*, these are the joys and hopes, the griefs and anxieties of the followers of Christ."[24] In other words, while all of human experience is of concern to Christians, the experiences of those who suffer ought to receive priority attention.

The preferential option for the poor reminds people of faith that, as shown throughout the scriptures, God desires justice for the oppressed and help for those who suffer. James Cone explains it this way: "It seems clear that the overwhelming weight of biblical teaching, especially the prophetic tradition in which Jesus stood unambiguously, is upon God's unqualified identification with the poor precisely because they are poor. The kingdom of God is for the helpless, because they have no security in this world."[25] This reality of divine concern has implications then for how humans who are devoted to God regard the poor and oppressed. Cone puts this emphatically: "Knowing God means being on the side of the oppressed, becoming one with them, and participating in the goal of liberation."[26] The wealthy and the powerful are those in the position to use their resources to help those in need, and if they are in touch with the heart of God for oppressed humanity, they embrace their responsibility to do so.

---

[24] Gaudium et Spes (Pastoral Constitution on the Church in the Modern World; December 7, 1965), 1. Accessed at http://www.vatican.va/archive/hist_councils/ii_vatican_council/documents/vat-ii_const_19651207_gaudium-et-spes_en.html (italics added).

[25] Cone, *Black Theology*, 117.

[26] Cone, *Black Theology*, 65.

The Rich Man and Lazarus (Luke 16:19–31)

Importantly, though, this preferential option is not a one-way street. Instead, it is a reciprocal relationship of giving and receiving, even if the poor and the wealthy bring different things to the table. Jon Sobrino explains, "The option for the poor is not just a matter of giving to them, but of *receiving from them.*"[27] In giving to Lazarus, the rich man could also have received an invitation into a fuller human experience and, ultimately, experienced salvation himself.

The metaphor of a person in extreme poverty and of an unbridgeable gap between the poor and the rich may describe the way things are. But it does not describe the way things can be different in the kingdom of God. Perhaps in offering this challenge parable, Jesus was inviting his listeners to see the extremely poor and the extremely wealthy, along with themselves, in a new light. In this way of thinking this is not a parable addressed to the obscenely wealthy or to those suffering unimaginably, but to people in any situation. As Levine notes, "This parable interrogates our priorities as well."[28]

Recognizing that the message of Jesus was not simply a set of rules to follow (or negative examples to avoid) but more so a declaration of the kingdom, we may consider how this metaphor works as a declaration on behalf of the disinherited. As a part of Jesus's declaration of the kingdom this is certainly a reversal intended to provoke. And knowing how reversal parables function, using one specific situation to speak to a more general one, we can extend this parable to more than just these two individuals. In a way similar to the parable of the Pharisee and the tax collector we can generalize to situations where one has power and privilege, and the other is powerless, without any agency. In the proclamation of Jesus, the disinherited and marginalized can be assured by the nature of the God who is a God of reversals, that God is on their side (recall the song of Mary, who celebrates God's bringing down the powerful and lifting up the lowly; cf. Luke 1:52). This was in essence what the mission and message of Jesus demonstrated.

---

[27] Sobrino, *Principle of Mercy*, 53. Italics added for emphasis.
[28] Levine, *Short Stories*, 295.

Chapter 9

7. Our Fifth Step: Articulate the Challenge

Ultimately the reversal of this parable is a call to recognize that there is an opportunity for those with power and privilege to be enlightened and saved by the powerless and marginalized. Cone again helps us here: "Being human means being against evil by joining sides with those who are the victims of evil. Quite literally it means becoming oppressed with the oppressed, making their cause one's own cause by involving oneself in the liberation struggle. *No one is free until all are free.*"[29] In the case of this parable, the postmortem judgment of the rich man revealed the reality of his life: despite his lavish lifestyle of conspicuous consumption, Lazarus's experience of dehumanizing suffering with no response from the rich man shows that the rich man was not living in freedom himself. He just did not realize it until it was too late. Had he exercised his ability to act on behalf of Lazarus, he would have experienced a fuller and deeper human freedom that was liberating to both himself and Lazarus.

In this parable, then, it is not a matter of doing the right thing and being rewarded. It is rather the reality of human experience that having open eyes, an open heart, and open hands toward others are the practices that support the well-being of others. These same practices enable the ultimate well-being of all—even those who practice them. For Cone this is why "Christians can never be content as long as their sisters and brothers are enslaved. They must suffer with them, knowing that freedom for Jesus Christ is always freedom for the oppressed."[30]

The basic story of this parable as it stands is quite sad. On the one hand, Lazarus suffered greatly in his earthly life, and no one had mercy on him. This is mitigated, to a certain extent, by the reversal in which he has a peaceful afterlife. However, the reality of a life of suffering in hunger, misery, sickness, and poverty is disturbing whatever happens in the next world. Hope for the afterlife is a thin comfort in the moment when the dogs are licking wounds and crumbs from the table are being discarded rather than shared. On the other hand, the parable is also quite sad in the outcome for the rich man. Though we are not generally inclined to feel pity for the rich man, his ultimate end in an afterlife of unaided

[29] Cone, *Black Theology*, 88.
[30] Cone, *Black Theology*, 101.

The Rich Man and Lazarus (Luke 16:19–31)

suffering, torment, and agony is disturbing as well. He literally begs Father Abraham for mercy. However, he can receive no comfort, and he can do nothing to prevent his five brothers from ending in a similar fate. Maybe we do feel a little bad for the rich man, and wonder if he is getting a fair shake after all. He literally asked for mercy but did not receive it.

Regardless of how we feel about the characters, there is a deeper tragedy in this story that we have already touched on: the rich man had the ability and resources to prevent both of their sufferings. Had he shown compassion and aided Lazarus in his suffering, Lazarus's suffering would have been relieved. At the same time, in the logic of the story, by showing compassion when he had the opportunity the rich man would have secured a better fate for himself in the afterlife. This imaginary alternate ending is dependent on one thing alone: the rich man's having compassion on the poor man at his gate. What would it have taken for the rich man to have had compassion? His request for his brothers gives a clue to what is needed: "If someone goes to them from the dead, they will repent" (v. 30). Repentance is what is needed. The Greek concept here is *metanoia*—a change of mind. The rich man, like his brothers, needed a change of mind toward the painful suffering of people in his immediate community.

And this takes us to the point of many of Jesus's parables: listeners then (and readers now) are challenged to "change their minds" about something. Here all are challenged to change their minds about wealth and poverty. In the world we experience on a daily basis, the poor are marginalized and ignored; sometimes even blamed for their poverty and thus condemned to continue in it.[31] Yet in the parable a poor man is the one God favors, while the rich man is the one who is condemned. The rich are thereby challenged to have compassion on the poor and suffering, as God does. This first entails seeing them. It may also entail unlearning the social stigmas around poverty, sickness, and suffering, and rejecting the rationalizations that insulate us, so that we can activate the natural human response of compassion. And as we saw in the parable of the Good Samaritan, the response of compassion is what drives action: action to alleviate the suffering of another.

Sister Marilyn Lacy, RSM, has engaged deeply with these realities and, in the spirit of contemplation and action that defines the Sisters of

---

[31] On this, see Harrington and Holbert, *No Mercy, No Justice.*

Chapter 9

Mercy, has been moved to action. After decades of work with refugees around the world, in 2008 she founded Mercy Beyond Borders. With operations in South Sudan and Haiti, Mercy Beyond Borders works with more than 1,400 women and girls annually by providing educational, economic and empowerment opportunities where there are few options to escape extreme poverty. In 2017 Sister Marilyn received the Opus Prize, one of the world's largest faith-based awards for social entrepreneurship, and was designated an Opus Laureate. In reflecting on the parable of the Rich Man and Lazarus she articulates the challenge in a way that focuses on this world rather than the next:

> Jesus wants us to understand that God pays attention to here and now. Jesus invites us to wake up, to open our gates, to notice our suffering brothers and sisters. Jesus invites us to share our resources before it is too late, before the chasm between rich and poor grows so wide that it cannot be bridged, before our wealth walls us off from the Holy One who stands outside our gate: unnoticed, unkempt, unwanted. We have the choice: stay within our own comfort zone, or take the risk to move beyond safe borders. Mercy nudges us toward those unknown edges, toward encountering the "other" as beloved of God. Then as our ways begin to align more with God's ways, then we begin to experience paradise.[32]

The invitation of this parable is thus to take the risk, to make the choice to move outside of our comfort zones, and to be open to engage with those in need. To be nudged by Mercy. And to begin to experience paradise as a result.

When reading this parable through the lens of mercy, the challenge is clear: in this life is the time to recognize the humanity in all people, and to respond to the suffering of fellow humans with mercy. In particular, to become aware of those in our own community who are in need of mercy but that we may be unwilling to see. And, surprisingly, having compassion on others and showing mercy not only restores the humanity of the one in need; it has the potential to restore the humanity of the one showing the compassion. In this sense, the poor offer salvation to the wealthy. Becoming the beloved community has the potential to bring life and dignity to all, regardless of status.

---

[32] Marilyn Lacey, RSM, "The Rich Man and Lazarus," 2019. See her complete reflection in Appendix 1.

The Rich Man and Lazarus (Luke 16:19–31)

8. Our Final Step: Consider Implications

As we consider the implications of this parable we can return to a concept we have already encountered: the corporal works of mercy. James Keenan explicitly connects this parable with the work of mercy of feeding the hungry.[33] He identifies the ideas of fellowship and inclusivity as being critical in order to address the needs of the poor who do not have enough to feed themselves or their families. For Keenan, it was not that the rich man necessarily had any malice in withholding the crumbs from his table from Lazarus. The barriers simply conveniently and consistently prevented him from being "a part of the rich man's fellowship."[34] In the end then, this is a parable about creating that fellowship, including people, so that their needs can be seen, and their needs can be met.

While hunger is clearly an element of this parable, we can also recognize that Lazarus's needs went much deeper than simply the need for food. He needed medical care, clothing, and shelter. There is thus quite a bit more that can be said in relation to this parable and the works of mercy such as caring for the sick and clothing the naked. Keenan calls us to consider ways of creating inclusive fellowship so that all can be seen and their needs can be met. As we noted in considering issues related to ecological awareness and concerns about environmental justice, humans are not separate from earth's environment, but rather part of it. And because of that, issues relating to the environment impact humans and in particular, their ability to have enough food, clean water, and stability. As for issues relating to hunger and creating room at the table for all, Keenan cites climate change, volatile markets (globalization), and food wastage as major challenges to be addressed. In addition to being vigilant about meeting our own needs, "We are called to be vigilant about the needs of our neighbor.... We are called to develop a new sense of, expectation, *a sense of being ready for someone else's difficulties.*"[35] This is another important dimension of an ethic of love, mercy, and justice: readiness to respond to the needs of others.

Also from a Christian foundation, but approaching from a different angle, Cone calls humans to freedom as a key aspect of their

---

[33] Keenan, *Works of Mercy*, 31–35.

[34] Keenan identifies "barriers" in other contemporary contexts, particularly in his chapter on responses to AIDS crisis (see pp. 127–131).

[35] Keenan, *Works of Mercy*, 83 (italics original).

Chapter 9

humanity. But this freedom is not freedom for the purpose of indulging one's interests, but rather a freedom to give attention and consideration to the concerns of the oppressed. Cone writes, "Inherent in freedom is the recognition that there is something wrong with society, and those who are free will not be content until all members of society are treated as persons."[36] In our parable, it is fair to say that Lazarus, lying at the gate and being ignored by rich man, his family, and his guests, was not being treated as a person, but as an obstacle. Such a situation, then and now, ought to call forth human emotion, response, and action on behalf of the suffering one(s). Cone explains, "To be human is to be in the image of God—that is, to be creative: revolting against everything that is opposed to humanity."[37] Furthermore, "The image of God refers to the way in which God intends human beings to live in the world.... In a world in which persons are oppressed, the image is human nature in rebellion against the structures of oppression. It is humanity involved in the liberation struggle against the forces of inhumanity."[38]

The rich man in the parable, and those who fall prey to similar views of the present world, have an opportunity to perceive the world differently. "The beginning of freedom is the perception that oppressors are the evil ones, and we must do something about it."[39] And beyond this, to take an additional step: "They also recognize that freedom becomes a reality when they throw in their lot with an oppressed community by joining with it in its cause, accepting whatever is necessary to be identified with the victims of evil."[40] Looking at the parables of Jesus we can suggest that the Samaritan embodied this idea of true humanity and human freedom. At least in the scope of the parable, he threw in his lot with the wounded man on the side of the road, who was a victim of evil. In a similar vein, the master of the vineyard threw in his lot with the workers he hired throughout the day. Though not everyone was able to work a full day, he provided each one a full day's wage—to the delight of those hired later, and to the chagrin of those who worked

[36] Cone, *Black Theology*, 88.
[37] Cone, *Black Theology*, 93.
[38] Cone, *Black Theology*, 94.
[39] Cone, *Black Theology*, 94.
[40] Cone, *Black Theology*, 94.

The Rich Man and Lazarus (Luke 16:19–31)

the whole day. Though perhaps not in a position to reimagine the whole social structure, within his sphere of ability he was able to at least provide work, a wage, and a sense of dignity for those who did not have additional job security but who labored on his behalf. In the parable of the rich man and Lazarus, however, the rich man emphatically did not throw in his lot with his suffering neighbor, Lazarus.

In the era in which James Cone was writing in the 1960s the Civil Rights movement was drawing critical attention to the injustices of racism, segregation, and other legal forms of discrimination that favored whites and disadvantaged peoples of color. In such a context during which time many corners of the Christian community failed to call out these injustices and evils, Cone offered an important message. If God was truly on the side of the oppressed, then persons created in the image of God, who fully lived into that reality, would themselves use their human freedom and energy to work for the liberation of the oppressed persons that God loved. In a racist society, Cone described the implication in ways that are worth quoting at length. The following three quotes capture this idea powerfully:

> Freedom means taking sides in a crisis situation, when a society is divided into oppressed and oppressors. In this situation we are not permitted the luxury of being on neither side by making a decision that only involves the self. Our decision affects the whole of society, and it cannot but be made in view of either oppressed or oppressors. There is no way to transcend this alternative.[41]
>
> The truly free are identified with the humiliated because they know that their own being is involved in the degradation of their brothers and sisters. They cannot stand to see them stripped of their humanity. This is not so because of pity or sympathy, but because their own existence is being limited by another's slavery.[42]
>
> Christians can never be content as long as their sisters and brothers are enslaved. They must suffer with them, knowing that freedom for Jesus Christ is always freedom for the oppressed.[43]

---

[41] Cone, *Black Theology*, 94–95.
[42] Cone, *Black Theology*, 95.
[43] Cone, *Black Theology*, 101.

Chapter 9

Returning to the rich man and Lazarus, as a parable of Jesus we see here an expression of Jesus's message and teaching. As such, this parable is an invitation to follow his example and to join in solidarity with the poor, oppressed, suffering, and marginalized. It also invites us to interrogate our understandings of wealth and poverty, and our assumptions about both the rich and the poor. The symbol of the gate and the symbol of the great chasm challenge us to imagine the possibility of a world in which those distances can be narrowed, human fellowship can be restored, and basic needs can be met so that all may be free to live and thrive.

Works Cited in Chapter 9

Blomberg, Craig L. *Interpreting the Parables*. Second ed. Downers Grove, IL: IVP Academic, 2012.

Carey, Greg. *Stories Jesus Told: How to Read a Parable*. First ed. Nashville: Abingdon, 2019.

Cone, James H. *A Black Theology of Liberation*. 20th anniversary ed. Maryknoll, NY: Orbis Books, 1990.

Crossan, John Dominic. *The Power of Parable: How Fiction by Jesus Became Fiction about Jesus*. New York: HarperOne, 2012.

Farley, Margaret A. "Wisdom, Dignity, and Justice: Higher Education as a Work of Mercy." *The MAST Journal* 16 (2006): 3–8.

Gowler, David B. *The Parables after Jesus: Their Imaginative Receptions across Two Millennia*. Grand Rapids: Baker Academic, 2017.

Harrington, Brooks and John C. Holbert. *No Mercy, No Justice: The Dominant Narrative of America Versus the Counter-Narrative of Jesus' Parables*. Eugene, OR: Cascade Books, 2019.

Herzog, William R. *Parables as Subversive Speech: Jesus as Pedagogue of the Oppressed*. Louisville, KY: Westminster/John Knox, 1994.

Hultgren, Arland J. *The Parables of Jesus: A Commentary*. The Bible in its World. Grand Rapids: Eerdmans, 2000.

Keenan, James F. *The Works of Mercy: The Heart of Catholicism*. Third ed. Lanham: Rowman & Littlefield, 2017.

Lacey, Marilyn, RSM. "The Rich Man and Lazarus." 2019.

Levine, Amy-Jill. *Short Stories by Jesus: The Enigmatic Parables of a Controversial Rabbi*. New York: HarperOne, 2014.

The Rich Man and Lazarus (Luke 16:19–31)

Schottroff, Luise. *The Parables of Jesus*. Minneapolis: Fortress, 2006.
Snodgrass, Klyne. *Stories with Intent: A Comprehensive Guide to the Parables of Jesus*. Second ed. Grand Rapids: Eerdmans, 2018.
Sobrino, Jon. *The Principle of Mercy: Taking the Crucified People from the Cross*. Maryknoll, NY: Orbis Books, 1994.
Sobrino, Jon. *No Salvation Outside the Poor: Prophetic-Utopian Essays*. Maryknoll, NY: Orbis Books, 2008.

Conclusion: Living into Our Humanity and Cultivating an Ethic of Love, Mercy, and Justice

1. Introduction

Throughout this book we have engaged in a process of studying an individual parable, considering its message to the original hearers, and exploring its challenge in our contemporary context. We worked through an intentional sequence of reflective steps involving grasping the features of each parable, asking good questions to clarify meaning, identifying the narrative twist or surprise within the parable, and considering the metaphors in play and their significance. On that foundation we then sought to translate the challenge of the parable from its narrative mode into propositional statements, sensitive to the ways that elements of meaning and affective impact could be lost in this process of translation from one genre to another. From there we moved away from, or rather, looked through the world of the text to a consideration of implications in our contemporary context with particular attention to issues of social justice.

In following such an approach this volume has been an exercise in biblical interpretation and ethics that engages the "then and there" of the New Testament world as well as the "here and now" of North American society in the 2020s. In this sense the volume participates in the process of ethical interpretation of the New Testament outlined by Richard B. Hays.[1]

[1] Hays, *Moral Vision*.

Social Justice in the Stories of Jesus: The Ethical Challenge of the Parables, First Edition.
Matthew E. Gordley.
© 2024 John Wiley & Sons Ltd. Published 2024 by John Wiley & Sons Ltd.

Living into Our Humanity and Cultivating an Ethic of Love

For each parable, in our process of seeking to read each passage carefully and understand what it actually says we engaged in what Hays called the "descriptive task." We saw this to be a critical foundation for any further engagement. We also sought to understand each parable in its multiple contexts. These included the broader cultural and religious context of first-century Judaism within the Roman Empire; the specific literary context of a particular parable in a particular Gospel; and the context of the teaching of Jesus as captured in the Gospels and early Christian writings. With this contextual work we moved into what Hays referred to as the "synthetic task": placing the particular text in conversation with the rest of the Bible in light of the guiding focal images of the New Testament. Of necessity we did so only in a limited way and could not provide an exhaustive accounting of this synthetic task, but rather highlighted key elements of the broader context that shed light on the particular parable. Finally, we moved to the process of relating the text to our current situation through an integrative act of the imagination. This is what Hays referred to as the hermeneutical task.[2]

Having worked through this intentional process we now see clearly why parables were such a powerful tool when used by Jesus to engage his audiences in critical reflection on their lives and the world around them. As a form of instruction, parables gently but insistently invite the listener to become aware of assumptions through the means of short, memorable stories grounded in the concrete realities of first-century rural life. By helping people to face their unexamined assumptions about the world, themselves, and others the parables are themselves an embodiment of one of the seven "spiritual works of mercy": to instruct the ignorant. Instructing the ignorant as parables do is not simply about helping people gain knowledge. It is rather about helping people to become aware of realities that are true about their lives but that they may never have realized. James F. Keenan describes this work of instructing the ignorant as one of the practices that enable us to "focus our attention rightly."[3]

---

[2] Hays's fourth and final task is the pragmatic one, and one which goes beyond the scope of any book: living out the text in the context of our daily lives individually and as individuals-in-community.

[3] Keenan, *Works of Mercy*, 83.

Conclusion

Focusing attention rightly certainly seems to be a goal of the parables of Jesus.

Along similar lines Sidney Callahan explains, "One of the most important things that one can teach another is to pursue an awareness of the hidden frameworks and prior assumptions which may be constricting one's vision or confining one's range of solutions."[4] Through Jesus's use of vignettes of everyday life with a whole range of different twists and turns, the parables invite readers to reflect on their assumptions and question their otherwise constricted vision of reality. Thus we might say that Jesus used an instructional tool which was less oriented toward conveying information, and more suited to creating awareness and openness to other perspectives. Jesus's parables themselves are a work of mercy as they enlighten those who are willing to learn from them.

As merciful and mercy-filled as the parables are, they do not appear to have been designed to comfort or confirm the listener's current mode of living or thinking. Rather, through their surprises, reversals, and defying of expectations they seem to be intended to provoke, challenge, and get people thinking in new ways about things that really matter. As narrative fiction, the stories themselves draw people into reflection on the drama within the narrative (what we have been referring to as the "in meaning"). In addition, as with all great literature, readers almost automatically begin making connections between the world of the parable and their own worlds, seeing their world anew through the lens of the parable (the "through meaning").

In addition to the meaning *within* the parable and its connections to the real world *outside* of the parable we also saw that there is a world of assumptions *behind* each parable—the worldview or what Via calls the "implied understanding of existence."[5] The internal meaning of the parable as a story works with this "existential understanding" behind the parable, and yields a unique "through meaning" of the parable for a listener at any time to consider, in relation to their own circumstances. At the time of Jesus, a given parable may have held one particular through meaning as readers connected the parable to events

---

[4] Sidney Cornelia Callahan, *With All our Heart and Mind: The Spiritual Works of Mercy in a Psychological Age* (New York: Crossroad, 1988), 47.

[5] Via, *Parables*, 95.

284

Living into Our Humanity and Cultivating an Ethic of Love

in the ministry of Jesus or in their own experiences; in differing circumstances and cultures as well as in our own day, there could naturally be another meaning. We have thus seen that each generation has the opportunity to engage the parables as they do their work of creating awareness, challenging prevailing assumptions, and offering new ways to imagine one's place in the world individually and as a community. And that is what we have sought to do in this book for our time and our place.

As we reach the end of our journey we can now look back at some of the paths we have traveled and draw some conclusions about the message of Jesus as conveyed to us through the parables. We will first take a moment to summarize the eight parables we have explored together, highlighting some of their key elements. Next, we will identify eight themes that permeate the parables and call for our continued attention. Third, we will revisit some of the conversation partners who helped us consider social implications of these parables from a wide range of perspectives. Finally, based on all of the above, we will outline the elements of an ethic of love, mercy, and justice which Jesus teaches as central to living into one's truest and deepest humanity.

2. Summary of the Parables

We began with the parable of the Good Samaritan (Luke 10:25–37) in which Jesus challenged his listeners to consider what it truly means to be a neighbor to a person in need. Through the story of a wounded man left for dead by the side of the road and three different individuals who come upon him, Jesus invited his audience to envision a world in which compassion toward those in need superseded divisions and hatred. The Samaritan who showed mercy on the wounded man despite the socially conditioned animosity they likely harbored toward one another is an image which suggests that mercy, compassion, and solidarity are the embodiment of genuine human concern for a fellow human who is suffering. Thus, Jesus challenged his listeners then and now to consider what it means to be a neighbor qualitatively rather than geographically. Jon Sobrino and others helped us to extend this challenge into our contemporary world of suffering peoples. In addition to reacting to the

Conclusion

suffering of another, we also noted the challenge of being ready to respond to the needs of others, predisposed to mercy and actively seeking to be a neighbor.

We next turned to the twin parables of the lost sheep and lost coin (Luke 15:4–10). In these short vignettes from rural life Jesus invited listeners to consider the inherent value of every member within a community and to recognize that God's highest joy is experienced in the fullness of the human community. In a way comparable to a shepherd seeking a lost sheep and a woman seeking a lost coin, where both individuals call their friends and neighbors together to celebrate the return of the lost, we are to understand that God likewise seeks, saves, and restores individuals to a meaningful place in community—and invites all people to celebrate their return as well. Implicit in these parables is also a challenge to our unexamined commitment to individualism and an invitation to us to begin see ourselves as individuals-in-community. Emilie Townes, Vivek Murthy, and Bryan Massingale helped us engage the concept of the common good and envision social structures, policies, and institutions that would support inclusive community for the good of all persons.

The parable of the lost sons (Luke 15:11–32) followed the lost sheep and lost coin and concluded what was a trio of parables focused on a vision of community in which the lost are not only found but celebrated by the community on their reintegration into their social context. Through a socially situated male-centered drama of a father and two sons, Jesus provided a challenge to embrace the life promoting power of participation in loving community, and to see ourselves as individuals-in-community with an inseparable link to others that will impact all of us one way or another. Through the departure, destitution, and return of the younger brother the parable brings into sharp relief the life sustaining power of community and the life threatening potential of its absence. Furthermore, through the resentment, refusal, and complaints of the older son who had always obeyed and never left, the parable showcases that one's proximity to the community may not necessarily be indicative of one's grasp of what it means to be a valued part of the community. For all persons, the mercy of God invites a deeper and more intentional experience of what it means to be together and experience the life-giving power of connection. In this context Howard Thurman helped us to consider the interconnectedness of all life and the resulting understanding that the well-being of others is linked to

Living into Our Humanity and Cultivating an Ethic of Love

my own well-being. Implications for our divisive social context of the 2020s suggest the need to engage in practices that reconnect us, that rehumanize those we view as our adversaries, and that help create the societal conditions in which all may thrive. These practices include things like active listening, understanding our opponents, extending anticipatory forgiveness, and engaging in compassion-based activism using the principles of peacebuilding. Inherent in all of these approaches was also the expectation of setting firm limits on abuse and preventing harm, so that progress in community building could be made.

We next examined the parable of the mustard seed (Mark 4:30–32; Matthew 13:31–32; Luke 13:18–19). This was our first look at a nature parable in which humans are surprisingly absent; there is no mention in this parable of any people, but only of natural phenomena. Through this metaphor Jesus invited listeners to see God's kingdom not as an other-worldly spiritual realm but rather embodied and on display in the natural world around them. Such an image is like a "school of nature" through which listeners are challenged to develop an ecological awareness: a sensitivity to the hospitable provision of the needs of and space for all of God's creatures. When we recognize that humans also are God's creatures and *a part of* rather than *distinct from* the natural world, we recognize that environmental issues and environmental justice concern all of us. We also saw the extent to which the environmental challenges of the twenty-first century have a decidedly more negative impact on the poor and marginalized.

We turned our attention next to the parable of the Pharisee and the tax collector (Luke 18:9–14). In this parable of reversal Jesus challenged listeners to recognize that all humans are connected by their shared dependence on God and God's mercy. The possibility that justification was available to both men, despite their significant contrasts in profession, religion, morals, and commitment to the community, suggests to us that we may need to reconsider our judgments on groups of people who are not like "us" and instead embrace that "all of us" are us. Just as the parable of the mustard seed suggests human interconnectedness with our natural environment, so this parable demonstrates the interconnectedness of all persons with one another—and our shared need for mercy. In the assessment of the kingdom of God, such a recognition invites us to compassion rather than judgment on those who neither see nor experience the world as we do.

Conclusion

The parable of the laborers in the vineyard (Matthew 20:1–16) put on display a generous landowner who continuously invited unemployed day-laborers into his vineyard. Most surprising of all was his decision to pay each one a full day's wage—to the delight of some and to the concern of those who worked the full day for the same pay. This parable challenged us in several ways: to accept the generous mercy of God toward all (including ourselves and others we think may be "less" deserving of mercy); to consider where we can extend that same generous mercy to others within our sphere of influence; and to examine our values relative to competition and collaboration in order to develop the spirit of the kingdom that will undergird our actions of generosity in this present world. Themes of solidarity and the common good came to the foreground in this parable.

Our final parable was that of the rich man and Lazarus (Luke 16:19–31). Through a reversal of fortunes of an extremely wealthy man and an extremely poor man who lay at the rich man's gate, Jesus reminded listeners that their earthly life is the time to recognize the humanity in all people, and to respond to the suffering of fellow humans with mercy. With this story Jesus affirmed the teaching of the Jewish scriptures, particularly the theme that God is on the side of the poor, the oppressed, and the marginalized, and that God's people must be too if they are to experience life to the full. Surprisingly, the parable implies that having compassion on others and showing mercy not only restores the humanity of the one in need; it also includes the potential to restore the humanity of the one showing the compassion. In this sense, the poor offer invaluable gifts to the wealthy including illumination and salvation. For the wealthy to receive these gifts requires eyes open to the needs of others and a heart ready to be moved to compassion and action.

3. Shared Themes throughout the Parables of Jesus

While the subjects of parables are wide-ranging, and no two parables make the same exact point, we have been able to see some clear themes, assumptions, and values that are promoted throughout the specific parables we have explored. Here we outline eight of the most significant.

Living into Our Humanity and Cultivating an Ethic of Love

First, the parables assert the value of every person. Regardless of societal position, economic status, gender, class, or ethnic or religious background, the dignity of all persons is affirmed. Without naming the biblical creation narratives specifically, this inherent dignity is grounded in an understanding of the origins of humanity as reflected in the Jewish scriptures and is a critical part of the worldview behind the parables. While expressed in the parables in metaphors and images integrally linked to the first-century context, the message of the inherent dignity of each person is a theme that conveys across time and location. Such an understanding is expressed powerfully in the modern world in the United Nations' 1948 document "The Universal Declaration of Human Rights." Grounded in the "recognition of the inherent dignity and of the equal and inalienable rights of all members of the human family," this document suggests that such a belief forms "the foundation of freedom, justice and peace in the world."[6] Expressed in this way, the dignity of every person is a value shared by many religions, and one that finds strong support in the teaching of Jesus.

Second, and closely tied to the first, is the theme of concern and responsibility for the needs of those whose dignity is compromised or overlooked. In the world of the parables Jesus introduced a range of fascinating types of characters, many of whom were individuals facing adversity. For some like Lazarus, the wounded man by the road, and the day laborers still waiting to be hired, their agency was severely limited as a result of injustices or hardships. In the parables these individuals are noteworthy for their situation of need and for Jesus's expression of concern for their well-being. This concern is seen through the inclusion of characters with agency who bear responsibility for their actions toward others. There is an expectation that the generosity of divine concern for those in such need would be expressed in actions by those who have an ability to act and meet the needs of others. It is not insignificant that when Jesus gives the command to "go and do likewise" (Luke 10:37) he was not speaking about morality or religious activity but about caring for a fellow human being in crisis.

---

[6] United Nations General Assembly, *The Universal Declaration of Human Rights (UDHR)* (United Nations General Assembly, 1948 [Accessed December 16, 2022]); available from https://www.un.org/en/about-us/universal-declaration-of-human-rights.

Conclusion

Third, compassion is a thread that is explicit in several parables and strongly implied in others. Rather than an obligation to help those in need, compassion erupts as a visceral response to the suffering of others and motivates action to relieve the suffering. The Samaritan acted on behalf of the wounded man because he was moved with compassion. The father of the lost son was also filled with compassion toward the son returning home broken and destitute. The vineyard owner saw that there were many individuals without work and without means to support themselves or their families. The actions each of these individuals took on behalf of others were a result of their compassion: to see, feel, and respond to the need of another. In other parables it is the lack of compassion that is noteworthy, as we saw in the case of the rich man and Lazarus and the Pharisee and the tax collector. This theme of compassion within the parables works on several levels. First, at the level of the story, through a verbal picture we see compassion in action, as example and illustration, and are attracted to it as inherently valuable. Second, through the metaphorical reach of the parable we understand that the parable in some sense tells us about the compassionate nature of God, from whom such a quality originates. Third, listeners are challenged to understand that God is a God of compassion, and that compassion in our interactions with others is a part of what it means to live into our full humanity as children of God. The absence of compassion, on the other hand, is a warning sign that our own humanity may be diminished and is not yet fully realized.

A fourth theme cutting across the parables relates to the first three. It is the reality of the interconnectedness of all persons, whether recognized or not. Pope Francis puts it concisely: "We are all really responsible for all."[7] Parables like the mustard seed, the rich man and Lazarus, the Pharisee and the tax collector, and the laborers in the vineyard help us grapple with this theme. And the parables of the lost sheep, lost coin, and lost sons make this explicit: a community is diminished when any of its members do not experience the life-giving power of connection with others. This theme invites all to a stance of solidarity with others. It also invites us to consider ourselves not just as individuals but as individuals-in-community, which is what we truly are whether we recognize it

---

[7] Cited in Massingale, *Racial Justice*, 116.

Living into Our Humanity and Cultivating an Ethic of Love

or not. To use a different metaphor to express this, mystic and philosopher Pierre Teilhard de Chardin writes: "We are not like the cut flowers that make up a bouquet: we are like the leaves and buds of a great tree on which everything appears at its proper time and place as required and determined by the good of the whole."[8] In light of this understanding of reality the parables support a commitment to the notion of the common good.

Fifth, the parables bring to our attention issues of justice. The *dike* (Greek term for "justice") word group finds its way into a number of parables asking the reader to judge what is just, right, and fair, and to consider who is righteous and who is justified. Despite our propensity to treat righteousness as an individual characteristic associated with piety, the scriptures indicate that this word group has more to do with one's obligations to others in community. When those obligations are not met, injustice is present. The distinction between the metaphorical sheep and goats in the parable in Matthew 25 is their action or inaction on behalf of those in situations of need in their community. Thus, it is appropriate to define justice not as a punitive concept but rather as "primarily the desire for opportunity equality, liberation, and right relationship."[9] Such an understanding of justice cannot be an ideal that we simply mentally assent to, however. It leads to giving attention to the diversity of human experience, interrogating and uncovering where oppression has effaced the dignity of some persons, and caring enough to take steps to address injustice.[10] This is the connection between justice and mercy. Although justice and mercy have at times been considered opposites (such as when mercy is understood simply as *not* giving out the just punishment that is deserved), such an understanding represents a diminished view of both mercy and justice. True mercy attends to matters of justice and

---

[8] Teilhard de Chardin, *Hymn of the Universe*, 93.

[9] Baldwin, *Taking It to the Streets*, viii.

[10] Townes captures this well: "Justice leads to public policies that claim rights as a part of the assertion of our dignity and well-being. It is relational, not autonomous, and leads to a sense of caring.... It recognizes the interdependence in which we all actually live." Townes, *Womanist Ethics*, 135. She adds, "Justice, then, is more than giving to each what is due or treating all cases equally. It requires attention to our diversities, particularly to those most marginalized. Simply put, justice involves uncovering, understanding, and rejecting oppression—which is but another way of saying that it involves structural evil" (135).

Conclusion

injustice and, in particular, seeks to remedy injustice out of concern for those who suffer as a result.

Sixth, expanding on the interconnectedness of all persons, we encounter in the parables the interconnectedness of humans with all of the natural world. Nature parables, in which Jesus gives attention to the beauty and intricacy of the created world, invite readers to see themselves as part of this larger community of life. Pope Francis, in his encyclical *Laudato Si'*, speaks at different times of *all* things being connected, related, interrelated, and interconnected. He writes, "Everything is related, and we human beings are united as brothers and sisters on a wonderful pilgrimage, woven together by the love God has for each of his creatures and which also unites us in fond affection with brother sun, sister moon, brother river and mother earth."[11] Not only so, but he understands Jesus as promoting this understanding as well. Jesus was "able to invite others to be attentive to the beauty that there is in the world because he himself was in constant touch with nature, lending it an attention full of fondness and wonder. As he made his way throughout the land, he often stopped to contemplate the beauty sown by his Father, and invited his disciples to perceive a divine message in things."[12] Humans are thus not separate from their environments but are literally a part of the environment themselves, making environmental concerns human concerns.

Seventh, across all of the parables we learn that the small moments, actions, and choices of daily life are, in the divine economy, the big moments. Seemingly insignificant moments are actually where God's kingdom is enacted or contradicted. It is in the going about of our daily work and interactions that we honor human dignity, demonstrate concern for others, and join in solidarity with others. Every moment thus has the potential to be a moment of significance as we choose which values will guide our choices in the present circumstances. This is what Emilie Townes refers to as the "everydayness of moral acts." Her call to people of faith is to "live your faith deeply. This is not a quest for perfection, but for what we call in Christian ethics the everydayness of moral acts."[13] In

---

[11] Francis, *Laudato Si'*, 68.
[12] Francis, *Laudato Si'*, 70–71.
[13] Townes, *Womanist Ethics*, 164.

Living into Our Humanity and Cultivating an Ethic of Love

this sense the parables bring into the present moment an opportunity to choose to live in a way that enacts the kingdom of God, or to act in a way that fails to do so. The kingdom of God is thus not a future coming concept, but a present reality. The parables at times explicitly use a metaphor of future judgment to highlight the critical importance of actions in the present world. The focus there is not on what happens in the future, but drawing attention to the critical significance of what happens in readers' day-to-day lives.

Eighth, despite their simplicity, there are no simple parables: the parables do not give up their treasures easily. Rather than giving easy answers about the right thing to do in a given situation, the parables point instead to a deeper and richer kind of approach. As with stories in general, the parables seem more suited to shaping readers' character and imagination than to giving exact prescriptions on how to handle each ethical question. In this way the parables support virtue ethics more so than normative ethics. "In the field of Christian ethics," writes, Alain Thomasset, "the Bible's major contribution may well be as a means of forming our characters and of nourishing particular virtues that predispose our action in the world."[14] This assertion captures the reality we find specifically in the parables as well. Their message, like that of the Bible, is addressed to the readers' imaginations, tapping into their ability to see their world in new ways: "Imagination is the mediation between the world of the text and the reader's appropriation" and in the shaping of the imagination we discover "the power of the biblical text to transform the ways in which its readers imagine reality and live in the world."[15] As Louise Schottroff expresses it in relation to the parable of the Good Samaritan, "The parable becomes a window through which the new creation becomes visible."[16] Reading parables well invites readers to imagine their world differently and then to live differently.

---

[14] Alain Thomasset, "The Virtue of Hospitality according to the Bible and the Challenge of Migration," in *The Bible and Catholic theological Ethics* (ed. Chan; *Catholic Theological Ethics in the World Church*; Maryknoll, NY: Orbis Books, 2017), 34.

[15] Thomasset, "Virtue of Hospitality," 36.

[16] Schottroff, *Parables*, 137.

Conclusion

This process of transformation through engaging the mind and the heart is powerful; it is also complex and defies easy explanation. It also suggests that the consideration of what a parable "means" is a reflective process that must be entered into by persons in a particular time and place in view of their specific circumstances. The interpretations of theologians from other times and other places, as insightful and instructive as they may be, cannot be a substitute for the imaginative engagement of each new generation of readers in their own social locations.

Ultimately the parables offer an imaginative vision of a just and merciful world in which readers are invited to contribute to human flourishing. It is a world where all creatures are reverenced and respected as a part of all that exists. It is also a world in which pain, suffering, and injustice exist and must be faced. In such a world of chaos and struggle, compassion for others and a concern for the well-being of others motivates a response of love and concern for all such suffering. In addition, the response of love is one that faces reality head on, while recognizing the limited scope of our individual grasp of it. In such a way, the person who lives in mercy recognizes their need of others, and even the need of the oppressor to receive and experience mercy, so that the community can be restored and achieve its highest potential. The parables do not seem to assume that all will embrace this mercy and live into it; but they present the listener with the reality that the time to choose it is the present moment, and the place to experience it is wherever one is at the moment. Baldwin uses the parable of the sheep and the goats in Matthew 25 to make this very point: "True prosperity includes a sustainable, healthful life in which all of the basic needs of life are adequately met and many of the joys of life are accessible—this is the true measure of life, liberty and pursuit of fulfillment/happiness. This is the vision Jesus offers in Matthew 25."[17]

4. Conversation Partners

Throughout our exploration of the parables we have connected our analysis with conversation partners from a range of backgrounds who provided unique insights into the social dynamics at work in the parables and in their application today. Beyond the discipline of biblical

[17]   Baldwin, *Taking It to the Streets*, viii.

Living into Our Humanity and Cultivating an Ethic of Love

scholarship we considered perspectives on social realities and societal forces from the vantage point of liberation theology, black theology, feminist theology, womanist theology, as well as authors writing from a position that was not explicitly religious at all.

In terms of biblical scholarship we benefited immensely from the work of Amy-Jill Levine who provides a model for reflecting on the parables that attends responsibly to their original contexts. Importantly, Levine's model includes paying careful attention to the persistence of anti-Jewish readings of the parables and resisting those in favor of a more informed picture of the Jewish context in which Jesus lived and taught. This approach yields two valuable results. First, it draws attention to biases and misinformation about early Judaism that have contributed to the growth of anti-Semitism and violence against Jews. Such an awareness allows us to resist such distortions and stand against negative stereotypes. Second, this approach enables a fuller grasp of the message of Jesus in terms of what Jesus was actually getting at as a Jewish teacher in a Jewish context drawing on the rich tradition of the Jewish scriptures. Rather than hearing the parables as "new Christian teaching" in contrast to "bad Jewish practice," we can appreciate the message of Jesus as a message with deep meaning to his original audience: first-century Jews living within an advanced agrarian economy under the shadow of Roman imperial domination. To such an audience the parables of Jesus provoked and challenged even as they announced a message of good news to the disinherited—a message which came in and through the matrix of early Judaism.

Jon Sobrino, a Latino liberation theologian, introduced us to what he referred to as the principle of mercy. From Sobrino we learn that true mercy is not one-sided or paternalistic, but rather communal and affirms the human dignity of the ones needing mercy and the ones showing mercy. It involves both giving and receiving on the part of those offering mercy and on the part of those in need of mercy. Mercy thus invites solidarity with those in need and offers an alternate vision to the materialistic, competitive, consumer-driven culture that is so prominent in the West. Such a vision of mercy is not neutral in regard to social issues but necessarily comes into conflict with forces that seek to maintain the status quo. Mercy also recognizes the reality of anti-mercy in the world. Thus, for Sobrino, living out the principle of mercy

Conclusion

"means necessarily stepping into society's conflicts, running personal and institutional risks."[18] To be merciful in this sense is a challenging call to be ready to observe where human dignity is being compromised in the world around us, to identify with those in need, and to work alongside them to restore their dignity as fellow human beings.

Howard Thurman, a teacher, scholar, clergyman, and mentor to the leaders of the Civil Rights movement, invited us to consider self-in-community, which entails understanding one's own dignity, purpose, and potential as a child of God. This understanding also carries an obligation to recognize the dignity of others and promote the flourishing of all for the good of all. Thurman developed these insights through his engagement with the teaching of Jesus, viewing it as a message for the disinherited. As a Jewish teacher in a colonized and occupied land, Jesus spoke to his fellow Jews about what it meant to live out the kingdom in a context of suffering and disempowerment. To the extent that the institution of the Christian church evolved from embodying a message of good news to the disinherited into a religion of the powerful, Thurman instead focused on the "religion of Jesus." For Thurman this was a way to see through the distortions that over time have become part of the religion that is now called Christianity and focus on what was central in the teaching and life of Jesus.

James Cone, a black liberation theologian who began his career in the 1960s, more explicitly invited us to consider the experiences and perspectives of those on the margins as an important corrective to the white framework which has been privileged not only in American society but in the church and academy. On issues of racism, Cone invited all persons to come to a better understanding of how racist perspectives are embedded, intertwined, and protected within Christianity as commonly practiced in the United States. For Cone the life of Jesus demonstrated that God is emphatically on the side of the oppressed. So important is this reality for Cone that he could say, "To understand the historical Jesus without seeing his identification with the poor as decisive is to misunderstand him and thus distort his historical person."[19] This reality invites us to attend more closely to Jesus's teaching as it

[18] Sobrino, *Principle of Mercy*, 179.
[19] Cone, *Black Theology*, 113.

Living into Our Humanity and Cultivating an Ethic of Love

related to the poor, marginalized, and oppressed, something which we can see now in the parables themselves. Accordingly, those who claim to be followers of God, followers of Jesus, most naturally demonstrate their allegiance to God by throwing in their lot in solidarity with all who are oppressed—and particularly those oppressed within their own communities.

Bryan Massingale, examining racism specifically within the Catholic church today, further amplified the concept of solidarity as a means through which to destabilize the culture of racism. He drew our attention to Christian practices that can promote a fuller understanding of human community and which support collective equality, love, and solidarity within the human family. Massingale also advocates a model of racial reconciliation which includes the critical elements of "truth telling" (which involves recognition and naming of past harms and taking responsibility for addressing their ongoing impacts) and of "affirmative redress" (which involves the even more challenging concepts of reconstruction and reparation).[20]

Lisa Sowle-Cahill, a Catholic ethicist and scholar, invites us to understand human rights as derived from natural law and fundamental to any approach to ethical decisions about the crises in our world. Cahill also notes theologian Jon Sobrino's linking of orthodoxy (right thinking) and orthopraxis (right acting) with *orthopathy* (right feeling): "To do what is right requires an attraction to the good, commitment to its reality, and the imagination to see possibilities of goodness that stretch beyond present conditions."[21] In this light the parables move not only our thinking and acting, but our emotions and imaginations through the power of story.

Ethicist and Sister of Mercy Margaret Farley invited us to see the connection between mercy and justice as inseparably interrelated. Capturing the multiple dimensions of mercy she describes mercy as the love for one in need; the gift to the one in need; and the action of giving to the one in need. Farley also explains the interrelatedness of justice and mercy eloquently:

---

[20] Massingale, *Racial Justice*, 97–102.
[21] Cahill, *Global Justice*, 7.

Conclusion

> Mercy—if it is not to be a false mercy, if it is to be a genuinely healing mercy—must be normatively *shaped* by a justice that does not miss its call and response. Without justice, mercy has no power to meet the truly wounded or to give hope to the truly broken. Only with merciful justice and just mercy will there be mutual illumination, and requisite new ways of seeing, required for at least some things to be put right.[22]

Her expression relating to mutual illumination and new ways of seeing helps to capture the power of parables to achieve these purposes—or at least to startle us into awareness to begin to envision them as reality.

Emilie Townes, a womanist theologian and ethicist, invited us to consider not only our individual actions as good or bad, but also the reality of larger systems of oppression and injustice. It is only when individual and communal perspectives are taken together that justice can be achieved. Her understanding of justice falls in line with the other perspectives we have noted above from Sobrino to Cone, as well as what we see in the parables. Townes explains, "Justice is the notion that each one of us has worth, and that each one of us has the right to have that worth recognized and respected. In short, justice lets us know that we owe one another respect and the right to our dignity."[23]

For our purposes, in terms of the contemporary implications of this understanding, Townes points not only to individual actions (as important as they are) but also to public policy. She explains,

> Justice leads to public policies that claim rights as a part of the assertion of our dignity and well-being. It is relational, not autonomous, and leads to a sense of caring that is actualized in accessible and affordable health care and childcare, and to the development of a federal and rural development policy that is systemic rather than episodic. It recognizes the interdependence in which we all actually live.[24]

This idea of justice as relational helps us understand the importance of healthy community for supporting the kinds of justice that support all members. It also helps us understand the critical importance of public

[22] Farley, "Mercy and Its Works," 38.
[23] Townes, *Womanist Ethics*, 135.
[24] Townes, *Womanist Ethics*, 135.

Living into Our Humanity and Cultivating an Ethic of Love

actions of affirmative redress for those who suffer the burden of systemic injustices. Ultimately, Townes like others points to the common good as a guiding concept for ethical thinking and acting. She explains, "Perhaps the simplest way to think about the common good is in terms of having the social structures on which all depend work so that they benefit all people as we strive to create a genuinely inclusive and democratic social and moral order."[25] Embracing the common good is an important step on the path to creating a truly just society where all can thrive.

Pope Francis has also been vocal on issues of social justice not only in the Catholic Church but in the natural world which people of all faiths share. Francis invites solidarity, especially with the poor and marginalized, to promote a culture of encounter. He promotes the importance of creating a culture of encounter and openness to others that can enable societies to find meaningful solutions to their problems, and to find ways to move toward public policies that promote the good of all. Recognizing our dependence on the natural world and on one another invites us to see our lives as truly interconnected with others and to see that when the well-being of anyone is compromised, the health of all of us is diminished.

James Keenan, a Jesuit theologian and scholar of mercy, offered multiple insights about the works of mercy and their significance today. The corporal works of mercy and the spiritual works of mercy invite our engagement with the people around us in ways that derive directly from the parables of Jesus. Keenan also emphasized not only responding to need but being actively ready and watchful to help those in need. From the parable of the Rich Man and Lazarus to the parable of the Good Samaritan, Keenan finds that "the Gospels prompt Christians to see that we are called to be vigilant about the needs of our neighbor.... We are called to develop a new sense of expectation, *a sense of being ready for someone else's difficulties.*"[26] In this way, the call of Jesus connects us with the needs of others.

In addition to theologians and ethicists, we benefited from the insights of social analyst Heather McGhee who discussed cross-racial solidarity as being in everyone's interest. Rather than embrace a

---

[25] Townes, *Womanist Ethics*, 137.
[26] Keenan, *Works of Mercy*, 83.

Conclusion

zero-sum approach to life, we can embrace the solidarity dividend where we can all benefit from our collective gifts and abilities. In a similar vein, former surgeon general Vivek Murthy showed us the importance of connection for human well-being. Supporting what we understand theologically, Murthy argues that connection, community, and service to others are essential elements of human health. He thus calls for all of us to help create a culture of connection. This is not unlike Pope Francis's call to create cultures of encounter. Murthy explains that thinking "tribally" or seeking to isolate ourselves from other cultures (both of which are practices that support the continuation of racism and white supremacy, even unintentionally) are ways of living that put us at great risk. He notes, "The simple reality is that we no longer have the luxury of thinking and acting tribally. Not only is it becoming harder to isolate ourselves from members of different cultures, but isolation costs us in terms of perspective and experience, which are ever more valuable resources in our global society."[27] Though we in the United States may have veered from collective to individual approaches, Murthy argues that we now need to find ways to invest in the collective aspects of our societal life that can sustain and nurture all of us.

Linking the above themes together, the Sisters of Mercy cited in this volume have invited us to consider their approach of contemplation and action in the application of God's mercy in practical ways in this world. To contemplate is to reflect deeply on our world, its challenges, and our individual and collective place within it. To act is to move intentionally into the space in which we live, and to do so in ways that address concrete needs, embodying mercy in our lives. The cycle of contemplation and action invites us continually to reflect and act, and then reflect on those actions, and act anew. That these actions begin from an acknowledgment of the dignity of every person, and an intention to see that dignity respected, means that mercy in action is a dynamic exchange based on relationships, understanding, and a recognition that we all have something to give.

The gritty realness of the parables grounds an understanding that the concreteness of daily life is the place where the kingdom is experienced. Yes, the parables invite consideration of spiritual realities, but those

---

[27] Murthy, *Together*, 96.

Living into Our Humanity and Cultivating an Ethic of Love

realities are not other-worldly. Those realities are unavoidably embedded in situations and social interactions in the physical world. This suggests that if we are leaning too heavily on a spiritual interpretation that is removed from this world, we need to allow the concreteness of the parables to pull us back down to earth. On the other hand, if we seek the comforting certainty of the concreteness of a particular parable, we may need to make room for an understanding that there is more than just the concrete world: there is also the world of the spirit in which we can see ourselves and others according to a set of values that may be counter to what is in our current reality.

Much like Moses at the burning bush, who recognized that he was in the presence of God, the parables invite us to embrace that reality whether we are outdoors, indoors, working, or worshipping. Bishop Michael Curry explains this reality by noting that "sometimes the *extra* is hidden right there in the ordinary"—an apt expression for the power of parables.[28] As a personal example he shares his experience of learning from the wisdom of his grandmother at work in the kitchen, a situation which is both ordinary and common, and at the same time extraordinary and touched with divine inspiration. Curry goes on to quote Elizabeth Barrett Browning to this same effect:

Earth's crammed with heaven,
And every common bush afire with God;
But only he who sees, takes off his shoes;
The rest sit round it and pluck blackberries.[29]

These lines, and Curry's reflection, are similar also to Gerard Manley Hopkins who describes the wonders of the created world as reflecting the glory of God. Nowhere is this expressed more clearly than in his poem "Hurrahing in Harvest":

These things, these things were here and but the beholder
Wanting.[30]

---

[28] Curry and Grace, *Love is the Way*, 58.
[29] Cited in Curry and Grace, *Love is the Way*, 57.
[30] Gerard Manley Hopkins, *Poems and Prose of Gerard Manley Hopkins* (Baltimore, MD: Penguin Books, 1953), 31.

Conclusion

In other words, the concrete and visible world around us and in which we live is the world in which the divine is active and present. But do we have the eyes to perceive it? From the parables, our conversation partners, and our own experiences of the divine in our lives, we are challenged to consider the truth of these sentiments and the kind of ethic they invite us to embody.

5. An Ethic of Love, Mercy, and Justice

To suggest that the parables promote an ethic of love, mercy, and justice is to situate them within a tradition of virtue ethics. Rather than providing clear-cut answers to specific ethical challenges, the parables point to the kinds of things that ought to be valued and practiced in a world in which God's ways prevail. The parables promote the importance of becoming people who are shaped by love, formed by mercy, and attentive to justice. To be attentive to justice does not simply mean avoiding injustice, but actively working against it in favor of justice for all persons.

An ethic of love, mercy, and justice is not a new idea. Our claim is that it can appropriately be traced to the teaching of Jesus in the parables and that it also precedes Jesus through the teaching of the Jewish scriptures on which Jesus drew heavily. An ethic of love alone (with no additional descriptors) could comfortably cover all the material we have found in the parables. However, drawing attention to the added concepts of mercy and justice, together with the concept of love, provides an important corrective to popular conceptions of love which highlight feelings but do not capture the rich complexity of the biblical notion of love. It also provides a needed focal point for the otherwise potentially "fuzzy" concept of love.[31]

Of course, love does not need to be abstract or generalized. Bishop Michael Curry makes it quite concrete: "Love is a firm commitment to act for the well-being of someone other than yourself."[32] At the same time, he shows how broad its scope can be: "It can be personal or

[31] See hooks, *All about Love*, 4–5.
[32] Curry and Grace, *Love is the Way*, 14.

Living into Our Humanity and Cultivating an Ethic of Love

political, individual or communal, intimate or public. Love will not be segregated to the private, personal precincts of life. Love, as I read it in the Bible, is ubiquitous. It affects all aspects of life."[33] Key for Curry though is that it always contains an interpersonal dimension, with a focus on the well-being of someone else. He adds, "Love is a commitment to seek the good and to work for the good and welfare of others."[34] Love and the common good are thus seen to be inseparable.

Feminist scholar bell hooks is very helpful for our purposes in defining love and the qualities that mark a love ethic. Eschewing the primacy of "love as a feeling" she, like Curry, focused instead on "love as action." In this way of thinking, genuine love is essentially an intention of the will to act on behalf of another's growth and well-being. It includes a combination of elements of care, commitment, trust, knowledge, responsibility, and respect.[35] Following psychologist M. Scott Peck she defines love as "the will to extend one's self for the purpose of nurturing one's own or another's spiritual growth."[36] Affection and positive regard are certainly important in shaping the will to act in these ways, but she notes, "To truly love we must learn to mix various ingredients—care, affection, recognition, respect, commitment, and trust, as well as honest and open communication."[37] If this captures a more holistic understanding of love, then a love ethic offers a set of values to live by, which can help to shape one's daily choices and actions, as well as impact larger issues in society including our institutions, policies, and laws.

Interestingly, hooks argues that a presupposition of a love ethic is what we have already discovered: the recognition of the dignity of every person and the implications of that in terms of what it means for human rights. In her approach, "A love ethic presupposes that everyone has the right to be free, to live fully and well."[38] This is another

---

[33] Curry and Grace, *Love is the Way*, 14–15.

[34] Curry and Grace, *Love is the Way*, 23.

[35] hooks, *All about Love*, 6–7.

[36] hooks, *All about Love*, 3.

[37] hooks, *All about Love*, 4. Hooks explains, "When we are loving we openly and honestly express care, affection, responsibility, respect, commitment, and trust" (14).

[38] hooks, *All about Love*, 87.

Conclusion

foundational element for envisioning a world of human flourishing in which all may thrive.

Both hooks and Curry find that a love ethic has strong historical roots in movements for social change. "Love as an action is the only thing that has ever changed the world for the better," writes Curry.[39] Curry offers a compelling series of examples in support of this claim ranging from Martin Luther King, Jr., to Gandhi, and from Malala Yousafzai to Fannie Lou Hamer. Similarly, hooks claims: "All the great social movements for freedom and justice in our society have promoted a love ethic. Concern for the collective good of our nation, city, or neighbor rooted in the values of love makes us all seek to nurture and protect that good."[40] This refrain is not just the insight of Curry or hooks but is something we have also encountered in our engagement with liberation theologians from a variety of traditions.

The idea of a love ethic is that it informs not only our romantic relationships but all of our relationships including family, neighbors, and all others: "When we see love as the will to nurture one's own or another's spiritual growth, revealed through acts of care, respect, knowing, and assuming responsibility, the foundation of all love in our life is the same. There is no special love exclusively reserved for romantic partners. Genuine love is the foundation of our engagement with ourselves, with family, with friends, with partners, with everyone we choose to love."[41] Regardless of the relationship, then, "the values that inform our behavior, when rooted in a love ethic, are always the same for any interaction."[42] With this understanding, we have a strong grounding for an ethic that can be applied across the range of human experiences and relationships. It is an ethic that, rather than prescribing specific actions, grounds our decisions and actions in values that center on the well-being of others.

In outlining what amounts to an almost universal kind of ethic, those of us in positions of privilege or who find ourselves in a majority culture run a very real risk of outlining values that protect the status quo,

[39] Curry and Grace, *Love is the Way*, 20.
[40] hooks, *All about Love*, 98.
[41] hooks, *All about Love*, 136.
[42] hooks, *All about Love*, 136.

Living into Our Humanity and Cultivating an Ethic of Love

and thereby protect "our" place in the social order. This is where looking to the works of theologians and ethicists like James Cone, Emilie Townes, and others enables us to broaden our view so that we are not screening out perspectives that have potential to challenge and disturb our comfort. In his work on black theology Cone discusses at length what it means to be fully human. For Cone, modeling his theology on Jesus who identified himself with the oppressed Jews of his day, to be fully human is essentially to identify oneself with the oppressed and to side with them in their struggle for liberation to enjoy the freedom for which God created them.

Cone also includes in his vision of humanity the very real presence of evil in the world. He explains, "The reality of evil is an ever-present possibility in our finite world, and to be (fully) human means to be identified with those who are enslaved as they fight against human evil."[43] With the recognition of the reality of human evil, the act of joining with the ones who suffer from it, and working alongside them for their true freedom, is what it means to be fully human. Cone explains, "Being human means being against evil by joining sides with those who are the victims of evil. Quite literally it means becoming oppressed with the oppressed, making their cause one's own cause by involving oneself in the liberation struggle. No one is free until all are free."[44] For Cone, this is the work of God and was the work of Jesus in his incarnation.

This notion of being fully human, for Cone, is linked to what it means to be formed in the image of God, as outlined in the creation account of Genesis. For Cone, the image of God is suggestive of creative generativity: "To be human is to be in the image of God—that is, to be creative: revolting against everything that is opposed to humanity."[45] Further, he writes, "The image of God refers to the way in which God intends human beings to live in the world.... In a world in which persons are oppressed, the image is human nature in rebellion against the structures of oppression. It is humanity involved in the liberation struggle

[43] Cone, *Black Theology*, 87–88.
[44] Cone, *Black Theology*, 88.
[45] Cone, *Black Theology*, 93.

Conclusion

against the forces of inhumanity."[46] The truly free person is the person who throws in their lot with the victims of oppression, joining in the cause for their freedom. It is not because it is logically right or just: it is because a fellow human is suffering, and someone in touch with their own humanity will be moved to act until they can be free as well. This sounds quite a bit like the Good Samaritan in our parable who was moved with compassion. And also like Jesus himself.[47] This is the love ethic which values the well-being of others to the extent that it generates a willingness to see the needs, to feel compassion, and to act for the good of others.

Thus, we suggest that Jesus's parables promote an ethic of love, mercy, and justice—each of which has a claim on those who wish to understand what it means to live into their full humanity. At this point, what is left is to return to where we began. We followed an interpretive process that led us from contemplating the parables of Jesus themselves to the creative and challenging task of relating the texts to our current situation through an integrative act of the imagination. This leaves but one step in Hays's approach to New Testament ethics: the pragmatic task of living out the message of good news in our lives, relationships, and communities. This is the "action" step of the contemplation and action cycle of the Sisters of Mercy. A task that is never finished and that will always benefit from a continual pattern of return to the teachings of Jesus, reflecting on them together in community, and working together to create a world in which love, mercy, and justice continue to increase for the benefit of all.

---

[46] Cone, *Black Theology*, 94.

[47] Cone adds: "The truly free are identified with the humiliated because they know that their own being is involved in the degradation of their brothers and sisters. They cannot stand to see them stripped of their humanity. This is not so because of pity or sympathy, but because their own existence is being limited by another's slavery" (95). Further, "Christians can never be content as long as their sisters and brothers are enslaved. They must suffer with them, knowing that freedom for Jesus Christ is always freedom for the oppressed" (101).

Living into Our Humanity and Cultivating an Ethic of Love

Works Cited

Baldwin, Jennifer. *Taking It to the Streets: Public Theologies of Activism and Resistance*. Lanham, MD: Lexington Books, 2019.

Cahill, Lisa Sowle. *Global Justice, Christology and Christian Ethics*. New Studies in Christian Ethics. New York: Cambridge University 2013.

Callahan, Sidney Cornelia. *With All Our Heart and Mind: The Spiritual Works of Mercy in a Psychological Age*. New York: Crossroad, 1988.

Cone, James H. *A Black Theology of Liberation*. 20th anniversary ed. Maryknoll, NY: Orbis Books, 1990.

Curry, Michael B. and Sara Grace. *Love is the Way: Holding onto Hope in Troubling Times*. New York: Avery, 2020.

Farley, Margaret A. "Mercy and Its Works: If Things Fall Apart, Can They Be Put Right?" *Proceedings of the Catholic Theological Society of America* 71 (2016): 33–40.

Francis, Pope. *Laudato Si': On Care for Our Common Home*. Vatican City: Vatican Press, 2015.

Hays, Richard B. *The Moral Vision of the New Testament: Community, Cross, New Creation: A Contemporary Introduction to New Testament Ethics*. First ed. San Francisco: HarperSanFrancisco, 1996.

hooks, bell. *All about Love: New Visions*. First ed. New York: William Morrow, 2000.

Hopkins, Gerard Manley. *Poems and Prose of Gerard Manley Hopkins*. Baltimore, MD: Penguin Books, 1953.

Keenan, James F. *The Works of Mercy: The Heart of Catholicism*. Third ed. Lanham: Rowman & Littlefield, 2017.

Massingale, Bryan N. *Racial Justice and the Catholic Church*. Maryknoll, NY: Orbis Books, 2010.

Murthy, Vivek H. *Together: The Healing Power of Human Connection in a Sometimes Lonely World*. New York, NY: Harper Wave, an imprint of HarperCollins, 2020.

Schottroff, Luise. *The Parables of Jesus*. Minneapolis: Fortress, 2006.

Sobrino, Jon. *The Principle of Mercy: Taking the Crucified People from the Cross*. Maryknoll, NY: Orbis Books, 1994.

Teilhard de Chardin, Pierre. *Hymn of the Universe*. New York: Harper & Row, 1965.

Thomasset, Alain. "The Virtue of Hospitality according to the Bible and the Challenge of Migration," Pages 34–44 in *The Bible and Catholic Theological Ethics*. Edited by Yiu Sing Lúcás Chan. of *Catholic Theological Ethics in the World Church*. Maryknoll, NY: Orbis Books, 2017.

Conclusion

Townes, Emilie Maureen. *Womanist Ethics and the Cultural Production of Evil. Black Religion, Womanist Thought, Social Justice.* New York: Palgrave Macmillan, 2006.

Via, Dan Otto. *The Parables: Their Literary and Existential Dimension.* Philadelphia: Fortress, 1967.

United Nations General Assembly. *The Universal Declaration of Human Rights (UDHR).* United Nations General Assembly, 1948 [Accessed December 16, 2022]. Available from https://www.un.org/en/about-us/universal-declaration-of-human-rights.

Appendix 1

Sisters of Mercy Reflections on the Parables

The Good Samaritan (Luke 10:29–37)

Anne Curtis, RSM

There are instances when something has become so familiar that I stopped paying attention. In all honesty, I have to admit that about the parable of the Samaritan. However, at some point I did hear with new ears the response to Jesus' question, "Which of these in your opinion, was neighbor to the robbers' victim?" In the Greek text, the response is literally "the one who did Mercy." I was used to hearing the one who had pity, and "pity" did not move me. However, as I have contemplated this parable I believe it goes to the heart of what it means to be, to do mercy.

A clear but likely unconscious movement seems to happen as the story unfolds. The Samaritan notices, sees the person lying by the side of the road. This is no small thing. There is a choice made to either see or not notice. To see, really see stirs or evokes something, a sense of compassion that draws one in and connects. In this case, the Samaritan connects with the person lying at the side of the road. That connection impelled action, not just awareness, and that is mercy. Mercy responds and acts from a place deep in the gut or heart.

Social Justice in the Stories of Jesus: The Ethical Challenge of the Parables, First Edition.
Matthew E. Gordley.
© 2024 John Wiley & Sons Ltd. Published 2024 by John Wiley & Sons Ltd.

Appendix 1

The Samaritan was "moved with compassion" and tended to the wounded traveler. He/she not only tended the wounds but also ensured there would be ongoing care. Contemplating the story calls me to ask anew the question posed by Jesus. In light of today's realities, who is my neighbor? Who or what am I to notice, to really see? With eyes wide open, I see not just my human sisters and brothers but also Earth and all of creation. What does that then portend if creation, Earth, is my neighbor? The ecological crisis we are experiencing calls me to notice and understand a new way of being neighbor. This inclusive view invites me to see not just humans, but also animals, trees and rocks, sunshine and sea, the stars and insects (yes, even mosquitoes!) as neighbor. To be neighbor calls me to see cosmically as well as locally. It means I must include the entire 13. 7 billion year story of our evolving universe. It means intimate connectedness to all of creation. It means that the very Earth itself, all God's creation, is my neighbor along with my fellow human beings.

God is present to us through both creation and the Incarnation, thus I see the face of the divine in my neighbor and in all of creation. Love for my neighbor cannot be separated from love for the planet. We are all made of the same stuff. All of life is intricately interrelated. As our Native American brother, Chief Seattle said, "Humankind has not woven the web of life. We are but one thread within it. Whatever we do to the web, we do to ourselves. All things are bound together. All things connect."

We form one community beyond all barriers of race and class and nation. We are deeply interconnected with all creatures, with the Milky Way Galaxy, with rain forests, with marine life, rocks and mountains, with ancient trees, with the flowering plants. Every creature is a word that reflects the wisdom of God, an icon of the divine. Each has its own integrity before God.

Seeing those who suffer and commitment to the well-being of our planet must go together. This is the cry of my neighbor, the other-than-human neighbor. It is a cry that is deeply connected to those in the human community who are lying at the side of the road bruised and battered. The urgent call to "do mercy" comes now with not only a social but also an ecological ring.

Mercy does not just invite me to see or feel, but also to be, to act differently. The gospel story of the Samaritan sets me on a new pathway, so that I might have mercy on our planet—my neighbor and to "Go and do likewise."

Anne Curtis, RSM, is the Executive Director of Mercy by the Sea Retreat and Conference Center, a sponsored work of the Sisters of Mercy which welcomes people of diverse faiths and backgrounds to nurture a relationship with the Sacred in self, others and creation in order to foster a just and compassionate world.

Lost Sheep, Lost Coin (Luke 15:4–10)

Cynthia Serjak, RSM

When I was quite young I loved to watch for my father's arrival home from work. When I saw his car coming up our long driveway I would tell my mother that I was going to hide, and would she please tell my father to come and find me. My favorite place to hide was in my closet where there was a wooden clothes hamper which was strong enough to hold me, so when my father came to find me I was at a height to be able to jump right into his arms. I loved that moment of "surprise" and the absolute delight I felt in being found.

I thought about my experience when I was musing about the sheep and the coin in these verses from Luke. What was it like for the sheep, who perhaps wandered too far off looking for the greener grass and then realized that all that was familiar had disappeared? Maybe some moments of terror followed, or at least a regret for what seemed a foolish lack of attention. Perhaps the moments stretched to days, and our distressed sheep thought all was lost.

And then there's the coin, accidentally dropped and seemingly disregarded in the busyness of a day's work. If it could, the coin might have felt rejection, sadness, even anger at being overlooked or forgotten.

The first story might remind you of times when you wandered away from your best self and into situations that proved to be harmful, when you were at risk of really being lost. And there may have been times in your life when you felt discarded, forgotten, even rejected, like the coin in the second story.

Then suddenly, in the midst of feeling hopeless, someone came to look for you and asked just what you thought you were doing anyway. It was enough of a jolt to bring you back to your senses. After a few moments of wondering at your own stupidity, you realized that

Appendix 1

particular joy of being found and were overwhelmed with gratitude that someone cared enough to come looking for you. What joy to be carried back to the flock, or returned to the pocket of a waiting garment, or to be welcomed back into the family or friend circle.

God's mercy is always searching for us, even when we think we are forgotten, even when we get distracted or lose track of ourselves. God's mercy goes beyond a quick look around for a little lost sheep. It is abundant and exceedingly generous, going as far and wide as need be to find a lost soul. There is an intensity in God's love for us that breaks through even our strongest defenses; this intensity opens the path for mercy to flow into us, even when we were not expecting it.

The best part for us may well be the exquisite joy we know in being found. But if our joy is unspeakable, imagine God's divine joy in doing the finding. And then think about how each time one of us is found, God's mercy is released even more widely into the world. Because of your joy in being found, you become an instrument of this divine impulse as you begin to find others who are suffering and looking for connection and you help them come back.

We become the Mercy of God by seeking out the one on the margins, the one who is looking to see if anyone cares, the one whose heart is so waiting and wanting to be found.

Cynthia Serjak, RSM, works with new members and Mercy staff development for the Sisters of Mercy of the Americas in Silver Spring, MD.

The Lost Sons (Luke 15: 11–32)

Judith Schubert, RSM

Throughout the Gospel of Luke, Jesus interacted with many castaways triggering some Jewish leaders to be frustrated and angered with him because he broke accepted social barriers. Such discontent caused these leaders to question, confront, and even condemn Jesus's behavior. Luke 15:11–32 demonstrates clearly that the ways of religious leaders do not always replicate the ways of God, who offers forgiveness, love and joy repeatedly to every human being. The Parable of the Two Lost Sons presents the father as totally open to his sons, non-judgmental of their disrespectful speech as well as vulnerable to their unexpected moods.

Sisters of Mercy Reflections on the Parables

In essence the father's behavior and speech exemplify the merciful ways of a loving God. It also calls its listeners to celebrate and be filled with joy because of this infinite mercy.

From the opening of the story, the younger son demands, not requests, his share of the property that will eventually be his. His speech appears cold and calculating. Culturally, in ancient Jewish society as well today, such an unusual verbal expectation would be considered irresponsible, crass, and reprehensible. No son or daughter has the right to expect any inheritance while the parent lives or even after death because it has not been earned. Entitlement destroys any sense of gratitude in life. Despite such crass behavior on the part of the younger son, what does the father do?

Instead of verbal reprimanding, the father does not speak at the beginning of the parable. On the contrary, he simply acts: "So he divided his property between them." Some may say that the father must have spoiled the son, while others may portray the father as a "wimp," one who appears too weak to challenge his son's unreasonable and expensive demand. Later in the parable, the son returns to his father after losing his inheritance and his dignity. He has already decided to ask forgiveness for his past wrongs and would ask to be treated as a hired hand rather than as his son. Whether the intentions of the son seem sincere or just practical because of his starvation, he does return to ask forgiveness from his father.[1]

As the father reenters the story, how does he respond to the son's return? This devoted father has been waiting and watching in the hope of his son's return. The absence of his younger son as well as his unknown whereabouts would have caused great pain to this gentle parent. Yet, his tender way allows him to wait for his younger son's return without animosity or anger.

Luke 15:20 declares that when the younger son "was still far off, his father saw him and was filled with compassion." Compassion ranks as one of the primary elements of mercy. A compassionate person demonstrates great wisdom and patience, as this caring parent does. Quickly, the father runs to greet him. His affectionate actions indicate that the

---

[1] In v. 17, the translated Greek phrase for "came to his senses" suggests that the younger son did act sincerely because he had a moment of realism about his bad behavior towards his father.

313

Appendix 1

younger son had never been disowned or abandoned by his father in any way. On the contrary, the warm embrace and kiss demonstrated that his son has been restored to his former status.

Total forgiveness and restoration of position continues as the forgiving father commands his servants: "Quickly, bring out a robe—the best one—and put it on him; put a ring on his finger and sandals on his feet…" These unexpected directives assure everyone that his son, not some hired hand or unforgiven child, has come home. All has been forgiven. As always, the father's clear directives exemplify his infinite mercy towards the younger son.

To clarify his benevolent intentions even further, the father instructs the servants "to get the fatted calf and kill it, and let us eat and celebrate; for this son of mine was dead and is alive again; he was lost and is found!" In other words, "Let's party!" Not only has the younger son been totally forgiven, but he has been showered with gifts of reinstatement, prestige, and family celebration. The spontaneous festivity offers an atmosphere of true joy!

Through these unexpected and generous actions, that father presents a complete demonstration of love. He has overlooked entirely the insulting disrespect and demands that his younger son originally made years ago. In a spirit of authentic mercy, the compassionate father has forgiven the unforgiveable and restored his broken son to his former status.

Now, how does the eldest son react to the unexpected situation? After returning from work in the fields, he learns the reason for all the "music and dancing." Instead of rejoicing, the older son becomes both angry and stubborn. He resents all the fuss over his brother who deserted the family in the past.

Resentment of any kind kills authentic joy and celebration. The older brother's bitterness toward his younger relative initiates his sudden burst of anger. In this instance he does not feel comfortable anymore in his surroundings. His refusal to enter the celebration suggests his unresolved animosity with the circumstances.

When the loving father came out "to plead with him" to enter the festivities, the older son reacted sharply and with great disrespect: "Listen! For all these years I have been working like a slave for you…" Without any proper address to his gentle parent, the son screams "Listen!" He describes his work on the farm in terms of a slave, even

Sisters of Mercy Reflections on the Parables

though his loving father would have seen him as a loving son. He protests that he had never been given a party to have fun with friends. He completes his aggressive complaints against his father and younger son by refusing to even acknowledge him as a brother.

All these accusations of the oldest son demonstrate frustration and anger, as well as many unresolved issues with both his father and younger brother. His pessimistic attitude throughout the past years on the farm must have affected this endearing father. Yet, the father responds with a deeply benevolent and sensitive reply to his resentful son: "Son, you are always with me, and all that is mine is yours." What a kindhearted reply to the son's indignant remarks!

While the eldest son protests with bitterness, the father responds in loving forgiveness. Truly, the father, who has experienced two lost sons, remains openly compassionate to both of them. He overlooks bad behavior in their demands as well as complaints or shameful remarks made to him. Through his superb listening skills, his eagerness to unite his family, as well as his patient waiting, the father's behavior signals acceptance, an invitation to celebrate and rejoice with unwavering compassion. In essence, the father models the boundless mercy of God!

Dr. Judith Schubert, RSM, is Professor of Theology and Religious Studies, Georgian Court University in Lakewood, New Jersey.

The Mustard Seed (Mark 4:30–32)

Sheila Carney, RSM

The story of the mustard seed is one of humility, interdependence and hospitality. In Luke's version of the parable, "a man took [the seed] and threw it into his garden" as if to discard it (Luke 13:19). It is cast off as if of no importance or consequence. But this tiny seed knows and embraces its purpose and from this groundedness, this humility, comes fulfillment. It grows into the biggest shrub of them all. The potential of the tiny seed is realized and the shrub lifts its arms to the sky, not only to receive the sun and rain needed for its own survival and growth but to signal its welcome for whatever may come. And what comes is "the other"—a bird seeking safety, a place where it can shelter and nurture new life.

Appendix 1

The word "shelter" appears in the Work of Mercy which urges us to make room. Shelter the homeless means more than put a roof over someone's head. The word is rich in meaning and challenge for it embodies a sense of protecting, safeguarding, wrapping, defending, shielding. To shelter is not an anonymous or impersonal gesture. It requires that one know and respond to the needs of the other, providing the resources and environment necessary for health and wholeness. The mustard seed doesn't simply tolerate a bird alighting on one of its limbs. It "puts out big branches so that the birds of the air can shelter in its shade" (Mark 4:32). It creates a place where the bird is kept safe from harmful conditions and predators. The parable of the Good Samaritan carries a similar message as a traveler encounters an "other" in distress, offers immediate care and provides for all that is needed to bring that person back to wholeness. This is a very personal, intimate and healing gesture of providing shelter in the richest sense of that word.

This same invitation to interdependence, humility, and hospitality is ours today as we respond to Pope Francis' call to care for our Common Home. Francis begins his encyclical Laudato Si with these words: "Our common home is like a sister with whom we share our life and a beautiful mother who opens her arms to embrace us" (Laudato Si, 1)—an image reminiscent of the mustard seed. A central message of the encyclical is the linkage created between the cry of the earth and the cry of the poor as we are reminded that those who suffer most from ecological degradation are those who live in poverty. Thus care for Earth becomes an issue of justice as we seek the rights of persons and of our planet as one indivisible cause.

We Sisters of Mercy have committed ourselves to embracing a new consciousness in regard to the needs of our Common Home and all who share it. We have undertaken "to work zealously toward the sustainability of all life by caring for Earth's ecosystems, addressing global climate change, advocating for the fundamental right to clean water and committing ourselves to an 'integral ecological conversion (Laudato Si, 4)'" (Call to a New Consciousness, Sisters of Mercy of the Americas, 2017). Engaging in the effort to eliminate single use plastics is one manifestation of our response as is investigation of destructive effects—on people and their lands—caused by extractive industries. We are challenging ourselves beyond contentment with recycling to the adoption of new styles of living and consuming.

Sisters of Mercy Reflections on the Parables

The many facets and evidences of the perils we face from ecological degradation are overwhelming and it is easy to fall into the "what difference can one person make?" syndrome. When I sink into that mindset, I am encouraged by Catherine McAuley, founder of the Sisters of Mercy, who advised her followers to be attentive to the daily, the ordinary, the commonplace. "The simplest and most practical lesson I know... is to resolve to be good today, but better tomorrow. Let us take one day only in hands, at a time, merely making a resolve for tomorrow, thus we may hope to get on taking short, careful steps, not great strides" (Letter to de Sales White, February 28, 1841). Catherine's words remind me that I am not responsible for solving the world's ecological crisis single-handedly, but that through attentiveness to my own surroundings and actions I can limit its effects. A first step may be declining a proffered straw in a restaurant. Perhaps a second step is telling the server and my companions why I am making this choice. These are small movements forward, but they are leading toward an ecological conversion.

The mustard seed embraced its purpose and potential and stretched itself until it became a blessing. It lived interdependently within its environment and contributed what, in its nature, it could to the wellbeing of all. This parable offers an invitation to us to live in humility and interdependence and hospitality, attending, in how we choose to live our lives, to the cry of the earth and the cry of the poor.

Sheila Carney, RSM, is a member of the Institute of the Sisters of Mercy of the Americas currently ministering as Special Assistant to the President for Mercy Heritage at Carlow University in Pittsburgh, Pennsylvania.

The Pharisee and The Tax Collector (Luke 18:9–14)

Diane Guerin, RSM

Marginalized within their cultures, treated as insignificant or peripheral, thus was the fate of the life of the Pharisee and the tax collector.

Part of an elite, separate group who set themselves above the majority, the Pharisee was a righteous man. He kept the law, gave alms and fasted; he did all that was required of him. But his self-righteousness arose from his perception that he was better than the tax collector and not a sinner.

Appendix 1

Charged with the collection of monies for the government, the tax collector was not looked upon favorably by much of the population. His occupation demanded his adherence to the law of Caesar which often earned him the contempt of others. A humble man, he felt unworthy of God's mercy.

It is doubtful that the paths of these two men crossed in their day-to-day lives. Little, if any, interaction occurred between them. One day, they find themselves both in the temple at the same time. Each one utters a prayer to God, but from very different vantage points.

What they do share is a need for God's mercy. The tax collector has no illusions about his need for mercy. The Pharisee is so intent on telling God of his good deeds, he misses his need for mercy. Each one of us needs God's abundant, unconditional mercy, many times during our lives, whether we recognize it or not. God never withholds mercy from anyone! Revelatory but disconcerting, one can easily envision herself/himself in all the roles presented.

With over 40 years of ministry in justice, conflict resolution, and race relations, it is easy for me to identify with the Pharisee. Indeed, the work focuses on righteousness and righteous indignation about inequities. Experiences of opposition and adversity can spark self-righteousness. How can "they" not see this? What is wrong with "them?" Why are "they" so stubborn and unyielding? Obviously, it is easy to fall into the trap that my view is the correct one.

The tax collector is a good example of cooperating with grace, leading him to proclaim "God, be merciful to me a sinner." The opposite approach as expressed by the Pharisee, hopefully leads to a deeper, more reflective stance and a realization of the universal need for mercy. Letting go of a strict adherence to only one perception, conceptualization or world view allows one's heart to be open to conversion.

Perception can only be changed by honest reflection and communication. Failure to do so leads to escalating conflict, resulting in alienation and little or no mercy for opposing viewpoints. Perhaps, if these two men were able to speak with each other about their experiences, they would realize their commonalities. Each in his need for mercy missed the longing in the other. The Pharisee's longing is deep within and still unrecognized; the tax collector is able to articulate his need, but feels he is unworthy.

As a Sister of Mercy, I struggle to understand needs and their underlying causes and address these challenges to bring about systemic change. We, Sisters of Mercy, also acknowledge our own contribution to global suffering and work with others, through direct service in the community, to advocate for change to unjust systems and exploitative behavior.

Pharisee, tax collector, or someone in between? The decision rests in the hands and hearts of each and every one of us.

Diane Guerin, RSM, is presently retired but continues her ministry of advocacy and social justice as she has done for 50 years.

The Laborers in the Vineyard (Matthew 20:1–16)

Mary Kay Dobrovolny, RSM

I love praying with parables. One of the reasons parables attract me is that over time the very same parable can have vastly different messages for me. I can enter into a parable from many different places, and where I place myself within the parable makes a difference in what message is being communicated to me. The parable of the laborers in the vineyard, or the parable of the charitable landowner (Matt 20:1–16), is one such example of a parable that has had multiple messages for me over my lifetime of praying with parables.

Some years back, I read a book by William Herzog entitled *Parables as Subversive Speech: Jesus as Pedagogue of the Oppressed* (Louisville: Westminster/John Knox Press, 1994). This book challenged me to ask what the message of this parable might be if I do not assume that God is the landowner. As I prayed with this parable and placed myself in the position of the landowner, I found my own ministerial perspectives being challenged.

At the time, I was living in Chicago and walked regularly in a place where several homeless people lived. I developed a relationship with one woman named Shirley. Shirley and I would often share a meal together, sometimes at McDonalds or another local fast-food place and sometimes out of my kitchen pantry and brought out to the street. I suspected that Shirley was addicted to drugs. One day, Shirley was in a

Appendix 1

particularly agitated state and she wanted the cash that I would otherwise spend on food for our shared meal. I refused. I calmly explained my "policy" of not giving money but never refusing food if I had the opportunity to share out of my abundance. She followed me for several blocks shouting expletives about me and my "policy" and I felt entirely justified by my reasoned charitable response. I didn't cave to Shirley's demands nor did she accept that day my offer to share a meal with her.

When I brought this experience into prayerful dialogue with the parable of the charitable landowner (Matt 20:1–16), I heard more challenge from Shirley's words. I sounded very much like the beneficent landowner: "Am I not allowed to do what I choose with what belongs to me?" (20:15). What, I wondered, might the message of the parable be if the answer to this rhetorical question was "No"? Might I be challenged to look beyond a world where some have an abundance and others do not have enough to meet their daily needs? Might I be challenged to look at my own ministry differently? How are my acts of charity supporting an unjust social structure, and what might the ministerial call be to look at ways of subverting the existing social structure and co-creating a world of shared power and authority and true kinship among all?

Those questions a decade or so later continue to challenge me. We continue to live in a world hugely divided by race, nationality, socio-economics, and other such factors. While I strive to live simply and while I strive to maintain an attitude of kinship and unity among all, I continue to use more than my fair share of Earth's resources and I continue to succumb unintentionally to white privilege.

This morning, as I prayed with this same parable anew, I found myself drawn to a more traditional interpretation. This time, I identified with the laborer hired last and paid a very generous wage.

Many people in all walks of life have a very profound relationship with God. For those of us like the Sisters of Mercy who choose vowed religious life, usually our primary motivating force is our God relationship. For me, I consider myself a slow learner or late bloomer. God has always been significant in my life and significant in my choice for vowed religious life. In many respects, however, God was secondary. I fell in love with the community and charism of Mercy and entered the Sisters of Mercy based on that love. God and the intentional focus on the spiritual life was part of the package.

Sisters of Mercy Reflections on the Parables

In the most recent decade of my life, the order of the primary loves of my life has reversed—God has become the central primary motivating force of my life, and my love for the community and charism of Mercy is my lived expression of that primary love. I feel like the laborer hired last. I have come to this vineyard of God at a late hour in the day, and God in God's abundant beneficent goodness is very generous in lavishing the full gift and grace of the spiritual life on me, a latecomer. Praying with the parable from this place, I am filled with gratitude as I soak in the generosity and gift and grace of God.

Ten or twenty years from now, what will this parable have to say to me? Will I become complacent with my God relationship and need the challenge provided to those who have been laboring in the vineyard for hours with the full heat of the day? Will I still be seeking the vision of a world where all have what they need for full flourishing and do not struggle to meet their daily needs? Will I feel the comfort and abundance of God's grace who gifts me, a latecomer, with more than I deserve and more than I could ever imagine? Whatever the message, the parable has the power to challenge the places in my life and heart that are too settled, and the power to comfort and heal the places in my life and heart that have lived too long being too unsettled. May I continue to be open to however God wants to work in my life as I pray with this and other parables.

Dr. Mary Kay Dobrovolny, RSM, serves as Minister in Residence at the University of Detroit-Mercy (Detroit, MI) and as Vocation Minister with the Sisters of Mercy of the Americas.

The Rich Man and Lazarus (Luke 16:19–31)

Marilyn Lacey, RSM

The parable of The Rich Man and Lazarus (Lk 16:19–31) is often cited as a cautionary tale: those who enjoy an easy life on earth will end up condemned for all eternity, and those who suffer now will finally find solace in heaven. I do not think that's the point at all.

Jesus in this parable describes a man so wealthy that he dressed in purple[2] and feasted splendidly every day. There is no mention as to his

---

[2] In those days purple dye was so rare and expensive that only royalty could afford it.

Appendix 1

character or morals, no indication that he was a bad or selfish person—only that he was extravagantly rich. Outside his gate lay "a man named Lazarus", starving, covered in sores and longing for scraps from the rich man's table.

The rich man dies and lands, much to his surprise, in hellish torment. Lazarus, by contrast, is welcomed to the bosom of Abraham at the heavenly banquet. Jesus' listeners would have been stunned by this confusing reversal of fortune, steeped as they were in the belief that wealth and health were certain signs of God's approval, while poverty and illness were proof positive that God punishes sinners.

Where exactly did the rich man go wrong? Nothing in the story says that he despised Lazarus or abused him or had guards drag him away. No. He simply didn't notice Lazarus, didn't pay attention to anyone outside his own gated lifestyle, didn't open the gate or share.

Is that so bad? Well, it's just not God's way. The clue is in the parable's opening line: Jesus calls the beggar Lazarus by his name. He does not name the rich man. God's attention is drawn to the one who is poor. God's compassion enfolds the outcast. God stands close to those who suffer. Their names, says Isaiah 49:16, are written on the palm of God's hand. In calling Lazarus by name, Jesus elevates Lazarus' status above that of the anonymous rich man. In God's eyes, the poor matter.

The point of this parable? Jesus wants us to understand what God pays attention to here and now. Jesus invites us to wake up, to open our gates, to notice our suffering brothers and sisters. Jesus invites us to share our resources before it is too late, before the chasm between rich and poor grows so wide that it cannot be bridged, before our wealth walls us off from the Holy One who stands outside our gate: unnoticed, unkempt, unwanted. We have the choice: stay within our own comfort zone, or take the risk to move beyond safe borders. Mercy nudges us toward those unknown edges, toward encountering the "other" as beloved of God. Then as our ways begin to align more with God's ways. Then we begin to experience paradise. Then we find ourselves surprised by joy.

Sister Marilyn Lacey, RSM, is the founder of Mercy Beyond Borders, a nonprofit lifting up thousands of women and girls through education, leadership training, and economic opportunities in countries of extreme poverty. In 2017 she received the Opus Prize, one of the world's largest awards for faith-based leadership.

Sisters of Mercy Reflections on the Parables

The Pearl of Great Price (Matthew 13:45–46)[3]

Mary-Paula Cancienne, RSM

In Matthew 13:45–46 Jesus tells the parable of the pearl. It is a very short story, two lines about a merchant and his single-pointed eyes for a valuable pearl. It is, in fact, an allegorical story about what the "kingdom of heaven" is like.

Jesus was a Jew and Jews traditionally do not refer to God directly by name, believing it arrogant of humans to do so. Rather, they allude to the deity and the broadest sense of the deity via metaphors, as with the "kingdom of heaven."

In addition, we have a second, more limited metaphor to help us explore who God is and what the reign of God is like, and this is the character of the merchant. The character and the situation invite us to imaginatively wonder how the merchant's passion for the pearl might be similar to God and God's reign in relation to humankind.

So, how is God something like a merchant who goes relentlessly after a valuable pearl, who sells all in order to obtain that pearl? Is God, indeed, filled with such passion? Is the whole of God's reign animated with such aliveness? Is God's reign imbued with energy, focus, and devotion, like that of a merchant wild for a beautiful pearl?

The resulting lovely pearl began as an irritant, a speck of sand in a barnacled oyster, but through its life process becomes layered with mother-of-pearl, transforming into the pearl itself. However, what if all of creation is represented by the pearl such that the pearl of God's eye, all of creation, is loved with an unimagined depth, passion, and devotion?

Jesus the storyteller is trying to convey to his listeners the love and affection that God has for them. In this parable he proclaims that it is God who seeks you like a valuable, irreplaceable, gloriously beautiful pearl, just like the merchant seeks that perfect pearl, or analogously, a baker that perfect cake, a fisherman that one big trout, a runner that perfect run. But for God it is you, you are the pearl for whom God is

---

[3] An originally planned chapter on the parable of the Pearl of Great Price did not make it into the final version of this volume, but I have included Sister Mary-Paula Cancienne's contribution since it provides a powerful concluding reflection for the entire book.

Appendix 1

willing to seek untiringly and with all God's resources, until you are one with God. It is you, me, us, all of creation. We are God's pearl. Stop and think about it. How does this kind of love affect us, change us, shape us, teach and call us to love as well?

But how does a parable about God's love pertain to the world today, a world with many troubling, critical issues, as well as opportunities to become a more peaceful Earth community? Some of the challenging issues include: migrating people on the road needing to escape violence; people who are condemned to the margins because of race, gender, poor education or lack of quality health care; a breakdown in society of simple civility; countries struggling under the cloud of graft and partisan ideologies; the risk of catastrophic events due to weapons-of-mass-destruction, including biological ones; a lack of appreciation for scientific method and the liberal arts when it comes to the craft of thinking clearly, creatively, and ethically; global warming and how we continue to pollute air, land, and water; the extinction of species; as well as religious and political patriarchal oppression. Really, what does a parable of God loving like a merchant's passion for a pearl have to offer us? But maybe, just maybe, if we bear down on our reflection of the pearl we might discover something more in Jesus's story.

The pearl is cozy in the oyster, but cannot be enjoyed truly until it is no longer within the shell. The pearl will never refract the light or shine as it can until it is outside of its nascent abode. Even to eat and enjoy the delicacy of the oyster, the pearl must first be removed from its shelter. In fact, the pearl does not have its value realized until the merchant sees it fully in the light outside of its shell, until it is itself in the world.

One way of interpreting the "kingdom of heaven" metaphor is that it represents God. In addition, it speaks to the reign of God, the glory of God's dynamic love that animates all of life. Thus, the pearl is seen in the light of God's love and devotion; in the light of God exist the pearl and the pearl reflects back the very light of God. Following this line, we can interpret the meaning of the pearl as a metaphor for all of humanity, and all of God's creation, the community of creation. When we live authentically who and what we are, we reflect something of the light of God.

The community realizes its worth when it appropriates for itself the knowledge that it is possessed by a God who loves the fullness of the community beautifully well. In today's awareness, we are learning that

Sisters of Mercy Reflections on the Parables

the planet community includes everyone and all kinds. We are the pearl whom God loves, and this love inspires and compels us to love each other, all others, justly, compassionately, and to shine without distortion, without blatant biases, greediness, ugliness and violence. We experience "love" through creation, through our very humanity when we live in right-relationship with ourselves, other people, other kinds, and with "God," or what some might name "ultimate reality."

If we as a collective of families, neighbors, towns, countries, and all kinds are represented by the pearl in this parable, then how are we called to live in the light of God, as in the eyes of the merchant who adores us without end? If we are this one magnificent "pearl" bathed in the stream of God's light, God's reign, then how is a pearl to be? No matter if you believe in "God" or not, are we, individually and as society, living attentively to non-violent practices and principles in harmony with the very wisdom of the universe, what we could call a "blue pearl"?

The great pearl purchased by the merchant might represent all of us living authentically who we are, not beyond ourselves and not encroaching on others, in ways that invite and support each other's contribution to the beauty of the pearl, to the reign of God, to the "kingdom of heaven" here and now, with a sense that there is more to come. Our desire to live and work for peace and justice and kindness and flourishing, for the "critical concerns," begins with a simple awareness that we, all of us together, are God's "pearl."

Dr. Mary-Paula Cancienne, RSM, facilitates mission related processes, is a contemporary iconographer, and writer on the twenty-first-century religious, spiritual landscape.

Appendix 2

Questions for Individual Study and Group Discussion

Chapter 1: Introduction: Reading the Parables through the Lens of Social Justice

1) How would you describe your current level of familiarity with the parables?
2) What are you curious about as you begin this exploration of the parables of Jesus?
3) Thinking about the power of stories in general to capture the imagination, what are some of the stories that have had an impact on you?
4) If you have encountered the parables previously, to what extent have you experienced the parables as delivering a spiritual message about faith and belief as opposed to delivering a challenge with regard to actions in this life toward others?
5) What human rights or social justice issues have caught your attention in recent months? How open are you to the idea that Jesus's ethic of love, mercy, and justice could have implications for how you view and respond to those issues?

Chapter 2: Encountering the World and Words of Jesus

1) Recognizing that one's own view of the world is shaped by many factors, what are some of the key cultural, social, physical, and historical elements that have shaped your own sense of identity? To really engage this question, consider spending ten minutes working on an identity

---

Social Justice in the Stories of Jesus: The Ethical Challenge of the Parables, First Edition.
Matthew E. Gordley.
© 2024 John Wiley & Sons Ltd. Published 2024 by John Wiley & Sons Ltd.

326

Questions for Individual Study and Group Discussion

mapping exercise (for example, the one found at the Center for Creative Leadership, https://www.ccl.org/articles/leading-effectively-arti cles/understand-social-identity-to-lead-in-a-changing-world).

2) In what ways do you think that understanding some of the social and cultural world of Jesus can help illuminate the meaning of parables?

3) The "kingdom of God" is a key phrase in the teaching of Jesus but also one that has been interpreted in many different ways. What have been your past associations with the phrase "kingdom of God"? How does recognizing that the phrase itself is a metaphor help create room for a broader understanding of it?

4) How does the Jewish expectation at the time of Jesus of a coming reversal, a "great divine clean up" foretold by the prophets, connect with issues of social concern?

5) The Christian belief in the incarnation of Jesus—born into this world as a Jew and crucified by the dominant power of imperial Rome—has important implications particularly as it demonstrates the extent to which God identifies with the poor, the oppressed, and the marginalized. Based on this example and the teaching of Jesus, James Cone claims, "Knowing God means being on the side of the oppressed, becoming *one* with them, and participating in the goal of liberation."[1] To what extent has this liberating element of solidarity with the oppressed been a part of your experience of Christianity?

Chapter 3: The Good Samaritan (Luke 10:25–37)

1) In your opinion, which aspects of the actions taken by the Samaritan help to clarify the meaning of mercy and compassion?

2) This parable can be seen as both an example to follow (be a neighbor to those in need, like the Samaritan) and a challenge to see the humanity and goodness of those outside of our social group (as the enmity between Jews and Samaritans creates the twist in this parable). With this awareness where do you see the emphasis in this parable, and why?

3) In the chain of events of seeing, feeling, and acting in response to the needs of others, where is your sense of mercy most in need of some revitalization?

[1] Cone, *Black Theology*, 65.

Appendix 2

4) Recognizing that the parable of the Good Samaritan is about mercy but also about overcoming cultural and other stereotypes that divide, who or what are the groups that you sometimes look at as "other" or "less than" ? How would you rate your willingness to examine issues of deep-seated and historically rooted antipathy from one group to another?
5) Looking at the world around you where do you see people suffering, whether in your community or outside of your community? Where is human dignity being compromised in the world around you?
6) In the situations you thought of above, where is mercy needed in this situation? What actions could you take to enact mercy where it is needed most?

Chapter 4: Lost Sheep, Lost Coin (Luke 15:4–10)

1) What elements of these twin parables stood out to you?
2) These parables have both an individual element (a person looking for a lost item of value) and a communal element (the gathering of friends and neighbors to celebrate the finding of that item). Do you see the emphasis in these parables falling more on the individual or more on the communal? Why?
3) In addressing social concerns in our world today, where do you see the emphasis being placed relative to individual responsibility versus our collective societal obligations to care for those who are in need?
4) These parables present the notion of being lost as very dire and being found as worth celebrating. In translating that into our world, what do you think it means to be lost—or to be found—today?
5) In this chapter we looked at an implication area of racism as a societal dynamic that creates marginalized groups and social disconnection. What do you think could help to foster connections across racial, ethnic, or other lines of division? What is the place of individual actions and the role of system-wide societal actions in addressing such a complex problem?

Chapter 5: The Lost Sons (Luke 15:11–32)

1) In this parable of a father and two sons, which do you take to be the main character? Why?
2) What do you identify as the key decision moments in this parable?

328

Questions for Individual Study and Group Discussion

3) What do you see as the significance of the extravagance of the father's welcome to the younger son?
4) In the process of reading a parable like this, readers almost automatically identify with one character more than others. With which character, if any, do you connect most closely—the younger son? the older brother? the father? none of them? Explain your answer.
5) The multiple references to life and death in this parable, related to whether one is isolated from or restored to the family, suggests the ultimate importance of social connection. The parable ends without letting us know whether the older brother will make the move toward reconnection with both his brother and his father. What do you think would need to happen for the older brother to overcome his alienation from his brother and father and find a more fulfilling connection to this small community?
6) In considering implications of this parable, we explored endeavors such as peacebuilding and compassion-based activism. These approaches to overcoming division include practices of setting firm boundaries against harm along with listening to others, being open to other perspectives, recognizing the dignity of every person, re-humanizing our opponents by sharing space together, and extending forgiveness. Which practices do you think hold the most promise for helping decrease the level of social disconnection people are experiencing today?

Chapter 6: The Mustard Seed (Mark 4:30–32; Matthew 13:31–32; Luke 13:18–19)

1) In this parable Jesus invites listeners to see the kingdom of God through a phenomenon in the natural world. What is one experience you have had in nature in which you had a sense of the divine or the transcendent?
2) Where do you see the focus of this parable? On the humble beginnings of the mustard seed? On its substantial and magnificent growth? On its provision of shelter for the birds of the air? Or do you see the focus as some combination of these? Based on what we have seen about how parables work, how would you support your answer?
3) What does ecological awareness mean in the context of this parable? What does ecological awareness mean in your community and current context?

Appendix 2

4) How would you assess your own ecological awareness at the moment? Think in terms of "never considered it," "mildly aware," "somewhat aware," "very aware," or "completely dialed in." Is there an aspect of your own environment that you would want to increase your understanding and awareness of?
5) What environmental issues are of greatest concern to you? What could you do to learn more about one issue and find ways to help address it?

Chapter 7: The Pharisee and the Tax Collector (Luke 18:9–14)

1) What stands out to you about the prayer of the Pharisee? What stands out to you about the prayer of the tax collector?
2) Although we do not have Pharisees and tax collectors today, what are two representative groups that may naturally fall into a similar pattern of judgement and shame with one another?
3) Think of a person or group that you generally have a negative view toward, whether you feel that it is justified or not. What would it take to adopt a more generous perspective?
4) In an interesting assessment of one of the key words in this parable, the tax collector may have been justified "alongside of" or even "on account of" the Pharisee. This raises the notion that the interconnectedness of all of us means that our own well-being cannot be disentangled from the well-being of others. What do you think of this notion, and do you see evidence of it, positively or negatively, in your world?
5) Thinking of implications, Bryan Massingale outlined four steps in the process of racial reconciliation: recognition, responsibility, reconstruction, and reparation. These steps have both an individual and communal component to them, and each one is increasingly more challenging. To what extent have you engaged with any of these? What thoughts do you have about individual or collective actions that could help you or your community to increase their awareness and capacity to promote racial reconciliation?

Chapter 8: The Laborers in the Vineyard (Matthew 20:1–16)

1) We have seen that Jesus uses many aspects of the ancient agrarian economy in his parables. What do you see as some of the significance of telling a parable about day laborers (expendables) and a landowner (a member of the wealthy elite) set in a vineyard?

Questions for Individual Study and Group Discussion

2) Some interpreters notice the detail that there are unhired laborers in the marketplace throughout the day as being suggestive of high employment (or at least a surplus of labor) and therefore limited bargaining power for those yet-to-be-hired laborers. To what extent do you think an understanding of the economic conditions in first-century Judaea could help shed light on the significance of this parable?
3) To what extent do you see this parable as an example of an individual (i.e., the landowner) using their resources for the benefit of all versus offering a spiritual analogy about divine generosity? Do you feel that it leans more toward one or the other, or could it work both ways?
4) In our world today who do you see as those at the mercy of the economic system, with little opportunity to provide for their own and their families' sustenance?
5) What would it mean to stand in solidarity with the poor and marginalized in your community, not just in spirit but in concrete ways?

Chapter 9: The Rich Man and Lazarus (Luke 16:19–31)

1) The rich man in this parable can serve as a reminder that people have ways of turning a blind eye to the realities of poverty and suffering around them. In what ways is our contemporary society structured to shield many of us from the realities of the sufferings of the poor and marginalized?
2) In the parable we are not given any of the details of the cause of the suffering of Lazarus in this life. But to what extent do you think people today view those in need (in poverty, sickness, extreme suffering) as responsible for their circumstances or stigmatize them as other or less than deserving?
3) If Jesus, following the Jewish scriptures, advocated compassion as a response to the suffering of others, what do you think keeps people today from being responsive to those in great need? To what extent do you think physical proximity to or distance from the poor contributes to current levels of responsiveness?
4) What were the "gifts of the poor" that Sobrino identified? How important is it to recognize the reciprocity that occurs when giving to those in need, and receiving from them?
5) What are some practical ways that the gulf between rich and poor could be bridged, and that people in need could be included in

Appendix 2

fellowship with those who have plenty? So that, in the words of Sobrino, "humanity will finally be healed, that there will be salvation for the poor, that we too will miraculously let ourselves be saved by them, and become truly a human family."[2]

Conclusion: Living into Our Humanity and Cultivating an Ethic of Love, Mercy, and Justice

1) As you review the parables we have studied together, which one stands out to you as having a message that carries implications for your life experience?
2) Having studied this subset of parables, to what extent do you see the parables overall as delivering a spiritual message about religious belief versus offering a challenge with regard to how one engages with others in this world?
3) In your opinion, which of the shared themes of the parables we studied is most needed in our world today?
4) In considering an ethic of love, mercy, and justice, how would you define each of those concepts?
5) What are the biggest challenges you see to living according to an ethic of love, mercy, and justice in the context in which you find yourself today?

[2] Sobrino, *No Salvation Outside the Poor*, xii.

Bibliography

Abu-Nimer, Mohammed. "Building Peace in the Pursuit of Justice," Pages 620–632 in *The Wiley-Blackwell Companion to Religion and Social Justice*. Edited by Michael D. Palmer and Stanley M. Burgess. Malden, MA: Wiley-Blackwell, 2012.

Anderson, Gary A. *Charity: The Place of the Poor in the Biblical Tradition*. New Haven: Yale University, 2013.

Bailey, Kenneth E. *Poet and Peasant, and Through Peasant Eyes: A Literary-Cultural Approach to the Parables in Luke*. Combined ed. 2 vols. Grand Rapids: Eerdmans, 1983.

Baker-Fletcher, Karen. "How Women Relate to the Evils of Nature," Pages 64–77 in *Womanist Theological Ethics: A Reader*. Edited by Katie G. Cannon, Emilie Maureen Townes, and Angela D. Sims. of *Library of Theological Ethics*. Louisville, KY: Westminster John Knox Press, 2011.

Baldwin, Jennifer. *Taking It to the Streets: Public Theologies of Activism and Resistance*. Lanham, MD: Lexington Books, 2019.

Barton, Stephen C. "Many Gospels, One Jesus?" Pages 170–183 in *The Cambridge Companion to Jesus*. Edited by Markus N. A. Bockmuehl. of *Cambridge Companions to Religion*. Cambridge: Cambridge University 2001.

Blomberg, Craig L. *Interpreting the Parables*. Second ed. Downers Grove, IL: IVP Academic, 2012.

Brantmeier, Edward J. and Noorie K. Brantmeier. *Culturally Competent Engagement: A Mindful Approach*. Charlotte, NC: IAP, Information Age Publishing, Inc., 2020.

Brobst-Renaud, Amanda. *Lukan Parables of Reckless Liberality*. Vol. 42, New Testament Monographs. Sheffield: Sheffield Phoenix, 2021.

Social Justice in the Stories of Jesus: The Ethical Challenge of the Parables, First Edition.
Matthew E. Gordley.
© 2024 John Wiley & Sons Ltd. Published 2024 by John Wiley & Sons Ltd.

Bibliography

Brown, Lerita Coleman. *What Makes You Come Alive: A Spiritual Walk with Howard Thurman*. Minneapolis: Broadleaf Books, 2023.

Brown, Raymond E. *New Testament Essays*. Garden City, NY: Image Books, 1968.

Cahill, Lisa Sowle. *Global Justice, Christology and Christian Ethics*. New Studies in Christian Ethics. New York: Cambridge University, 2013.

Callahan, Sidney Cornelia. *With All Our Heart and Mind: The Spiritual Works of Mercy in a Psychological Age*. New York: Crossroad, 1988.

Carey, Greg. *Stories Jesus Told: How to Read a Parable*. First ed. Nashville: Abingdon, 2019.

Carney, Sheila, RSM. "The Mustard Seed." 2019.

Cone, James H. *A Black Theology of Liberation*. 20th anniversary ed. Maryknoll, NY: Orbis Books, 1990.

Cook, Michael L. "Jesus' Parables and the Faith that Does Justice." *Studies in the Spirituality of Jesuits* 24, no. 5 (1992): 1–35.

Cousland, J. R. C. "Do 'The Birds of Heaven' in the Parable of the Mustard Seed Represent Gentiles?" *Catholic Biblical Quarterly* 85, no. 1 (2023): 53–74.

Crary, David. *Wave of Anti-Transgender Bills in Republican-Led States Divides U.S. Faith Leaders*. May 12, 2023. [Accessed May 21, 2023]. Available from https://www.pbs.org/newshour/nation/wave-of-anti-transgender-bills-in-republican-led-states-divides-u-s-faith-leaders.

Crossan, John Dominic. *The Power of Parable: How Fiction by Jesus Became Fiction about Jesus*. New York: HarperOne, 2012.

Curry, Michael B. and Sara Grace. *Love is the Way: Holding onto Hope in Troubling Times*. New York: Avery, 2020.

Curtis, Anne, RSM. "The Good Samaritan." 2019.

Danker, Frederick W. *Benefactor: Epigraphic Study of a Graeco-Roman and New Testament Semantic Field*. St. Louis, MO: Clayton Publishing House, 1982.

Day, Kristen. "Supporting Pregnant Women and Their Families to Reduce Abortion Rate," Pages 143–158 in *In Search of Common Ground on Abortion: From Culture War to Reproductive Justice*. Edited by Justin Murray, Meredith B. Esser, and Robin West. Burlington, VT: Ashgate, 2014.

Delio, Ilia. *A Franciscan View of Creation: Learning to Live in a Sacramental World*. Vol. 2, Franciscan heritage series. St. Bonaventure, NY: Franciscan Institute, St. Bonaventure University, 2003.

De Long, Kindalee Pfremmer. *Surprised by God: Praise Responses in the Narrative of Luke-Acts*. Vol. 166, Beihefte zur Zeitschrift für die neutestamentliche Wissenschaft. Berlin: Walter de Gruyter, 2009.

Dobrovolny, Mary Kay, RSM. "The Laborers in the Vineyard." 2019.

Dodd, C. H. *The Parables of the Kingdom*. Revised ed. Glasgow: Fount Paperbacks, 1961.

334

Bibliography

Doran, Robert. "The Pharisee and the Tax Collector: An Agonistic Story." *Catholic Biblical Quarterly* 69, no. 2 (2007): 259–270.

Edwards, Denis. "Humans and Other Creatures: Creation, Original Grace, and Original Sin," Pages 159–170 in *Just Sustainability: Technology, Ecology, and Resource Extraction*. Edited by Christiana Z. Peppard. Vol. 3 of *Catholic Theological Ethics in the World Church*. Maryknoll, New York: Orbis Books, 2015.

Elliott, John H. "Patronage and Clientage," Pages 144–158 in *The Social Sciences and New Testament Interpretation*. Edited by Richard L. Rohrbaugh. Peabody, MA: Hendrickson, 1996.

Evans, Craig A. "Context, Family and Formation," Pages 11–24 in *The Cambridge Companion to Jesus*. Edited by Markus N. A. Bockmuehl. of *Cambridge Companions to Religion*. Cambridge: Cambridge University 2001.

Farley, Margaret A. "Wisdom, Dignity, and Justice: Higher Education as a Work of Mercy." *The MAST Journal* 16 (2006): 3–8.

Farley, Margaret A. "Mercy and Its Works: If Things Fall Apart, Can They Be Put Right?". *Proceedings of the Catholic Theological Society of America* 71 (2016): 33–40.

Finnis, John. "Aquinas' Moral, Political, and Legal Philosophy." *The Stanford Encyclopedia of Philosophy* Edited by Edward N. Zalta. Stanford University: Metaphysics Research Lab. 2021. https://plato.stanford.edu/archives/spr2021/entries/aquinas-moral-political.

Francis, Pope. *Laudato Si': On Care for Our Common Home*. Vatican City: Vatican Press, 2015.

Francis, Pope. *Lettera enciclica Fratelli tutti del Santo Padre Francesco sulla fraternità e l'amicizia sociale*. Città del Vaticano: Libreria editrice vaticana, 2020.

Friedrichsen, Timothy A. "The Temple, a Pharisee, a Tax Collector, and the Kingdom of God: Rereading a Jesus Parable (Luke 18:10-14a)." *Journal of Biblical Literature* (2005): 89–119.

Getty-Sullivan, Mary Ann. *Parables of the Kingdom: Jesus and the Use of Parables in the Synoptic Tradition*. Collegeville, MN: Liturgical Press, 2007.

Gonzalez, Dennis T. "New Measures for Justice, Ecological Wisdom, and Integral Development," Pages 69–80 in *Just Sustainability: Technology, Ecology, and Resource Extraction*. Edited by Christiana Z. Peppard. Vol. 3 of *Catholic Theological Ethics in the World Church*. Maryknoll, NY: Orbis Books, 2015.

Gordley, Matthew E. "Parables and the Principle of Mercy: Reading Parables Alongside the Work of Jon Sobrino in a First-Year College Course." *Journal of Catholic Higher Education* 39 (2020): 15–36.

Gowler, David B. *The Parables after Jesus: Their Imaginative Receptions across Two Millennia*. Grand Rapids: Baker Academic, 2017.

Bibliography

Graham, Mark. "The Unsavory Gamble of Industrial Agriculture," Pages 105–116 in *Just Sustainability: Technology, Ecology, and Resource Extraction.* Edited by Christiana Z. Peppard. Vol. 3 of *Catholic Theological Ethics in the World Church.* Maryknoll, NY: Orbis Books, 2015.

Green, Barbara. *Like a Tree Planted: An Exploration of Psalms and Parables through Metaphor.* Collegeville, MN: Liturgical Press, 1997.

Green, Joel B. *Dictionary of Jesus and the Gospels.* Second ed. Downers Grove, IL: IVP Academic, 2013.

Greene, Graham. *Brighton Rock.* Deluxe ed., Penguin Classics. New York: Penguin Books, 2004.

Guerin, Diane, RSM. "The Pharisee and the Tax Collector." 2019.

Gutiérrez, Gustavo. *A Theology of Liberation: History, Politics, and Salvation.* Maryknoll, NY: Orbis Books, 1988.

Harrington, Brooks and John C. Holbert. *No Mercy, No Justice: The Dominant Narrative of America versus the Counter-Narrative of Jesus' Parables.* Eugene, OR: Cascade Books, 2019.

Hays, Richard B. *The Moral Vision of the New Testament: Community, Cross, New Creation: A Contemporary Introduction to New Testament Ethics.* First ed. San Francisco: HarperSanFrancisco, 1996.

Herzog, William R. *Parables as Subversive Speech: Jesus as Pedagogue of the Oppressed.* Louisville, KY: Westminster/John Knox, 1994.

Hill Collins, Patricia and Sirma Bilge. *Intersectionality.* Second ed., Key Concepts. Cambridge, UK; Medford, MA: Polity Press, 2020.

hooks, bell. *All about Love: New Visions.* First ed. New York: William Morrow, 2000.

Hopkins, Gerard Manley. *Poems and Prose of Gerard Manley Hopkins.* Baltimore, MD: Penguin Books, 1953.

Hultgren, Arland J. *The Parables of Jesus: A Commentary.* The Bible in its World. Grand Rapids: Eerdmans, 2000.

Kasper, Walter and William Madges. *Mercy: The Essence of the Gospel and the Key to Christian Life.* New York: Paulist Press, 2014.

Keenan, James F. *The Works of Mercy: The Heart of Catholicism.* Third ed. Lanham: Rowman & Littlefield, 2017.

Kelley, Shawn. *Racializing Jesus: Race, Ideology, and the Formation of Modern Biblical Scholarship. Biblical Limits.* New York: Routledge, 2002.

Lacey, Marilyn, RSM. "The Rich Man and Lazarus." 2019.

Levine, Amy-Jill. *Short Stories by Jesus: The Enigmatic Parables of a Controversial Rabbi.* New York: HarperOne, 2014.

Levine, Lee I. *The Ancient Synagogue: The First Thousand Years.* Second ed. New Haven: Yale University Press, 2005.

Bibliography

Levine, Lee I. "Temple, Jerusalem," Pages 1281–1291 in *The Eerdmans Dictionary of Early Judaism*. Edited by John J. Collins and Daniel C. Harlow. Grand Rapids: Eerdmans, 2010.

Loba-Mkolel, Jean-Claude. "Beyond Just Wages: An Intercultural Analysis of Matthew 20:1-16." *Journal of Early Christian History* 4, no. 1 (2014): 112–134.

Lustig, Andrew. "Beginning of Life," Pages 547–560 in *The Wiley-Blackwell Companion to Religion and Social Justice*. Edited by Michael D. Palmer and Stanley M. Burgess. Malden, MA: Wiley-Blackwell, 2012.

Massaro, Thomas. *Mercy in Action: The Social Teachings of Pope Francis*. Lanham: Rowman & Littlefield, 2018.

Massingale, Bryan N. *Racial Justice and the Catholic Church*. Maryknoll, NY: Orbis Books, 2010.

McGhee, Heather C. *The Sum of Us: What Racism Costs Everyone and How We Can Prosper Together*. New York: One World, 2021.

McKenna, Megan. *Parables: The Arrows of God*. Maryknoll, NY: Orbis Books, 1994.

Mealey, Ann Marie. "Feminism and Ecology," Pages 182–193 in *Just Sustainability: Technology, Ecology, and Resource Extraction*. Edited by Christiana Z. Peppard. Vol. 3 of *Catholic Theological Ethics in the World Church*. Maryknoll, New York: Orbis Books, 2015.

Murray, Justin, Meredith B. Esser, and Robin West. *In Search of Common Ground on Abortion: From Culture War to Reproductive Justice*. Gender in Law, Culture, and Society. Burlington, VT: Ashgate, 2014.

Murthy, Vivek H. *Together: The Healing Power of Human Connection in a Sometimes Lonely World*. New York, NY: Harper Wave, an imprint of HarperCollins, 2020.

Nabhan, Gary Paul. *Jesus for Farmers and Fishers: Justice for All Those Marginalized by Our Food System*. Minneapolis, MN: Broadleaf Books, 2021.

Neyrey, Jerome. "Meals, Food, and Table Fellowship," Pages 159–182 in *The Social Sciences and New Testament Interpretation*. Edited by Richard L. Rohrbaugh. Peabody, MA: Hendrickson, 1996.

Peppard, Christiana Z. *Just Water: Theology, Ethics, and Fresh Water Crises*. Revised ed., Ecology and Justice, an Orbis Series on Integral Ecology. Maryknoll, NY: Orbis Books, 2018.

Perrin, Norman. *Jesus and the Language of the Kingdom: Symbol and Metaphor in New Testament Interpretation*. Philadelphia: Fortress, 1976.

Peters, Rebecca Todd. *Trust Women: A Progressive Christian Argument for Reproductive Justice*. Boston: Beacon Press, 2018.

Powery, Emerson B. *The Good Samaritan: Luke 10 for the Life of the Church*. Touchstone Texts. Grand Rapids, MI: Baker Academic, 2022.

Bibliography

Reid, Barbara E. and Shelly Matthews. *Luke 10–24*. Vol. 43B, Wisdom Commentary. Collegeville, MN: Liturgical Press, 2021.

Rogers, Frank. "Warriors of Compassion: Coordinates on the Compass of Compassion-Based Activism," Pages 25–41 in *Taking It to the Streets: Public Theologies of Activism and Resistance*. Edited by Jennifer Baldwin. Lanham, MD: Lexington Books, 2019.

Rourke, Nancy M. "A Catholic Virtues Ecology," Pages 194–204 in *Just Sustainability: Technology, Ecology, and Resource Extraction*. Edited by Christiana Z. Peppard. Vol. 3 of *Catholic Theological Ethics in the World Church*. Maryknoll, New York: Orbis Books, 2015.

Ruether, Rosemary Radford. "The Female Nature of God," Pages 298–304 in *Exploring the Philosophy of Religion*. Edited by David Stewart. Upper Saddle River, NJ: Pearson Prentice Hall, 2007.

Ryken, Leland. *How to Read the Bible as Literature*. Grand Rapids: Zondervan, 1984.

Saldarini, Anthony J. *Pharisees, Scribes, and Sadducees in Palestinian Society: A Sociological Approach*. Grand Rapids, MI: W.B. Eerdmans, 2001.

Schaper, Joachim. "Levites," Pages 885–887 in *The Eerdmans Dictionary of Early Judaism*. Edited by John J. Collins and Daniel C. Harlow. Grand Rapids: Eerdmans, 2010.

Schottroff, Luise. *The Parables of Jesus*. Minneapolis: Fortress, 2006.

Schubert, Judy, RSM. "The Lost Sons." 2019.

Serjak, Cynthia, RSM. "The Lost Coin, the Lost Sheep." 2019.

Sievers, Joseph and Amy-Jill Levine. *The Pharisees*. Grand Rapids, MI: Eerdmans, 2021.

Smith, Luther E. *Howard Thurman: The Mystic as Prophet*. Revised ed. Richmond, IN: Friends United Press, 1992.

Snodgrass, Klyne. *Stories with Intent: A Comprehensive Guide to the Parables of Jesus*. Second ed. Grand Rapids: Eerdmans, 2018.

Sobrino, Jon. *The Principle of Mercy: Taking the Crucified People from the Cross*. Maryknoll, NY: Orbis Books, 1994.

Sobrino, Jon. *No Salvation Outside the Poor: Prophetic-Utopian Essays*. Maryknoll, NY: Orbis Books, 2008.

Teilhard de Chardin, Pierre. *Hymn of the Universe*. New York: Harper & Row, 1965.

Thiselton, Anthony C. *The Power of Pictures in Christian Thought: The Use and Abuse of Images in the Bible and Theology*. London: SPCK Publishing, 2018.

Thomas, Linda. "A Womanist Perspective on the Election of Donald Trump: What Pastors are Called to Do," Pages 15–23 in *Taking It to the Streets: Public Theologies of Activism and Resistance*. Edited by Jennifer Baldwin. Lanham, MD: Lexington Books, 2019.

Bibliography

Thomasset, Alain. "The Virtue of Hospitality according to the Bible and the Challenge of Migration," Pages 34–44 in *The Bible and Catholic Theological Ethics*. Edited by Yiu Sing Lúcás Chan. of *Catholic Theological Ethics in the World Church*. Maryknoll, NY: Orbis Books, 2017.

Thompson, Marianne Meye. "Jesus and His God," Pages 41–55 in *The Cambridge Companion to Jesus*. Edited by Markus N. A. Bockmuehl. of *Cambridge Companions to Religion*. Cambridge: Cambridge University 2001.

Thurman, Howard. *With Head and Heart: The Autobiography of Howard Thurman*. First ed. New York: Harcourt Brace Jovanovich, 1979.

Thurman, Howard. *Jesus and the Disinherited*. Boston, MA: Beacon Press, 1996.

Thurman, Howard. *Sermons on the Parables*. Maryknoll, NY: Orbis Books, 2018.

Tomson, Peter J. "Jesus and His Judaism," Pages 25–40 in *The Cambridge Companion to Jesus*. Edited by Markus N. A. Bockmuehl. of *Cambridge Companions to Religion*. Cambridge: Cambridge University 2001.

Townes, Emilie M. "Ethics as an Art of Doing the Work Our Souls Must Have," Pages 35–50 in *Womanist Theological Ethics: A Reader*. Edited by Katie G. Cannon, Emilie Maureen Townes, and Angela D. Sims. of *Library of Theological Ethics*. Louisville, KY: Westminster John Knox Press, 2011.

Townes, Emilie Maureen. *Womanist Ethics and the Cultural Production of Evil*. Black Religion, Womanist Thought, Social Justice. New York: Palgrave Macmillan, 2006.

United Nations General Assembly. *The Universal Declaration of Human Rights (UDHR)*. United Nations General Assembly, 1948 [Accessed December 16, 2022]. Available from https://www.un.org/en/about-us/universal-declaration-of-human-rights.

Van Eck, Ernest and John S. Kloppenborg. *The Parables of Jesus the Galilean: Stories of a Social Prophet*. Vol. 9, Matrix–The Bible in Mediterranean Context. Eugene, OR: Cascade Books, 2016.

VanderKam, James C. *An Introduction to Early Judaism*. Second ed. Grand Rapids: Eerdmans, 2003.

VanderKam, James C. "Judaism in the Land of Israel," Pages 57–76 in *The Eerdmans Dictionary of Early Judaism*. Edited by John J. Collins and Daniel C. Harlow. Grand Rapids: Eerdmans, 2010.

Via, Dan Otto. *The Parables: Their Literary and Existential Dimension*. Philadelphia: Fortress, 1967.

Wallis, Jim. *Christ in Crisis? Why We Need to Reclaim Jesus*. San Francisco: HarperOne, 2019.

Wells, Samuel, Ben Quash, and Rebekah Ann Eklund. *Introducing Christian Ethics*. Second ed. Hoboken, NJ: Wiley Blackwell, 2017.

White, Lynn. "The Historical Roots of Our Ecological Crisis." *Science* 155 (1967): 1203–1207.

Bibliography

Willis, Lawrence M. "Methodological Reflections on the Tax Collectors in the Gospels," Pages 251–268 in *When Judaism and Christianity Began: Essays in Memory of Anthony J. Saldarini.* Edited by Anthony J. Saldarini, Alan J. Avery-Peck, Daniel J. Harrington, and Jacob Neusner. Vol. 85 of *Supplements to the Journal for the Study of Judaism.* Leiden; Boston: Brill, 2004.

Wright, N. T. *Paul and the Faithfulness of God.* Minneapolis: Fortress, 2013.

Yinger, Kent L. and Craig A. Evans. *The Pharisees: Their History, Character, and New Testament Portrait.* Eugene, OR: Cascade Books, 2022.

Index

abortion 164, 252–254
Abraham, as patriarch 45–46, 49
   in the parables 260–261,
     267–268
Acts of the Apostles 88–89
advanced agrarian
   societies 54–57, 175,
     245–246
   bureaucracies 55–56
   cultural background 56–57
   day laborers 232, 234, 237–
     238, 239, 242–243
   pastoralism 113–114
   social stratification 56–57,
     154–155, 236, 243–244
   vineyards 238, 242
   wage levels 234, 238, 243
   women's role 122–123

Africa 250–251
afterlife imagery, in the
   parables 257–258, 261,
     267–268
   and reversal of circumstances
     261, 263–264
anti-Jewish biblical
   interpretation 18–19,
     43–44, 90–92, 96, 295
   contrast with Christianity
     19
   German scholarship 43
   parables *see* anti-Jewish
     parable interpretation
anti-Jewish parable
   interpretation 18–19, 90,
     92, 121, 208
   anachronistic 217, 241

Social Justice in the Stories of Jesus: The Ethical Challenge of the Parables, First Edition.
Matthew E. Gordley.
© 2024 John Wiley & Sons Ltd. Published 2024 by John Wiley & Sons Ltd.

Index

anti-Jewish parable
  interpretation (*cont'd*)
  contrast with Christianity 19,
    90–91, 149–150, 181–182,
    265
  good Samaritan 90–91, 92,
    240
  laborers in the vineyard 242
  lost coin 121
  lost sons 149–150
  mustard seed 181–182
  Pharisee and tax
    collector 208, 217
  rich man and Lazarus
    262–263, 264–266
anti-Judaism 18, 19, 91, 36, 295
  and allegory 97, 98
  definitions 18n28, 43
  and New Testament study *see*
    anti-Jewish biblical
    interpretation
  and racialized worldviews 44
  relation to anti-Semitism 43
  stereotypes 97, 121–122
anti-mercy 23, 102
anti-Semitism 18n28, 43, 265
apocalyptic writings 51–52
Apostle Paul 31, 49
  on Jesus 26
  on love 31
  on the Pharisees 209
Aquinas *see* Thomas Aquinas
Augustine of Hippo 96
  allegorical approach 96–97,
    217

Baker-Fletcher, Karen 189,
  198–199
Baldwin, Jennifer 165, 294
banquet, parable of 11–12,
  124–125
Barrett Browning, Elizabeth
  301
Barton, Stephen C. 63
Ben Sira 237
biblical interpretation 24, 43–44,
  280
  allegorical 97, 217
  anti-Jewish *see* anti-Jewish
    biblical interpretation
  euro-centricity 33
  parables *see* parables,
    interpretation of
black theology 27, 212, 305
Bonaventure 97
Bonhoeffer, Dietrich 5
Brobst-Renaud,
  Amanda 162–163
Brown, Kelly Douglas 75–76
Brown, Raymond 10

Callahan, Sidney 284
Cancienne, Mary-Paula 325
  reflection on the parable of
    the pearl of great
    price 323–325
Carey, Greg 11n15, 14, 16, 267
Carney, Sheila 176, 185, 193,
  197, 199, 317
  reflection on the parable of
    the mustard seed 315–317

342

Index

Catholic Social Teaching 100, 101–102, 250
  "common good" concept 101, 249
  economic justice 249, 272
Chief Seattle 105, 310
civilization of poverty 246–247
Civil Rights movement 29, 279, 296
classical Greek philosophy, and Christian thinking 26
climate change 4, 192, 196
  see also ecological awareness
common good, concept of 101, 199
  and community 223, 249
  and ethic of love 303
  and public policy 132, 299
  and social justice 299
communal rejoicing 115–116, 123–124, 130
  see also Jewish festivals
community, importance of 132–133, 147–148, 157–160
  across difference 164–165, 167, 171
  and the common good 223, 286
  as divine purpose 159, 160, 163, 286
  family 152
  inclusivity 202
  and individualism 132
  Jewish worldview 149, 150
  and nature 292, 310

  obligations to others 291
  in the parables 147–149, 152, 154, 157–158
  restoration 133, 134, 155, 229, 286, 294
  shift from competition 224
  and solidarity 251
  and well-being 158, 162, 276, 300
  see also forgiveness; individuals-in-community; interconnectedness
compassion 97, 140–141, 271, 322
  active 72, 90
    see also compassion-based activism
  beneficial effects 276, 288
  as element of mercy 140–141, 313
  fatherly 11, 138, 140, 141, 163, 314, 315
  of Jesus 74, 97, 306
  lack of 269, 275, 296
  as motivation 23, 89, 99, 188, 254, 271, 309
  as natural response to suffering 275, 276, 285
  obligation 91, 92, 97, 103, 106
  thread in the parables 5, 290
  toward the poor 100
compassion-based activism 167, 171, 287
Cone, James 212, 296
  on civil rights 212, 279

343

Index

Cone, James (*cont'd*)
  on freedom 77, 212, 279, 305–306
  on the kingdom of God 70, 74
  on the reality of evil 305
  on solidarity with the poor and oppressed 70, 71, 77, 78, 212, 272, 274, 296, 304
Cook, Michael 3, 244
covenant, Jewish
    understandings of 49
  Abrahamic 45–46, 49
  and exile 49
  and New Covenant 125
Crossan, J. Dominic 216n22
  on the day of the Lord 51
  on first-century Judaic thought 65, 65n31
  on the kingdom of God 65, 66–67, 69
  on the parables 15, 106, 216, 223, 266n16
  on violence 19, 92
crucifixion of Jesus 57, 75–77, 78, 80
  as act of compassion 76, 97
  Jewish leaders and 48, 88
  proclamation of 125
  Roman responsibility for 68
cultural hegemony 41–42
  in twentieth-century German scholarship 43, 43n44
  in Western philosophy 43
Curry, Bishop Michael 32, 301, 302–303, 304

Curtis, Anne 95, 311
  reflection on the good Samaritan 95, 105, 106, 309–310

Daniel, Book of 52, 65–66
David, king of Israel 46, 53–54
death
  and disintegration of community 152, 161–162
  imagery, in the parables 147, 152, 153
  of Jesus *see* crucifixion of Jesus
  as metaphor 153
de-colonial theology 27
Democratic Republic of the Congo (DRC) 250–251
Dobrovolny, Mary Kay 321
  reflection on the parable of the laborers in the vineyard 248, 319–321
Dodd, C.H. 13
Doran, Robert 216

ecofeminism 195
ecological awareness 105, 188–191, 192–196, 198
  and justice 193, 195
  see also sustainability
ecological humility 190–191
Ellacuría, Ignacio 246, 247
El Salvador 22
Enlightenment ideas 130
environmental justice 193, 195

344

Index

Esdras, Books of 124
ethical reflection, on the
parables 24–32
see also New Testament ethics,
discipline of
ethic of love 32, 35, 302–305
and common good 303
of enemies 96, 107
in Jesus's teaching 29–30, 80
and social change 304
universality 304–305
see also mercy
ethics, Christian 26n39, 32, 199,
292, 293
reflection 32
virtue 293, 302
see also ethic of love; New
Testament ethics, discipline
of; womanist theologies
euangelion see gospel message, the
Eucharist, the 125, 133–134
evil
agents of 22
confronting 23, 274
and forgiveness 22
racism *see* racism
reality of 305
structural 130–131, 291n10
victims of 274, 278
existential understanding
143–144, 148
in the parables 146–147, 155,
161, 284
Ezekiel, Book of 119
Ezra 124

Farley, Margaret 99–100,
170–171, 270, 297
fellowship 32, 168
barriers to 277
table *see* table fellowship
see also community,
importance of
feminist theologies 27, 120, 157
Floyd, George, murder of 4, 92,
228
focal awareness 142–143, 144
forgiveness 22, 171
and community 169
in the Jewish Scriptures 16
in the parables 141, 163,
313–314
and restoration 314
see also reconciliation
Francis of Assisi 190–191
"Canticle of the
Creatures" 191
freedom 77, 159, 277–278,
305–306
of choice 249
God's grant of 189, 212
and human rights 73
individual 130–132
and the oppressed 77, 212,
274, 278, 306
and wealth 274

Galilee 56, 59
Gbowee, Leymah 168
generosity
of God 245, 248

Index

generosity (*cont'd*)
  parable of the laborers in the
    vineyard 235, 239, 245–246,
    247–248
  parable of the lost
    sons 151n16, 162
  Second Temple literature 53
Genesis creation narratives 185,
  189, 191, 305
Getty-Sullivan, Mary Ann 9
global crises 4–5, 104, 197
  climatic 316, 324
  health 4, 93
  moral 5, 101, 199
  refugees 104
globalization 104, 249, 277
  inequities 192, 249
  and refugees 104, 197
global pandemic (2020s) 4, 93
good Samaritan, parable
  of 83–107
  allegorical
    interpretations 96–97
  anti-Jewish readings 90–91,
    92, 240
  and Catholic Social
    Teaching 100
  challenges 98–102
  characters in 49, 84, 87–90
  context 84, 122
  implications of 102–107
  invitation to "see" 95, 102
  mercy 21, 23, 98–99, 134,
    309–310
  as narrative metaphor 94–97

shelter 316
solidarity 278
summary 285–286
text of 85
and Torah 47
Gospel of John 61
Gospel of Luke 116, 125
  childhood of Jesus
    narratives 48
  and the covenant 46
  on the kingdom of
    God 62–63, 65
  narrative context 86–87
  parable applications
    123–124, 218, 222, 262
  see also individual parables
  and prophetic
    tradition 15–16, 62–63
  reversal motif 262
  women's role 120, 262
  see also synoptic gospels
Gospel of Mark 15, 45, 61, 63,
  116n8
  double questions 176
  emphasis on the natural
    world 177, 183, 186
  parables *see* parable of the
    mustard seed
  see also synoptic gospels
Gospel of Matthew 12, 16, 125
  parable applications 10, 235,
    291, 294
  and prophetic
    tradition 15–16, 51
  see also synoptic gospels

Index

gospel message, the
  as good news 61–62
  as message of liberation
    64, 78
Gospels, the 61
  diasporic composition 50
  and prophetic tradition 51,
    186
  source for Jesus's
    teachings 60–61
  summaries 61
  see also individual gospels
Graham, Mark 193–194
Green, Barbara 7, 34, 94
Guerin, Dianne 221–222, 224,
  319
  reflection on the parable of
    the Pharisee and the tax
    collector 317–319

Harrington, Brooks 247
Hays, Richard B. 25, 25n37, 33,
  282–283, 306
Hellenism, in the Roman
  Empire 40
Hellenization of Christianity 26
Herod the Great 46, 58, 59
Herzog, William 31, 69, 236
  Parables as Subversive
    Speech 54n13, 72–73, 319
historical Jesus, the 3, 58, 76,
  296
Holt-Lunstad, Julianne 162
homelessness 103–104
  and hospitality 197

hooks, bell 72n54, 303, 304
hospitality 197, 316
  of Jesus 209
  in the Jewish Scriptures 197,
    260
  in the parables 176, 178, 197, 199
  see also shelter
Hultgren, Arland 9, 16, 20, 142
humanization 170, 246–247, 305
human rights 73, 289
  and natural law 297
  see also Civil Rights movement
humility 176, 185, 206
  cultural 42, 43
  ecological 190–191

image of God, concept of 158,
  278
immasculation 120–121
individualism 130–131
  Christian tradition 133
  community context 223, 286
    see also individuals-in-
    community
  competitive 247
  and public policy 131
individuals-in-community 158,
  163, 283n2, 286, 290
industrialized
  agriculture 193–195
inheritance, in the
  parables 138–139, 153, 313
  entitlement to 139, 313
integral ecology 191–192, 193
  see also sustainability

347

Index

interconnectedness 106,
  290–291
  and forgiveness 171, 220
  in the natural world 178,
    188–189, 310
    see also integral ecology
  and well-being 162, 170
Isaiah, Book of 52, 270
  imagery 119, 124
  Jesus's quotations from 16,
    49, 63

Jerusalem
  destruction 48, 60
  and foreign domination 54
  importance of 48
  see also Second Temple, in
    first-century Judaism
Jesus 68, 69–71
  actions of 40, 73–74, 148–149
  crucifixion *see* crucifixion of
    Jesus
  as exorcist 74
  fulfillment of prophecy 51,
    60–61, 69, 118, 119
  historical context 30–31,
    39–60
  and Jerusalem 48–49
  and Jewish Scriptures 19, 47,
    86–87, 97–98
  as Jewish teacher 19, 29, 39,
    40, 42–43, 44, 92, 296
  messianic role 119
  miracles *see* miracles of Jesus
  and money 122

as prophet 70, 77, 272
quotations from Isaiah 16, 49,
  63
relations with Pharisees 120,
  127, 149–150
resurrection 76–77
and Roman Empire 68
solidarity with the poor and
  oppressed 75, 76, 78, 272,
  280, 297
as Son of Man 67n36
teachings *see* teachings of
  Jesus
use of parables 15–16, 18, 51
in the wilderness 65
see also historical Jesus, the
Jewish diaspora 49
Jewish festivals 50
Jewish worship *see* worship,
  Jewish
John the Baptist 66, 69, 88, 117
Judaism 42–43, 44–46
  apocalyptic tradition 51–52
  celebrations *see* Jewish
    festivals
  covenant understandings *see*
    covenant, Jewish
    understandings of
  and Davidic line 53, 65
  "day of the Lord"
    tradition 51
  Hellenistic 50
  importance of the Temple 46,
    47–48
  kingship 46, 46n4

348

Index

monotheism 44–45
and national identity 53–54
oral traditions 47
Palestinian 50
prophetic tradition 50–51, 70, 78
religious leaders 88–89
scriptures *see* Scriptures, Jewish
Second Temple period *see* Second Temple Judaism
worship *see* worship, Jewish
see also Jewish diaspora
justice 131–132, 291n10, 298
as parable theme 291–292
and public policy 298–299
relational 298
relationship with mercy 71, 291–292, 297–298
justification 214
in the parables 205, 213–214, 215, 218

Kaspar, Cardinal Walter 21
Keenan, James 100, 103–105, 196, 177, 283, 299
kingdom of God, in Jesus's teachings 63–67, 71, 223–224
collaborative nature of 67
as deliverance 65–66
in earthly activities 155, 292, 300–301
inclusivity 229
as metaphor 68, 175

and the natural world *see* natural world, in Jesus's teachings
as new age 16, 77, 116–117, 247
nonviolent nature of 67
parables of *see* parables of the kingdom
as present reality 293
symbolism 68

laborers in the vineyard, parable of 2–3, 10–11, 232–254
anti-Jewish readings 241–242
challenges of 245–248
characters 233–234
generosity 235, 239, 245–246, 247–248
implications of 248–254
justice 235, 242, 244
mercy 245
metaphor in 240–245
narrative context 233–240, 242
relationship with other parables 238, 241
repentance 237
solidarity 278–279
spiritualized interpretations 234, 240–241
summary 288
text of 233

349

Index

laborers in the vineyard,
parable of (*cont'd*)
themes from Jewish
Scriptures 242
Lacey, Marilyn 275–276, 322
reflection on the rich man and
Lazarus 321–322
landowner and his vineyard *see*
laborers in the vinehard,
parable of
Lazarus, as character in Jesus's
parable 259–261
see also rich man and Lazarus,
parable of
Levine, Amy-Jill 19, 121,
241–242, 295
on the good Samaritan 89
on the Pharisee and the tax
collector 207–208, 215,
217–218
on the rich man and
Lazarus 259, 263–264, 273
Short Stories of Jesus 36
Leviticus, Book of 91
liberation theology *see*
theologies of liberation
Liberia 168
Loba-Mkolel, Jean-Claude 250
loss, as human experience 116,
123
being lost 123, 153, 160
and redemption 127
lost coin, parable of 109–134,
238, 311–312
anti-Jewish readings 121

celebration 116, 122
challenges of 126–127
characters 111–112, 113,
121–122
compared to parable of lost
sheep 110–111
context 148–149
implications of 128,
129–134
mercy 312
narrative context 112
repentance 109, 110, 111,
112–113
summary 286
text of 110
lost sheep, parable of 109–134,
311–312
celebration 116
challenges of 126–127
characters 111, 113
compared to parable of lost
coin 110–111
context 148–149
in Gospel of
Matthew 117–118
implications of 128, 129–134
mercy 312
metaphor in 118–119
narrative context 112
repentance 109, 110, 111,
112–113
summary 286
text of 110
themes from Jewish
Scripture 119–120

350

Index

lost sons, parable of 122,
  136–172, 312–315
  anti-Jewish readings 149–150
  celebration 140, 148, 151, 154,
    160
  challenges of 157–162
  characters 138, 155–156
  context 148–149
  death references 153, 154
  forgiveness 313–314
  implications of 163–172
  mercy 141, 163, 312–314
  metaphor in 153–157
  narrative context 138–140
  older son 141–142, 314–315
  relationship with other
    parables 151–152, 158
  repentance 155
  summary 286–287
  text of 136–137
  themes from Jewish
    Scriptures 138, 139, 150
  younger son 138–142, 313–314

Manley Hopkins, Gerard 301
martyrdom, modern 22
Mary, mother of Jesus 65, 214,
  262, 273
Massaro, Thomas, *Mercy in
  Action* 249–250
Massingale, Bryan 297
  on racial reconciliation
    133–134, 225–226, 228, 297
  on solidarity 251–252, 254
  on truth telling 228–229, 297

McAuley, Catherine 317
McGhee, Heather, *The Sum of
  Us* 226–227, 299–300
McKenna, Megan 15
mercy 98, 126–127
  anti- *see* anti-mercy
  books on 21
  compassion element 140–141,
    313
  corporal works of 103–105, 196
  in Jesus's parables *see under
    individual parables*
  principle of *see under* Sobrino,
    Jon
  relationship with justice 71,
    291–292, 297–298
  Scriptural tradition 53, 71
  Second Temple
    almsgiving 53
  spiritual works of 171
  towards the Earth 105, 310, 316
Mercy Beyond Borders 276
Messiah, age of 16, 77, 116–117,
  247
  first-century expectations
    65n31, 66, 69, 77, 175
  prophecies of 116–117, 124
  as threat to authorities 59, 68
  see also kingdom of God, in
    Jesus's teachings; messianic
    banquet, the
messianic banquet, the 124–125
  and the Last Supper 125
  New Testament
    imagery 124–125

351

Index

messianic banquet, the (*cont'd*)
  Old Testament imagery 124
  and restoration 125
  see also banquet, parable of the
Micah, Book of 52–53, 119
miracles of Jesus 65, 73–74
motive attribution
    assymetry 225
Murthy, Vivek 132–133, 162,
    169–170, 224–225, 300
mustard seed, parable of
    174–199, 315–317
  anti-Jewish readings 181–182
  challenges of 187–192
  characters 179, 184
  context 178–179
  implications of 189–190
  invitation to "see" 188
  mercy 197
  metaphor in 179, 180–183,
    184–187
  narrative context 176–178
  relationship with other
    parables 174n2, 181
  shelter 178, 184, 197, 316–317
  summary 287
  text of 176
  themes from Jewish
    Scriptures 180–181, 184,
    185, 186–187

Nabhan, Gary P. 114n4, 175n6,
    179n12
narrative, ancient forms of 148,
    149, 154

narrative metaphor, parables
    as 34, 94–95, 144
natural world, in Jesus's
    teachings 174–183, 292
  birds 178, 180, 181, 184–186,
    315
  crops 174–175, 177–178
  the earth 105, 177
  and human existence 174, 183
  trees 184–185
  weeds 179n12
nature parables 187
  parable of the mustard seed
    see mustard seed, parable
    of *see also* natural world, in
    Jesus's teachings
Nazi Germany 5
new age *see* Messiah, age of
New Testament ethics,
    discipline of 25, 33
non-violence 67–68, 325

Old Testament *see* Jewish
    Scriptures
oppression 212–213, 247, 291
  first-century Palestine 30, 68,
    179
  in Jewish Scriptures 52, 66
  liberation from 77, 79, 278
  overcoming 68, 77
  of women 195 *see also*
    solidarity with the poor
    and oppressed
Opus Prize 276
orthopathy 297

Index

Palestine, first-century
Galilee 56, 59
rule by Romans 39–40, 53, 54,
59
socio-economic background
see advanced agrarian
economies
violent uprisings 59–60
parable interpretation 18,
33–36, 142–147, 280
allegorical 10, 96, 242n13
analytical 7, 126
anti-Jewish *see* anti-Jewish
parable interpretation
and context 3, 10–11, 33–34,
57, 84
in conversation 11
distorted 19, 241
and focal awareness 142–143,
144
intercultural 250
and modern assumptions 17,
18, 84
and Old Testament
prophecies of 16
over history *see* parables,
interpretation history of
spiritualized 3, 234
and translation 205, 219
typifications 57
see also ethical reflection, on
the parables
parables 8–12, 13–14
as allegories 10

as comparisons 9, 12–13
as counter-narrative 247
definition 9
as instructional tool 280
as metaphors 10, 14, 34,
94–95, 234
as narratives 9, 334
as short stories 8–9
parables, challenging nature
of 6–7, 11, 12, 14–15, 34–35
on character of God 11–12,
45, 126–127
emotional response to 14
and ethical concerns 3–4,
24–31
implications 35
on justification 219
and mystery 16
and participative
pedagogery 15, 284
and scriptural quotation 16
see also under individual
parables
parables, interpretation history
of 1, 2–3, 25–26
modern 27, 130
original understandings 7,
10, 17–19, 26, 156
and patriarchy 156
Patristic 10, 26, 182n16
see also Christian thinking,
history of
parables, shared themes
of 288–294

353

Index

parables, shared themes of (*cont'd*)
  compassion 290
  concern for those in need 289
  human value 289
  interconnectedness 290–291
  justice 291–292
  nature 292
parables of the kingdom 16–17,
    20, 127, 175, 183, 233
  see also banquet, parable of;
    laborers in the vineyard,
    parable of; mustard seed
    see mustard seed, parable
    of; pearl of great price,
    parable of
"participatory pedagogy" 14,
    216n22, 267
patriarchal culture
  first-century 114, 156
  modern 156–157
  in the parables 156
Paul of Tarsus *see* Apostle Paul,
    the
peacebuilding 167–170
pearl of great price, parable
    of 323–325
  kingdom metaphor
    323, 324
Peck, M. Scott 303
Peppard, Christiana Z., *Just
    Water* 194
Perrin, Norman 16–17
Pharisees 209–210, 317
  devotion to the Torah 209,
    210

Jesus's relations with 120,
    127, 149–150, 210
  in the parables 209, 210
  view of resurrection 263
Pharisee and the tax collector,
    parable of 91, 202–230,
    317–319
  anti-Jewish readings
    208, 217
  challenges of 204–205,
    219–221
  characters 204–205, 209–212,
    215, 317–318
  implications of 221–230
  mercy 205, 220, 318
  metaphor in 215–219
  narrative context 203–207,
    211–212
  as parable of reversal 202,
    213–214, 216
  and philanthropy 122, 204,
    211
  relationship with other
    parables 208
  repentance 205
  summary 287
  text of 203
  themes from Jewish
    Scriptures 214
Pope Francis 187, 197, 199,
    249–250, 299
  Laudato Si' 191, 193, 292, 316
  On Social Friendship 100–101
Pope John Paul II, *Gaudium et
    Spes* 272

354

Index

post-colonial theology 27
power dynamics, in society 28,
235–236
preferential option for the
poor 272–273
see also solidarity with the
poor and oppressed
prodigal son, parable of *see* lost
sons, parable of
prophetic writings,
Jewish 50–51, 52–53, 124,
185
see also Ezekiel, Book of;
Isaiah, Book of; Micah,
Book of; Zechariah, Book of
Protestant theology 218, 267
Psalms
imagery 119, 181, 186
quotations from 16, 186
Psalms of Solomon 53, 64, 209
public policymaking 131–132

racism 4, 92, 225–229
in the Catholic Church 133
institutional
embeddedness 133, 226
and marginalization 226
and political rhetoric 92–93,
163–164
and reconciliation 226, 228
subtlety of 228–229
and white privilege 101–102,
134, 227
see also white supremacy

reconciliation
and forgiveness 171
and justice 168, 169
racial 226, 228, 297
and truth telling 228,
254, 297
refugee crisis 104, 192, 197
repentance 70, 133, 149, 207,
275
laborers in the vineyard
parable 237
lost coin and lost sheep
parables 109, 110, 111,
112–113
lost sons parable 155
Pharisee and the tax collector
parable 205
rich man and Lazarus
parable 261, 275
resurrection of Jesus 76–77
resurrection, as theme in
parables 153–154
Revelation, Book of 52
rich man and Lazarus, parable
of 257–280, 321–322
afterlife 257–258, 261, 263
anti-Jewish readings 262–263,
264–266
challenges of 274–276
characters 257, 259–260,
274–275
freedom 277–278
implications of 277–280
justice 264

355

Index

rich man and Lazarus, parable
of (*cont'd*)
mercy 270, 275, 276, 277
metaphor in 268–273
narrative context 259–261
as parable of the
kingdom 273
as parable of reversal 259,
260, 267
relationship with other
parables 264, 269, 271, 278
repentance 261, 275
shelter 277
and socio-economic
distance 267–270, 271–272
summary 288
text of 258–259
themes from Jewish
Scriptures 262–263, 264,
269–270
tragic nature of 274–275
Roe v. Wade, 2022 reversal
of 164, 252
Roman Emperor, divine cult
of 39, 58–59
Roman Empire, first-
century 39–40, 58–60
cultural Hellenism 40
Judaism in 39, 49, 59, 68
patriarchal culture 155
rule of Palestine 39–40, 54,
68, 213
taxation 39–40, 179, 210–211,
213

Rourke, Nancy M. 188, 192,
195–196
Ruether, Rosemary
Radford 184, 198
Rwanda 250–251
Ryken, Leland 9

Sadducees 263
salvation, meaning of 64, 127,
159, 230, 267
Samaritans 89, 92
Schottroff, Louise 184, 217n26
on the parable of the good
Samaritan 188, 293
on the parable of the lost
coin 121–122
on the parable of the lost
sons 156
on the parable of the rich man
and Lazarus 266
Schubert, Judy 140–141, 163,
315
reflection on the lost
sons 312–315
Scriptures, Jewish 19, 46–47,
50–54
apocalyptic writings 51–52
expectation of new age 77,
116–117, 247
female imagery for God 120
messianic banquet 124
prophetic writings *see*
prophetic writings, Jewish
social justice tradition 52–53

Index

suffering servant 270
Torah *see* Torah
Wisdom 52
Second Temple Judaism 39,
    42–43, 46–53, 65
    literature 51, 53
    patriarchal culture 114
    popular thought 64–66
    religious leaders 88–89
    treasury of merit 218–219,
        220, 223
Serjak, Cynthia 312
    reflection on the lost sheep
        and lost coin 126–127, 134,
        311–312
sheep and goats, parable of 291,
    294
shelter
    parable of rich man and
        Lazarus 277
    parable of the good
        Samaritan 316
    parable of the mustard
        seed 178, 184, 197, 316–317
    as work of mercy 104, 187,
        197–198, 316
Shema, the 44, 45, 87
Sisters of Mercy 3, 275–276, 300, 306
    ecological
        commitment 316–317
    *Reflections on the
        Parables* 309–325
    see also Cancienne, Mary-
        Paula; Carney, Sheila;

Dobrovolny, Mary Kay;
    Guerin, Dianne; Serjak,
    Cynthia
Snodgrass, Klyne 126, 127
Sobrino, Jon 22–23, 80, 271
    civilization of
        poverty 246–247
    on Good Samaritan
        parable 98–99, 102
    principle of mercy 23, 99,
        102, 106, 295–296
social construction of reality 57,
    144n6
    and the parables 57, 144,
        145–146, 236
social justice concepts 27–28,
    235–236
    see also oppression;
        reconciliation; solidarity
        with the poor and
        oppressed
socio-economic background to
    Jesus's teachings *see*
    advanced agrarian
    economies
sociological insights 54–55, 58,
    222–223
solidarity with the poor and
    oppressed 71, 227, 271,
    249–253
    and the civilization of
        poverty 247
    cross-racial 134, 227, 299–300
    ...and economic justice 251

357

Index

solidarity with the poor and
oppressed (*cont'd*)
and freedom 274, 278
of Jesus 71, 75, 76, 78
as kingdom value 247–248
and socio-economic
distance 269–270
Solomon, king of Israel 52, 53
and Davidic line 46n4
reputation for wisdom 53
Temple builder 46, 46n4, 48
writings 53
sower, parable of the 10
Sowle-Cahill, Lisa 15, 71–72, 77,
167–168, 169, 297
St. Louis, Missouri 227
subsidiary awareness 143
sustainability 104, 193,
195, 316
synagogue worship 48, 49
synoptic gospels 52, 61, 186n21,
238
compared 61–62
see also Gospel of Luke;
Gospel of Mark; Gospel of
Matthew

table fellowship 125, 133–134
Taking It to the Streets (Baldwin
et al.) 165
tax collectors 210–211
see also Pharisee and the tax
collector, parable of
teachings of Jesus 40, 60–73,
176–177

anachronistic readings
of 30–31, 30n45, 92
and covenant tradition 46, 125
ethic of love 29–30, 80
on fatherhood of God 71
as good news 62–64
invitation to "see" 95, 102,
188
Jewish underpinnings 44, 51
kingdom of God 64–69
see also parables of the
kingdom
on the kingdom of God *see*
kingdom of God, in Jesus's
teachings
the natural world in *see*
natural world, in Jesus's
teachings
parable themes *see* parables,
shared themes
prophetic tradition 79
on social justice 30–31,
69–73
socio-economic background
see advanced agrarian
economies
sources 60–61
subversive nature of 72
through action 74
and wisdom tradition 53
Teilhard de Chardin, Pierre
291
theologies of liberation 22, 27,
78
Thomas, Linda 165–166

Index

Thomas Aquinas 101
Thomasset, Alain 293
Thompson, Marianne Meye 71
Thurman, Howard 14, 29–30, 78, 158–161, 296
  on divine purpose 159–160
  Jesus and the Disinherited 78–79
  on parable of the good Samaritan 107
  on parable of the lost sons 158–159
  on parables of the lost coin and lost sheep 126, 127
Tomson, Peter 63–64
Torah 46–47
  and God's concern for the poor 91
  Jesus's summary of 47
Townes, Emilie 28–29, 30, 292
  on the common good 223–224, 299
  on individualism 130–131, 298–299
  on justice 291n10, 298–299
  Womanist Ethics 131–132
transgender issues 93–94, 94n15
Tree of Life Synagogue, Pittsburgh 19
Trump, Donald 93, 163–164

United States
  hate crimes 93
  moral values 247

protest movements 78, 93, 167
racism 4
social divisions 92, 164, 221
Supreme Court 164
Trump presidency 163–164
white supremacy 163–164
Universal Declaration of Human Rights 289

Van Eck, Ernest 239, 243
Via, Dan Otto 13–14, 130
  "implied understanding of existence" *see* existential understanding
  literary approach 142–144, 145
vineyards, in Jesus's teachings 238, 242
  see also laborers in the vineyard, parable of
virtue ethics 293, 302

Wallis, Jim 5, 253n39
White, Lynn 190–191
white privilege 101–102, 134, 320
white supremacy 163–164
Wiesel, Elie 91
Wisdom literature 52, 53, 185–186
womanist theologies 27, 28, 165–166, 189, 298
women 164
  domestic work, status of 122n16
  in Jesus's parables 113, 114, 120–122

Index

women (*cont'd*)
  in poverty 114
  refugees 104
world tree 185, 187
worship, Jewish 47–49
  synagogues 48–49

tabernacle 48
temple system 46, 48,
  207–208, 213
Wright, N. T. 51

Zechariah, book of 119